The
COMPLETE GUIDE TO
GERMAN ARMORED VEHICLES

Copyright © 2019 by David Doyle

All rights reserved. No part of this book may be reproduced in any manner without the express written consent of the publisher, except in the case of brief excerpts in critical reviews or articles. All inquiries should be addressed to Skyhorse Publishing, 307 West 36th Street, 11th Floor, New York, NY 10018.

Skyhorse Publishing books may be purchased in bulk at special discounts for sales promotion, corporate gifts, fund-raising, or educational purposes. Special editions can also be created to specifications. For details, contact the Special Sales Department, Skyhorse Publishing, 307 West 36th Street, 11th Floor, New York, NY 10018 or info@skyhorsepublishing.com.

Skyhorse® and Skyhorse Publishing® are registered trademarks of Skyhorse Publishing, Inc.®, a Delaware corporation.

Visit our website at www.skyhorsepublishing.com.

10 9 8 7 6 5 4

Library of Congress Cataloging-in-Publication Data is available on file.

Cover design by Rain Saukas

Cover photo credits: Front, top row: Bundesarchiv; Front, bottom row: Patton Museum; Back, clockwise: Thomas Anderson, National Archives and Records Administration, Patton Museum, National Archives and Records Administration; Flap: National Archives and Records Administration

ISBN: 978-1-510716-575
Ebook ISBN: 978-1-510716-582

Printed in China

The COMPLETE GUIDE TO GERMAN ARMORED VEHICLES

PANZERS, JAGDPANZERS, ASSAULT GUNS, ANTIAIRCRAFT, SELF-PROPELLED ARTILLERY, ARMORED WHEELED AND SEMI-TRACKED VEHICLES, AND MORE

DAVID DOYLE

Skyhorse Publishing

Contents

Chapter 1 Tanks 3
    Panzer I 5
    Panzer II 14
    Panzer III 28
    Panzer IV 47
    Panther 71
    Porsche Tiger 79
    Tiger I 82
    Tiger II 88
    Maus 90
    Panzerkampfwagen 35(t) 90
    Panzerkampfwagen 38(t) 90
    FT-17 94
    Char I BiS 95
    S35 96

Chapter 2 Assault Guns and the *Sturmgeschütz* 99
    Sturmgeschütz 99
    Sturmhaubitze 112
    Sturmgeschütz IV 114
    Sturminfanteriegeschütze 33B 114
    Sturmpanzer 116
    Sturmmörserwagen 117

Chapter 3 *Jagdpanzers* 126
    Jagdpanzer 38 "Hetzer" 126
    Jagdpanzer IV 129
    Jagdpanzer IV (A) 133
    Jagdpanther 133
    Ferdinand/*Elefant* 135
    Jagdtiger 141

Chapter 4 *Panzerjäger* 144
    Aufklärungspanzerwagen 38 144
    Panzerjäger I 145
    Panzerjäger Lorraine Schlepper 7.5 cm PaK 40/1 (SdKfz 135) "Marder I" ... 147
    Panzerselbstfahrlafette 1 für 7.62 cm PaK 36(r) auf Fahrgestell ... 148
    7.5 cm PaK 40/2 auf Fahrgestell Panzerkampfwagen II (Sf)(SdKfz 131) ... 149
    Panzerjäger 38(t) für 7.62 cm PaK 36(r) (SdKfz 139) "Marder III" ... 151
    Panzerjäger 38(t) für 7.5 cm PaK 40/3 Ausf H (SdKfz 138) "Marder III" ... 151
    10.5 cm K. Panzer *Selbstfahrlafette* Iva 154

Nashorn	156
Other *Panzerjäger*	160

Chapter 5   *Flammpanzers*   168

Chapter 6   Flakpanzers—Antiaircraft Tanks   174

Chapter 7   Self-Propelled Artillery   189

15 cm sIG auf PzKpfw I Ausf B	189
15 cm sIG33 auf Fgst PzKpfw II (Sf)	191
Geschützwagen 38 für sIG 33/1 (Sf) (SdKfz 138/1) "Grille"	191
Geschützwagen 38 M f für sIG 33/2 (Sf)(SdKfz 138/1) "Grille"	194
15 cm sIG 33/2 (Sf) on *Bergepanzerwagen* 38	196
LgsFH 13 (Sfl) auf Lorraine-*Schlepper*	196
15 cm s Pz H 18/1 auf Fgst Pz III/IV (Sf) (SdKfz 165) "Hummel"	196
10.5 cm leFH 16 *Geschützpanzer*	197
10.5 cm leFH 16 auf gepSfl FCM	200
Geschützwagen IVb für 10.5 cm leFH 18/1(Sf) (SdKfz 165/1)	201
10.5 cm leFH 18/3 (Sf) auf *Geschützwagen* B2	201
Geschützwagen Lorraine-Schlepper für leFH 18/4	204
10.5 cm leFH 18/6 (Sf) auf *Geschützwagen* III/IV "Heuschrecke IVB"	205
Geschützpanzer 39H(f) leFH 16 & 18 Hotchkiss	206
leFH 18/40/2 (Sf) auf *Geschützwagen* III/IV	207
Gerät 040 and Gerät 041, "Karl"	208

Chapter 8   Armored Engineer and Support Vehicles   213

Abwurfvorrichtungen on Panzerkampfwagen I	213
Brückenleger II	221
Land-Wasser-Schlepper	224

Chapter 9   Armored Recovery Vehicles   226

Chapter 10   Armored Semi-Track Vehicles   238

Leichter Gepanzerter Kraftswagen (SdKfz 250)	238
mittlerer *Schützenpanzerwagen* (SdKfz 251)	257
Le gep *Munitionskraftwagen* (SdKfz 252)	277
Le gep *Beobachtungskraftwagen* (SdKfz 253)	279
M gepanzerter *Beobachtungskraftwagen* (SdKfz 254)	281
Mun Kw fur Nebelwerfer (SdKfz 4) and 15 cm Panzerwerfer 42 auf Sf (SdKfz 4/1)	281
7.5 cm *Selbstfahrlafette* L/40.8 Modell 1	282
3.7 cm *Selbstfahrlafette* L/70	282
Schwerer Wehrmachtschlepper (gep Ausf)	282

Chapter 11   Armored Cars   286

SdKfz 223	288
SdKfz 232 (6-Rad)	297
(SdKfz 231 8-Rad)	297
Schwerer Panzerspähwagen (5 cm) (SdKfz 234/2) Puma	310

Acknowledgments

It would be impossible to compile a book such as this alone. Rather, pulling together this much information requires a great deal of help and cooperation from friends and colleagues, often, as in this case, spanning a number of years, sometimes decades. Counter to what many think, locating and putting this information together does not require merely sitting behind a computer, scrolling through search engine results looking for photos and documentation; rather, it requires in-person visits to archival repositories ranging from dusty storage units to gleaming research centers.

The Internet has been inordinately helpful in making new friends in faraway places who can lessen the travel burden, and also in rapidly moving information from continent to continent.

That the archival material survived at all is remarkable. Not only were there wartime bombing efforts, but also the deliberate destruction of material to prevent it from falling into enemy hands—efforts that thankfully did not always succeed. As an example, as WWII wound down, US troops captured what is believed to be about one-half of the images taken by *kriegsberichters*—the German equivalent of US Signal Corps photographers. These were spirited away by the US Army for intelligence purposes. By 1947 they had been transferred to the US National Archives, who is also the official custodian of US military-created photographs of the WWII era. In 1968 the captured *kriegsberichter* were returned to the Federal Republic of Germany, where they are held today by the Bundesarchiv. However, prior to returning the photos, the National Archives made copies, which remain in US custody.

In addition to the National Archives and Bundesarchiv, frequent visits to the former Patton Museum at Fort Knox, Kentucky, totaling over two hundred days of on-site research, yielded a wealth of material.

Part of that material was from a collection assembled by Robert J. Icks over a period of decades. Colonel Icks, a career Ordnance officer, was also one of the earliest authors of books on military vehicles.

The late Richard Hunnicutt, who was generous in assisting with many of my projects, assisted with this one as well. Richard, a long-time friend of Walter Spielberger, had copies of much of Walter's collection of materials—so much so that when Walter's home burned, destroying many records, Richard was able to provide copies which were the basis for rebuilding the collection. Richard connected me to Walter, and both were gracious in assisting me with assembling my own collection.

Beyond the invaluable help provided by the staffs of the National Archives and the Patton Museum, I am indebted to Tom Kailbourn, Scott Taylor, Pat Stansell, Eric Mueller, David Fletcher, Thomas Anderson, and Hans-Heiri Stapfer. Charles Kliment, the staff of the Bundesarchiv, and the late Stefan De Meyer. Their generous and skillful assistance adds immensely to the quality of this volume. Finally, the Lord has blessed me with my wonderful wife Denise, who has scanned thousands of photos and documents for this and numerous other books. Even more importantly, she has been an ongoing source of encouragement and inspiration.

Introduction

There is little question that during World War II, Germany's military and industry produced a number of formidable fighting machines. However, it is also true that Nazi Germany's propaganda machine was equally formidable. During the war, and certainly over the years since, a number of myths have arisen concerning these vehicles. Through the following pages, we will present the facts concerning Germany's World War II armored fighting vehicles.

The tank, arguably the most fearsome of armored fighting vehicles, was initially developed by the British during World War I as a means of breaking the stalemate of trench warfare. Germany soon responded with a tank of their own, the boxy A7V.

As part of the terms of surrender that Germany signed, bringing to an end World War I, the nation was explicitly forbidden from developing tanks. However, even before Hitler's rise to power, the nation had embarked on a rearmament program, including tanks, which were created and tested clandestinely with the aid of Soviet Russia.

Ultimately unleashed on the world through the *blitzkrieg*, German armored formations startled the world. However, the simple, reliable armored vehicles deployed initially by Germany soon gave way to increasingly complex, expensive, difficult-to-manufacture, and often unreliable designs. Those engineering difficulties were compounded by ever-increasing pressure on the nation's manufacturing capacity brought on by the Allied strategic bombing campaign. Add to this the almost constant intervention in the arms program by Adolf Hitler himself, who had no engineering or manufacturing background (and little military background), and it is little surprise that the Germany military fielded an almost bewildering array of designs, often produced in low numbers, leading to a logistical nightmare for those tasked with supplying and maintaining an army in the field.

In addition to the numerous tanks fielded by the German military, so too was an array of fully tracked combat vehicles ranging from tank destroyers to self-propelled artillery and combat engineer vehicles. Armored half-track vehicles filled roles as personnel carriers and munitions transports and served an array of other uses. Armored cars were produced in four-, six-, and eight-wheel configurations. All of these vehicles are explored in the following pages.

Popularly known as the A7V, but actually designated Sturmpanzerwagen, this 1918 vehicle was Germany's first tank. Over the next twenty years Germany's armored vehicles would evolve considerably, as seen in the following pages. Only twenty A7Vs were produced, and today only one survives. Bundesarchiv

Chapter 1
Tanks

Panzerkampfwagen I

The peace terms that the Allies dictated to the Germans at the end of World War I in the Treaty of Versailles were clear about Germany's future armament. The November 11, 1918, Armistice represented a cease fire, but the Versailles Treaty set the actual terms of Germany's surrender, and German delegates to the Paris Peace Talks signed the treaty only reluctantly on June 28, 1919, under threat of invasion by the combined Allied armies.

The Treaty imposed severe restrictions on Germany's military, designed to prevent the German army—then called the *Reichswehr*—from the possibility of mounting any kind of offensive action. Article 198 of the treaty directly prohibited Germany from maintaining an air force or manufacturing aircraft. Article 171 banned the production and purchase of armored cars and tanks.

Versailles limited the German army to one hundred thousand men, with seven infantry and three cavalry divisions, and it also banned the draft. Importantly, the Versailles limitations were open-ended—Germany was expected to remain perpetually subject to the narrow limitations it imposed.

Today it is widely believed among scholars that it was precisely the Versailles Treaty's punitive nature and limitations that would lead to the rise of Adolf Hitler. Even the Weimar Republic government covertly disregarded and circumvented many of the Versailles restrictions. After the Nazis came to power, however, in March 1935, Berlin proclaimed outright that it would no longer abide by parts 5 and 6 of the treaty—the parts dealing with disarmament.

The history of the creation of the Panzer I amounts to a case study of how German leaders were already deliberately violating the imposed Treaty of Versailles under President Paul von Hindenburg, and then openly and more intensively under Hitler.

The LaS and Panzer I *Ausführung* A

Since the Versailles Treaty prohibited Germany from having armored weapons, the vehicle that eventually gained the name Panzer I was developed covertly under the designation *Kleintraktor* (light tractor). Indeed, early discussion of the vehicle focused on its use as a light prime mover, weapons carrier, and scout vehicle.

Prüfwesen 6—the automotive design office of the *Waffenamt* (ordnance department), or WaPrw 6, assigned the task of designing the vehicle to the Krupp firm. Krupp would carry out the engineering of the chassis and come up with wooden models of various proposed superstructures. Krupp's annual report for October 1930–September 1931 records that the company had been hired to design a 3.5-ton light tractor, in addition to manufacturing suspension parts. The report also notably said that the company would be building a wooden mock-up of a turret for the *Kleintraktor*—a giveaway that a decision had been reached to construct some of the vehicles as tanks, in spite of concerns, some expressed as early as February 1930 about the practicality of the diminutive vehicle in that capacity.

Initially envisioned as including a 20 mm cannon, the turret had evolved by September 1932—on paper at least—into one featuring both a 20 mm cannon and a 7.92 mm machine gun. The following month, the cannon was dropped and replaced with a second 7.92 mm machine gun.

A front-engine, rear-drive vehicle was the original Krupp conception, but it came to be known that similarly designed

Above: *The* Grosstraktor *(great tractor) was a medium tank, of which six were built in 1929 and 1930 by three different companies: two each were completed by Krupp, Rheinmetall-Borsig, and Daimler-Benz. The vehicles were constructed of 13 mm mild steel and had as the main gun a 75 mm cannon. Covert tests were conducted on the Grosstraktor, in violation of the Versailles Treaty, in the Soviet Union, and they saw only limited operational service. Seen here is one of the Krupp-built tanks, displayed at the camp of Armored Regiment 5 in Wünsdorf, Germany. Protruding through the bow is a machine gun.* Bundesarchiv

vehicles were known to throw tracks. In addition, planners had a chance to familiarize themselves with the Vickers-Carden-Loyd carrier, and in particular its suspension, and in September 1931 Krupp received a request to redesign the *Kleintraktor* to accommodate an engine in the rear with frontal drive.

Krupp advanced such a proposal and on March 5, 1932, received contract V/66906 to produce a single example to be delivered to the German army's proving ground at Kummersdorf, Brandenburg, near Berlin, by June 20, 1932.

The debut of the *Kleintraktor* was repeatedly set back, however, in many cases due to the army changing its specifications regarding such crucial features as the final drive, steering unit, and transmission. For its part Krupp suffered from a shortage of skilled tradesmen due to layoffs occasioned by the generally slow business of the Depression era. Accordingly, the *Kleintraktor* was first demonstrated at the Krupp facility in Essen, in the Prussian Rhineland, on July 29, 1932. Another demonstration took place the following month at the Krupp facility in Meppen, in northwestern Prussian territory near the Dutch border.

Government officials were satisfied with the *Kleintraktor*'s suspension and transmission, but the performance of the four-cylinder, air-cooled Krupp model M engine left them unimpressed. In fact, the engine was so underpowered that the vehicle could not even operate in high (fifth) gear. The automotive design office, therefore, suggested that Krupp investigate the possibility of replacing the weak engine with a water-cooled, four-cylinder Büssing-NAG Model G engine.

With the Nazis now at the helm of the German Reich, Krupp was told on July 1, 1933, that an order for 150 additional *Kleintraktor* chassis, code named *Landwirtschafliche Schlepper* (LaS) or "farm tractor," were to be expected even though the design of the superstructure and turret had not yet been finalized. To be used to train tank drivers, these vehicles were to be delivered in 1934. The chassis would ultimately be retrofitted with superstructures and turrets. Meanwhile, on the same day, Krupp was instructed to prepare a carbon steel superstructure and turret for testing by October 10, 1933. That date was later put back to July 1, 1934.

Although in the end the plan to arm these 150 chassis fell through, the authorities' intent to place an order for a second batch of 150 chassis in April 1934 was announced on July 1, 1933. All the vehicles were to be painted in *Feldgrau* (field gray), the *Reichswehr*'s color for its commercial vehicles. Combat vehicles then in service would have received a three-color camouflage paint scheme.

In order to ensure that the chassis would still meet specifications after they had been eventually fitted with superstructures and turrets, the vehicles were to be completed and tested with cast steel weights that simulated the heaviness and center of gravity of the missing components.

Shortly thereafter, on July 14, 1933, Krupp learned that the order for the LaS chassis had been reduced to 135 units. The remaining fifteen chassis would be built by other firms—three each by Daimler-Benz, Henschel, Maschinenfabrik Augsburg-Nürnberg (MAN), Krupp-Grusonwerk, and Rheinmetall. Krupp and all the other firms successfully completed their respective allotment of chassis by October 1934.

Production of the turret and superstructure made slower progress, however. When Krupp's first experimental armor superstructure was tested by being fired at in January 1935, it was rejected. Though it had extensive experience in turning out heavy armor plating for ships and fortifications, Krupp had more trouble making the relatively light 13 mm armor for the LaS—the first attempt was found to be brittle.

After the test failure and rancorous discussions, Krupp conceded in February that it would not be able to conform to the time line set by German ordnance. Ordnance canceled Krupp's contract for 150 armored turrets and superstructures, replacing it with a new contract for twenty mild-steel versions of both.

As already announced in July 1933, the *Reichswehr* was ready to order another batch of LaS chassis and their structures and turrets on April 1, 1934. A meeting that took place on February 12, 1934, established that Krupp-Essen would be the design firm for the order, but that other factories would be contracted to do the majority of the chassis production. Krupp would turn out the engines for all the participating contractors. In June, however, Krupp was asked for a quote on 650 engines, indicating that the planned order would far exceed the earlier mentioned 150 vehicles.

Fifty vehicles were initially planned to be produced at Krupp-Essen, but as things ultimately worked out, the second series LaS—which would soon be renamed the

Panzerkampfwagen I Ausf A

Production	
Make	Grusonwerk
Chassis (Fahrgestell) number	9001–9405
Make	MAN
Chassis (Fahrgestell) number	9501–9700
Make	Rheinmetall
Chassis (Fahrgestell) number	9801–9960
Make	Henschel
Chassis (Fahrgestell) number	10001–10249
Make	Daimler-Benz
Chassis (Fahrgestell) number	10301–10476
Specifications	
Length	4.02 m
Width	2.06 m
Height	1.72 m
Weight	5.4 tons
Fuel capacity	140 liters
Maximum speed	37.5 km/hr
Range, on-road	140 km
Range, cross-country	93 km
Crew	2
Communications	FuG 2
Armament	
Weapon, main	2 x 7.92 MG 13k
Ammo stowage, main	2,250 rounds
Automotive	
Engine make	Krupp
Engine model	H 305
Engine configuration	4-cylinder, air-cooled
Engine displacement	3.5 liter
Engine horsepower	60 @ 2500 rpm

6   THE COMPLETE GUIDE TO GERMAN ARMORED VEHICLES

Above: *In the early 1930s, in contravention of the Versailles Treaty, Germany began to build up its armored force by several means, including contracting with five firms to construct a lot of fifteen tank chassis, designated* Landwirtschaftlicher Schlepper *(agricultural tractor). This vehicle is one of three Krupp-built chassis, and it would serve as the prototype for the chassis of the* Panzerkampfwagen I *light tank.* Patton Museum

Above: *Produced by Henschel, MAN, Krupp-Gruson, and Daimler-Benz, the* Panzerkampfwagen I Ausf A *was the first mass-produced German tank. It was a two-man light tank with a turret housing two 7.92 mm MG13s. Its armor ranged from 6 mm to 13 mm in thickness. Power was provided by the Krupp M305 engine through a gearbox with five forward gears and one reverse. A total of 818 were produced between July 1934 and June 1936. The example shown here is an early-production* Panzerkampfwagen I Ausf A. *The machine guns have been dismounted.* Patton Museum

Above: *A mid-production* Panzerkampfwagen I Ausf A *features a Bosch headlight on the left side of the glacis and a cover over the grille on the engine deck that was introduced in 1937. Attached to the top of that cover are two angle irons that served as supports for a* Nebelkerzenabwurfvorrichtung *(NAKV) smoke-grenade dispenser (not installed). Each fender had a muffler and fishtail exhaust. Vision ports, some of which included vision slots, were provided on the turret and upper hull. Patton Museum*

Panzerkampfwagen I *Ausführung* A—would consist of 863 units.

The army originally intended to field one thousand Panzer I tanks by retrofitting the original 150 LaS vehicles with superstructures and turrets. When that plan was abandoned, a new contract was issued for additional Panzer I vehicles on a Series 3 chassis to meet the need for one thousand vehicles.

In December 1935, contracts went out for a fourth series of 175 more Panzer I Ausf A vehicles, the last to be constructed with the Krupp air-cooled engine.

Panzer I Ausf B

Although theoretically the Panzer I Ausf A's air-cooled engine should have had many tactical and logistical advantages, it proved in practice to be seriously deficient in horsepower and longevity, despite Krupp's ongoing effort to fix problem after problem.

Several water-cooled engines were considered as replacements for the Krupp air-cooled power plant, including a Krupp 80-hp V-8 and the Büssing-NAG engine alluded to above. Some evidence suggests that a Krupp V-8 engine was fitted into a vehicle for comparison tests with the Maybach NL 38 Tr 6-cylinder engine. In any case the Maybach power plant seemed to promise a definite performance improvement, and together with its radiator and fan, it was fitted into the same space that the air-cooled Krupp engine had taken up. Once equipped with the 100-horsepower, 3000 rpm Maybach, the vehicle received the designation *Panzerkampfwagen* I Ausf B (Panzer I Ausf B). The first contract vehicles were built on the series 5a chassis.

Besides the above-mentioned tanks with turrets, forty-seven small *Panzerbefehlswagen* (command tanks) were also constructed on the new series 5a liquid-cooled chassis. In addition, at the same time, contracts went

Above: *The Panzerkampfwagen I Ausf B incorporated several changes over the Ausf A, including an increase from four bogie wheels and three track-support rollers per side to five bogie wheels and four rollers; the trailing idler of the Ausf A was changed to a raised one; and the two fender-mounted mufflers were exchanged for a single muffler on the rear of the hull. This example was photographed during the invasion of Poland in 1939.* National Archives and Records Administration

Above: *A Panzerkampfwagen I Ausf B from the 36th Panzer Regiment, 4th Panzer Division, is viewed from the right rear at an assembly area in France during the 1940 blitzkrieg. The difference in the layout of the engine deck compared to that of the Ausf A is illustrated. As a modification, a steel rod had been installed between the idler supports, to reinforce them.* National Archives and Records Administration

Above: *Based on the* Panzerkampfwagen I Ausf A *chassis, the* Leichte (Funk) Panzerwagen *was the first armored, tracked command vehicle to go in service with the* Wehrmacht. *It had an armored superstructure by Daimler-Benz, which was attached to the upper hull, and it contained only a single FuG 2 receiver set, making it of limited utility.* Patton Museum

out for another group of 146 turret-equipped tanks to be constructed using series 6a chassis. Originally planned as a batch of 150 vehicles, this second group lost four of its chassis when four *Kleine Panzerbefehlswagen* vehicles were diverted to be shipped to Spain and four chassis were then pulled from the batch of 150 to build replacement *Kleine Panzerbefehlswagen*.

In the second half of the 1930s, Germany's rearmament accelerated, producing a need for even more vehicles for training tank drivers, beyond the 150 vehicles misleadingly dubbed *Landwirtschaftliche Schlepper*. A series of 295 open-top vehicles were therefore ordered, these constructed upon the Maybach-engined chassis.

Although the original concept of retrofitting turrets and superstructures on those first 150 LaS vehicles fell through (because of Krupp's difficulties in manufacturing tough enough tank armor) the idea persisted and reemerged in 1937 in a new guise—147 new-style vehicles called LaS *Fahrgestell für Umsetz-Fahrzeuge* (light tractor chassis for vehicle conversions).

Open-topped like the *Schulfahrzeuge* on LaS-Maybach, these driver-training vehicles had armored engine decks (unlike the mild-steel engine decks on the *Schulfahrzeuge*) and slip-ring contacts in the electrical system. These features would allow the LaS *Fahrgestell für Umsetz-Fahrzeuge* to be easily converted to combat tanks, merely by the installation of a turret and superstructure.

Military units were authorized to take the superstructures and turrets off of as many as twenty-four Panzer I Ausf A vehicles to mount them on the new conversion

Above: *The* Leiche Panzerbefehlswagen (SdKfz 265) *was a radio-equipped armored command vehicle based on the* Panzerkampfwagen I *chassis. A Daimler-Benz-produced armored superstructure over the stock upper hull contained two-way radio equipment—an FuG 6 transmitter-receiver and an FuG 2 receiver—as well as a chart table. A ball mount for an MG 34 was on the right front of the superstructure. The vehicle shown here had a cupola on the right side of the superstructure roof, an addition dating to 1938. Here, a soldier is peering into the left side door of a* Kleine Panzerbefehlswagen. *National Archives and Records Administration*

Above: *A crewman of a* Leiche Panzerbefehlswagen *from Panzer-Abteilung z.b.V.40 and a Finnish officer observe the action during a battle in Finland on July 1, 1941. This vehicle has a late, low-profile cupola, which replaced an early, higher cupola. The angled object on the right side of the vehicle is a trough-shaped rack for storing the antenna when folded down for travel.* Patton Museum

Above: *A* Leiche Panzerbefehlswagen *modified for use in the tropics was available by early 1941. This example is being unloaded from a ship at Tripoli, Libya, in February of that year. The tropical version included revamped ventilation for the engine deck and a larger radiator. A storage bin has been attached to the rear of the superstructure, and on the rear of the muffler is a NAKV smoke-grenade dispenser. Jutting from the side of the cupola is a hatch-door stop.* National Archives and Records Administration

chassis with Maybach engines. The Ausf A chassis released from superstructures were then to be used as vehicles for tank driver training. These rearrangements ensured that the combat vehicles ended up with the newer, more powerful chassis.

Panzerkampfwagen I Ausf B

Production	
Make	Daimler-Benz
Chassis (Fahrgestell) number	10478-10567
Make	Henschel
Chassis (Fahrgestell) number	12501-12656
Make	MAN
Chassis (Fahrgestell) number	13501-13600
Make	Grusonwerk
Chassis (Fahrgestell) number	14501-14566, 14687-14720
Specifications	
Length	4.42 m
Width	2.06 m
Height	1.72 m
Weight	5.8 tons
Fuel capacity	146 liters
Maximum speed	40 km/hr
Range, on-road	170 km
Range, cross-country	115 km
Crew	2
Communications	FuG 2
Armament	
Weapon, main	2 x 7.92 MG 13k
Ammo stowage, main	2,250 rounds
Automotive	
Engine make	Maybach
Engine model	NL 38 Tr
Engine configuration	6-cylinder, liquid cooled
Engine displacement	3.8 liter
Engine horsepower	100 @ 3000 rpm

Panzerkampfwagen I Ausf C

Krupp was the design source for all the vehicles so far discussed, although the turret and superstructures had been designed by Daimler-Benz, with the specifications set by the automotive branch of Germany's ordnance department. In contrast, the Ausf C was the result of a conception by engineer Heinrich Ernst Kniepkamp, a specialist in tank development, in his effort to give vehicular form to what he understood were the priorities of the German General Staff.

Kniepkamp first approached Krupp in 1937 with a new general contract for tank development. Krupp however was unwilling to go along with provisions in the proposed contract that would have moved much of the decision-making

Panzerkampfwagen I Ausf C

Production	
Make	Krauss-Maffei
Chassis (Fahrgestell) number	150101-150140
Specifications	
Length	4.195 m
Width	1.92 m
Height	1.945 m
Weight	8 tons
Fuel capacity	170 liters
Maximum speed	79 km/hr
Range, on-road	300 km
Range, cross-country	190 km
Crew	2
Communications	Fu Spr Ger A
Armament	
Weapon, main	1 x 7.92 MG 34 1 x 7.92 mm EW 141
Ammo stowage, main	2,100 rounds
Automotive	
Engine make	Maybach
Engine model	HL 45 P
Engine configuration	6-cylinder, liquid cooled
Engine displacement	4.678 liter
Engine horsepower	150 @ 3800 rpm

Above: *The Panzerkampfwagen I Ausf C, of which only forty were assembled by Krauss-Maffei, was designed as an airborne, light, high-speed reconnaissance vehicle. It was a complete departure from the Ausf A and B, and featured a new hull and running gear by Krauss-Maffei as well as a superstructure and turret designed by Daimler-Benz. The turret contained a 7.92 mm MG 34 on the right side of the mantlet and a Mauser EW 141 semiautomatic gun on the left.* Patton Museum

Above: *The Panzerkampfwagen I Ausf C had a turret similar to that of the Panzerkampfwagen II, with an external mantlet and a cupola. It was powered by a Maybach HL45P engine and had a top speed of over 40 mph. To the front of the storage boxes on the right fender is an array of three N.b.K. smoke dischargers. The large bogie wheels were mounted on torsion bars. The tracks were KGS 62/290/90. Patton Museum*

Panzerkampfwagen I Ausf F

Production	
Make	Krauss-Maffei
Chassis (Fahrgestell) number	150301-150330
Specifications	
Length	4.375 m
Width	2.64 m
Height	2.05 m
Weight	21 tons
Fuel capacity	180 liters
Maximum speed	25 km/hr
Range, on-road	150 km
Range, cross-country	110 km
Crew	2
Communications	FuG 2
Armament	
Weapon, main	2 x 7.92 MG 34
Ammo stowage, main	5,100 rounds
Automotive	
Engine make	Maybach
Engine model	HL 45 P
Engine configuration	6-cylinder, liquid cooled
Engine displacement	4.678 liter
Engine horsepower	150 @ 3800 rpm

on designs out of the hands of Krupp engineers and into the offices of the automotive design office. Undeterred, Kniepkamp took the tank contract to Munich-based Krauss-Maffei—with which firm he had previously worked successfully on half-track projects.

Krauss-Maffei agreed, leading to a series of concept designs that resulted in the VK (*Vollketten*, or "fully tracked") 6.01. Featuring large, interleaved roadwheels, the VK 6.01 was powered by a Maybach HL 45 high-output engine and had an eight-speed semiautomatic transmission. Armament consisted of a self-loading Mauser 7.92 mm EW 141 cannon and an MG 34 machine gun. With World War II having just begun, Krauss-Maffei received a contract for forty chassis of such vehicles on September 15, 1939. A few months later, on February 17, 1940, Daimler-Benz was contracted to make the tanks' superstructure and turrets. March through September 1941 was the expected delivery period. It was deemed of relatively low priority compared to other vehicles, however, and output suffered from some delays.

Panzerkampfwagen I Ausf F

Another Krauss-Maffei product featuring interleaved roadwheels, the *Panzerkampfwagen* I Ausf F bore a certain resemblance to the Ausf C. Though armed only with two 7.92 mm MG 34 machine guns, the Ausf F was envisioned as a heavily armored breaching vehicle, a vehicle to be tasked with taking on heavy border fortifications, while remaining within the limits of 18-ton portable bridges.

On December 22, 1939, the German ordnance department authorized production of thirty of the new vehicles that Krauss-Maffei had designated the VK 18.01. Krauss-Maffei was to build the Ausf F chassis and Daimler-Benz the turrets and superstructures—a repeat of the arrangement regarding the Ausf C. In April 1942, final assembly of the thirty vehicles got underway. In December that same year, the last of the vehicles was completed.

Panzerkampfwagen II

Regardless of the Versailles Treaty restrictions, Germany began an ambitious—but secret—rearmament program in the early 1930s. The arms program, now widely known, was

Above: The Panzerkampfwagen I Ausf F was an infantry-support tank boasting excellent armor protection, with 80 mm armor on frontal surfaces and 50 mm and 25 mm armor elsewhere. The turret contained two 7.92 mm MG 34s. The suspension included interleaved bogie wheels on torsion bars. The driver had a substantial armored visor as well as a binocular periscope. The engine was the Maybach HL45P. Patton Museum

Above: A prominent splash guard was on the hull roof to the front of the Daimler-Benz–designed turret of the Panzerkampfwagen I Ausf F. Five periscopes were provided for the commander/gunner. The fenders on both sides of the vehicle were interrupted to provide clearance for round hatches on the sides of the hull. Krauss-Maffei assembled a total of thirty of these vehicles, from April to December 1942. Patton Museum

PzKpfw II Ausf a/1, a/2, and a/3 (SdKfz 121)

Production	
Make	MAN
Chassis (Fahrgestell) number	20001-20075
Specifications	
Length	4.38 m
Width	2.14
Height	1.95
Weight	7.6 tons
Fuel capacity	170 liters
Maximum speed	40 km/hr
Range, on-road	190 km
Crew	3
Communications	FuG 5
Armament	
Weapon, main	2 cm KwK 40 L/55
Weapon, coaxial	7.92 mm MG 34
Ammo stowage, main	180 rounds
Ammo stowage, secondary	2,250 rounds
Automotive	
Engine make	Maybach
Engine model	HL57TR
Engine configuration	straight 6-cylinder
Engine displacement	5.7 liter
Engine horsepower	130 @ 2600 rpm

already extensive even before Hitler came to power in 1933. It grew exponentially thereafter.

One part of the rearmament program involved producing a 6-ton light tank. Just as the true nature of the Panzer I had been concealed under the misleading code name *Kleintraktor*, the 6-ton tank received a designation for agricultural equipment—*Landwirtschaft Schlepper 100* (LaS 100) or "farm tractor with 100-horsepower engine."

Krupp was widely expected to receive the contract for the "tractor," and indeed presented rough designs for the vehicle's chassis to the *Waffenamt* (German Ordnance Department) on February 24, 1934.

Rather than rubber-stamp Krupp's proposal, however, the *Waffenamt* requested additional proposals for construction of such a chassis from Krupp's competitors Henschel and Maschinenfabrik Augsburg-Nürnberg (MAN). *Waffenamt* reviewed all the proposals and issued contracts to all three companies to build and deliver two chassis each by the end of calendar year 1935.

In the event, MAN won the contract for production of the chassis, which was to be combined with a superstructure and turret designed by Daimler-Benz. Seventy-five of the new tanks were ordered in October 1935, with chassis production broken down into three series of twenty-five each, to be designated Ausf a/1, Ausf a/2, and Ausf a/3. The hulls of the seventy-five chassis were made of high-nickel armor, a composition that allowed for plating that could be thinner than armor of lower quality, yet equally protective.

The pretense that these vehicles were farm equipment was dropped on April 3, 1936, when the LaS 100 was redesignated *Panzerkampfwagen* II (hereafter referenced as the Panzer II or PzKpfw II). The seventy-five vehicles were scheduled for delivery between April and September 1936.

Meanwhile, it was decided by June 1936 that an additional 425 vehicles would be needed. The Panzer II was a combat-capable vehicle and served effectively in that capacity, particularly in the early stages of World War II. But there were also other reasons why demand steadily rose for the PzKpfw II. A total of 460 of the Panzer II vehicles had been ordered by September 30, 1936.

In the beginning, MAN produced the Panzer II chassis, while Daimler-Benz turned out the vehicle's turret and superstructure. When time for the fourth series—dubbed the Panzer II Ausf A—rolled around, however, two other assembly plants were added to the list of makers. The Versailles Treaty banned Germany from manufacturing tanks in the years after World War I and as a result the country suffered from a shortage of manufacturing and, to some extent, engineering expertise for the large-scale production of what were then regarded as heavy tanks, such as the Panzer III and IV.

Regular industrial production of the Panzer II not only supplied Germany with a combat-capable light tank, but it also provided training for an expanding pool of skilled labor—from machinists to assembly workers to engineers—whose experience would translate into greater efficiency and higher quality when heavier, more

TANKS 17

Left: *The Panzerkampfwagen II was designed as a light tank that would work in conjunction with the Panzerkampfwagen I, but with more powerful weapons: specifically, a 2 cm KwK30 L/55 automatic cannon and a coaxial 7.92 mm MG 34. The first development or preproduction model was the Ausf a (with emphasis on the lowercase "a"), an example of which is portrayed here, armed with a nonstandard weapon, apparently a 37 mm type. A total of seventy-five Ausf a vehicles were completed by MAN from 1936 to 1937. The suspension featured six bogie wheels per side, mounted in pairs, with a steel beam connecting the bogie assemblies. Armor on the front, sides, and rear of the vehicle was 13 mm thick, with 15 mm armor on the mantlet.* Patton Museum

Above: *The standard armament of a 2 cm KwK30 L/55 automatic cannon and a coaxial 7.92 mm MG 34 is mounted in the turret of a Panzerkampfwagen II Ausf a, preceding a Panzerkampfwagen I in a parade through Chomutov, Sudetenland, on October 9, 1938. A trough for holding a radio antenna when lowered for travel is on the left fender. The bracket on the roof of the turret was for an antiaircraft machine gun.* Bundesarchiv

Above: *Two Panzerkampfwagen II Ausf a vehicles from Panzer Regiment 1 are crossing a bridge during the invasion of France on June 15, 1940. Both vehicles have sunscreens over the driver's front vision ports. A dummy periscope head is visible on the turret roof, as is the driver's hatch on the glacis to the front of the driver's visor.* National Archives and Records Administration

Above: *The second development model of the Panzerkampfwagen II was the Ausf b, of which one hundred were completed by MAN in February and March 1937. This tank was similar to the Ausf a, but with new sprockets and track-support rollers, wider bogie wheels, strengthened suspension, improved ventilation for the engine compartment, and hinged rear mudguards. Armor protection remained the same as for the Ausf a, except with slightly thicker armor on the top and bottom of the turret and hull. This Panzerkampfwagen II Ausf b was photographed in an unidentified town.* Patton Museum

Above: Panzerkampfwagen II Ausf b chassis number 21022 has a Notek blackout light to the side of the left headlight: a modification introduced in October 1940. The mantlet was designed to fit inside, rather than over, the front of the turret. The front of the hull of the Ausf b was of a different design than that of the Ausf a, to fit around a new steering unit. The hull and the engine deck were slightly longer than on the Ausf a. Patton Museum

costly armored vehicles went into large-scale production. Having acquired skilled tradesmen, a manufacturing firm had the vital need to retain that staff on the job and on the payroll. In manufacture, the overall rate of production is limited by the component with the lowest production rate. To keep skilled workers on the job, production had to be continuous, and to that end assembly rates would be adjusted and additional orders placed. Germany's leaders sought to keep the Panzer II on the assembly lines so that the skilled workforce would be in place and at the ready when the time came for mass production of larger Panzers.

Nazi Germany's industry was not unique in this respect. In the United States, General Motors and Chrysler used similar tactics to forestall laying off skilled work staff. American manufacturing plants' final assembly rates never attained the maximum capacity of either the plant or the workers. In fact, assembly rates often fell far below those maximum quantities, due to problems in securing various components.

In February 1937, Panzer III engineering and testing had not progressed sufficiently to allow a launch of production before the anticipated date of October 1, 1938. Accordingly, it was decided to continue output of the Panzer II to ensure the availability of skilled manufacturing staff at such time as bigger Panzers could be produced. In that interim period, then, contracts for chassis production in the 5th, 6th, and 7th series were issued. The chassis manufacturing pool, by this time, now included not only MAN, but also Henschel, Mühlenbau-Industrie AG (MIAG), Fahrzeug- und Motoren-Werke (FAMO), and others. Where Daimler-Benz had in the beginning been solely responsible for Panzer II turrets and superstructures,

Above: *The third and final development model of the* Panzerkampfwagen *II was the* Ausf c, *an example of which is in the front in this photograph. This model retained the flat driver's visor with no vision slot and introduced a new running gear, with individually sprung suspension arms supporting five large bogie wheels, and four track-support rollers per side instead of the previous three.* Bundesarchiv

PzKpfw II Ausf b (SdKfz 121)

Production	
Make	MAN
Chassis (Fahrgestell) number	21001-21100
Specifications	
Length	4.76 m
Width	2.14
Height	1.96
Weight	7.9 tons
Fuel capacity	170 liters
Maximum speed	40 km/hr
Range, on-road	190 km
Crew	3
Communications	FuG 5
Armament	
Weapon, main	2 cm KwK 40 L/55
Weapon, coaxial	7.92 mm MG 34
Ammo stowage, main	180 rounds
Ammo stowage, secondary	2,250 rounds
Automotive	
Engine make	Maybach
Engine model	HL57TR
Engine configuration	straight 6-cylinder
Engine displacement	5.7 liter
Engine horsepower	130 @ 2600 rpm

Wegmann joined the production team, beginning with series 4 vehicles. Later, some of the chassis makers also started turning out superstructures and turrets.

Panzer II Ausf J

With Germany's Communist nemesis, the Soviet Union, steadily building heavier and more powerful weapons, it was clear to Berlin in 1939 that German armor was going to have to be significantly upgraded. In line with this thinking, Daimler-Benz and MAN were tasked with engineering yet another version of the Panzer II, featuring 80 mm frontal armor. Based on the VK 1601 chassis, the resulting vehicle was to have a Maybach HL 45 150-horsepower engine and interleaved roadwheels and was to be fitted with the 2 cm KwK 38.

Because the VK 1601 was highly similar to the VK 1801 (Panzer I Ausf F), MAN was instructed to work with the VK 1801's contractor Krauss-Maffei. The arrangement between the two firms involved Krauss-Maffei providing steering gear and final-drive components, while MAN would build four trial VK 1601 vehicles. In June 1940, a mild-steel chassis was ready for inspection.

Authorization for the construction of thirty of the vehicles came through on December 22, 1939, and contracts went out to MAN and Daimler-Benz. MAN, however, only turned out three trial chassis by August 1941, despite estimated series production being imminent. Concerns were still being voiced about the absence of turret deliveries.

Turret and armor difficulties indeed were a persistent problem. Such shortages, together with the decline in the project's priority, meant that only eight vehicles were completed in 1941. The last twenty-two vehicles of the initial thirty-vehicle order were not finished until December 1942. Before that time, in July 1942, a follow-on order for one hundred more of the Ausf J was canceled.

The twenty-two Panzer II Ausf J vehicles that were completed saw sporadic service in the area around Leningrad and also in France and Yugoslavia.

Panzerspähwagen II (SdKfz 123)

Originally called the *Panzerkampfwagen II neu Art* (VK 1301), this vehicle with a full tracklaying design later received a re-designation as an armored car rather than a tank. Like the ill-fated VK 901 (Panzer II Ausf G), which it resembled, the VK 1301 was a product of MAN and Daimler-Benz, with MAN designing the chassis and Daimler-Benz responsible for the turret and superstructure. The two designs differed in their crew size, however: the Panzer II Ausf G had a three-man crew, while the VK 1301 would have a crew of four.

Since the VK 1301 was intended as a reconnaissance vehicle, emphasis in its design was placed on off-road mobility and high speed, especially in reverse. Powered by the 150-horsepower Maybach HL 45, the vehicle was to be armed with a 2 cm KwK 38 with a coaxial MG 34 machine gun.

Left: *The Ausf B was the second production model of the Panzerkampfwagen II. A total of 629 were built. The Ausf A and Ausf B were similar; both had a new, peaked visor for the driver. A splash guard on the hull roof to the front of the turret was standard for the Ausf B, and some Ausf A vehicles had a splash guard installed during production.* Bundesarchiv

Left: *As German Panzers met increasingly effective antitank weapons on the battlefields, it became necessary to uparmor the Panzerkampfwagen II Ausf A, B, and C. By early 1940, a supplemental armor kit was being installed on these vehicles to beef up the frontal armor of the bow, glacis, and the upper hull. This Panzerkampfwagen II of the executive officer of the 3rd Panzer Regiment has been equipped with the supplemental armor.* Bundesarchiv

PzKpfw II Ausf c, A, B and C (SdKfz 121)

Production	
Make	MAN
Chassis (Fahrgestell) number	21101-21131, 22001-22044, 23001-23160, 24401-24569, 26301-26380
Make	Henschel
Chassis (Fahrgestell) number	23301-23328, 24001-24102, 26101-26215
Make	Alkett
Chassis (Fahrgestell) number	24201-24232, 26401-26415
Make	Miag
Chassis (Fahrgestell) number	26501-26539
Make	Famo
Chassis (Fahrgestell) number	26601-26635
Specifications	
Length	4.81 m
Width	2.22
Height	1.99
Weight	8.9 tons
Fuel capacity	170 liters
Maximum speed	40 km/hr
Range, on-road	200 km
Crew	3
Communications	FuG 5
Armament	
Weapon, main	2 cm KwK40 L/55
Weapon, coaxial	7.92 mm MG 34
Ammo stowage, main	180 rounds
Ammo stowage, secondary	2,250 rounds
Automotive	
Engine make	Maybach
Engine model	HL62TR
Engine configuration	straight 6-cylinder
Engine displacement	6.2 liter
Engine horsepower	140 @ 2600 rpm

PzKpfw II Ausf D and E (SdKfz 121)

Production

Make	MAN
Chassis (Fahrgestell) number	27001-27085 (Ausf. D), 27801-27807 (Aust. E)

Specifications

Length	4.65 m
Width	2.30
Height	2.06
Weight	10.0 tons
Fuel capacity	200 liters
Maximum speed	55 km/hr
Range, on-road	200 km
Crew	3
Communications	FuG 5

Armament

Weapon, main	2 cm KwK 40 L/55
Weapon, coaxial	7.92 mm MG 34
Ammo stowage, main	180 rounds
Ammo stowage, secondary	2,250 rounds

Automotive

Engine make	Maybach
Engine model	HL62TR
Engine configuration	straight 6-cylinder
Engine displacement	6.2 liter
Engine horsepower	140 @ 2600 rpm

PzKpfw II Ausf F (SdKfz 121)

Production

Make	Ursus
Chassis (Fahrgestell) number	28001-28204, 28305-29489
Make	Famo
Chassis (Fahrgestell) number	28205-28304, 28820-28839

Specifications

Length	4.81 m
Width	2.28
Height	2.15
Weight	9.5 tons
Fuel capacity	170 liters
Maximum speed	40 km/hr
Range, on-road	200 km
Crew	3
Communications	FuG 5

Armament

Weapon, main	2 cm KwK 40 L/55
Weapon, coaxial	7.92 mm MG 34
Ammo stowage, main	180 rounds
Ammo stowage, secondary	2,250 rounds

Automotive

Engine make	Maybach
Engine model	HL62TR
Engine configuration	straight 6-cylinder
Engine displacement	6.2 liter
Engine horsepower	140 @ 2600 rpm

An order for fifteen experimental VK 1301 chassis was placed, but none of the vehicles had been finished by the time it was decided to substitute for it the VK 1303 with a 160-horsepower Maybach HL66P engine that would produce a road speed of 60 km/h and a cross-country speed of 30 km/h when coupled to the SSG 48 six-speed transmission.

Long before testing of the VK 1303 was complete, orders for production began to come in. Alternately designated the Panzer II Ausf L or *Panzerspähwagen* II, orders and change orders came in a flurry, pushing the desired number of the vehicles from 250 to 500 to 800. In the end, though, by February 1943, it had been resolved to manufacture only one hundred of the VK 1303. MAN began delivering the *Panzerspähwagen* II— popularly called the *Luchs* (Lynx or Bobcat) in September 1942. The firm continued to turn out the vehicle until January 1944. The *Luchs* was first deployed on the

Above: *German Army transporter trucks and trailers are carrying a mix of* Panzerkampfwagen Is *and* IIs *in a parade on June 2, 1939. In the foreground is a* Panzerkampfwagen II Ausf D, *a light tank designed for cavalry use, which, along with the Ausf E, had a distinctive hull unlike that of any other PzKpfw II model, but the same turret as the Ausf C. The Ausf D and E also had torsion-bar suspensions, four double-bogie wheels, new sprockets and idlers, and new lubricated-pin tracks.* Patton Museum

Above: *The* Panzerkampfwagen II Ausf F *featured several new improvements, including a bow constructed of flat armor plates; 30 mm frontal armor for the superstructure, with a dummy visor on the right side; and a cupola furnished with periscopes. Ursus, of Poland, built 389 Ausf F vehicles from March 1941 to July 1942, while FAMO completed 120 of them from August 1941 to June 1943, for a total of 509 units. Shown here is a* Panzerkampfwagen II Ausf F *crossing a bridge in the Soviet Union in June 1942.* Bundesarchiv

26 THE COMPLETE GUIDE TO GERMAN ARMORED VEHICLES

Above: *The second tank in this column of SS-Panzergrenadier Division "Liebstandarte Adolf Hitler," which has paused in the suburbs of Kharkov, Ukraine, in March 1943, is a* Panzerkampfwagen II Ausf F *with a coat of whitewash winter camouflage. The divisional insignia and a Balkenkreuz are painted on the armored housing of the smoke-grenade rack, to the right of which is the muffler and its perforated shield.* Bundesarchiv

Above: *This is one of two pilot* Panzer Selbstfahrlafette *(armored self-propelled carriage) light tank destroyers built in 1941 on* Panzerkampfwagen II Ausf G *chassis. They had a 50 mm PaK 38 antitank gun in a superstructure with an open top. These vehicles were to have had a four-man crew. The frontal armor was 30 mm, and the side armor was 20 mm. The project never went into production, and both pilots were sent to the Eastern Front for service in August 1942.* Patton Museum

Above: The Panzerkampfwagen II Ausf J, of which thirty were produced by MAN, was designed as a heavily armored reconnaissance tank. It was protected by 80 mm armor plate on the front and 50 mm armor on the sides and rear. The fenders had gaps in them on each side of the tank for clearance for a round hatch in the hull. The driver and the radio operator to his right had heavily armored visors and, for side vision, a round plate with a vision slot. Armaments consisted of a 2 cm KwK 38 L/55 cannon and a 7.92 mm MG 42. Patton Museum

Above: Usually referred to as the "Luchs" (Lynx), the Panzerkampfwagen II Ausf L also was referred to as the VK 1303. Designed as a reconnaissance tank, it had the same lower hull as the Panzerkampfwagen II Ausf G but with solid bogie wheels, and the upper hull was enlarged to provide for a larger turret ring. The turret housed a 2 cm KwK 38 L/55 cannon and a 7.92 mm MG 34. Shown here is chassis number 200164 and turret number 200143 after it was captured by the British. This tank survives at the Tank Museum, Bovington, England. Patton Museum

Panzerspähwagen II SdKfz 123

Specifications	
Length	4.63 m
Width	2.48 m
Height	2.21 m
Weight	11.8 tons
Fuel capacity	235 liters
Maximum speed	60 km/hr
Range, on-road	260 km
Range, cross-country	155 km
Crew	4
Communications	FuG 2, Fu Spr Ger f, intercom
Armament	
Weapon, main	2.0 cm KwK 38
Weapon, coaxial	7.92 mm MG 34
Ammo stowage, main	320 rounds
Ammo stowage, secondary	2,250 rounds
Automotive	
Engine make	Maybach
Engine model	HL66P
Engine configuration	inline 6, liquid cooled
Engine displacement	6.6 liters
Engine horsepower	180 @ 3200 rpm

Eastern Front, but some *Luchse* were sent to Normandy in the summer of 1944.

Panzerkampfwagen III

In the mid-1930s the German military had an armored strategy that provided for two types of tank carrying an offensive forward. One type would be armed with a reasonably heavy weapon used for destroying enemy fortifications some distance away. The *Panzerkampfwagen* IV could play this role. The other tank type was to be armed with a cannon firing armor-piercing shells to knock out enemy tanks and machine guns to neutralize infantry. This type of tank was to be present in much greater numbers than the first—at a ratio of three companies to one. The actual tank that conformed to this second type was the *Panzerkampfwagen* III.

Contracts went out from the *Waffenamt* in 1934 for the *Panzerkampfwagen* III under the code name *Zugführerwagen* (ZW, "platoon leader's vehicle"). Krupp AG (Essen), Daimler-Benz AG (Berlin-Marienfelde), MAN (Nürnberg), and Rheinmetall-Borsig (Berlin) were all contacted for design proposals. Rheinmetall-Borsig in the end designed the turret, while Krupp and Daimler-Benz produced designs for the entire vehicle.

Initially a desire to standardize weapons and ammunition prevailed in planning and it was expected that the new tank was to be fitted with a 3.7 cm main gun. The Inspector for Mechanized Troops, familiar with international and technological trends, saw that this caliber would be insufficient and insisted that the new vehicle feature a turret ring sufficiently large to permit the use of a heavier cannon.

The *Panzerkampfwagen* III was to be operated by a five-man crew: commander, gunner, and loader—all in the turret—and the driver and radio operator in the front of the hull. To facilitate communication among the crewmen, an intercom was provided.

At Kummersdorf, near Berlin, and Ulm, in southwestern Germany's state of Württemberg, tests were run comparing the Daimler-Benz and Krupp prototypes. As a result, production of the Daimler-Benz design was ordered in early 1936.

Featuring what is now regarded as "traditional" German tank styling, the *Panzerkampfwagen III* had a boxy superstructure, the engine in the rear, and a gearbox at the front with the driver and radio operator positioned just behind it. The turret was basically in the center of the vehicle.

Panzerkampfwagen III Ausf A

A total of ten of the I.Serie ZW, the *Panzerkampfwagen* III Ausf A, were constructed and served in troop tests. The Ausf A had five large roadwheels on each side of the vehicle, and coil springs served for suspension. Although trials with troops showed that the coiled-spring suspension was unable to carry the tank—which weighed in excess of fifteen tons—through rough terrain, this vehicle served with the 1st Panzer Division in the Polish campaign. A redesign of the suspension followed, however,

Above: *A Panzerkampfwagen III Ausf A negotiates an obstacle during testing. Built in small numbers by Daimler-Benz in 1935, the A model of the Panzer III is recognizable by its oversized roadwheels and coil spring suspension.* Patton Museum

Above: *Although generally considered to be unreliable, a few Ausf A models of the Panzer III did see service in the Polish campaign. The two prominent return rollers are visible here, as are the two square transmission access hatches on the lower front hull.* Patton Museum

Panzerkampfwagen III Ausf A

Production	
Make	Daimler-Benz
Chassis (Fahrgestell) number	60101-60110
Specifications	
Length	5.69 m
Width	2.81 m
Height	2.34 m
Weight	15.4 tons
Fuel capacity	300 liters
Maximum speed	32 km/hr
Range, on-road	165 km
Range, cross-country	95 km
Crew	5
Communications	FuG 5
Armament	
Weapon, main	3.7 cm KwK L/46.5
Weapon, coaxial	2 x 7.92 mm MG 34
Weapon, ball-mounted	7.92 mm MG 34
Ammo stowage, main	120 rounds
Ammo stowage, secondary	4,425 rounds
Automotive	
Engine make	Maybach
Engine model	HL108TR
Engine configuration	V-12, liquid cooled
Engine displacement	10.8 liters
Engine horsepower	250 @ 3000 rpm

Panzerkampfwagen III Ausf B

Production	
Make	Daimler-Benz
Chassis (Fahrgestell) number	60201-60215
Specifications	
Length	6.00 m
Width	2.87 m
Height	2.45 m
Weight	15.9 tons
Fuel capacity	300 liters
Maximum speed	35 km/hr
Range, on-road	165 km
Range, cross-country	95 km
Crew	5
Communications	FuG 5
Armament	
Weapon, main	3.7 cm KwK L/46.5
Weapon, coaxial	2 x 7.92 mm MG 34
Weapon, ball-mounted	7.92 mm MG 34
Ammo stowage, main	120 rounds
Ammo stowage, secondary	4,425 rounds
Automotive	
Engine make	Maybach
Engine model	HL108TR
Engine configuration	V-12, liquid cooled
Engine displacement	10.8 liters
Engine horsepower	250 @ 3000 rpm

for the next series as the Ausf A was withdrawn from combat service.

Panzerkampfwagen III Ausf B
Eight roadwheels mounted on leaf springs were the hallmark of a new series—the Ausf B—which did away with the Ausf A's five wheels and coil springs. At one end of a leaf-spring assembly on the new tank were mounted the first two wheel stations. At the other end of that leaf-spring assembly were the second two wheel stations. Toward the rear of the tank was another leaf spring assembly on which were mounted in similar fashion the fifth and sixth wheel stations and the seventh and eighth at the very end. Dubbed the 2.Serie or Ausf B, a dozen of these tanks were manufactured for use in tests. Other than the spring and roadwheel configurations, this tank was virtually unchanged from the Ausf A.

Panzerkampfwagen III Ausf C
Daimler-Benz continued to work on the suspension and after further refinements came up with the 3a.Serie, also called the *Panzerkampfwagen* III Ausf C. This series

Above: *The next step in the development of the Panzer III was the Ausf B. This vehicle mounted eight roadwheels per side suspended with two leaf springs, four to a set. The wheels were mounted in pairs on bogie trucks. An additional return roller provided stability. The drive sprocket and idler wheel were unchanged.* Patton Museum

consisted of fifteen produced vehicles, which, like the earlier examples, saw service in the invasion of Poland.

Testing showed the Ausf B wheel and spring configuration to be better than the configuration on the Ausf A, but still less than optimal. Accordingly, a third version, the Ausf C, was developed, featuring three sets of leaf springs. Mounted on one leaf spring were the first two wheel stations, while the last two were mounted on the rearmost leaf spring. In the middle of each side of the vehicle was a third and longer leaf spring on which were mounted the four middle wheel stations.

Panzerkampfwagen III Ausf D

Modifications continued still, and in January 1938 the 3b.Serie or *Panzerkampfwagen* III Ausf D was introduced. Boasting increased armor protection, 30 mm plate replaced the previously used 14.5 mm armor thickness. A six-speed ZF SSG transmission was used instead of the earlier five-speed ZF SFG 75 employed in previous versions. Suspension was changed yet again—the leaf-spring assemblies that supported the first and last pairs of roadwheel stations were now installed at an angle rather than horizontally. In place of the fabricated steel cupola fitted to earlier versions of the *Panzerkampfwagen* III, the Ausf D had a cast commander's cupola. As had been the case with the Ausf C, a total of fifteen examples of the Ausf D were constructed.

Panzerkampfwagen III Ausf E

The *Panzerkampfwagen* III running gear continued to be modified over the course of 1938 so that by December of that year a new design had been devised that featured six roadwheels on each side, mounted on

Panzerkampfwagen III Ausf C

Production	
Make	Daimler-Benz
Chassis (Fahrgestell) number	60301-60315
Specifications	
Length	5.69 m
Width	2.81 m
Height	2.34 m
Weight	15.9 tons
Fuel capacity	300 liters
Maximum speed	35 km/hr
Range, on-road	165 km
Range, cross-country	95 km
Crew	5
Communications	FuG 5
Armament	
Weapon, main	3.7 cm KwK L/46.5
Weapon, coaxial	2 x 7.92 mm MG 34
Weapon, ball-mounted	7.92 mm MG 34
Ammo stowage, main	120 rounds
Ammo stowage, secondary	4,425 rounds
Automotive	
Engine make	Maybach
Engine model	HL108TR
Engine configuration	V-12, liquid cooled
Engine displacement	10.8 liters
Engine horsepower	250 @ 3000 rpm

Panzerkampfwagen III Ausf D

Production	
Make	Daimler-Benz
Chassis (Fahrgestell) number	60221-60225, 60316-60340
Specifications	
Length	5.92 m
Width	2.87 m
Height	2.45 m
Weight	15.9 tons
Fuel capacity	300 liters
Maximum speed	35 km/hr
Range, on-road	165 km
Range, cross-country	95 km
Crew	5
Communications	FuG 5
Armament	
Weapon, main	3.7 cm KwK L/46.5
Weapon, coaxial	2 x 7.92 mm MG 34
Weapon, ball-mounted	7.92 mm MG 34
Ammo stowage, main	120 rounds
Ammo stowage, secondary	4,425 rounds
Automotive	
Engine make	Maybach
Engine model	HL108TR
Engine configuration	V-12, liquid cooled
Engine displacement	10.8 liters
Engine horsepower	250 @ 3000 rpm

a torsion-bar suspension. This version, designated the *Panzerkampfwagen* III Ausf E, assumes the form that is usually remembered as that of this particular tank. With this version too, more assembly plants involved themselves in manufacturing the vehicle, because demand was on the increase. Besides Daimler-Benz, Henschel and MAN were now beginning to turn out the *Panzerkampfwagen* III.

The first five *Ausführungen* all incorporated the Maybach HL 100 TR power plant. All carried the 3.7 cm KwK 35/36 L/46.5 gun and three 7.92 mm MG 34 machine guns, with one hull-mounted machine gun and the other two fitted to the right of the main gun.

Panzerkampfwagen III Ausf F
When the *Panzerkampfwagen* III was improved yet again, by September 1939, most noticeably with the addition of brake cooling air intakes atop the glacis, the result was dubbed the Ausf F. Internally the vehicle was also up-engined, with fitting of the Maybach HL 120TRM

Above: *A new drive sprocket and idler wheel were introduced with the* Panzerkampfwagen III Ausf C. *The leaf-spring system was also redesigned, with three sets on each side: a large central set and two smaller ones to the front and rear. The smaller sets were further strengthened with the Ausf D model, an example of which is seen here serving in Poland.* Patton Museum

power plant, a magneto-ignition engine with more horsepower than the earlier HL 108TR could produce. The new engine's greater horsepower helped the vehicle cope with the steadily increasing weight of the frequently "improved" tank. To transfer the now greater power to the tracks, a Maybach Variorex 10-speed transmission was installed in the Ausf F.

Another change was that with the production of the Ausf F, two more companies joined the pool of *Panzerkampfwagen* III producers. Now Alkett and FAMO joined Daimler-Benz, Henschel, and MAN to produce more than four hundred of the Ausf F tanks. As with the previous *Ausführungen*, the first 335 Ausf F vehicles were armed with the 3.7 cm KwK 35/36 L/46.5 gun and three 7.92 mm MG 34 machine guns. With the war now underway, combat was highlighting the inadequacy of the 3.7 cm cannon in battle with enemy armor. Accordingly, it was decided to begin arming the Panzerkampfwagen III with 5.0 cm cannon. The tanks armed with the 5.0 cm KwK 38 L/42 also featured external mantlets and one, coaxial MG 34 machine gun. Approximately one hundred of these 5.0 cm-armed tanks were constructed.

Above: *This Ausf D model is seen while serving in Finland during the winter of 1941/42. In spite of its shortcomings as a main battle tank by this date, it still was capable of providing valuable infantry support with its three rapid-firing MG 34 machine guns.* Patton Museum

In August 1940, a program was launched to rearm the early Ausf F and also earlier Ausf E tanks with a 5.0 KwK 38 L/42 gun. This program continued throughout all of 1941 and into 1942. At the same time, 30 mm supplemental armor plating was added to the front and rear of the hull and to the front of the superstructure.

Panzerkampfwagen III Ausf G

Meanwhile, starting in April 1940, manufacture of the *Panzerkampfwagen* III moved on to the Ausf G. Produced by Alkett, Daimler-Benz, FAMO, Henschel, MAN, MNH, and Wegmann, in the end some six hundred units of this model would be produced. For reasons as yet unexplained, the first few Ausf G models produced were armed with obsolete 3.7 cm KwK 35/36 L/46.5 guns mounted in an internal mantlet. The majority of the production models were fitted with the more powerful 5.0 cm KwK 38 L/42. Ausf G production continued until February 1941.

The Ausf G turret was redesigned to feature longer sides, allowing the commander's cupola to fit entirely on the top of the turret, no longer protruding from the turret's rear as in previous models. The thickness of the armor at the hull's rear was increased and the driver's visor was improved.

Panzerkampfwagen III Ausf H

Some six months after production of the Ausf G began, concurrent manufacture of the Ausf H commenced. Alkett,

Above: *The* Panzerkampfwagen *III Ausf E was a complete redesign of the original concept. Perhaps its most significant improvement was the innovative torsion-bar suspension. This eliminated the vulnerable external leaf springs and better distributed the weight of the now 19-ton tank. The Ausf E can be easily identified by the circular openings of the drive sprockets and the fan-shaped pattern of the idler wheels.* National Archives and Records Administration

Above: *Many additional external and internal modifications of the Panzer III followed, prompting another variant, the Ausf F. The defining feature of that model can be seen here, the armored brake cooling intakes. They are located just to the inside of the headlight housings. Many of the new features were incorporated during refit, making older variants disappear quickly.* National Archives and Records Administration

Panzerkampfwagen III Ausf E

Production	
Make	Daimler-Benz
Chassis (Fahrgestell) number	60401-60441
Make	MAN
Chassis (Fahrgestell) number	60442-60496
Specifications	
Length	5.38 m
Width	2.91 m
Height	2.44 m
Weight	19.5 tons
Fuel capacity	320 liters
Maximum speed	40 km/hr
Range, on-road	165 km
Range, cross-country	95 km
Crew	5
Communications	FuG 5
Armament	
Weapon, main	3.7 cm KwK L/46.5
Weapon, coaxial	2 x 7.92 mm MG 34
Weapon, ball-mounted	7.92 mm MG 34
Ammo stowage, main	120 rounds
Ammo stowage, secondary	3,600 rounds
Automotive	
Engine make	Maybach
Engine model	HL 120 TRM
Engine configuration	V-12, liquid cooled
Engine displacement	11.9 liters
Engine horsepower	265 @ 2600 rpm

Production	
Make	MAN
Chassis (Fahrgestell) number	61001-61096
Make	Daimler-Benz
Chassis (Fahrgestell) number	61101-61195
Make	Famo
Chassis (Fahrgestell) number	61201-61228
Make	Henschel
Chassis (Fahrgestell) number	61301-61420
Make	Miag
Chassis (Fahrgestell) number	61501-61560
Make	Alkett
Chassis (Fahrgestell) number	61601-61636
Specifications	
Length	5.38 m
Width	2.91 m
Height	2.44 m
Weight	15.9 tons
Fuel capacity	320 liters
Maximum speed	40 km/hr
Range, on-road	165 km
Range, cross-country	95 km
Crew	5
Communications	FuG 5
Armament	
Weapon, main	3.7 cm KwK L/45
Weapon, coaxial	2 x 7.92 mm MG 34
Weapon, ball-mounted	7.92 mm MG 34
Ammo stowage, main	120 rounds
Ammo stowage, secondary	4,450 rounds
Automotive	
Engine make	Maybach
Engine model	HL 120 TRM
Engine configuration	V-12, liquid cooled
Engine displacement	11.9 liters
Engine horsepower	265 @ 2600 rpm

Henschel, MAN, MNH, MIAG, and Wegmann made the Ausf H, which remained in production until 1941. Supplemental armor plates of 30 mm thickness were bolted on the vehicle to try to enhance protection from increasingly efficient enemy antitank guns.

The Ausf H also got a new transmission—the ten-speed Variorex transmission, which had caused some difficulties, was replaced on the Ausf H by a six-speed Maybach SSG 77

Above: *This overhead view provides a good perspective on the new design. The Ausf E/F retained the 3.7 cm main gun and the coaxially mounted MG 34s within an internally mounted mantlet. The twin signal ports to either side of the commander's cupola are yet another feature of the new tank. Hatches on the top of the front hull permitted access to the transmission.* Patton Museum

Panzerkampfwagen III Ausf G with 5.0 cm gun

Production	
Make	MAN
Chassis (Fahrgestell) number	65001-65090
Make	Henschel
Chassis (Fahrgestell) number	65101-65255
Make	Famo
Chassis (Fahrgestell) number	65365-65379
Make	Alkett
Chassis (Fahrgestell) number	65401-65550
Make	Miag
Chassis (Fahrgestell) number	65720-65799
Make	Daimler-Benz
Chassis (Fahrgestell) number	65801-65860
Make	MNH
Chassis (Fahrgestell) number	65901-65950
Specifications	
Length	5.38 m
Width	2.91 m
Height	2.44 m
Weight	19.8 tons
Fuel capacity	300 liters
Maximum speed	40 km/hr
Range, on-road	165 km
Range, cross-country	95 km
Crew	5
Communications	FuG 5
Armament	
Weapon, main	5.0 cm KwK 38 L/42
Weapon, coaxial	7.92 mm MG 34
Weapon, ball-mounted	7.92 mm MG 34
Ammo stowage, main	99 rounds
Ammo stowage, secondary	3,750 rounds
Automotive	
Engine make	Maybach
Engine model	HL 120 TRM
Engine configuration	V-12, liquid cooled
Engine displacement	11.9 liters
Engine horsepower	265 @ 2600 rpm

Above: *Another leap forward in the design of the Panzer III was the Ausf G. In order to counter Allied tanks such as the T-34 and the Sherman, which had thicker armor, the main gun was changed to the 5 cm KwK L/42. This was now mounted within an external mantlet that also offered improved armored protection. The Ausf G added extra protection for the driver with the installation of an armored visor and block known as a* Fahresehklappe. Thomas Anderson

Above: *This* Panzerkampfwagen III Ausf G *has been outfitted as a* Tauchpanzer *amphibious tank. The frames around the gun mantlet and MG port allowed for the installation of waterproof covers, and covers over the air intakes could be closed for deep fording (seen at the left). Air intake for the crew and engine was by means of a floating buoy and hose. Thus prepared, the tank moved along the bottom of a water obstacle. Although originally designed for the invasion of Britain, a few were used in the Soviet Union.* Patton Museum

Above: *The Ausf H model saw the addition of 30 mm armor plates to the front hull, as well as new 40 cm tracks to help distribute the extra weight. This is a* Panzerbefehlswagen *Ausf H command tank. The* befehlswagen *was outfitted with the FuG 6 radio set and either the FuG 2, FuG 8, or FuG 7 command net radio set. The main gun and traverse system were omitted to create more room in the turret, which was bolted in place. Additional pistol ports and vision devices were added, as was a TSF1 periscope, which was mounted in the turret roof. In order to disguise its purpose, the vehicle mounted a realistic dummy gun in the gun mantlet.* Patton Museum

gearbox. The new model was also fitted with new sprockets and idler wheels.

Armament on production Ausf H tanks—like that on most of the Ausf G—consisted of the 5.0 cm KwK 38 L/42. In the course of the years 1942–1943, that armament was replaced on many Ausf H tanks with the 5.0 cm KwK39 L/60 gun.

Panzerkampfwagen III Ausf J

As combat progressed in World War II, it became increasingly evident that the existing *Panzerkampfwagen* III versions had insufficient armor protection for current battlefield conditions. This reality prompted a total redesign of the vehicle with an eye to upgrading its protection. This redesign resulted in the *Panzerkampfwagen* III Ausf J.

The Ausf J entered production in March 1941, being designated both the last SdKfz 141 and the first SdKfz 141/1 *Panzerkampfwagen* III tank. Since fully 2,700 of the tanks were being sought, a large pool of companies received contracts for the vehicle—Alkett, Daimler-Benz, Henschel, MAN, MNH, MIAG, and Wegmann. Indeed, by July 1942, a total of 2,616 of the tanks had rolled off the assembly lines.

Although improved armor was the Ausf J's main virtue, the vehicle also featured a new driver's visor (*Fahrersehklappe* 50) and a ball mount (*Kugelblende* 50) for the hull-mounted 7.92 mm MG 34 machine gun. Armor plating was further enhanced when, beginning in April 1942, 20 mm spaced armor was added to the gun mantlet and front of the superstructure. The first 1,549 production vehicles carried the 5.0 cm KwK 38 L/42 gun and two MG 34 machine guns. These tanks were the last vehicles to receive the designation PzKpfw III Ausf J/SdKfz 141. From December 1941 to July 1942, 1,067 tanks were produced that were armed with 5.0 cm KwK 39 L/60 guns and two MG 34 machine guns. These vehicles were listed as PzKpfw III Ausf J/SdKfz 1451/1. British forces confronting the Germans in North Africa had their own designation for the long-barreled versions of these tanks: "Mark III Special."

Panzerkampfwagen III Ausf H

Production	
Make	Daimler-Benz
Chassis (Fahrgestell) number	70001-70175
Specifications	
Length	5.52 m
Width	2.95 m
Height	2.50 m
Weight	21.8 tons
Fuel capacity	320 liters
Maximum speed	40 km/hr
Range, on-road	165 km
Range, cross-country	95 km
Crew	5
Communications	FuG 5
Armament	
Weapon, main	5.0 cm KwK 38 L/42
Weapon, coaxial	7.92 mm MG 34
Weapon, ball-mounted	7.92 mm MG 34
Ammo stowage, main	99 rounds
Ammo stowage, secondary	3,750 rounds
Automotive	
Engine make	Maybach
Engine model	HL 120 TRM
Engine configuration	V-12, liquid cooled
Engine displacement	11.9 liters
Engine horsepower	265 @ 2600 rpm

Panzerkampfwagen III Ausf L

Beginning in June 1942, a version boasting improvements to the gun mount and turret armor entered production under the designation *Panzerkampfwagen* III Ausf L. Alkett, Daimler-Benz, Henschell, MAN, MIAG, MNH, and Wegmann joined to manufacture 653 of these tanks. Armament on the Ausf L, like that on the earlier Ausf J, consisted of a 5.0 cm KwK 39 L/60 main gun and two 7.92 mm MG 34 machine guns. Most production models

Panzerkampfwagen III Ausf J as initially produced

Production	
Make	Daimler-Benz
Chassis (Fahrgestell) number	68001-68134
Make	MAN
Chassis (Fahrgestell) number	68201-68333
Make	Miag
Chassis (Fahrgestell) number	68401-68533
Make	MNH
Chassis (Fahrgestell) number	68601-68700
Make	Henschel
Chassis (Fahrgestell) number	68701-68979
Specifications	
Length	5.56 m
Width	2.95 m
Height	2.50 m
Weight	21.5 tons
Fuel capacity	320 liters
Maximum speed	40 km/hr
Range, on-road	145 km
Range, cross-country	85 km
Crew	5
Communications	FuG 5
Armament	
Weapon, main	5.0 cm KwK 38 L/42
Weapon, coaxial	7.92 mm MG 34
Weapon, ball-mounted	7.92 mm MG 34
Ammo stowage, main	99 rounds
Ammo stowage, secondary	3,750 rounds
Automotive	
Engine make	Maybach
Engine model	HL 120 TRM
Engine configuration	V-12, liquid cooled
Engine displacement	11.9 liters
Engine horsepower	265 @ 2600 rpm

Left: *The* Panzerkampfwagen *III Ausf J discarded the supplemental armor of the Ausf H in favor of a new 50 mm armored glacis plate. The transmission access hatches were also simplified. The Ausf J featured the much more potent 5 cm L/60 main gun immediately recognizable by its longer barrel. The mantlet of the J model was also thickened to improve protection.* Patton Museum

Right: *This Ausf J of the SS Wiking Division is moving forward in the summer of 1943 on the Eastern Front. The improved and smooth-faced 50 mm visors on the mantlet are a distinctive feature of the* Panzerkampfwagen *III Ausf J.* National Archives and Records Administration

Panzerkampfwagen III Ausf L

Specifications	
Length	6.41 m
Width	2.95 m
Height	2.50 m
Weight	21.3 tons
Fuel capacity	320 liters
Maximum speed	40 km/hr
Range, on-road	155 km
Range, cross-country	95 km
Crew	5
Communications	FuG 5
Armament	
Weapon, main	5.0 cm KwK 39 L/60
Weapon, coaxial	7.92 mm MG 34
Weapon, ball-mounted	7.92 mm MG 34
Ammo stowage, main	78 rounds
Ammo stowage, secondary	4,950 rounds
Automotive	
Engine make	Maybach
Engine model	HL 120 TRM
Engine configuration	V-12, liquid cooled
Engine displacement	11.9 liters
Engine horsepower	265 @ 2600 rpm

lacked hull side escape hatches as well as the front visor for the loader and turret side ports. For the first time on a *Panzerkampfwagen* III, defense against aerial attack was taken into consideration with the Ausf L. An antiaircraft machine-gun mount (*Fliegerbeschußgerät* 41/42) was mounted on the commander's cupola. It was also retrofitted on older tanks. An additional air filter, improved oil filters, and a different reduction ratio were features on those Ausf L tanks supplied to the German *Afrika Korps*. This sub-variant received the tropical designation Ausf L (Tp).

Panzerkampfwagen III Ausf M

Some four months after the Ausf L started rolling off assembly lines, yet another upgrade of the *Panzerkampfwagen* III, the *Panzerkampfwagen* III Ausf M, had entered production. A production pool of MAN, MIAG, MNH, and Wegmann turned out 250 Ausf M vehicles by the time production came to a halt in February 1943. The Ausf M could wade through hard-bottom water crossings about 1.5 meters deep—a half-meter deeper than earlier models could handle. It was fitted with a 90 mm three-tube NbK discharger mounted well to the front on both sides of the turret. Armament on the Ausf M, like that on the Ausf J and Ausf L, consisted of a 5.0 cm KwK 39 L/60 gun and two 7.92 mm MG 34 machine guns, one coaxial with the main gun and another in the bow. In March 1943, the practice of hanging armored skirts, or *Schürtzen*, from the sides of the hull began. Similar armor plates were also hung from the sides of the turret.

Left: *The Panzerkampfwagen III Ausf L can be distinguished by the presence of even more supplemental armor. Spaced plates of 20 mm thickness were added to the glacis. Additional spaced armor was also seen on the mantlet, although this had appeared on some late Ausf J models. This tank is an Ausf M and incorporates several new features, such as the smoke launchers on the turret and the fording covers for the air intakes. The latter was used in conjunction with modification around the exhaust to enable the tank to ford a depth of 1.5 meters.* Patton Museum

Panzerkampfwagen III Ausf M

Specifications	
Length	6.41 m
Width	3.41 m w *Schürzen*
Height	2.50 m
Weight	21.3 tons
Fuel capacity	320 liters
Maximum speed	40 km/hr
Range, on-road	155 km
Range, cross-country	95 km
Crew	5
Communications	FuG 5
Armament	
Weapon, main	5.0 cm KwK 39 L/60
Weapon, coaxial	7.92 mm MG 34
Weapon, ball-mounted	7.92 mm MG 34
Ammo stowage, main	84 rounds
Ammo stowage, secondary	3,800 rounds
Automotive	
Engine make	Maybach
Engine model	HL 120 TRM
Engine configuration	V-12, liquid cooled
Engine displacement	11.9 liters
Engine horsepower	265 @ 2600 rpm

Panzerkampfwagen III Ausf N

Specifications	
Length	5.65 m
Width	3.41 m w *Schürzen*
Height	2.50 m
Weight	23 tons
Fuel capacity	320 liters
Maximum speed	40 km/hr
Range, on-road	155 km
Range, cross-country	95 km
Crew	5
Communications	FuG 5
Armament	
Weapon, main	7.5 cm KwK L/24
Weapon, coaxial	7.92 mm MG 34
Weapon, ball-mounted	7.92 mm MG 34
Ammo stowage, main	64 rounds
Ammo stowage, secondary	3,450 rounds
Automotive	
Engine make	Maybach
Engine model	HL 120 TRM
Engine configuration	V-12, liquid cooled
Engine displacement	11.9 liters
Engine horsepower	265 @ 2600 rpm

Panzerkampfwagen III Ausf N
Exasperated by the increasing superiority of Soviet tanks, Hitler finally denounced the *Panzerkampfwagen* III as "inferior" and put a halt to further production so that plants could totally change over to manufacture of the *Sturmgeschütz*. The last version of the *Panzerkampfwagen* to be built—the Ausf N—was constructed by Henschel, MAN, MIAG, MNH, and Wegmann from June 1942 through August 1943.

Armament on the Ausf N consisted of the short 7.5 cm KwK 37 L/24 gun, which had been taken off the PzKpfw IV Ausf A to F1 tanks when they were rearmed with the longer-barreled 7.5 cm guns. The Ausf N retained the two MG 34 machine guns.

Envisioned as close support vehicles, 663 Ausf N tanks were manufactured using the chassis types originally intended for the Ausf J (3), L (447), and M (213). The Ausf N was produced without spaced armor on the mantlet as a weight-saving measure. Ausf N tanks carried varying quantities of ammunition, depending upon the chassis on which the particular tank was constructed. Ausf N tanks built on Ausf L chassis carried 56 rounds of 7.5 cm ammunition. Ausf N versions built on the Ausf M chassis could carry 64 rounds.

Later production Ausf N tanks featured a one-piece commander's cupola hatch rather than the two-piece hatch utilized on earlier examples. The cupola on the final Ausf N

Left: *The final variant of the Panzer III was the Ausf N. This was armed with the short-barreled 7.5 cm L/24 gun originally used in the Panzer IV and Sturmgeschütz. This vehicle was now to fulfill the infantry support intended for those earlier vehicles. The most recognizable feature is, of course, the shorter weapon, but other notable changes are the larger and solid mantlet and full complement of* Schürzen *panels. Many of the Ausf Ns were converted from Ausf J, L, or M models, giving them a mixture of features. Much of these are in evidence on these vehicles surrendering to British forces in 1945.* National Archives and Records Administration

vehicles was taken over from the *Panzerkampfwagen* IV Ausf G.

As was the case with other tanks in this series, *Schürzen* were installed prior to shipment after March 1943. *Zimmerit* antimagnetic mine paste was also applied to those vehicles.

Panzerbeobachtungswagen III

Between February 1943 and April 1944, 262 *Panzerkampfwagen* III tanks were reconstructed as artillery observation vehicles or *Artillerie-Panzerbeobachtungswagen* III. The vehicles were rebuilt in order to have a way to insert forward artillery observers in Panzer formations, while at the same time disguising their purpose and protecting their crewmen.

Reconstructing the vehicles required removal of the main gun and mantlet and installing a slightly thicker fixed plate in place of it. A ball-mounted MG 34 machine gun was installed in the middle of the new fixed plate, and a dummy main gun was welded just to the right of the machine gun. An extendable TBF2 artillery observation periscope was installed, by piercing the turret roof. There were also provisions for installing additional periscopes in the commander's cupola.

The ball-mounted machine gun in the hull was eliminated, opening up space in the vehicle's interior for added

Panzerbeobachtungswagen III

Specifications	
Length	5.52 m
Width	2.95 m
Height	2.50 m
Weight	23 tons
Fuel capacity	310 liters
Maximum speed	40 km/hr
Range, on-road	155 km
Range, cross-country	95 km
Crew	5
Communications	FuG 8, FuG 4, Fu Spr Ger f
Armament	
Weapon, main	7.92 mm MG 34
Automotive	
Engine make	Maybach
Engine model	HL 120 TRM
Engine configuration	V-12, liquid cooled
Engine displacement	11.9 liters
Engine horsepower	265 @ 2600 rpm

Above: *Panzerkampfwagen III Ausf E, F and G all were used as basis for constructing* Panzerbeobachtungswagen III. *Rather than building the observation vehicles new from the ground up, older tanks were converted in the course of their rebuilding after extensive use or damage in the field.* Ordnance Museum

Above: *Although only in water up to the commander's cupola in this view, the* Tauchpanzer *was designed to operate in depths up to 15 meters. Ultimately, they were not used for their intended purpose, the invasion of England, and were modified slightly and used for river crossing on the Russian Front.* Patton Museum

Above: *Intended to play a key role in Operation Sea Lion, the planned invasion of England, was the* Panzerkampfwagen III als Tauchpanzer. *The large hose wrapped around this* Tauchpanzer *was its snorkel. Check valves prevented water from entering the exhaust during submerged operation. When that operation was canceled, the vehicles were transferred to the Eastern Front and used for river crossing.* Patton Museum

radio equipment—a FuG 8, FuG 4, *Funksprechgerät* f, and a dismountable *Tornisterfunkgerät*. The hull ball mount was replaced with a pistol port, facilitating some sort of protection in desperate situations.

Panzerbeogachtungswagen III vehicles, which served throughout the war, were attached to forward observers with *Hummel* and *Wespe* batteries.

Panzerkampfwagen III *als Tauchpanzer*

Another somewhat unusual adaptation of the *Panzerkampfwagen* III, indeed one that enjoyed some measure of success, was the *Panzerkampfwagen* III *als Tauchpanzer*—i.e., an underwater version of the tank. More that 150 examples of this diving tank were developed in preparation for Germany's planned invasion of England—*Unternehmen Seelöwe* (Operation Sea Lion). *Panzerkampfwagen* III vehicles of various *Ausführungen* were converted to dive tanks, equipped to operate submerged to depths of as much as 15 meters. With the Luftwaffe failing to acquire air superiority over Britain, Hitler ordered Sea Lion postponed indefinitely in September 1940 and then, on October 12, 1940, the German leader ordered dispersal of the forces that had been gathering for the operation. The *Tauchpanzer* went on to see service in river crossings on the Eastern Front.

Panzerbefehlswagen III

Daimler-Benz also built command tanks on the *Panzerkampfwagen* III chassis. These vehicles, known as *Panzerbefehlswagen* III, were manufactured in the Ausf D1 (30), Ausf E (45), and Ausf H (175) (SdKfz 266-268) versions from June 1938 through February 1943. To serve in the command role, the interior of these tanks was packed with added communications gear, and to supply the needed space for this equipment, the vehicle's main gun and ammunition were deleted and a dummy weapon installed.

Above: *During wartime there existed a need to place commanders on the front line of the action, yet keep them in communication with their subordinates. The* Panzerbefehlswagen *was intended to do just that. Modified combat tanks, such as this Ausf E, were used in this capacity. The dummy guns were quite convincing looking, but the array of radio antennae clearly signals this* Afrika Korps *vehicle's purpose.* Patton Museum

Above: *A* Panzerbefehlswagen *based on the* Panzerkampfwagen *III Ausf H leads a column of gun tanks through snow-covered terrain. The blanked-out hull ball mount is visible in this view; only the 7.92 mm MG 34 in the former turret armed the command vehicles.* Patton Museum

Above: *The number of men in the crew remained the same whether a gun tank or command tank, with the additional radio equipment being operated by "extra" crewman.* Patton Museum

In addition, a new form of command tank was created, beginning in August 1942. Known as the *Panzerbefehlswagen* III *mit 5 cm KwK L/42 / SdKfz 141*, the vehicles were both new production and made by retrofitting older vehicles. These command tanks retained the 5.0 cm main gun but reduced the amount of ammunition stowage and eliminated the hull machine gun to make room for the added radio gear.

Never advancing beyond the trial stage was an unusual *Panzerkampfwagen* III version that was based on the Ausf N. Produced in October 1943, the three prototypes of the vehicle were Ausf N tanks adapted to run on railroad tracks. The aim of the experiment was to create a vehicle that could protect railway lines on the Eastern Front. The vehicles had a maximum on-rail speed of 100 km/hr but never advanced beyond the experimental stage.

Panzerkampfwagen IV

Commonly called the Panzer IV, the *Panzerkampfwagen* IV played a key role in Nazi Germany's World War II armor strategy. Armed with what was at the start of the war a fairly heavy 75 mm main gun, the Panzer IV was expected to constitute heavy tank companies of tank battalions. Each battalion was expected to comprise one heavy tank company and three companies of medium tanks—the *Panzerkampfwagen* III. While the Panzer III tanks would take on enemy tanks and infantry, the Panzer IV tanks would confront heavy enemy fortifications and similar targets.

As often happens with weapons systems, the role of the *Panzerkampfwagen* IV evolved over time. A longer, higher-velocity 75 mm gun replaced the earlier main gun, and the Panzer IV became the core of Germany's armored forces. It was Germany's only tank to remain in production throughout all of World War II, and was the most produced tank in the arsenal of the Third Reich. Moreover, the Panzer IV was also exported to Germany's Axis allies and to countries with which Germany sought friendly relations—Romania

Above: *The* Neubaufahrzeug *(new construction vehicle) was a Rheinmetall-Borsig prototype for a medium tank, based on experience gained from the earlier* Grosstraktor. *Two initial* Neubaufahrzeug *vehicles constructed of mild steel were produced in 1935, and three additional, experimental examples built with armor plate were finished in 1935. They had a main turret designed by Krupp, with a 7.5 cm KwK L/24 cannon and a 3.7 cm KwK L/45 cannon. There also were two small turrets with 7.93 mm MG13 machine guns. Seen here is one of the three armored vehicles.* Patton Museum

receiving 126, Bulgaria receiving 91, Hungary 84, Spain 20, Finland 15, Turkey 15, and Italy 12. Considering its central role in the campaigns of Hitler's *Wehrmacht*, it is a somewhat surprising fact that the Panzer IV's development began well before World War II, indeed even before Hitler came to power.

Under threat of invasion and possible dismemberment, the German delegation reluctantly signed the Treaty of Versailles on June 28, 1919, bringing an end to World War I, which had begun on that day five years earlier. Named in that Treaty as the main aggressor and bearer of war guilt, Germany was forced to renounce forever the production and purchase of armored cars and tanks.

Notwithstanding the treaty provisions, by 1926 Germany was already working on tank designs, albeit clandestinely. The next year, contracts were issued for the manufacture of prototype tanks under the code name *Grosstraktor* or "large tractor." Six examples were eventually constructed—two each from Krupp, Daimler-Benz, and Rheinmetall—and completed in 1929, after which they were dispatched to a secret German training facility set up in the Soviet Union. Located in the city of Kazan on the Volga, the clandestine *Panzerschule Kama* or "Kama Tank School" operated from 1929 to 1933. The school was the product of a conspiracy between Weimar Germany and the Soviet Union to conceal the German tank program from the remaining Allied powers. It gave the Germans a way to evade the Versailles prohibition on the development of armor and aircraft and enabled the Soviet Red Army to benefit from cutting-edge German military technology and tactics.

Significantly, the designer of Krupp's "large tractor" was Senior Engineer Erich Woelfert, a specialist who would remain a key figure in the Panzer IV program until its final demise. As a result of the training and testing undertaken in Kazan, by 1932, Germany had started to think about manufacture of a new medium tank. At first, in keeping with the practice of concealing the nature of these tank projects, the vehicle was code named the *mittlere Traktor*—medium tractor. By October 1933, however, the name had been changed to *Neubaufahrzeug*—new build vehicle. Around the same time, the new Nazi government in Germany ordered the closure of the Kama school in Kazan, Russia, following diplomatic gains by Germany at the Geneva Conference and increasing tension between Moscow and Berlin.

To start with, two contracts for mild-steel prototypes of the *Neubaufahrzeug* were issued, one for a tank with turret and chassis designed by Rheinmetall, and a second tank to have a turret from Krupp mounted on a Rheinmetall chassis. The tank was to be armed with a 75 mm KwK 37 L/24 or 75 mm *Kampfwagenkanone*, or "tank gun," whose barrel was to be 24 calibers (75 mm) long. As secondary armament, the tank was to be fitted with a 37 mm KwK 36 L/45.

Completed in 1934 and early 1935, those mild-steel prototypes were followed by three more examples—armored this time—all with the Krupp turret. These tanks were finished in 1935 and 1936. These armored tanks were deployed during the German invasion of Norway in April 1940.

A *Begleitwagen* or "escort vehicle" (BW) represented the next stage in the evolution of medium tank design. Rheinmetall and Krupp were approached in 1934 for preliminary designs for such a vehicle. Then, on February 26, 1935, Rheinmetall received a contract for a wooden mock-up and mild-steel prototype of that firm's chassis design. Krupp was awarded a similar contract.

Unlike all the tanks previously discussed in this section, the BW had to be driven through front-mounted drive sprockets and therefore required a specially designed tank engine. Aircraft engines that drove through rear-mounted

Left: *The* Begleitwagen *(escort vehicle) prototype for a medium tank was constructed by Rheinmetall. It featured a Maybach Type HL 100 TR engine and a round enclosure on the top of the hull; it was intended that this enclosure would be replaced by a turret containing a 7.5 cm cannon and two machine guns.* Patton Museum

drive sprockets served as the power plant for all the tanks discussed up to this point.

The BW was powered by a Maybach 10-liter liquid cooled V-12 gasoline engine, model number HL 100 TR, that developed 300 horsepower at 3,000 rpm.

Suspension components that were originally designed for the *Neubaufahrzeug* were employed in the Rheinmetall prototype. The two Krupp prototypes, on the other hand, had differing types of suspensions. Krupp's BW I incorporated, on each side, eight pairs of roadwheels that were 420 mm in diameter. Two pairs were mounted via leaf springs per bogie. The BW II, also from Krupp, featured torsion-bar suspension and six pairs of larger roadwheels on each of the vehicle's sides.

The Krupp BW I prototype was finished and operational as early as April 30, 1936. The Krupp BW II, however, was only tested as a chassis, initially not being finished with a turret. Only in mid-1938 was a turret installed on the BW II, and then the experiment was a brief one, as by 1939 the BW II chassis was serving as a test article for bridge-laying vehicles. In testing, the torsion-bar suspension proved problematic, and it was soon resolved that BW vehicles would feature the BW I prototype's leaf-spring suspension.

Panzer IV Ausf A

In 1936 a general army bulletin standardized the nomenclature of armored vehicles. So by the end of that year, when the BW I chassis had accumulated more than 1,500 miles in tests, there were few improvements to be made and a production contract for 35 1.Serie/BW (first-series, escort vehicles) was awarded to Krupp-Grusonwerk. Officially designated *Panzer* IV *Ausführung* (type) A, the vehicles looked nearly identical to the BW I, although nearly all the components had been newly engineered. The vehicle was powered by a V-12 Maybach HL 108 TR gasoline engine that was driven through a *Zahnradfabrick* SFG 75 five-speed synchronized transmission. Homogenous, nickel-free PP694 armor of thicknesses ranging from 5 mm to 14.5 mm protected the vehicles from incoming shells up to 7.92 mm armor piercing.

The German army accepted the first two Panzer IV Ausf A tanks on November 30, 1937. Stowage for 140 rounds of main gun ammunition was provided in the two tanks—the greatest stowage capacity provided in any of the Panzer IV series vehicles. In later Ausf A tanks, ammunition storage was reconfigured to make reloading the bow machine gun easier. That reconfiguration, however, resulted in main-gun round stowage being cut down to 122 rounds—a figure that still represented the second greatest stowage in any of the Panzer IV tanks. The Ausf A remained in production until June 1938. A distinguishing feature of almost all Ausf A tanks was a machine-gun ball mount in setback armor located in front of the compartment of the radio operator. This setback armor was not, however, a feature of the last five Ausf A tanks produced. Harkort, Essen, was unable to deliver the hulls for these last Ausf A vehicles by the deadline

Panzerkampfwagen IV *Ausführung* A, 1.Series BW (*Begleitwagen*)

Production	
Make	Krupp Grusonwerk
Chassis (Fahrgestell) number	80101–80135
Quantity	35
Dimensions	
Length	19 feet, 5.07 inches
Width	9 feet, 3.42 inches
Height	8 feet, 9.51 inches
Wheelbase	7 feet, 10.9 inches
Track Contact	11 feet, 6.58 inches
Weight	39.690 pounds
Automotive	
Engine	Maybach HL 108 TR
Configuration	V-12, water-cooled
Displacement	10.8 liters
Power output	230 @ 2,600 rpm
Fuel capacity	124 gallons
Transmission	ZF S.S.G.75
Speeds	5 + reverse
Steering	differential
Track	Kgs 6110/380/120
Links per side	99
Performance	
Crew	5
Maximum speed	20 mph
Cruising speed	12.5 mph
Cross country	6 mph
Range, on-road	130 miles
Range, cross-country	80 miles
Fording depth	31.5 inches
Trench crossing	7.5 feet
Armament	
Main Gun	7.5 cm KwK37 L/24
Range	2,000 meters
Coaxial	7.92 mm MG 34
Elevation	-10 to +20 degrees
Ball mount	7.92 mm MG 34
Ammo, 7.5 cm	122 rounds
Ammo, 7.92 mm	3,000 rounds

set and accordingly, Krupp opted to put the last five Ausf A tanks together using upper hulls originally intended for the Ausf B. These hulls, which were already available in the plant, did not have the ball-mount machine gun or the setback armor of the compartment of the radio operator.

Panzer IV Ausf B
The initial Ausf A tanks had not yet been accepted when production of forty-two follow-on tanks—the Series 2, Ausf B—was ordered in another contract awarded once again to Krupp Grusonwerk. These tanks were significantly heavier, boasting armor that could now protect the tank's front plates from 2 cm rounds—rather than the 7.92 mm rounds of earlier vehicles. These heavier tanks received a more powerful engine as well—the Maybach-designed HL 120 TR gasoline power plant that provided 285 horsepower and was linked to a six-speed SSG76 transmission, instead of the five-speed transmission employed in the Ausf A. Another measure taken to cope with the increased weight of the vehicle was the reduction of main-gun ammunition stowage to 80 rounds. In addition the superstructure was narrowed. Whereas the superstructure on earlier versions was almost as wide as the vehicle track width, the Ausf B superstructure only reached approximately half of the way across the tracks.

Also serving to mitigate weight gain from heavier armor was the deletion of the ball mount from the single-plane front armor plate of the superstructure. As noted above, the front plate on the Ausf A featured a ball turret and a setback at the position of the radio operator. The Ausf B turret incorporated the same type of commander's cupola as that used on the Panzer III Ausf C.

The Panzer IV Ausf B remained in production from May through October 1938.

Although the above remarks serve to delineate the intended configuration of the Ausf B, some variation did slip in. As noted above, Ausf B hulls were fitted to the last five Ausf A tanks due to the delayed arrival of Ausf A hulls. When the Ausf A hulls showed up, they were fitted on Ausf B tanks. Then, when Harkort's output of 18 Ausf B hulls lagged behind schedule, and another 12 Ausf B hulls from Eisen- und Hüttenwerke were also delayed, Krupp built thirty Ausf B chassis—numbers 80213 through 80242—using Ausf C hulls so as to keep output moving forward with no interruptions. In fact, as a result of such exigencies, of the forty-two Ausf B tanks that were ordered, only seven were actually finished with Ausf B hulls.

Left: *Crewmen from 4.Kompanie, 1.Panzer Regiment, 1.Panzer Division are sitting or standing in the hatches of an example of the first production model of the Panzerkampfwagen IV Ausf A as it rolls through a village in Poland. The main armament was a 7.5 cm KwK 37 L/24 cannon. The bogie wheels, eight double wheels per side, were mounted on four bogie assemblies. Note the jogged front of the upper hull, with the driver's compartment on the vehicle's left jutting farther forward than the right side.* Patton Museum

Above: *Only forty-two examples of the second production model of the Panzerkampfwagen IV, the Ausf B, were completed, all by Krupp-Grusonwerk, from May to October 1938. Changes from the Ausf A included a straight-across frontal plate on the upper hull to the front of the driver's and radio operator's compartments; thicker frontal armor (from 14.5 mm to 30 mm) on the turret, upper hull, and bow; splash guards for the turret; improved side visors; and a new cupola with thicker (30 mm) armor.* Patton Museum

Panzerkampfwagen IV Ausf B, 2.Series BW (*Begleitwagen*)

Production	
Make	Krupp Grusonwerk
Chassis (*Fahrgestell*) numbers	80201–80242
Quantity	42
Dimensions	
Length	19 feet, 5.07 inches
Width	9 feet, 3.42 inches
Height	8 feet, 9.51 inches
Wheelbase	7 feet, 10.9 inches
Track Contact	11 feet, 6.58 inches
Weight	40,793 pounds
Automotive	
Engine	Maybach HL 120 TR
Configuration	V-12, water-cooled
Displacement	11.9 liters
Power output	265 @ 2600 rpm
Fuel capacity	124 gallons
Transmission	ZF S.S.G.76
Speeds	6 + reverse
Steering	differential
Track	Kgs 6110/380/120
Links per side	99
Performance	
Crew	5
Maximum speed	26 mph
Cruising speed	15.5 mph
Cross country	12.5 mph
Range, on-road	130 miles
Range, cross-country	80 miles
Fording depth	31.5 inches
Trench crossing	7.5 feet
Armament	
Main Gun	7.5 cm KwK37 L/24
Range	2,000 meters
Coaxial	7.92 mm MG 34
Elevation	-10 to +20 degrees
Ammo, 7.5 cm	80 rounds
Ammo, 7.92 mm	2,500 rounds

Panzer IV Ausf C

Not only was the contract for the Ausf B awarded before the Ausf A had been completed, but the contract for the Ausf C went out before the completion of the Ausf A as well. A total of 140 vehicles—chassis numbers 80301 through 80440—of the 3.Serie/BW were ordered in October 1937. Initially the intention was that the Ausf C vehicles would have a different chassis from that which had been previously used. The Daimler-Benz chassis equipped with torsion-bar suspension that was intended for that company's Panzer III Ausf E was to be employed on the Panzer IV Ausf C as well. In line with that intention, the army design office ordered Krupp to halt further development of the chassis for the Panzer IV on June 1, 1937.

The new chassis suffered repeated production delays, however. On May 2, 1938, Erich Woelfert reported on what was happening with Daimler: "The major setback was caused by using newly designed components that were insufficiently tested . . . series production won't occur for the foreseeable future."

With the aim of avoiding interruptions in Panzer IV output, it was decided to use the Ausf B-type chassis as the basis for the Ausf C, with only a handful of changes receiving government authorization.

An improved engine was one of those changes. The Ausf B's HL 120 TR engine was fitted onto the first 40 Ausf C chassis. Thereafter, however, the improved HL 120 TRM went into the Ausf C vehicles. As with other models of the engine, the abbreviation HL stood for *Hochleistungsmotor* (high-performance motor) and the TR signified *Trockensumpfschmierung* (dry sump lubrication). The added letter M referred to the addition of *Schnappermagnet* or magneto ignition, which not only increased the engine's reliability but also allowed hand cranking as a means for starting the power plant, when necessary. An engine with magneto ignition could also function without external (battery or generator) electric power.

More obvious improvements to the Ausf C than the new engine included enveloping the barrel of the MG 34 coaxial machine gun in an armored sleeve and reshaping the mantlet's top leading edge.

The Ausf C remained in production from October 1938 through August 1939. As with earlier versions of the Panzer IV, some of the Ausf C tanks were constructed using hulls originally intended for other *Ausführungen*. Producing companies received instructions to modify 30 Ausf B hulls that had been delivered late so that they could meet Ausf C standards and be used to meet Ausf C output goals. In

Above: *Members of the 5th Panzer Division relax for a moment in their* Panzerkampfwagen IV Ausf B *during a lull during one of the 1940 campaigns. The divisional symbol, an inverted Y with a dot to its lower left, is on the sponson to the upper rear of the Balkenkreuz. An antenna deflector is attached to the underside of the 7.5 cm gun. A folded boarding ladder is alongside the rear of the sponson.* National Archives and Records Administration

Above: *In most respects, the* Panzerkampfwagen IV Ausf C *was similar to the Ausf B, but the Ausf C had an armored sleeve on the mantlet to protect the barrel of the coaxial 7.92 mm MG 34, a feature that is quite noticeable in this photo of a vehicle from the 6th Panzer Division. The "XX" symbol of that division is to the left of the driver's visor. On the right front of the turret, the armored cover of a vision port is open.* Patton Museum

Panzerkampfwagen IV Ausf C, 3.Series BW (*Begleitwagen*)

Production	
Make	Krupp Grusonwerk
Chassis (*Fahrgestell*) numbers	80301–80440
Quantity	140
Dimensions	
Length	19 feet, 5.07 inches
Width	9 feet, 3.42 inches
Height	8 feet, 9.51 inches
Wheelbase	7 feet, 10.9 inches
Track Contact	11 feet, 6.58 inches
Weight	40,793 pounds
Automotive	
Engine	Maybach HL 120 TRM
Configuration	V-12, water-cooled
Displacement	11.9 liters
Power output	265 @ 2600 rpm
Fuel capacity	124 gallons
Transmission	ZF S.S.G.76
Speeds	6 + reverse
Steering	differential
Track	Kgs 6110/380/120
Links per side	99
Performance	
Crew	5
Maximum speed	26 mph
Cruising speed	15.5 mph
Cross country	12.5 mph
Range, on-road	130 miles
Range, cross-country	80 miles
Fording depth	31.5 inches
Trench crossing	7.5 feet
Armament	
Main Gun	7.5 cm KwK37 L/24
Range	2,000 meters
Coaxial	7.92 mm MG 34
Elevation	-10 to +20 degrees
Ammo, 7.5 cm	80 rounds
Ammo, 7.92 mm	2,500 rounds

addition, in keeping with secret orders issued on February 22, 1939, the last six Ausf C chassis were to be put together without turrets so that they could serve as bridge-laying vehicles. In February 1940 these test tanks were delivered, although one of them, chassis 80436, was sent back to Krupp after March 1940 testing so that it could be completed as a standard Panzer IV Ausf C after all. In June three more of the experimental bridge-layer vehicles were also returned to be transformed back into standard Ausf C tanks. Thus only chassis 80435 and 80438 remained as bridge-laying vehicles. Meanwhile, starting in July 1940, the three tanks that had been converted back from bridge-layers were fitted with Ausf E bow armor and Ausf C turrets, rear armor, and chassis.

During production, there were some minor modifications made to the Ausf C. One such change involved the Panzer III commander cupola being introduced, starting with the thirty-first turret. A rain deflector was welded over the driver's visor, starting with the fifty-eighth vehicle.

In all, there were 217 Panzer IVs produced through the Ausf C. Of these, 211 began life as tanks. When German forces invaded Poland in September 1939, 198 of those tanks took part in the action. The remaining tanks served as training vehicles or sat in reserve in storage depots. The Ausf C generally impressed both crews and the German military command with its performance, though nineteen of the tanks later needed a total overhaul, and experience brought to light a number of the vehicle's design flaws. These weaknesses were addressed in later *Ausführungen*.

Panzer IV Ausf D

A contract for production of 200 examples of the Fourth Series *Begleitwagen* (4.Serie/BW), also known as Panzer IV Ausf D, was delivered to Krupp on July 1938. Manufacture of the Ausf D was to start in October 1939, but before that date could arrive, another forty-eight vehicles were ordered in December 1938 under the designation 5.Serie/BW but also labeled Panzer IV Ausf D. Four *Waffen*-SS regiments with medium tank companies were to be the recipients of those forty-eight new tanks. The vehicles were turned out at a rate of five every month, starting in January 1940, concurrently with the tanks of the 4.Serie; they were issued to the army rather than the *Waffen*-SS as originally intended. The *Waffen*-SS received the *Sturmgeschütz* instead.

Several design changes accompanied the introduction of the Ausf D. A new tank track with a taller guide horn was introduced. The number of suspension bump stops rose to one bump stop for each bogie, with yet another bump

Above: *This Panzerkampfwagen IV Ausf C is numbered 414 on the sponson, indicating it was the 4th vehicle in the 1st Platoon of the 1st Company. A bit to the rear of that number is the symbol of the 6th Panzer Division for 1940, consisting of an inverted Y with two dots to its right.* Patton Museum

Above: *The Panzerkampfwagen IV Ausf D marked a return to a superstructure with a jog in the front, with a ball-mounted MG 34 on the right side. Other changes included a new type of track with a taller guide horn, and an increase in the thickness of the armor on the hull front, sides, and rear from 14.5 mm to 20 mm. The frontal armor of the superstructure was increased to 30 mm and was of face-hardened steel. The vehicle in this photo bears, to the upper right of the Balkenkreuz, the tactical symbol of the 7th Panzer Division specifically in 1940.* National Archives and Records Administration

Panzerkampfwagen IV Ausf D, 5 and 5.Series BW (*Begleitwagen*)

Production	
Make	Krupp Grusonwerk
Chassis (*Fahrgestell*) numbers, 4.Series BW	80501–80700
Chassis (*Fahrgestell*) numbers, 5.Series BW	80701–80748
Quantity, 4.Series BW	200
Quantity, 5.Series BW	48
Dimensions	
Length	19 feet, 5.07 inches
Width	9 feet, 3.42 inches
Height	8 feet, 9.51 inches
Wheelbase	7 feet, 10.9 inches
Track Contact	11 feet, 6.58 inches
Weight	44,100 pounds
Automotive	
Engine	Maybach HL 120 TRM
Configuration	V-12, water-cooled
Displacement	11.9 liters
Power output	265 @ 2600 rpm
Fuel capacity	124 gallons
Transmission	ZF S.S.G.76
Speeds	6 + reverse
Steering	differential
Track	Kgs 6111/380/120
Links per side	99
Performance	
Crew	5
Maximum speed	26 mph
Cruising speed	15.5 mph
Cross country	12.5 mph
Range, on-road	130 miles
Range, cross-country	80 miles
Fording depth	31.5 inches
Trench crossing	7.5 feet

Continued

Armament	
Main Gun	7.5 cm KwK 37 L/24
Range	2,000 meters
Coaxial	7.92 mm MG 34
Elevation	-10 to +20 degrees
Ball mount	7.92 mm MG 34
Ammo, 7.5 cm	80 rounds
Ammo, 7.92 mm	2,700 rounds

stop behind the rear roadwheel pair. In the past these bump stops were only installed together with the roadwheels in the front and rear.

A more obvious change was the return of the radio operator's setback position with the ball-mounted machine gun. Not readily apparent was the use of thicker armor on the front of the hull and on the rear and side of the vehicle. Armor thickness rose from 14.5 mm to 20 mm. The superstructure's frontal armor was now fully 30 mm thick and was constructed of face-hardened PP494 cemented armor plate. The term "cemented" in the context of steel plates and armor connotes carburizing—the introduction of carbon into steel after the plate has been made. Since this molecular carbon is deposited most heavily toward the plate's surface and decreases gradually toward the center of the cross section, the resulting metal has a surface that is hard but an interior that is malleable enough to deform rather than shatter when hit. Another feature of the Ausf D was a newly designed, 35 mm thick external mantlet, 5 mm thicker than that on the Ausf C.

Combat experience in Poland, however, impressed on the German military that even that thickening of the Ausf D's armor was insufficient. Accordingly, on December 18, 1939, the army requested Krupp to further augment the vehicle's frontal armor. The last sixty-eight Ausf D hulls were to be fitted with homogenous PP794 armor 50 mm thick. In July 1940, Krupp started screwing on to the front and sidewalls of tank hulls additional armor plates that were 20 mm to 30 mm thick. In addition, the military hoped also to retrofit such additional armor to vehicles that had already been delivered.

In all, 232 Panzer IV Ausf D vehicles were produced, out of initial orders for 248 of the tanks. The sixteen remaining

Left: *A Panzerkampfwagen IV Ausf D with the hatches buttoned up proceeds through a clearing. The plate over the ball mount for the radio operator's machine gun is nearly square with rounded corners and is bolted to the face-hardened armor of the front of the superstructure. A four-faceted armored cover is provided for a small viewing port on each side of the mantlet. Krupp Grusonwerk manufactured 248 Ausf D vehicles starting in October 1938.* National Archives and Records Administration

Left: *Photographed after being captured by the Allied forces, this Panzerkampfwagen IV Ausf D was one of those that was rebuilt in the early 1940s, being refitted with new sprockets made for 40 cm tracks; supplemental armor on the front and sides of the superstructure; and a long-barreled 7.5 cm KwK 40 L/43 cannon.* National Archives and Records Administration

chassis were diverted for conversion into bridge layers, but then, once completed in that form, orders were received to convert the bridge layers into gun tanks instead.

In the first half of 1940 a number of Ausf D vehicles were equipped with tropical gear to make them *tropenbeständig* ("suitable for use in the tropics"), readying them for action in North Africa. During July and August 1940, 48 Ausf D tanks were fitted out for deep-water fording with *Tauchpanzer* gear, in preparation for an expected landing in Britain. The Ausf D *tropen* vehicles deployed to North Africa and served in combat as intended. In the event, however, no invasion of Britain ever took place, and the only known instance in which the Germans employed submersible tanks was during Operation Barbarossa, when German forces crossed the Bug River at Patulin on June 22, 1941. Meanwhile, in October 1940, as manufacture of the Ausf D was drawing to a close, at least one vehicle was put together using Ausf E bow armor, but the documentation regarding this exceptional vehicle is unclear.

Panzer IV Ausf E

While the original plan was for 223 Ausf E tanks to be manufactured as the 5.Serie/BW, the order of forty-eight Ausf D vehicles for the SS as 5.Serie made it necessary to redesignate the Ausf E as the 6.Serie/BW. Manufacture of these vehicles was contracted for in July 1939, and in October 1940 the assembly lines began to operate. In March 1941, a mere month before the end of Ausf E production, seventeen tanks were cut from the order, leaving the total sought at 206. German experience in Poland had taught them that it was important to have 50 mm of armor on the front of the superstructure, but these tanks were unable to meet this target. On July 12, 1940, it was determined, instead, that the Ausf E would carry on using the 30 mm faceplate with another 30 mm of supplemental armor—the same arrangement that had been made with the Ausf D tanks. The front of the superstructure in front of the radio operator's position continued to be set back.

The introduction of the Ausf E involved a change in the top of the turret. The Ausf E utilized the commander's cupola with five vision ports employed on the Panzer III Ausf G. The turret's back end no longer featured a bulge to accommodate that cupola, but instead rose to a point immediately to the rear of the cupola.

On the left side of the turret's roof, forward of the cupola was this model's only signal opening, in contrast to the turrets on earlier models that had signal openings on both sides, forward of the cupola. Excess gas buildup from firing the main gun had been a frequent complaint regarding earlier models, so the Ausf E added a ventilator in the turret roof, significantly forward and to the cupola's right. Also introduced with the manufacture of the Ausf E were new-style drive sprockets and cast steel roadwheel hubs. Internal changes featured on the Ausf E included a new type of auxiliary generator that received power from an Auto Union ZW500 two-cylinder engine, instead of the PZW600 that all earlier models had used. Radio equipment on the Ausf E was like that fitted to all Panzer IC starting with the Ausf B—the FuG 5 10-watt transmitter and FuG 2 receiver, which had a range of 2.5 to 4 miles, depending on the lay of the land.

An armored box at the tank's rear, just above the muffler, now enclosed the smoke-grenade discharger. In March 1941, a baggage box started to be installed on the turret's rear. Previously delivered vehicles also received that baggage box as a retroactive addition.

As had been the case with the Ausf D, after production, a few Ausf E vehicles were fitted out with deepwater fording or tropical gear. A total of 206 Ausf E tanks had been ordered, but only 200 were turned out as gun tanks. Four Ausf E chassis were turned into bridge layers and the last two Ausf E vehicle chassis, 81005 and 81006, were sidelined for experiments on the running gear.

Panzer IV Ausf F

The first order for the Panzer IV Ausf F, placed in December 1938, called for only 128 units. After the German invasion of Poland and the beginning of World War II, the ordered quantity was increased to 500 in November 1939. Orders for 100 Panzer IV Ausf F vehicles were directed to two new manufacturing plants: Vomag in Saxony and Nibelungenwerk (Steyr) in Lower Austria. Then in January 1941 Krupp received a contract for 300 additional Ausf F vehicles.

The single-plane face of the front of the superstructure returned with the Ausf F, this time with face-hardened, thicker armor of 50 mm that afforded protection against 37 mm rounds. Directly in front of the radio operator and incorporated into the front of the superstructure was a ball mount for the MG 34 machine gun. The thickness of the Ausf F's side armor was increased to 30 mm and a visor developed for the *Sturmgeschütz* was now provided for the driver.

Added armor protection meant that the Panzer IV Ausf F weighed more—now nearly five tons more—than the Ausf A. It was therefore decided that larger tracks were needed so as to maintain the heavier tank's off-road mobility. The tracks—20 mm wider—in turn required a different drive sprocket. Meanwhile, the rubber tires on the roadwheels also increased in width from 75 mm to 90 mm.

The muffler, at the rear of the Ausf F, was now shortened and the auxiliary motor now received its own, small muffler, instead of exhausting as previously into the main engine muffler. The discharger for smoke grenades was now positioned over the smaller muffler.

Earlier *Ausführungen* featured one large hatch on both sides of the turret. The Ausf F, however, had a pair of smaller hatches—originally designed for the Panzer III turret—on each side of its turret.

Although the Ausf F already incorporated 50 mm of frontal armor, an additional 20 mm of supplemental armor began to be added to the hull front and turret face—per a request from Adolf Hitler himself—starting in February 1942. Meanwhile, based on field reports of their ineffectiveness, manufacturers stopped installing smoke grenade dischargers also around February 1942.

Manufacture of the Ausf F was curtailed following a decision to begin replacing the short 75 mm KwK L/24 barrel with a long 75 mm KwK 40 L/43 barrel as of March 1, 1942. In all, therefore, instead of the one thousand Ausf F vehicles

Panzerkampfwagen IV Ausf E, 6.Series BW (*Begleitwagen*)

Production	
Make	Krupp Grusonwerk
Chassis (*Fahrgestell*) numbers	80801–81006
Quantity	206
Dimensions	
Length	19 feet, 5.07 inches
Width	9 feet, 5.39 inches
Height	8 feet, 9.51 inches
Wheelbase	8 feet, .85 inches
Track Contact	11 feet, 6.58 inches
Weight	48,510 pounds
Automotive	
Engine	Maybach HL 120 TRM
Configuration	V-12, water-cooled
Displacement	11.9 liters
Power output	265 @ 2600 rpm
Fuel capacity	124 gallons
Transmission	ZF S.S.G.76
Speeds	6 + reverse
Steering	differential
Track	Kgs 6111/380/120
Links per side	99
Performance	
Crew	5
Maximum speed	26 mph
Cruising speed	15.5 mph
Cross country	12.5 mph
Range, on-road	130 miles
Range, cross-country	80 miles
Fording depth	31.5 inches
Trench crossing	7.5 feet
Armament	
Main Gun	7.5 cm KwK 37 L/24
Range	2,000 meters
Coaxial	7.92 mm MG 34
Elevation	-10 to +20 degrees
Ball mount	7.92 mm MG 34
Ammo, 7.5 cm	80 rounds
Ammo, 7.92 mm	3,150 rounds

Left: *The Panzerkampfwagen IV Ausf E was produced by Krupp Grusonwerk, which completed a total of 206 from October 1940 to the end of production in April 1941. Changes from the Ausf D included improved armor, capable of defeating antitank projectiles up to 37 mm; installation of a ventilator in the turret roof; a revised cupola; and new driver's visor, sprockets, and hubcaps for the bogie wheels. In some cases, as on this vehicle, supplemental armor was fastened to the front of the superstructure.* Patton Museum

Above: *A Panzerkampfwagen IV Ausf E serving with 13th Panzer Division has 20 mm supplemental armor bolted onto the stock 20 mm armor on the side of the superstructure. Supplemental armor also is bolted to the front of the superstructure.* Patton Museum

Above: *A heavily damaged Panzerkampfwagen IV Ausf E from the 3rd Panzer Regiment, 2nd Panzer Division, nicknamed "Elfrieda" or "Elfriede" on the front of the turret, is lying alongside a dirt road in mountainous terrain. Note the location of the ventilator to the right front of the cupola, and the sections of track affixed to the superstructure for added protection.* National Archives and Records Administration

originally ordered, only 395 of the vehicles rolled off Krupp assembly lines, while Vomag had produced sixty-five and Nibelungenwerk (Steyer) had made thirteen of the vehicles.

Panzer IV Ausf G

With Germany's foes and potential enemies increasing the armor on their vehicles, the German military leadership decided that their tanks needed to be up gunned. As regards the Panzer IV, the first directive—which came from Hitler on February 19, 1941—was to install a 50 mm gun on the vehicle. Ausf D chassis 80668 received such a gun, but then, within weeks, it was decided to try out the installation of the new 75 mm gun.

After trying several versions, German planners decided on the 7.5 cm KwK 40 L/43, which began to figure in Panzer IV production in March 1942. The vehicles fitted with that gun were variously designated the 7./BW-Umbau, the Panzer IV Ausf F-Umbau, the Panzer IV Ausf F2, and various other names, until on July 1, 1942, the official label 8./BW Panzer IV Ausf G was chosen.

There still remained 527 Ausf F vehicles that had been contracted for, but never built, and these were now completed as Ausf G tanks. New orders for an additional 1,400 units of the Ausf G were also issued.

Above: *The Panzerkampfwagen IV Ausf F marked several departures from the Ausf E. The D-shaped side doors of the turret were replaced by two-panel doors. The front of the superstructure was straight across. The armor was upgraded: 50 mm face-hardened armor was on the fronts of the superstructure and turret; the sides of the superstructure and hull were increased to 30 mm face-hardened armor; and the mantlet was made of 50 mm armor. Production of the Ausf F was from May 1941 to February 1942, with Krupp completing approximately 395, Vomag sixty-four, and Nibelengenwerk thirteen.* Patton Museum

Panzerkampfwagen IV Ausf F, 7.Series BW (*Begleitwagen*)

Production	
Make	Krupp Grusonwerk
Chassis (*Fahrgestell*) numbers	82001–82395
Make	Vomag
Chassis (*Fahrgestell*) numbers	82501–82565
Make	Nibelungenwerk
Chassis (*Fahrgestell*) numbers	82601–82613
Quantity	473
Dimensions	
Length	19 feet, 5.07 inches
Width	9 feet, 5.39 inches
Height	8 feet, 9.51 inches
Wheelbase	8 feet, .85 inches
Track Contact	11 feet, 6.58 inches
Weight	49,170 pounds
Automotive	
Engine	Maybach HL 120 TRM
Configuration	V-12, water-cooled
Displacement	11.9 liters
Power output	265 @ 2600 rpm
Fuel capacity	124 gallons
Transmission	ZF S.S.G.76
Speeds	6 + reverse
Steering	differential
Track	Kgs 61/400/120
Links per side	99
Performance	
Crew	5
Maximum speed	26 mph
Cruising speed	15.5 mph
Cross country	12.5 mph
Range, on-road	130 miles
Range, cross-country	80 miles
Fording depth	31.5 inches
Trench crossing	7.5 feet

Armament	
Main Gun	7.5 cm KwK 37 L/24
Range	2,000 meters
Coaxial	7.92 mm MG 34
Elevation	-10 to +20 degrees
Ball mount	7.92 mm MG 34
Ammo, 7.5 cm	80 rounds
Ammo, 7.92 mm	3,150 rounds

Continued

Above: *Visible on the engine deck of this* Panzerkampfwagen IV Ausf F *at a ceremonial function are grilles, a modification made to some Ausf F tanks (and earlier models) for improving engine ventilation in the tropics. On the turret roof under the right elbow of the crewman to the left is a round signal port with a hinged cover. At the bottom left is the exhaust port on top of the muffler.* Patton Museum

Above: *The short-barreled 7.5 cm gun of the* Panzerkampfwagen *IV up through the Ausf F was a good weapon for infantry support but was not useful against harder targets. Thus, experiments were conducted with mounting a more potent, longer-barreled cannon in the turret. In a feasibility study, this* Panzerkampfwagen *IV Ausf F was furnished with a wooden mock-up of a 5 cm KwK L/60 gun.* Patton Museum

The differences between the first Panzer IV Ausf G tanks and their Ausf F predecessors were limited to features directly linked to the main gun, gun mantlet, internal tavel lock, gunsight, and ammunition stowage racks. KwK 40 ammunition was different from the earlier 75 mm ammunition and from PaK 40 ammo as well, despite the fact that the KwK 40 was a derivative of the antitank PaK 40.

That said, the Ausf G only favored the KwK 40 L/43 gun for part of the tank's production run. In April 1943 the longer KwK 40 L/48 replaced the L/43. The L/48 was easier to produce, since if featured a consistent rifling twist of 7 degrees, whereas the L/43 twist began at 6 degrees and transitioned to 9 degrees.

Manufacture of the Ausf G wound up in June 1943. Several changes were introduced to the vehicle during the time it was still in production, however. In April 1942 its turret side and right front visors were deleted. A rack for spare roadwheels was mounted on a running board and a glacis rack for spare track links was also added to the Ausf G, starting in June 1942. In addition, 30 mm of additional armor plate began to be added to the superstructure fronts of some tanks, starting in May 1942.

A new commander's cupola with a one-piece hatch replaced the earlier cupola with a split hatch, beginning in February 1943. During the period of February through May 1943, a three-barreled smoke grenade launcher was fitted to the area near the upper front of the right and left sides of the turret. For better protection against antitank weapons, *Schürtzen*, or armor plate skirts, began to be fitted to hull sides and turret of the Ausf G in April 1943.

Issued in July 1942, orders stated that when older Ausf D through Ausf F tanks were brought in for depot-level overhaul they should be rearmed with the longer 75 mm KwK 40 gun and should also receive chassis updates.

Panzer IV Ausf H

In July 1942 it was decided that, on the basis of internal improvements made to the drivetrain of the Panzer IV, a new version, the Ausf H, would appear in 1943. In the event, however, when Vomag turned out its last Ausf G and began

Panzerkampfwagen IV Ausf G, 8.Series BW (*Begleitwagen*)

Production	
Make	Krupp Grusonwerk
Chassis (*Fahrgestell*) numbers	82396–82500
	82701–83000
	83201–83400
	83651–83950
Make	Vomag
Chassis (*Fahrgestell*) numbers	82566–82600
	83001–83100
	83401–83550
	83951–84100
Make	Nibelungenwerk
Chassis (*Fahrgestell*) numbers	82614–82700
	83100–83200
	83551–83650
	84101–84400
Quantity	1927
Dimensions	
Length	21 feet, 9 inches
Width	9 feet, 5.39 inches
Height	8 feet, 9.51 inches
Wheelbase	8 feet, .85 inches
Track Contact	11 feet, 6.58 inches
Weight	52,038 pounds
Automotive	
Engine	Maybach HL 120 TRM
Configuration	V-12, water-cooled
Displacement	11.9 liters
Power output	265 @ 2600 rpm
Fuel capacity	124 gallons
Transmission	ZF S.S.G.76
Speeds	6 + reverse
Steering	differential
Track	Kgs 61/400/120
Links per side	99

Performance	
Crew	5
Maximum speed	26 mph
Cruising speed	15.5 mph
Cross country	12.5 mph
Range, on-road	130 miles
Range, cross-country	80 miles
Fording depth	31.5 inches
Trench crossing	7.5 feet
Armament	
Main Gun	7.5 cm KwK 40 L/43
Range, direct fire	1,800 meters
Coaxial	7.92 mm MG 34
Elevation	-10 to +20 degrees
Ball mount	7.92 mm MG 34
Ammo, 7.5 cm	87 rounds
Ammo, 7.92 mm	3,150 rounds

producing the Ausf H in May 1943, the new final drives were not yet ready. Old-style final drives were therefore fitted into the first thirty Ausf H tanks produced by the Vomag facility. The new final drives were ready, however, when Krupp and Nibelungenwerk started to produce the Ausf H in June 1943, so those firms' H models did incorporate the new final drives.

The Ausf H boasted another major improvement over the Ausf G, namely its thicker turret roof armor. The front roof plate was thickened from 10 mm to 16 mm and the rear plate from 10 mm to 25 mm. The modification afforded the vehicle better protection against low-flying fighter attack, an increasing problem as the Luftwaffe lost control of the skies.

Vulnerability to air attack was not the only issue faced by German Panzers. In February 1943, even before the Ausf H went into production there were discussions about boosting the thickness of the frontal armor plates to 80 mm. On the Ausf A the armor on that part of the tank was 14.5 mm thick, but this was periodically increased over the following *Ausführungen*. During June 1943, the second month of production of the Ausf H, the thicker armor plating was incorporated into the tanks, meaning that the vast majority of the approximately 2,400 Ausf H vehicles were protected by

Continued

Above: *The gun eventually chosen to replace the short-barreled 7.5 cm KwK 37 L/24 cannon in the* Panzerkampfwagen IV Ausf F *was the 7.5 cm KwK 40 L/43. At that point in early 1942, the* Panzerkampfwagen IV Ausf F *was redesignated Ausf F1, while the new vehicle with the long 7.5 cm gun was designated the Ausf F2. The Ausf F2 had other improvements, including revamped storage for 87 7.5 cm rounds of ammunition and a revised mantlet and gun mount. On July 1, 1942, the designation of these vehicles was changed from* Panzerkampfwagen IV Ausf F2 to Ausf G. Patton Museum

that heavier armor. When, in December 1943, the front and hull side plates began to be interlocked, the armor protection was further enhanced.

Magnetic mines remained a threat, however, despite the thickening armor plating. Accordingly, starting in September 1943, a coating of antimagnetic *Zimmerit* paste was applied to all tanks prior to leaving the factory. By means of its thickness and the rough texture of application to the external surfaces of the tank, this paste was intended to make it impossible for a magnetic mine to stick to the tank's steel. Applied by hand, the *Zimmerit* set and dried after application. The process added days to the time needed for production of the vehicle—days that were already precious to the faltering German war effort.

In October 1943, it was decided to give up the rubber-tired track return rollers that had been a characteristic of the Panzer IV from the beginning. That same month it was also decided to switch to a cast idler wheel. The considerations that brought about these decisions included material shortages resultant from the war and the need to cut the amount of labor input—both in terms of time and of cost—that went into production.

Vomag launched production of the Panzer IV Ausf H in May 1943, and Krupp and Nibelungenwerk started their output of the Ausf H the month after that. Krupp, however, was ordered in December 1943 to start producing the StuG IV, after having turned out 379 of the five hundred Ausf H vehicles that they had contracted to manufacture. Those 379 tanks became Krupp's final Panzer IV vehicles.

Panzerkampfwagen IV Ausf H, 9.Series BW (Begleitwagen)

Production	
Make	Krupp Grusonwerk
Chassis (*Fahrgestell*) numbers	84401–84791
Make	Vomag
Chassis (*Fahrgestell*) numbers	84901–85350
	86151–86393
Make	Nibelungenwerk
Chassis (*Fahrgestell*) numbers	85351–85750
	86601–87100
	89101–89530
Quantity	about 2,325
Dimensions	
Length	23 feet, .377 inches
Width	9 feet, 5.39 inches
Height	8 feet, 9.51 inches
Wheelbase	8 feet, .85 inches
Track Contact	11 feet, 6.58 inches
Weight	55,125 pounds
Automotive	
Engine	Maybach HL 120 TRM
Configuration	V-12, water-cooled
Displacement	11.9 liters
Power output	265 @ 2600 rpm
Fuel capacity	124 gallons
Transmission	ZF S.S.G.76
Speeds	6 + reverse
Steering	differential
Track	Kgs 61/400/120
Links per side	99
Performance	
Crew	5
Maximum speed	23.6 mph
Cruising speed	15.5 mph
Cross country	12.5 mph
Range, on-road	130 miles
Range, cross-country	80 miles

Fording depth	31.5 inches
Trench crossing	7.5 feet
Armament	
Main Gun	7.5 cm KwK 40 L/48
Range, direct fire	1,800 meters
Coaxial	7.92 mm MG 34
Elevation	-10 to +20 degrees
Ball mount	7.92 mm MG 34
Ammo, 7.5 cm	87 rounds
Ammo, 7.92 mm	3,150 rounds

Meanwhile, starting in October 1943, Nibelungenwerk also had to devote a part of its output to assault gun manufacture. February 1944, one month after Vomag stopped making the Ausf H, Nibelungenwerk appears to have concluded its output of that *Ausführung*.

Panzer IV Ausf J

In many ways a simplified variant of the Ausf H, the last production Panzer IV model was the Ausf J. The Ausf J dispensed with the electric turret traverse and associated auxiliary generator that had been features on the Panzer IV design since it was introduced. A two-speed manual traverse system was installed instead on Ausf J vehicles.

It was originally thought that eliminating the generator would leave extra space in the hull rear to accommodate an additional 53-gallon fuel tank. Since Germany was suffering ever more serious fuel shortages as the war progressed, it is questionable how much use could have been made of such a large fuel capacity. However that may be, when the Ausf J began to be produced, those new fuel tanks were not yet available and the area to the back of the hull remained vacant until July 1944, when those fuel tanks finally started to show up. Chassis number 91501 was the first to receive the new fuel tanks, but then the fuel tanks were found to leak. The lines that to the fuel tanks had to be plugged and the fuel tanks themselves were discontinued. Only in September 1944 were the fuel tanks reintroduced when non-leaking tanks were finally supplied.

The relentless Allied bombing campaign forced other changes to be introduced to the design as well. The requirement that the vehicle's armor be face-hardened was

Continued

TANKS 67

Left: *The Panzerkampfwagen IV Ausf H varied from the Ausf G principally in two areas: the installation of a new final drive; and an increase in the thickness of the armor of the turret roof, from 10 mm to 16 mm on the front plate and from 10 mm to 25 mm on the rear plate. The strengthening of the turret roof was in response to the increased peril of Allied aerial attacks on tank columns. Early in Ausf H production there was a transition to 80 mm armor on the fronts of the superstructure and the hull. Also, as seen on this example, chassis number 84559, in September 1943 the application of Zimmerit began. This was a cement applied to the vehicle to defeat magnetic mines.* Patton Museum

Above: *Panzerkampfwagen IV Ausf H chassis number 84599, which Krupp Grusonwerk completed in September 1943, is viewed from above. Note the presence of Zimmerit on the roof of the fighting compartment, glacis, turret front and mantlet, and fenders, but not on the remainder of the turret or the engine deck. The cylinder and pipe on the center of the right sponson is a felt-bellows air filter.* Patton Museum

68   THE COMPLETE GUIDE TO GERMAN ARMORED VEHICLES

Above: *New sprockets with deep recesses in the six spokes were introduced with the* Panzerkampfwagen IV Ausf H, *as seen on this tank marked with the tactical number 200 on the turret skirt. The idler is the old style: during Ausf H production a new type with seven spokes with deep recesses would be introduced.* Patton Museum

Above: *Several characteristics distinguished the final production model of the* Panzerkampfwagen IV, *the Ausf J, from its predecessor, the Ausf H: the replacement of the electric turret traversing mechanism for a manual one, and the omission of the auxiliary generator, with the space being used for a 200-liter fuel tank. Accounts vary concerning the number of Ausf J tanks completed: the number was somewhat over three thousand, with production divided between Nibelungenwerk and Vomag. Production lasted from February 1944 to the surrender of Germany. This photo shows an Ausf J painted in* Dunkelgelb *(dark yellow), produced by Nibelungenwerk in August or September 1944.* Patton Museum

Panzerkampfwagen IV Ausf J, 10.Series BW (*Begleitwagen*)

Production	
Make	Vomag
Chassis (*Fahrgestell*) numbers	~86394–86573
Make	Nibelungenwerk
Chassis (*Fahrgestell*) numbers	~89531–90600
	91300–93250
	110001–110272
Quantity	about 3,400
Dimensions	
Length	23 feet, .377 inches
Width	9 feet, 5.39 inches
Height	8 feet, 9.51 inches
Wheelbase	8 feet, .85 inches
Track Contact	11 feet, 6.58 inches
Weight	55,125 pounds
Automotive	
Engine	Maybach HL 120 TRM
Configuration	V-12, water-cooled
Displacement	11.9 liters
Power output	265 @ 2600 rpm
Fuel capacity	124 gallons
Transmission	ZF S.S.G.76
Speeds	6 + reverse
Steering	differential
Track	Kgs 61/400/120
Links per side	99
Performance	
Crew	5
Maximum speed	23.6 mph
Cruising speed	15.5 mph
Cross country	12.5 mph
Range, on-road	130 miles
Range, cross-country	80 miles
Fording depth	31.5 inches
Trench crossing	7.5 feet

Continued

Armament	
Main Gun	7.5 cm KwK 40 L/43
Range, direct fire	1,800 meters
Coaxial	7.92 mm MG 34
Elevation	-10 to +20 degrees
Ball mount	7.92 mm MG 34
Ammo, 7.5 cm	87 rounds
Ammo, 7.92 mm	3,150 rounds

abandoned in June 1944, after the Krupp works in Essen had suffered damage. Roller bearings were deleted from the track return rollers in October 1944. Then in December the rollers themselves were affected; the number of return rollers per side were cut from four to three. This economy measure rounded out an initiative, launched six months previously, with the intent to save an annual two thousand roller-bearing sets.

At times, security trumped economy, however and so in July 1944 it was decided that the superstructure roof needed to be thickened to 16 mm. To improve nighttime concealment, a flame-arresting muffler (*Flammenvernichter*) was introduced in August 1944.

The functionality of the tank was improved in September 1944 when armor skirt plates or *Schürzen* were replaced by *Drahgeflecht Schürzen* or "Thoma shields," skirts made of mesh. Mesh shields were lighter than solid armor plates and also reduced the amount of dust buildup on the running gear. Sockets and knobs (*Pilze*) for mounting maintenance jibs began to be installed in the Ausf J in June 1944. Also in that same month a single S-hook replaced the two C-tow hooks that had facilitated towing.

In spite of all these constant refinements, the German leadership planned to phase out the Panzer IV and replace it with the Panther tank. The number of Panzer IV Ausf J chassis diverted to production of *Sturmpanzer*, *Jagdpanzer* IV, and *Flakpanzer* IV saw an increase. Vomag discontinued manufacture of the Panzer IV in May 1944. Since Krupp had exited Panzer IV production with the Ausf H, only Steyer's Nibelungenwerk in St. Valentine, Austria, continued making the Ausf J, and those vehicles were still rolling off the assembly lines when Germany surrendered in May 1945. Exact output figures for the Ausf J are not available due to the fog of wartime conditions, but total production of the final Panzer IV model was in the range of 3,400 units.

Left: *A Panzerkampfwagen IV Ausf J, tactical number 203, halted in a village likely on the Eastern Front exhibits Zimmerit, a feature that was discontinued on these vehicles in September 1944. Beginning in that same month, the steel Schürzen (skirts) on the sides of the hull were replaced by wire-mesh skirts, which were lighter, just as effective, and trapped less dust in the running gear.* Patton Museum

Left: *Two Panzerkampfwagen IV Ausf Js of the 2nd SS Panzer Division "Das Reich" lie abandoned along a road while a Sherman tank rolls past them. On the rear of the Ausf J in the foreground is the muffler that was in production up to July 1944, following which it was replaced by two vertical Flammentöter (flame-killer) exhausts.* Patton Museum

Panzerkampfwagen V (Panther)

It may not enjoy the reputation and repute of the fearsome Tiger, but the Panther tank was very possibly the more effective of the Third Reich's two well-known "cats." The *Panzerkampfwagen* V or Panther made its debut as the new German medium tank in 1943. It was designed to replace the Panzer III and Panzer IV, both of which had by that time been outclassed by the Soviet T-34 and KV-1. Boasting superb firepower and protection for their era, the early Panthers were, however, plagued by mechanical problems, which often stemmed from the vehicles' being hurried into production and off to the front before troops could be adequately trained on them. In the summer of 1943 the Soviet Union launched a counteroffensive, and the Germans had to rush to shore up their collapsing lines.

Troop training and some other issues were corrected, at least for the time being. Some mechanical issues, however, in particular difficulties with the transmission, plagued the Panther until the German surrender in 1945. Relentless Allied bombing only made things worse for the Germans, since the bombing targets included not only the main tank-manufacturing plants, but also factories where key parts and subassemblies were turned out. The use of slave labor in the production of tanks and components added to the difficulties. Putting enemy prisoners to work in factories was aimed at reducing the 117,100 *Reichsmark* vehicle cost, but sabotage by the hostile workers was common and, as a 1947 study later showed, effective.

The Panther's sloping armor—which deflected shot and increased the plates' effective thickness—gave the vehicle a look that still appears modern now, some seventy-five years after its debut. Unfortunately, the tank's actual performance did not meet its full potential. In the beginning a 30-ton vehicle whose engine and transmission were matched to its mass (as was standard for German tank designs), the Panther soon began to put on weight as battlefield challenges continued to mount. Ultimately, later versions of the Panther weighed more than 45 tons—almost equal to the design weight of the huge Tiger tank.

Many voices among modern students of the history of armored warfare have pronounced the Panther the best medium tank that took to the field during World War II. A few Panther tanks did serve in various armies after the end of World War II. Fifty Panthers deployed as part of the French Army's 503e *Régiment de Chars de Combat* and postwar Romania's 1st Armored Brigade possessed thirteen Panthers. British forces captured the Maschinenfabrik Nidersachsen Hannover (MNH) plant. Though damaged, the factory's tools and equipment for tank production were located and moved to Laatzen, south of Hannover, where the British oversaw the resumption of Panther production using MNH. employees. Nine "British" Panthers and twelve *Jagdpanthers* were turned out for study, but Britain curtailed output at that point, neither making any tanks for Britain or other countries to use. For the record, however, the British-made Panthers were the final examples of the tank produced.

Panther Ausf D

The first Panther model to be produced was actually the *Ausführung* D (model D). An order for one thousand of these

Left: *The Panther tank was, at its time, a state-of-the-art design, which was armed with a potent 7.5 cm KwK 42 L/70 gun and made wise use of sloped armor, in imitation of the Soviet T-34 tank. The first production model of the Panther tank was Ausf D. A total of 842 of these vehicles were completed, with production split between four firms: Maschinenfabrik Augsburg-Nürnberg (MAN); Daimler-Benz, Maschinenfabrik Niedersachsen-Hannover (MNH), and Henschel und Sohn, in Kassel. As seen in this photo, the Panther Ausf D had a viewing port for the driver on the upper left of the glacis, and, barely discernible here, a "letterbox" aperture with rectangular cover for the bow machine gun on the opposite side of the glacis.*
Patton Museum

Above: *The Panther Ausf D had a prominent jog on the bottom of the rear part of the sponson, a feature that added materials and man-hours to the manufacturing process. This feature is apparent on the tank in the foreground, thanks to the absence of some of the Schürzen (skirt) panels. The two curved tailpipes of the exhaust system are on the rear of the hull. The suspension constituted interleaved bogie wheels on torsion bars.* Bundesarchiv

Left: *Members of the RAF are inspecting a captured Panther Ausf D in northern Greece around November 1944. The vehicle lacks Zimmerit, and the barrel of the 7.5 cm gun appears to be missing. The cupola of the Ausf D was drum shaped, with the top inch or two recessed compared with the bottom. On this vehicle, a partial ring has been attached to the upper part of the cupola to support an antiaircraft machine-gun mount. The cylinder on the left sponson contained a cleaning staff for the main gun. Two sheet-metal storage boxes were to the sides of the engine exhausts.* National Archives and Records Administration

Panther Ausf D (SdKfz 171)

Production	
Make	MAN
Chassis (Fahrgestell) number	210001-210254
Make	Daimler-Benz
Chassis (Fahrgestell) number	211001-211250
Make	Henschel
Chassis (Fahrgestell) number	212001-212130
Dimensions	
Make	MNH
Chassis (Fahrgestell) number	213001-213220
Length	8.86 m
Width	3.27 m
Height	2.99 m
Weight	44.8 tons
Fuel capacity	730 liters
Maximum speed	55 km/hr
Range, on-road	200 km
Crew	5
Communications	FuG 5 and FuG 2
Automotive	
Weapon, main	7.5 cm KwK 42 L/70
Weapon, coaxial	7.92 mm MG 34
Ammo stowage, main	79 rounds
Ammo stowage, secondary	5,100 rounds
Armor	
Glacis	80mm/50 degrees
Superstructure side	50mm/29 degrees
Turret front	100mm/12 degrees
Turret sides & rear	45mm/25 degrees
Performance	
Engine make	Maybach
Engine model	HL 210, later HL 230
Engine configuration	V-12
Engine displacement	21 (or 23) liter
Engine horsepower	650 @ 1000 rpm

new tanks had been divided up among Maschinenfabrik Augsburg-Nürnberg (MAN), Daimler-Benz, Maschinenfabrik Niedersachsen-Hannover (MNH) and Henschel und Sohn in Kassel. Henschel, however, would only manufacture chassis, but would use turrets produced by Wegmann, another firm in Kassel. The other companies all produced chassis and turrets.

The order for those one thousand tanks was reduced to only 850 before the first Panther rolled off the assembly lines. Some chassis were diverted to *Bergepanther* manufacture and in the end only 842 Panther Ausf D vehicles were produced as combat tanks.

Hitler wanted production to proceed quickly due to the urgent situation on the front. Nevertheless, the first Panthers—twenty-six of them—were completed by the four manufacturing firms only in January 1943. Then, the introduction of the tanks into combat was further delayed as problems—particularly with the engines—arose and required the rebuilding of the tanks.

Having with difficulty overcome these setbacks, *Panzer-Abteilung* 51 deployed on the Russian Front, was issued ninety-six of the new Panther tanks on June 24–25, 1943. Ninety-six more of the Panthers together with two *Bergepanthers* were provided to *Panzer-Abteilung* 52, also on the Eastern Front, some days later.

Then, just a few days after that, on July 5, 1943, 184 Panthers were sent into battle at Kursk. A report later prepared by *Generaloberst* Heinz Guderian—the then *Inspekteur der Panzertruppen*—and submitted to the Chief of Staff revealed that within two days of their deployment, only forty Panthers were still operational. After five days only ten of the tanks were still functioning. Of those tank "casualties," twenty-five were complete losses, fifty-six had suffered damage in combat, and forty-four had simply broken down. The remaining out-of-commission Panthers littered the battlefield, their exact condition being unknown.

Panther Ausf A

In August 1943, the second production model of the Panther began to roll off assembly lines—the Panther Ausf A. Although many Panther tanks were damaged or lost at Kursk, the blame was largely assigned not to the design of the tanks but to inadequate training of crews and inadequate proper field trials prior to sending the vehicles into major combat. It is noteworthy that although Panther losses were substantial, the Germans recorded 140 Soviet tanks eliminated in return. They even reported destroying a T-34 at a distance of three thousand meters!

Left: *The second production model of the Panther was the Ausf A, which made its debut in August 1943 and continued in production to July 1944. The manufacturers remained the same as for the Panther Ausf D, with approximately 2,200 vehicles completed. The main differences between the Ausf A and Ausf D were in a new, improved turret. In September 1943, there were several new modifications to the Ausf A, including a new cupola with seven periscopes, a redesigned mantlet, inclusion of a periscope for the loader on the turret roof, application of Zimmerit antimagnetic paste, and new bogie wheels with 24 bolts around the rim. This example, photographed at the MAN factory, has a coating of Zimmerit and is fitted with the improved cupola with periscopes.* Patton Museum

Left: *Infantry troops are crouching on the engine deck of a Panther Ausf A, tactical number 622, during combat. The vehicle has a subtle camouflage pattern of wavy lines over the Dunkelgelb base color. On the rear of the hull is a pipe with a curved top on each side of the left exhaust. These were for cooling the left exhaust manifold and were initiated on the Ausf A in January 1944.* National Archives and Records Administration

TANKS 75

Left: *In the cupola of a Panzerbefehlswagen Panther Ausf A, tactical number "0," is Willy Langkeit, commander of Panzer Regiment "Grossdeutschland," who is conferring with Gen. Hasso von Manteuffel, in a Schwimmwagen. The Panzerbefehlswagen* Panther Ausf A *was a command tank that worked with Panther units. It carried a FuG 5 radio in the turret and a FuG 7 or FuG 8 radio set in the hull above the gearbox. To make space for the extra radio equipment, the tank carried fewer 75 mm rounds.* Patton Museum

Left: *Watching to his rear for signs of enemy aircraft is the commander of a Panzerfefehlswagen* Panther Ausf A. *A* Sternantenne *(star antenna), a mast with outward-radiating rods at the top, is mounted on a drum-shaped base on the center rear of the engine deck.* Patton Museum

Panther Ausf A (SdKfz 171)

Production	
Make	MAN
Chassis (Fahrgestell) number	210255-210899
Make	Daimler-Benz
Chassis (Fahrgestell) number	151901-152575
Make	MNH
Chassis (Fahrgestell) number	154801-155630
Make	Demag
Chassis (Fahrgestell) number	158101-158150
Specifications	
Length	8.86 m
Width	3.42 m
Height	3.10 m
Weight	45.5 tons
Fuel capacity	730 liters
Maximum speed	55 km/hr
Range, on-road	200 km
Crew	5
Communications	FuG 5 and FuG 2
Armament	
Weapon, main	7.5 cm KwK 42 L/70
Weapon, coaxial	7.92 mm MG 34
Ammo stowage, main	79 rounds
Ammo stowage, secondary	5,100 rounds
Armor	
Glacis	80mm/50 degrees
Superstructure side	40mm/40 degrees
Turret front	100mm/12 degrees
Turret sides & rear	45mm/25 degrees
Automotive	
Engine make	Maybach
Engine model	HL 230
Engine configuration	V-12
Engine displacement	23 liter
Engine horsepower	700 @ 1000 rpm

In view of such findings, it is not too surprising to learn that the Panther Ausf A was but little different from the Ausf D, externally, at any rate. Internally too, the hulls were the same, at least in the beginning. The HL 230 TRM V-12 engine that had replaced the HL 210 after production of the first 250 Ausf D vehicles remained the power plant on the Ausf A and, in fact, on all later Panthers as well, despite plans to introduce a fuel-injected HL 234 that failed to make it into production by war's end.

The turret of the Ausf A was extensively redesigned from that of the Ausf D. The turret shape itself was largely unchanged, but most of its mechanics were modified. At first the turret kept the same drum cupola that was used on the Ausf D, but, in place of the drum cupola, a cast commander's cupola with seven periscopes was introduced.

The tank's hull was changed too in late November or early December. On the glacis, a ball-mount machine gun replaced the so-called letterbox machine-gun port.

Panther Ausf G

With the weapons of war becoming ever more powerful and destructive, the Panther's armor grew inadequate. But as armor was thickened, the vehicle's weight rose, and more and more strain was put on the Panther's drivetrain that was originally designed for a lighter tank. Meanwhile, Allied bombing was systematically battering German industry, deeply complicating efforts to develop and improve vehicles. In 1943 work began on the design of the Panther II, which was to be a heavier-armed but more easily produced tank than its predecessor, with greater parts commonality with the Tiger tank.

One prototype of the Panther II was manufactured, but the tank never went into regular production. The field experience and research that went into developing the Panther II was, however incorporated in the Panther Ausf G. The Ausf G boasted side armor of 50 mm in thickness, with armor in other places, such as the bottom and lower front of the hull, was slightly reduced to minimize the overall weight increase and to streamline production. Ausf G production, begun at MAN in March 1944, was simplified in other ways as well. Daimler-Benz and M.N.H. later came on line as Ausf. G producers later.

Many voices among modern students of the history of armored warfare have pronounced the Panther the best medium tank that took to the field during World War II. A few Panther tanks did serve in various armies after the end of World War II. Fifty Panthers deployed as part of the French Army's 503e Régiment de Chars de Combat and

Above: *The Panther Ausf G featured a new upper hull that eliminated the jog at the lower rear of the sponsons, opting instead for a straight lower edge for the entire sponson. This greatly simplified the construction of the upper hull. The turret remained the same as for the Ausf A. A total of 2,953 Panther Ausf Gs were completed by three manufacturers from March 1944 to the end of the war: Maschinenfabrik Augsburg-Nürnberg (MAN), Daimler-Benz, and Maschinenfabrik Niedersachsen-Hannover (MNH). This Panther Ausf G was chassis number 121052, completed by MAN around September 22, 1944, by which time the application of Zimmerit to Panther tanks in the factories had ceased. A newly added feature at the time, an early iteration of the* Kampfraumheizung *(crew-compartment heater), is on the engine deck. The camouflage scheme was the so-called "ambush" type and consisted of* Dunkelgelb *(dark yellow),* Olivgrün *(olive green), and* Rotbraun *(reddish brown). Noteworthy is the fact taht this is one of 24 Panther Ausf Gs completed with all-steel roadwheels. Patton Museum*

post-war Romania's 1st Armored Brigade possessed thirteen Panthers. British forces captured the Maschinenfabrik Nidersachsen Hannover (MNH) plant. Though damaged, the factory's tools and equipment for tank production were located and moved to Laatzen, south of Hannover, where the British oversaw the resumption of Panther production using MNH employees. Nine "British" Panthers and 12 *Jagdpanthers* were turned out for study, but Britain curtailed output at that point, neither making any tanks for Britain or other countries to use. For the record, however, the British-made Panthers were the final examples of the tank produced.

Panther II

With the weapons of war becoming ever more powerful and destructive, the Panther's armor grew inadequate. But as armor was thickened, the vehicle's weight rose, and more and more strain was put on the Panther's drivetrain that was originally designed for a lighter tank. Meanwhile, Allied bombing was systematically battering German industry,

Left: *A Panther Ausf G doing service as a battle taxi for Panzergrenadiers has paused in a town during the final phase of World War II. Zimmerit, discontinued in September 1944, is on the vehicle, and brush has been arranged on the tank for camouflage. The thin, straight object on the side of the sponson is a fender, to which armored skirts would be attached, but the skirts often were discarded or damaged in battle or normal operations.* Bundesarchiv

Left: *Outside of Bures, France, around the summer of 1944, a Panther Ausf G camouflaged with tree branches has diverted from a road. The armor protection for the Ausf G was virtually identical to that of the Ausf A, with a few small changes. Other new features for the Ausf G included revamped hatch doors for the driver and the radio operator, with external leaf hinges on the sides; a rotating periscope for the driver and omission of the driver's visor; revised engine deck; and other progressive improvements.* Bundesarchiv

deeply complicating efforts to develop and improve vehicles. In 1943 work began on the design of the Panther II, which was to be a more heavily armed but more easily produced tank than its predecessor, with greater parts commonality with the Tiger tank.

While the Panther II would never enter into series production, a single prototype was produced. However, many of the changes that were made with the introduction of the Panther Ausf. G were borne from the development and testing of the Panther II.

Left: *Toward the end of World War II, the Germans developed infrared night-vision equipment for use in night combat. They began to install this equipment on a few Panther tanks beginning in September 1944. The Panther Ausf G shown here had an FG 1250 infrared searchlight and scope mounted on the cupola. This vehicle was completed by Daimler-Benz in mid-September 1944 and had an "ambush" camouflage scheme that was Daimler-Benz's own, featuring small dots of contrasting paint on the* Dunkelgelb, Rotbraun, *and* Olivgrün *camouflage paint.* Patton Museum

Left: *The Panther Ausf F, of which only a handful were built, represented an effort to mount a newly designed* Schmalthurm *(narrow turret) to the Panther Ausf G chassis. One of the Panther Ausf Fs is seen here in an August 20, 1944, photo. The* Schmalthurm *had a small frontal plate, making it more difficult for enemy gunners to score a head-on hit on the turret. The mantlet was designed to deflect shots and prevent any projectiles that struck the bottom of the mantlet from penetrating the superstructure roof. Jutting from the sides of the turret were range finder hoods.* Thomas Anderson

Porsche Tiger

Development of the Tiger tank can be traced back to 1937, when Daimler-Benz, Henschel, and MAN all presented heavy-tank designs. Porsche joined the development pool late in 1939. As things worked out, the Daimler-Benz and MAN designs led to the production of the Panther tank while the Porsche and Henschel designs formed the basis for the Tiger.

The initial concept that Henschel submitted included a main gun with a bore tapering from 7.5 cm to 5.0 cm, a *Waffe* 0725, but this planned armament was later discounted due to the shortage of tungsten available to German manufacturers due to the war.

Panther Ausf G (SdKfz 171)

Production	
Make	MAN
Chassis (Fahrgestell) number	120301-121443
Make	Daimler-Benz
Chassis (Fahrgestell) number	124301-125304
Make	MNH
Chassis (Fahrgestell) number	128301-129114
Specifications	
Length	8.86 m
Width	3.42 m
Height	3.10 m
Weight	45.5 tons
Fuel capacity	700 liters
Maximum speed	46 km/hr
Range, on-road	200 km
Crew	5
Communications	FuG 5 and FuG 2
Armament	
Weapon, main	7.5 cm KwK 42 L/70
Weapon, coaxial	7.92 mm MG 34
Ammo stowage, main	82 rounds
Ammo stowage, secondary	4,800 rounds
Armor	
Glacis	80mm/55 degrees
Superstructure side	50mm/29 degrees
Turret front	100mm/12 degrees
Turret sides & rear	45mm/25 degrees
Automotive	
Engine make	Maybach
Engine model	HL 230
Engine configuration	V-12
Engine displacement	23 liter
Engine horsepower	600 @ 1000 rpm

Panzerkampfwagen VI P Tiger

Production	
Make	Nibelungenwerk
Chassis (Fahrgestell) numbers	150001-150014
Specifications	
Length	9.54 m
Width	3.4 m
Height	2.9 m
Weight	60 tons
Fuel capacity	520 liters
Maximum speed	35 km/hr
Range, on road	105 km
Range, cross country	48km
Crew	5
Communications	FuG 5, FuG 2, and intercom
Armament	
Weapon, main	8.8 cm KwK 36 L/56
Weapon, coaxial	7.92 mm MG 34
Weapon, ball mounted	7.92 mm MG 34
Ammo stowage, main	80 rounds
Ammo stowage, secondary	4350 rounds
Automotive	
Engine make originally, 2 x Porsche	
Engine model	Typ 101
Engine configuration	V-10, air cooled
Engine displacement	15 liters each
Engine horsepower	310 hp each

All measurements are given in the metric system.

Above: *The VK 45.01 (P), also referred to as the Tiger (P), was Porsche's proposal in response to a* Wehrmacht *requirement in July 1941 for a new heavy tank. The turret, designed by Krupp, featured the 8.8 cm KwK 36 gun; a similar turret would be included on the early-production Tiger I, for which Henschel would receive the contract. The VK 45.01 (P) chassis would serve as the basis for the Ferdinand heavy tank destroyer. One of the ten VK 45.01 (P) vehicles equipped with the Krupp turret and 8.8 cm gun is seen here during testing.* Patton Museum

Above: *Dr. Ferdinand Porsche, founder of the Porsche corporation, is in the right foreground of this view of the rear of a VK 45.01 (P). The turret in its particulars, from the mantlet and hoisting lugs, to the vision slot on the side and the drum-shaped cupola with vision slots, would become very familiar on the production Tiger I.* Patton Museum

For his part, Dr. Ferdinand Porsche strongly believed that the standard mechanical powertrain was too weak to bear the high loads imposed by a heavy tank, so his firm offered a new system.

Porsche's *Typ* 100, also called the VK 3001 (P), provided for the use of a gas-electric drivetrain. Driven by two large, air-cooled V-10 gasoline engines, generators would power electric motors that would serve as final drives. Railroad engines frequently used (and still use) the same propulsion method, so Porsche's concept was not, perhaps, as radical as it might seem. In any case, the Porsche firm received an order for one wooden mock-up and three trial vehicles, but in the event, Porsche only completed the mock-up and a single trial vehicle that was unarmed.

In May 1941, just weeks before the invasion of the USSR, Hitler ordered that frontal armor on the new heavy tank be thickened to fully 100 mm. Although he would have preferred better penetration, the German Führer also ordered that the VK 3001 (P)'s 8.8 cm armament be retained. The redesigned heavy tank received the army designation VK 4501 (P), while the Porsche company called it *Typ* 101. A little over a year later, in June 1942, the vehicle was redesignated *Panzerkampfwagen* IV Tiger and the twin air-cooled engines' displacement was raised from 10 liters to 15 liters.

Reworked or modified *Typ* 100 components accounted for much of the *Typ* 101. The basic turret design and the unusual longitudinal torsion-bar suspension of the *Typ* 100, for example, were incorporated into the *Typ* 101. The fundamental turret design, which originated from Krupp, also served the Henschel-designed Tiger tank.

The project had come to be called the *Tigerprogramm* by August 1941, and a push was made to complete the prototypes, with an initial order issued for 100 of the vehicles.

Defects in the newly designed engines from Simmering led to delays, but after those were overcome, a trial vehicle arrived at Hitler's Rastenburg headquarters in East Prussia for a competition with the Henschel vehicle. Delivery and Hitler's first chance to view the vehicle took place on April 20, 1942, as part of the Führer's birthday celebrations. Although Hitler and other German leaders had initially inclined toward the Porsche design, that tank's performance at trials was plagued with difficulties. The tanks frequently broke down, they often became mired in soft earth, their engines proved to have a short service life, and they consumed excessive amounts of oil.

In the end, of the one hundred Porsche Tiger tanks initially ordered, only a few were completed, and most of them were used for testing and training. They had, however, consumed a sizeable amount of investment of money and resources.

Tiger I

Billed as an invincible tank by Nazi propaganda, the Tiger was possibly the most feared tank of World War II. Though a massive, well-armed, and well-protected combat vehicle, the Tiger was a burden on the German manufacturing base and was plagued by automotive and maintenance deficiencies. Hitler issued a ban on the designation "Mark VI tank" on February 27, 1944, insisting instead on the designation

Panzerkampfwagen VI Ausf. E (Tiger)

Production	
Make	Henschel
Chassis (Fahrgestell) numbers	250001-251346
Specifications	
Length	8.45 m
Width	3.70 m
Height	2.93 m
Weight	57 tons
Maximum speed	38 km/hr
Range, on road	140 km
Crew	5
Communications	FuG 5
Armament	
Weapon, main	8.8 cm KwK 36 L/56
Weapon, coaxial	7.92 mm MG 34
Weapon, ball mounted	7.92 mm MG 34
Ammo stowage, main	93 rounds
Ammo stowage, secondary	4,800 rounds
Automotive	
Engine make	Maybach
Engine model	HL210P45
Engine configuration	V-12, liquid cooled
Engine displacement	21.0 liters
Engine horsepower	700

All measurements are given in the metric system.

Above: *Henschel completed the first Tiger prototype vehicle, designated the VK 45.01 (H), in April 1942. It featured a Krupp-designed hull and turret, the latter being very similar to that of the Porsche VK 45.01(P), armed with an 8.8 cm KwK 36 gun. Lying on the glacis of this vehicle is an experimental Vorpanzer (frontal shield) that could be lowered to protect the tracks and hull front.* The Tank Museum

Left: *Above the holes for tow shackles on the forward portion of the extended hull side plates of an early-production Tiger I are notches designed to give clearance to the Vorpanzer. The extended side plates were manufactured before the Vorpanzer was discontinued.*

This vehicle lacks the side mudguards and their mounting points, which became standard in August 1942. Patton Museum

84 THE COMPLETE GUIDE TO GERMAN ARMORED VEHICLES

Left: *Not long before the German defeat in North Africa in 1943, the remaining Tiger Is of Schwere Panzer-Abteilung 501 were reassigned to the 10th Panzer Division. Here, local inhabitants have gathered around Tiger I tactical number 732, of the 7th Company, 7th Panzer Regiment, 10th Panzer Division. Formerly, this tank had had tactical number 132 of the 501st Battalion.* Bundesarchiv

Left: *Tiger I hull number 250234 is being rolled out of the factory during May 1943. It is painted overall in Dunkelgelb and lacks visible markings. This mantlet is reinforced across the area where the gunner's binocular sight apertures are located. The loader's periscope on the turret roof entered production in March 1943. Spare-track brackets are protruding from the turret.* National Archives and Records Administration

Left: *A mid-production Tiger I has been unceremoniously pushed aside on an Italian road. Not much of the vehicle is visible for identification purposes, but the absence of the bow machine-gun-cover bolts and the presence of the cast commander's cupola indicate production sometime after July 1943.* Patton Museum

"Tiger Tank *Ausführung* E" (Ausf E). In August 1944, the last Tiger Ausf E rolled off the assembly lines.

The projected weight of the Tiger continued to rise as engineering progressed. Finally, an additional roadwheel had to be added to the design. Located outboard of the initially planned roadwheel stations, the addition of a roadwheel also involved widening the track from 520 mm to 725 mm, which, in turn, made the tank too wide for railroad loading limitations. To cope with this difficulty, a second set of tracks, known as *Verladeketten* (transportation tracks) and only 520 mm wide, was developed for installation prior to railroad transport. To switch to the *Verladeketten*, the operational *Marschketten* (combat tracks) together with the outer roadwheels had to be removed. After the tanks had reached their destination, they were offloaded from railroad cars and the process was reversed. An experienced crew needed about thirty minutes to switch the tracks out.

The suspension on the Tiger tanks was torsion-bar suspension and after approximately eight hundred tanks had been manufactured, in January 1944, makers started putting what are known as "steel roadwheels" on the Tigers. The Germans had learned of steel roadwheels from captured Russian vehicles.

Prior to the invasion of the Soviet Union, the German roadwheels featured a heavy rubber tire applied to a metal wheel, similar to familiar forklift wheels and tires. The Soviet-based design involved use of a steel tire basically separated from the steel wheel by O-ring rubber cushions. Introduction of the so-called steel roadwheels allowed for cutting the number of roadwheels per axle from three to two.

Maybach HL 210 P30 power plants with a 21-liter, 650-horsepower rating drove the first 250 Tiger tanks. After that, the Maybach HL 230 P45 engine with a 23-liter, 700-horsepower rating was installed instead.

After 391 Tigers had been produced, the turret was redesigned to include a new commander's cupola that was based on the Panther cupola. Also introduced on the turret at that point were a gun barrel clamp and an escape hatch. Then in July 1943, a better cupola mount for the MG 34 machine gun was fitted to the Tiger. Two months after that, the number of headlights on Tiger tanks was reduced to one, only. Finally, the last fifty-four of the 1,346 Tigers produced were unique models. Most were extensively rebuilt tanks that resulted from a project that used the hulls of tanks salvaged from irreparably damaged vehicles. Twenty-two new turrets were built for use on these rebuilt tanks. Started in August 1942, Tiger I manufacture came to an end in August 1944.

Powerfully armed and formidably protected, the Tiger's colossal weight of 56 tons pushed suspensions and powertrains to their limits. It is considered probable that the Germans themselves destroyed more Tiger tanks—after exhausting their fuel supplies or running out of spare parts—than were eliminated by Allied armor. Tigers were not invulnerable, of course. Seasoned Allied tank crews eventually learned how to take on the Tiger successfully, but victory depended on skill and cunning because in a simple, straightforward duel, the Tiger was more than a match for Allied armor.

Panzerkampfwagen VI Ausf. B (Tiger II)

Production	
Make	Henschel
Chassis (Fahrgestell) numbers	280001-280489
Specifications	
Length	10.30 m
Width	3.76 m
Height	3.08 m
Weight	68 tons
Maximum speed	35 km/hr
Range, on road	170 km
Crew	5
Communications	FuG 5
Armament	
Weapon, main	8.8 cm KwK 43 L/71
Weapon, coaxial	7.92 mm MG 34
Weapon, ball mounted	7.92 mm MG 34
Ammo stowage, main	72 rounds
Ammo stowage, secondary	5,850 rounds
Automotive	
Engine make	Maybach
Engine model	HL 230 P30
Engine configuration	V-12, liquid cooled
Engine displacement	23 liters
Engine horsepower	700 @ 3000 rpm

All measurements are given in the metric system.

Left: *Officially known as the* Panzerkampfwagen Tiger Ausf B, *the second production variant of the Tiger is most commonly known as the Tiger II. The first fifty tanks produced by Henschel mounted a turret inherited from the aborted Krupp VK 45.02. It is often referred to as the Porsche turret, although it was not manufactured by that firm. It can be recognized by its distinctive curved mantlet and noticeable bottom gap. This design was not considered optimal due to these ballistic shortcomings.* Patton Museum

Left: *A group of Tiger IIs of the* Schwere Panzerabteilung 503 *practice gunnery on a range in France in late July 1944. All visible vehicles mount the earlier turret. The segmented turret ring guard of this variant can be clearly seen on the tank in the foreground. The tank in the middle distance mounts a one-piece barrel, common in early production Tiger IIs.* National Archives and Records Administration

TANKS 87

Left: *Tiger IIs of the* Schwere Panzerabteilung *503 are again depicted; but this time slightly later models mounting the purpose-built Henschel turret. This part was much more economical to produce as its overall shape was simpler. Per its original design specifications, it had no shot traps around its lower edge, or around the mantlet.* National Archives and Records Administration

Left: *The forward corners of the production turret were chamfered to allow it to clear the driver's and radio operator's hatches. The flat front face of the turret and the bell-shaped gun base are evident here. The absence of the side skirts also provides a useful perspective on the suspension system of the Tiger B.* National Archives and Records Administration

Left: *Yet another tank of the Schwere Panzerabteilung 503, this time serving in Hungary in October 1944. This close-up portrait reveals a number of interesting features of the turret. Visible at the upper right is the L-shaped commander's vane sight. Also seen clearly here on the top of the gun mantlet is one of three mounts for poison gas detection panels. The other two were located on the rear of the turret.* National Archives and Records Administration

Tiger Ausf B, or Tiger II

Probably the best-armed and protected tank to take the field in World War II, the Tiger II suffered from low production numbers, a relatively weak power train, and German tactical decisions that worked to the benefit of the Allies.

Designed by Henschel, the Tiger II was originally fitted with a turret of Krupp's design. Three prototypes and the initial forty-seven production vehicles had turrets that were originally intended for Porsche's ill-fated *Typ* 180. On orders from the German Führer himself, Tiger II armament was based on the 88 mm FlaK 41, which now had the form of the 8.8 cm L/71 KwK 43.

Though the original intent was for the Tiger II to be based on the Tiger I, in the event the Tiger II relied for much of its design and components as well on the stillborn MAN Panther II project. As things finally played out, the only Tiger II component taken over from the Tiger I was the transmission, and even this was slightly modified.

Ultimately, although the Tiger II entered production in January 1944 and remained in production through March 1945, only 474 of the vehicles were constructed.

Even though the number of Tiger II vehicles was relatively low, those that were produced exhibited several variations. As noted above, the first 50 Tiger II tanks incorporated Krupp turrets originally intended for the Porsche heavy tank project and therefore called "Porsche" turrets. Krupp turrets designed specifically for the Henschel Tiger B were used on the remaining Tiger II vehicles.

A few of the earliest Tiger II vehicles featured a telescoping snorkel for fording, but this was soon discontinued. In April 1944, changes were made near the two shackles on the front and rear hull extensions so as to allow the use of "C" hooks. Other changes occurring at about the same time included the addition of a four-segment turret ring guard and a notch that was added to the glacis in the area of the radio operator's periscope. At the same time, the screens on the rear deck of the tank had to be modified to accommodate the new ring guard. Meanwhile the left hole in the turret face was plugged so that the binocular TZF 9b/1 gunner's sight could be replaced with the monocular TZF 9d sight.

Most of the tanks constructed after April 1944 incorporated a two-piece stepped gun barrel, in place of the earlier single-piece tapered tube.

In May 1944, the very flexible original track design, which featured small bar links, was replaced with a new track that had a solid-bar connecting link and was more rigid. This feature exacerbated rolling resistance, but decreased the likelihood of a track working its way off the sprocket. The change to the new track necessitated a switch to a new drive sprocket that had only nine teeth, instead of the eighteen on the sprocket used with the earlier track. Meanwhile, a vane sight was incorporated in the roof of the turret for the commander to use.

June 1944 saw major changes in Tiger II manufacture. In order to mount a jib boom crane with a 2-ton lifting capacity, three sockets were added to the tank's turret roof.

A shorter muzzle brake was incorporated at about the same time. But the biggest change that June was the new turret that was introduced. This turret, known as the "production turret" or "series turret," was very different from its predecessor. The Porsche turret had featured a rounded face and a left-side bulge to accommodate the cupola. In the new series, the turret's face was flat and the turret's side armor was less steeply sloped, a design that obviated the need for the bulged side.

The commander's cupola began to be bolted, rather than welded, onto the turret, beginning in August 1944. The weld seam, a prominent feature on earlier models, obviously is absent from the tanks with the cupola bolted in place. That same month, Tiger II tanks started to roll off the assembly line wearing a three-color factory camouflage scheme.

Already in September, however, that three-color scheme was abandoned and the new Tigers were left in their red oxide primer to which patches of dark yellow, reddish brown, and olive green were added. That same month the *Zimmerit* antimagnetic mine coating was dispensed with.

In October 1944, the 20-ton jack and the corresponding mounting brackets were discontinued.

Things remained largely the same, then, for nearly three months—apart from changes in the design of the latches on the hull personnel hatches and the intermittent use of a rain shield over the gunner's sight aperture.

Then in January 1945, Henschel's assembly plant began to receive the armor components prepainted in RAL 6003 olive green. After assembly, RAL 8017 red brown and RAL 7028 were sprayed on to the vehicles in a hard-edge camouflage scheme.

Finally, in March 1945, came the final major change: another change of the track. In place of the earlier double-link track, the track introduced in March 1945 was a single-link version. Once again the drive sprocket needed to have eighteen teeth. Only a few vehicles were actually produced with

Left: *The heaviest tank ever built by the Germans in World War II was the Panzerkampfwagen VIII Maus. This superheavy design was intended to fulfill the breakthrough role originally envisioned for the Panzer IV and Tiger I. It utilized a unique propulsion system, not unlike a modern train engine. A large Diesel engine was used to power two electric generators, which in turn powered the drivetrain. It was to be armed with both a 12.8 cm and 7.5 cm guns with a total weight of 185 tons. This photo depicts one of two prototypes during testing.* Patton Museum

Left: *The Maus prototype as seen from the rear. A large concrete structure was put in place to mimic the turret during trials. Fuel capacity was enormous as well, with over 700 gallons within the vehicle and another 400 gallons in an external rear-mounted tank. In spite of this, range was only about 100 miles on the road and a little less than forty miles cross-country. The second prototype was tested with the turret in place and was undergoing trials when the war ended. Parts of both tanks are now on display at the Kubinka Tank Museum in Russia.* Patton Museum

this track, since it was in March 1945 that US troops seized control of Henschel's Kassel factory, the Tigers' home.

Maus

Attaining near mythic status in postwar armor accounts, the *Maus* was an enormous vehicle designed by Ferdinand Porsche in answer to a personal request from Adolf Hitler himself. Two trial chassis were actually completed but only one turret was ever made.

Work began on superheavy tanks in Germany in 1941, but it was not until May 1942 that Porsche's VK 10001 project got underway. A 100-ton tank in its initial conception, designs for the vehicle developed in such a way that in the end it would weigh more than 180 tons. Armament of various types was proposed for the giant vehicle, but the only turret ever made for it was equipped with a 12.8 cm KwK 44 L/55 gun with a coaxial 7.5 cm KwK 44 L/36.5 gun and 7.92 mm MG 34 machine gun.

The first of these giants was slated for delivery in May 1943. That trial tank was to be followed by five production models every month. The huge vehicle received many names during the course of its development—a fate it shared with many other German tanks. Porsche *Typ* 205 ("Mammoth") and VK10001 were the designations employed through April 1942. It was renamed *Mäuschen* ("mousy," "little mouse") in December that year and then in February 1943 acquired its now familiar name of simply *Maus* (Mouse).

In response to an initial order for 150 vehicles, Krupp worked fabricating the armor plate, with Alkett undertaking to do the assembly. In October 1943, however, the order for 150 vehicles was canceled and in November development was ordered to stop. On Christmas Eve 1943, the first chassis was finally completed, seven months behind deadline.

Two MB 509 engines supplied the first vehicle's power. Each of the MB 509 power plants, derivatives of the Daimler-Benz DB 603, drove a generator that powered the traction motors that were typical features of the heavy tanks designed by Porsche. Even with these massive engines, the tank had a top speed of just 13 km/h during trials, considerably less than the designed top speed of 20 km/h.

Trials began with prototype number one without turret. Upon the completion of the first turret, that feature was installed and then the trials recommenced.

Prototype number two was finished and shipped with neither turret nor engines. As soon as they were ready, Diesel engines were fitted into the vehicle, Diesel being preferred to gasoline due to worsening gasoline shortages in wartime Germany. The Soviet Red Army managed to capture the second prototype before it had received a turret.

German tank crewmen destroyed prototype number one after they saw they would be unable to escape the Soviet advance. Soviet forces recovered the turret from the demolished first prototype and had it installed on the second vehicle, which was then sent back to the USSR for evaluation.

Panzerkampfwagen 35(t) and 38(t)

Following the Munich Conference in which leaders of Germany, Italy, Britain, and France decided the fate of Czechoslovakia—whose representative was excluded from the conclave—Hitler's Germany received the largely ethnic-German Sudetenland region.

When Czechoslovakia was left without its border defenses and abandoned by its former allies, political chaos descended. President Edvard Beneš resigned and the First Czechoslovak Republic collapsed. Political leaders willing to comply with German instructions formed a Second Republic that granted Slovakia autonomy and officially hyphenated the country's name to Czecho-Slovakia. Conservative Catholic Emil Hácha was named President of the federated country and Roman Catholic priest Jozef Tiso took over as leader of Slovakia.

In October 1938, Poland, then aligned with Germany, seized the Czech border region of Český Těšín. The next month Hungary, another of Germany's partners, seized a third of Slovak territory along its border with the country. The now pliant leaders of Czecho-Slovakia did little more than sign over the territories to their ambitious neighbors.

As 1939 dawned, Hitler was increasingly concerned with subduing Poland and, to secure his flank, was determined to eliminate the last vestige of Czech independence. On the eve of the planned German absorption of what remained of that country, Hitler summoned Czecho-Slovak leader Hácha to Berlin. In a late-night meeting Hitler told Hácha that Germany was seizing his country and instructed Hácha to order Czech troops to stand down. Hácha fainted on the spot and went into cardiac arrest, prompting an urgent call to Hitler's personal physician, Dr. Theodor Morell. Morell revived the Czech leader sufficiently with injections so that he could be pressed and brow beaten until he finally agreed to his country's death sentence at five minutes before 4:00 a.m. Two hours later, at 6:00 a.m. on March 15, 1939, German troops occupied the Czech lands, which were annexed to the Reich by Hitler's personal proclamation later

Left: *After the annexation of Czechoslovakia, the German integrated the excellent LT vz. 35 medium tanks into the Wehrmacht, where it was known as the Panzerkampfwagen 35(t), the "t" designation referring to the German word for Czech: Tschechien. The most significant modification was the addition of a loader, which freed up the commander, the common* Wehrmacht *practice of the time. A German radio set was also added along with a few minor external changes.* Patton Museum

Left: *A fully stowed 35(t) advances toward the city of Pskow on July 8, 1941. This vehicle is serving in the 7th Company of the 6th Panzer Division. They were the primary user of the 35(t) during the war. The* Wehrmacht *fielded only a single variant of the 35(t). After becoming obsolete as battle tanks in 1942, some turretless 35(t) were used as tugs for towing artillery piece and ammunition vehicles.* National Archives and Records Administration

92 THE COMPLETE GUIDE TO GERMAN ARMORED VEHICLES

Left: *Another weapon gained by Germany during the annexation of Czechoslovakia was the robust and dependable 38(t). Known as the LT vz. 38 in Czech service, several hundred joined the ranks of the Panzerwaffe for the Polish, French, and Russian campaigns. Very minor differences separated Ausf A–D and Ausf E–G were also quite similar in outward appearance. This latter group did have an additional 25 mm installed on the front surface of the tanks, increasing the protection there to 50 mm. A concerted effort was made over time to use welding rather than riveted construction.* Patton Museum

Above: *This factory shot taken at the Czech firm of ČKD, shows a row of LT vz. 38s being prepared for service in the Czech army. Ironically, these tanks were originally intended to protect the country against their aggressive German neighbors. Like the LT vz. 35, the LT vz. 38 received a loader when in German service, along with modifications to the ammunition stowage.* Patton Museum

TANKS 93

Above: *The riveted construction of the 38(t) is clearly evident on this range-testing vehicle. Rivets created a hazard inside the tank, as they would violently shear off after an impact. The large roadwheels are also clearly seen here. They were suspended by large leaf springs, two per spring. Patton Museum*

Left: *Two types of Panzerbefehlswagen were created from the 38(t). The first was the SdKfz 266, which carried the FuG 5 and FuG 6 radio sets. The Fu5 was standard in all 38(t)s. The second, pictured here, was the SdKfz 267, and it utilized the FuG 5 and FuG 8 radios in conjunction with a large frame antenna. In order to accommodate the larger FuG 8, the main gun was removed and replaced with a wooden mock-up. Patton Museum*

Left: *The Renault FT light tank, sometimes referred to the FT-17, saw service in the last half-year of World War I. During the invasion of France in 1940, the Germans reportedly captured approximately 1,700 FTs, many of which they put to use in patrol activities in occupied areas on the Eastern Front. The FT had a crew of two: a driver and a commander/gunner. Some FTs were armed with a 3.7 cm gun; the ones seen here in German service are armed with a machine gun in the turret.* Bundesarchiv

Left: *Two American soldiers examine a captured FT light tank with German markings. The glacis comprised two entry/exit doors, which are open in this photo. Note the muffler on the rear of the upper hull.* National Archives and Records Administration

Above: *The French Char B1 was conceived as an assault tank specializing in breaking through enemy lines and fortifications. The first order for these vehicles was in 1935. It was of an impressive size: 21 feet, 5 inches in length, 9 feet, 2 inches high, and armed with a 7.5 cm ABS SA 35 howitzer in the hull and a 4.7 cm gun in the turret. In 1940 the Germans captured and put back into service a number of these tanks. This vehicle, Char 1B bis number 114, was captured from the Germans and is now on display at the Tank Museum at Bovington.* Patton Museum

Left: *The captured Char B1 bis, number 114, is viewed from the right side. This vehicle retained its original cupola, which the Germans often replaced or removed completely. Features of the Char B1 bis included armor up to 6 cm thick, a long-barreled SA35 4.7 cm gun, and the APX4 turret.* Patton Museum

Above: *The S35 tank was manufactured by the Société d'Outillage Mécanique et d'Usinage d'Artillerie (SOMUA) as a medium tank for mechanized cavalry use. Mounted in the turret was the 4.7 cm SA 35 gun. The Germans captured and subsequently operated large numbers of SOMUA S35s in World War II, some of which are seen here during a military parade, painted in* Dunkelgrau *(dark gray).* Bundesarchiv

that day. Meanwhile, Germany recognized Tiso's Slovakia as an "independent" country, albeit subject to German dictate.

In addition to securing his right flank as he turned to face Poland, Hitler perhaps also desired the Czech region's raw materials and, more importantly, highly advanced armament manufacturing facilities that two decades before had constituted much of the Austro-Hungarian empire's munitions industry. Not only did the Germans take control of famous munitions plants, they also secured some highly advanced armament designs.

One of these spoils was Škoda's *Lehký tank vzor* 35 (LT vz. 35 or "light tank, model 35"), which the Germans would rename the *Panzerkampfwagen* 35(t). Another was the Českomoravská Kolben Daněk (ČKD) light tank, LT vz. 38, known in German service as *Panzerkampfwagen* 38(t).

The Czechoslovak vehicles were on a par with German light tanks and, in some ways, superior to them. The LT vz. 35 light tank's armor and armament outdid that of Germany's *Panzerkampfwagen* II and the *Panzerkampfwagen* III. The armor and armament of the LT vz. 38 was even more formidable than that of the LT vz. 35.

Riveted construction was the main drawback of the Czech vehicles, though that was less of a problem with the LT vz. 38 than with the LT vz. 35, which was virtually covered in rivets. If an incoming shell severed the head of a rivet, its shank could be blasted into the interior of the tank like a ricocheting bullet, inflicting casualties and damaging equipment.

Although designed by Škoda, the LT vz. 35, now renamed *Panzerkampfwagen* 35 (t), was also produced

Above: *A SOMUA S35 in German markings is advancing along a road. There were separate mantlets on the turret for the 4.7 cm main gun and a machine gun. Like the turret, the hull was of cast armor; the hull was in four sections that were bolted together. On the glacis is a raised manufacturer's plate that reads "SOMUA."* Bundesarchiv

in equal numbers by ČKD. All the vehicles, regardless of maker, were fitted with the Škoda A3 3.7 cm gun that was mounted in the tank's manually traversed turret. Coaxial with the A3 was a Zbrojovka Brno ZB vz. 35 heavy machine gun. A second ZB vz. 35 was ball mounted in the front of the tank's hull. In tanks produced later, the ZB vz. 37 heavy machine gun replaced the ZB vz. 35. The later machine gun was also retrofitted to earlier vehicles.

The pneumatically shifted transmission of the LT vz. 35 functioned nearly flawlessly in Czech, German, and French climatic conditions, but frequently failed in the harsh Russian winter. This weakness resulted in the loss of many tanks.

Total output of the LT vz. 35 was 298 for the Czechoslovak army, 126 for Romania, and 10 earmarked for Afghanistan but later turned over to Bulgaria. After the German takeover of Czechoslovakia, no new LT vz. 35 tanks were produced either by Škoda or ČKD (BMM).

Rushed into production, the LT vz. 35 suffered from developmental problems that caused the Czechoslovak army to seek a replacement even as the vehicle continued to roll off factory assembly lines.

Czechoslovak authorities settled on the ČKD-designed LT vz. 38 as the replacement. The LT vz. 38 featured on each side four large roadwheels mounted in tandem pairs with leaf-spring suspensions. The LT vz. 35's roadwheels were small. Though of riveted construction like the vz. 35, the vz. 38 had fewer joints and rivets, enhancing the safety of the crew.

The LT vz. 38 was armed with a new type of Škoda 3.7 cm gun that the Czechoslovak military designated as *Útočná vozba ÚV vz. 38*. Mounted coaxially in a ball mount in the manually operated turret was a ZB vz. 37 heavy machine gun. Another ball-mounted ZB vz. 37 was fitted into the front of the tank's hull.

In 1938, the first 15 LT vz. 38 tanks of the initial 150-tank order were made for the Czechoslovak government. After the German occupation, The German military bought the 150 tanks and reclassified them *Panzerkampfwagen* 38(t), and proceeded to order yet more of the vehicles. Production came to an end in 1942, by which time more than 1,400 had been constructed as gun tanks. Production of the chassis continued for employment in other uses, in particular for self-propelled guns.

Chapter 2
Assault Guns and the *Sturmgeschütz*

In 1936 Colonel (later Field Marshal) Erich von Manstein began advocating the development of an artillery assault weapon. The new vehicle was intended specifically to support the infantry, and the crews would be trained as part of the artillery force, not as a tank unit. The vehicles, given the broad classification *Sturmartillerie*, would be deployed at platoon strength, and were to be capable of defeating enemy tanks with superior armor protection.

Five trial vehicles, fully operational and armed with the 7.5 cm StuK L/24, but manufactured of mild steel rather than armor, were completed by Daimler-Benz beginning in mid-1937.

In 1938 a production contract for 30 combat-capable vehicles, designated *Sturmgeschütz* Ausf A, was issued to Daimler-Benz as well. These vehicles were to carry the same armament as the five trial vehicles. The firm completed production of this group of *Sturmgeschütz*, or StuG as the vehicles came to be known, by May 1940.

The next contract, which was for 250 *Sturmgeschütz* Ausf B, was awarded to Alkett even before the first Ausf A had been delivered. Whereas the last of the *Sturmgeschütz* Ausf A was built upon the Panzer III Ausf G chassis, the Panzer III Ausf H chassis was used for the *Sturmgeschütz* Ausf B. With a further fifty examples ordered beyond the initial contract, the *Sturmgeschütz* Ausf B was in production from July 1940 through March 1941. The vehicles saw combat in the Balkans as well as in Operation Barbarossa.

While combat in Barbarossa proved the soundness of the concept, it also revealed some weaknesses in the *Sturmgeschütz* Ausf B design. Accordingly, the next two models, the *Sturmgeschütz* Ausf C and the *Sturmgeschütz* Ausf D, sought to remedy the chief problem. The first of these, the shot trap caused by the sight aperture in the left front superstructure, was corrected by redesigning the superstructure and adding a periscopic sighting system. The redesigned vehicle was designated the *Sturmgeschütz* Ausf C.

The second issue, having to do with armor protection, was addressed in the outwardly identical *Sturmgeschütz* Ausf D by introducing face-hardened frontal armor. Finally, for better self-protection, the vehicles began to be equipped with the MG 34 machine gun. Production of the fifty Ausf C vehicles began in April 1941, and was followed immediately by the first of the 150 Ausf D vehicles the next month. The Ausf D remained in production into October 1941.

As the use of the *Sturmgeschütz* expanded, so too did the lessons learned. One of the areas in which the Germans learned a painful lesson was in command and control. Early on, the platoon leaders and *Sturmartillerie* battery commanders were provided with SdKfz 253 armored observation vehicles equipped with extensive radio suites. These vehicles, however, were relatively lightly armored and distinctive, causing them to both draw, and be particularly vulnerable to, enemy fire. Beginning with the *Sturmgeschütz* Ausf E, the StuG itself was equipped to serve as a command

Above: *The* Sturmgeschütz *came to be the single most plentiful armored vehicle of the World War II German army. The series began with production by Daimler-Benz of five mild-steel pilot vehicles based on PzKpfw III Ausf B chassis, including this one. Designated the PzSfl III (s PaK), sometimes referred to as the O-Series* Sturmgeschütz, *all five of the 7.5 cm StuK-armed vehicles were delivered to the* Wehrmacht *by 1939.* Patton Museum

Above: *The first combat-capable version of the* Sturmgeschütz *was the Ausführung A (Ausf A) model, thirty of which were produced by Daimler-Benz. These vehicles bore chassis numbers 90001 to 90030. The two apertures, tapered in a stepped fashion, visible above the driver's visor, are for the driver's binocular periscope.* Thomas Anderson

Above: *This StuG III Ausf A is attached to motorized regiment Liebstandarte SS "Adolf Hitler" (hereafter referred to as Liebstandarte SS "Adolf Hitler") circa 1940–41. Stowed in a rack above the fender can be seen a two-piece bore-cleaning staff. Behind the folded-back front mudguard is a Notek blackout headlight. Protruding from the side of the superstructure is an armored enclosure for the radio.* Thomas Anderson

Above: *This early Ausf B StuG III was attached to Sturmbatterie 667, deployed to the Normandy coast in 1940 during rehearsals for the planned invasion of England. The eight-hole sprockets, 40 cm Kgs 61/400/120 type track, and the unarmored smoke-grenade rack on the right rear of the hull are typical of early Ausf B vehicles.* National Archives and Records Administration

Above: *During Operation Barbarossa, the invasion of the Soviet Union, the crew of this early-production StuG III Ausf B enjoys some relaxation near a shoreline. Clearly visible are the 40 cm Kgs 61/400/120 tracks, which were introduced with the Ausf B. This type of track is distinguished by the two noticeable indentations around the raised tread, giving that tread a three-segment appearance.* National Archives and Records Administration

Above: *This StuG is a typical Ausf B vehicle with a six-spoke sprocket, which replaced the eight-hole sprocket early in the production run. This vehicle sports a field modification - an improvised brush guard for the position light. These small lights were somewhat fragile and thus frequently were damaged in service by limbs, boots, etc.* National Archives and Records Administration

Above: *The Sturmgeschütz superstructure of the almost-identical Ausf C and D had several features that were significantly different from earlier models of StuG III, but were in common with each other. The area above the driver's compartment was redesigned, eliminating the gunner's sight port and shot deflectors and forming a straight rather than dogleg-shaped top edge of the outer plate of the superstructure in that position. Instead, in the SfZ.F.1/1a periscopic sight for the gunner was mounted in an opening in the top of the vehicle. The lack of raised lock covers between the brake access hatch hinges identifies this particular vehicle as an Ausf D.* Patton Museum

Above: *Sections of spare track are stored against the superstructure and on the front hull of this StuG Ausf C/D serve not only as replacement parts in the event of damage, but also serve as makeshift supplemental armor. Such armor may just be useful soon, as the vehicle commander studies the area before him and battle smoke rises in the background.* Thomas Anderson

Above: *The design of the StuG III was revised for the Ausf E to include space for additional radio equipment. This was accomplished by adding an enlarged radio enclosure on the left side of the superstructure as well as a similar radio enclosure on the right side. This allowed the Ausf E to serve as platoon or battery command vehicles when equipped with the appropriate radios. Use as such would be evidenced by a radio antenna on each side of the rear of the superstructure. Also improved on the Ausf E were new low-profile, internally mounted hinges on the brake-access hatch doors, with just the tops showing on the glacis.* National Archives and Records Administration

Above: *The lines of the StuG III Ausf E superstructure as well as the left radio enclosure and the rack for the two-piece bore-cleaning rod are clearly visible on this vehicle. The beveled top edge of the radio enclosure can be seen, as can the vertical weld bead where the front plate of the enclosure was butt-jointed to the side plate. Also visible are the interiors of the commander's hatch doors, and his scissors telescope with extensions. The head of the gunner's periscopic sight protrudes through an opening in the superstructure roof in front of the commander's scissors telescope.* National Archives and Records Administration

ASSAULT GUNS AND THE *STURMGESCHÜTZ* 105

Above: *With the German army facing increasingly well-armored Soviet tanks, the need arose for more powerful armament on the Sturmgeschütz. It was decided to experimentally install a higher velocity gun in the vehicle. Accordingly, this vehicle was converted from a standard Ausf E, which has been equipped with a 7.5 cm StuK 40 L/43 cannon.* Patton Museum

Above: *The rearmed vehicle, which would serve as the prototype StuG III Ausf F, is shown with the StuK 40 L/43 gun elevated. On the production vehicles, the StuK had a range of elevation of +20 to -6 degrees and could traverse 10 degrees to each side of the centerline. A new, box-type mantlet was designed to enclose the recoil cylinders of the 7.5 cm StuK 40 L/43.* Patton Museum

Above: *This vehicle is an early StuG III Ausf F as evidenced by the 7.5 cm StuK 40 L/43 gun. This weapon was used on the first 120 StuG III Ausf F vehicles and had a shorter barrel relative to the StuK 40 L/48 gun introduced later in Ausf F production. Although the right headlight and its cover are missing, the armored cover for the left headlight is visible, along with other early Ausf F features such as the long, hinged front mudguards. Sandbags have been piled on the sloping frontal armor above the driver's compartment of this vehicle, and a lone sand bag placed to the front of the radio enclosure. Additional sandbags, visible beneath the StuK 40 L/43 barrel, are on the right front of the superstructure.* National Archives and Records Administration

Above: *Brush has been positioned on the front of this early StuG III Ausf F advancing along a dusty road on the Eastern Front. The StuG appears to be painted in* Dunkelgelb. Patton Museum

Above: *Beginning in May 1942, the final 246 StuG III Ausf Fs would be armed with the 7.5 cm StuK 40 L/48 gun, which had a barrel that was 37.5 cm (14.76 inches) longer than the barrel of the L/43. In September of that year, the chassis changed as well, and subsequent vehicles are known as StuG III Ausf F/8. One such vehicle, assigned to the 303rd Sturmgeschütz Brigade, is shown here passing through the town of Lappeenranta, Finland. In addition to welded supplemental 30 mm frontal armor, this crew of this vehicle has poured concrete into the upper front of the superstructure for extra protection, and the recess around the openings for the driver's binocular periscope has been filled in.* SA-Kuva

Above: *Concurrently with the creation of the prototype StuG III Ausf F, a second StuG III Ausf E was modified through the installation of a howitzer. This created a prototype self-propelled 10.5 cm Sturmhaubitze (StuH) 42 L/28 howitzer. Externally, it could be distinguished from the prototype StuG III Ausf F by its thicker, stubbier barrel and much larger muzzle brake.* Patton Museum

Above: *The howitzer-armed vehicle, or Sturmhaubitze, was created to compensate for the increasing use of the Sturmgeschütz, now rearmed with the 7.5 cm StuK 40, as a tank destroyer, leaving the infantry without needed fire support. The howitzer of the prototype is shown here at or near its maximum elevation of 20 degrees; it could be depressed to -6 degrees. The total range of traverse was 20 degrees.* Patton Museum

Above: *The final, and most abundant, version of the StuG III was the Ausf G, which entered production in December 1942 and remained in production for the duration of the war. The vehicle was armed with the potent StuK 40 7.5 cm L/48 gun, which had been introduced on the StuG Ausf F. The Ausf G had a slightly enlarged superstructure as compared to its predecessor. The vehicle shown here is one of thirty the Germans transferred to the Finnish army in 1943. Produced by Alkett in May or June 1943, it features 80 mm frontal armor on the hull and 50 mm basic armor with 30 mm armor bolted on in front of the driver's compartment. Painted on the hull front is the* hakaristi, *the Finnish national insignia, which is similar to the German swastika. Beside the main gun is stenciled Ps. 531-5, the vehicle's Finnish identification number.* SA-Kuva

Above: *The muzzle brake, which has been damaged by an Allied round, is the type with an oval face and a circular rear ring: a feature on Alkett StuG III Ausf Gs produced between June and October 1944, frequently referred to as the "oval/round muzzle brake." Painted on the gun tube are more than 20 rings, signifying a like number of kills. On the front center of the glacis the folded-down gun travel lock can be seen. The StuG was protected from magnetic mines by waffle-pattern Zimmerit and featured Schürzen: side skirts of 5 mm armor designed to detonate antitank shells before they struck the hull. National Archives and Records Administration*

Above: *Advancing across the steppes on the Eastern Front, this early StuG Ausf G was produced by Alkett. The ventilator just visible on the roof between the hatches is a characteristic of the early Ausf G. Just ahead of the loader's hatch is a pintle mount for an MG 34. The faintly visible rhomboid with an upward-pointing arrow superimposed on the upper left, displayed on the left mudguard, is the tactical symbol for a Stürmgeschutz company. National Archives and Records Administration*

Above: *The same StuG Ausf G viewed from behind exposes a large wooden crate on the rear deck. The large, hinged mud flaps of this vehicle were discontinued on the Alkett production line in March 1943, while the tubular taillight seen on the left fender was introduced in same month, thus this vehicle appears to have been manufactured in March 1943. The StuG is equipped with early-type armored skirts. On the rear of the hull is the number 211, indicating 2nd Company, 1st Platoon, 1st vehicle.* National Archives and Records Administration

Above: *In addition to Alkett, MIAG manufactured StuG III Ausf Gs, including this vehicle, built in April or May 1943. Here, a Commonwealth tanker peers in the cupola of the StuG shortly after its September 1943 capture in or near Battipaglia, Italy. The chassis number, 95219, is visible in small numerals on the right frontal plate of the superstructure, revealing its origin. Ultimately, the StuG was shipped to Aberdeen Proving Ground, and from there to Canada, where it was destroyed as a target.* National Archives and Records Administration

Above: *Armored skirts with triangular brackets were introduced to MIAG StuG III Ausf Gs in March 1944, while the hinged machine-gun shield was discontinued at MIAG in May 1944. Thus, this vehicle was produced in March, April, or May 1944. The vehicle wears a finely applied, squiggly camouflage pattern on the armored skirt.* Patton Museum

Above: *This StuG III Ausf G, painted overall in* Dunkelgelb *while serving on the Eastern Front, shows features that indicate its date of production as March 1943. The tubular fender supports were introduced to production in March 1943, and the 30 mm supplemental armor bolted to the stock 50 mm armor, also dates to March 1943. Side skirts and their associated brackets were introduced in April 1943, thus the lack of these features dates the completion of this StuG to before April 1943.* National Archives and Records Administration

vehicle. To do this, an armored pannier was added to each side of the fighting compartment in order to accommodate additional radio equipment, which was installed as needed by Army depots.

Production of the *Sturmgeschütz* Ausf E began in September 1941 and carried on through February of the next year. Delays in the delivery of the 7.5 cm StuK L/24 main gun meant that the final nine Ausf E weren't actually delivered until March and April.

As the German army pressed deeper into Russia, they encountered increasingly more powerful Soviet tanks, notably the T-34. The armor of these vehicles were such that the 7.5 cm StuK L/24 was inadequate to fulfill von Manstein's initial premise, that the *Sturmartillerie* "must be capable of defeating enemy tanks that have better armor protection."

To counter the new Soviet tanks, in late 1941 the German Army Ordnance Test Board (WaPrüf), began efforts to equip a StuG Ausf E with a high-velocity gun. The weapon developed for this installation was a combination of a Krupp-designed short chamber and a Rheinmetall PaK 40 L/46 barrel. Designated 7.5 cm StuK 40 L/43, the new gun was installed and the associated modifications completed in February 1942.

Satisfied with the initial tests, contracts were issued and production of 7.5 cm StuK 40 L/43-armed *Sturmgeschütz* began in March 1942. The new model was designated the *Sturmgeschütz* Ausf F. However, in May 1942 the design was modified to include an even longer weapon, the 7.5 cm StuK 40 L/48, a change that also required a change to the gunsight port.

A more substantial change came in September 1942, when the chassis of the vehicle was improved to the standard set for the *Panzerkampfwagen* III 8./Z.W., and are known as *Sturmgeschütz* Ausf F/8. These improvements included the lengthening of the armored hull sides to include towing brackets, heavier, 50 mm rear armor, shorter front track guards, and improved engine cooling through larger louvers. Because of production difficulties, many StuG Ausf F/8s were produced with hulls originally assembled for Panzer III Ausf L and M tanks. These vehicles can be distinguished by the added 30 mm supplemental armor. Production of the *Sturmgeschütz* Ausf F/8 continued into December 1942.

Seeking to improve the *Sturmgeschütz* still further, in December 1942 Alkett began production of the Ausf G. The Ausf G had a slightly larger superstructure than its predecessor, with a slightly raised roof, and utilized the same chassis as had been used on the Ausf F/8. The *Sturmgeschütz* was the most produced armored vehicle in Germany's arsenal—and the Ausf G was the most-produced variant of the *Sturmgeschütz*. Demand for the vehicles was so great that a second firm was engaged to augment Alkett's production. The new firm, Mühlenbau und Industrie AG, or MIAG, assembled *Sturmgeschütz* not only on chassis that they produced themselves, but also on chassis produced by Maschinenfabrik Augsburg-Nürnberg (MAN). Production of the StuG at MIAG began in February 1943, as Panzer III production by the firm was being terminated. *Sturmgeschütz* production by MIAG utilizing MAN chassis began at the same time.

In March 1945, Allied bombing raids brought the end to *Sturmgeschütz* production by MIAG. Production at Alkett, a subsidiary of Rheinmetall-Borsig in Berlin, continued until April 25, 1945, a week before Berlin fell. Nearly 3,000 prisoners from the Sachsenhausen concentration camp were used as slave labor in *Sturmgeschütz* production at Alkett, in addition to the regular employees.

Sturmhaubitze

In addition to the assault guns discussed previously in this chapter, the German army produced a limited number of assault howitzers. The vehicles, known as *Sturmhaubitze*, look strikingly similar to the *Sturmgeschütz*, differing in the weapons. Guns, whether in *Sturmgeschütz*, tanks or artillery, are intended to be fired on a nearly flat, line-of-sight, trajectory. Howitzers, on the other hand, have lower velocities and are intended to rather lob shells, firing over rises in terrain or other obstructions. The first *Sturmhaubitze* was built by the German Army Ordnance Test Board (WaPrüf) concurrently with the production of the first of the long-barrel *Sturmgeschütz*, and like that StuG, was based on a *Sturmgeschütz* Ausf E. The *Sturmhaubitze* was armed with the 10.5 cm LeFH 18 howitzer, which was known to be very effective against fortifications and pillboxes. The increasing use of the *Sturmgeschütz* as an antitank weapon was leaving the infantry without the assault artillery that they needed—the very reason the StuG was created to begin with—and it was hoped that the *Sturmhaubitze* would return that firepower.

Production of the *Sturmhaubitze* began with the first twelve vehicles, rebuilt from *Sturmgeschütz* by Alkett. Nine of the vehicles were provided to 3.Batterie of *Sturmgeschütz-Abteilung* 185 for use near Leningrad.

Series production of the *Sturmhaubitze* began by Alkett, the sole producer of the type, in March 1943. But for the initial prototype, the *Sturmhaubitze* was based on the *Sturmgeschütz* Ausf G. The chassis of the two types were intermingled, as were the chassis numbers.

Above: *In part because the* Sturmgeschütz *was being employed increasingly as an antitank weapon, the infantry were compelled to come up with an alternate fire support vehicle. As a result, this vehicle, based on the Alkett StuG III Ausf G chassis, was created. Known as the* Sturmhaubitze 42 (StuH 42) *the new vehicle was armed with a version of the 10.5 cm leFH 18 howitzer, and was capable of both direct- or indirect-fire.* Sturmhaubitze *were built with either cast mantlets, as seen here, or mantlets of bolted-together armor plate.* SA-Kuva

Above: *This* Sturmgeschütz *features bolted 30 mm supplemental bow armor; and small, fixed front mudguards, indicative of early production.* National Archives and Records Administration

Sturmgeschütz IV

The Allied bombing campaign targeted the German arms industry with increasing effect, and on November 26, 1943, Alkett, primary producer of the StuG, received 1,400 tons of bombs delivered by the Allies. This brought about an almost 90 percent drop in StuG production—and then the plant was bombed twice more the next month.

By this time, the German ground forces were being pushed back by the Soviets, and the StuG was increasingly important as an antitank weapon. With StuG chassis production crippled, in early December 1943 the decision was made to mount a *Sturmgeschütz* Ausf G superstructure on a Krupp-produced Panzer IV 7./BW chassis.

In order to accomplish this, a driver's compartment had to be added to the front left side of the superstructure, and a plate fabricated to fill the gap between the transmission cover and the leading edge of the StuG superstructure.

Shown the new vehicle in mid-December, Hitler approved the *Sturmgeschütz* IV, as the new hybrid was dubbed, for production, which began immediately.

Initially, the vehicle utilized the chassis of the Panzer IV Ausf H, but in time this transitioned to the Panzer IV Ausf J chassis instead. By the time of the Allied victory, 1,141 *Sturmgeschütz* IV had been produced.

Sturminfanteriegeschütze 33B

The German assault on Stalingrad pointed to the need for an armored, self-propelled assault gun with heavier armament than the 7.5 cm gun of the StuG. The *Sturminfanteriegeschütze* 33B was created to fill that void. These vehicles featured the chassis and lower hull of a *Sturmgeschütz* upon which was installed a new, larger superstructure housing a 15 cm sIG 33, or 150 mm heavy infantry support gun.

This was not the first attempt to mount this weapon on a mechanized chassis, as prior efforts had utilized the Panzer I and Panzer II chassis, without full armor enclosure. However, the earlier efforts were not entirely satisfactory.

Therefore when the *Führerkonferenz* of September 1942 closed on the 22nd of that month, it was directed that within fourteen days a new design would be presented. Protection for the crew was considered of highest importance. After failed attempts at mounting the big howitzer in the turret of the Panzer III and Panzer IV, the design settled on was that utilizing the StuG chassis.

The directive of the 22nd required that at least six, and preferably twelve, of the new vehicles, dubbed *Sturminfanteriegeschütze* 33B, be produced. Incredibly, Alkett completed the first six by October 7, with a second group of six completed by October 10. A further batch of twelve were completed by the end of the month.

The first twelve vehicles were deployed in the assault on Stalingrad, where six each were assigned to *Sturmgeschütz-Abteilung* 177 and *Sturmgeschütz-Abteilung* 244 of the 23rd Panzer DIvision. The *Sturminfanteriegeschütze* 33B reached Stalingrad in early November 1942, but all six were lost there.

The vehicles were in the area of Stalingrad by November 8, 1942. None of them survived the combat there. Remarkably, the 23rd Panzer Division escaped being encircled at Stalingrad, and when the unit was reformed, it was issued the twelve remaining *Sturminfanteriegeschütze* 33B, which it took with them to Kursk in July 1943.

Ultimately only one of the *Sturminfanteriegeschütze* 33B survived, and is today on display at the Russian tank museum in Kubinka.

Specifications	
Length	5.4 m
Width	2.90 m
Height	2.3 m
Weight	21 tons
Fuel capacity	310 liters
Maximum speed	20 km/hr
Range, on-road	110 km
Range, cross-country	85 km
Crew	5
Communications	Fu Spr Ger d
Armament	
Weapon, main	15 cm sIG33/1
Weapon, secondary	7.92 mm MG 34
Ammo stowage, main	30 rounds
Ammo stowage, secondary	600 rounds
Automotive	
Engine make	Maybach
Engine model	HL 120 TRM
Engine configuration	V-12, liquid cooled
Engine displacement	11.9 liters
Engine horsepower	265 @ 2600 rpm

Above: *Faced with a shortage of Sturmgeschütz, and with Alkett's plant in shambles following Allied bombing, this makeshift StuG was created by mounting a Sturmgeschütz Ausf G superstructure on a Panzer IV chassis. Here, General Field Marshal Albert Kesselring, in the light-colored coat, observes a firing demonstration of a StuG IV in Italy in 1944. Fabric covers the mantlet, and in an effort to increase protection, concrete has been added to the front of the driver's frontal armor.* Patton Museum

Above: *Among this group of captured German and Italian vehicles in Italy in the summer of 1944 is a StuG IV, followed to the rear by a StuG III Ausf G, and a variety of other shot-up vehicles, all of which are being looked over by British troops.* Patton Museum

Left: *The Sturminfanteriegeschütze 33B was the third wartime design to incorporate the venerable 15 cm sIG 33 L/11 infantry gun. This time it was mounted within a fully enclosed superstructure built on the chassis of a StuG Ausf E or F/8. The weapon was mounted in a sliding aperture slightly right of center. The chassis were those that had been returned for overhaul at the Alkett factory. Two rear escape hatches and a hatch for the commander were provided. Twenty-four conversions were made between December 1941 and October 1942.* Bundesarchiv

Left: *This photo and the previous one both depict guns of the Infanterie Geschütze Battery assigned to Panzer Regiment 201 of the 23rd Panzer Division in the summer of 1943. Originally conceived as urban demolition vehicles for use in the battle of Stalingrad, the Sturminfanteriegeschütze 33 was eventually used in a role similar to that of the Sturmgeschütze—infantry assault support. Guns from this unit are known to have had vivid tactical markings. One was captured by the Russians and survives to this day at the armor museum at Kubinka.* Patton Museum

Sturmpanzer

While the *Sturminfanteriegeschütze* 33B was not as successful as German strategists had hoped, the need for such a vehicle was still existent in the fall of 1942. With the continued insistence of Hitler to develop a heavily armed, full-enclosed armored assault gun suitable for urban environments, Alkett was tasked with the design. The resultant vehicle was designated the *Sturmpanzer*, but after WWII it became popularly known as the *Brummbär*, or grumbling bear.

The design which Alkett advanced, and which was approved, featured a special short barreled 15 cm StuH 43 L/12 howitzer in a ball mount. This weapon fired the same round as the 15 cm sIG 33 heavy infantry gun. The superstructure, though box-like, was well armored and mounted on the proven Panzer IV chassis.

The vehicle was built not by an industrial firm, but rather the vehicles were assembled in the army's own workshops starting in Vienna in 1943.

Approximately three hundred of the vehicles were produced in four distinct production groups.

Production of the first group of sixty vehicles began in 1943. Initially, new Panzer IV G chassis were used, but the final eight were built upon remanufactured Panzer IV Ausf E and F chassis.

The second series production began in December 1943 (coincidentally, the same month surviving vehicles of the first series were rebuilt). Second series Sturmpanzers were built on new Ausf H chassis, with production of these sixty vehicles running through March 1944. These vehicles can be distinguished from the first series by reinforced driver's compartment, lack of gunner's hatch, addition of a ventilator and introduction of steel-rimmed roadwheels on the forward suspension.

In May 1944, at the beginning of fourth series, production was transferred to workshops in Duisberg. Production continued there until March 1945, during which time 162 vehicles were produced.

As a result of successful infantry attacks against the Sturmpanzers, a later improvement involved the mounting of a MG 34 in a Kugelblende 80 ball mount on the face of the superstructure.

The Sturmpanzers first saw combat at Kursk, and were used throughout the rest of the war.

Sturmmörserwagen

While the *Sturminfanteriegeschütze 33B* and the *Sturmpanzer* were effective, the were not as effective as was desired – specifically, a heavier weapon was needed in order to achieve the goal of demolishing large structures with a single round. Further, while the *Sturmpanzer* was considerably better protected than was the *Sturminfanteriegeschütze 33B*, the armor was far short of what was felt was needed, especially in urban settings, where the ranges were likely to be close.

Thus in in mid-1943 work began on developing an even more formidable weapon. Based on the Tiger I chassis, it was intended that the new vehicle be armed with a 210 mm howitzer, then under development. Owing to delays, the decision was made to adapt a naval weapon instead. The adapted weapon was designated *Raketenwerfer* 61, and fired a short-range rocket-propelled round. Breach loading, the 1.5 meter round weighed up to 829 pounds, and had a range of up to 6,000 meters. Both high explosive and shaped charge rounds were manufactured. For self-defense, a MG 34 was mounted through the front 150mm-thick armor. Known as the *Sturmtiger* or *Sturmmörser*, the prototype of the new vehicle was displayed to Hitler in October 1943.

Although approval was given to place the vehicle in production, and Alkett began fabricating the superstructures. As originally planned, these vehicles would be built on new Tiger I chassis, by the time production commenced, the decision had been made to utilize rebuilt Tiger I chassis instead. The first three of the vehicles were completed in August 1944, followed by ten the next month, with the final five being completed in December 1944.

Three new Panzer companies were formed to operate the new vehicle. They were Panzer Sturmmörser Kompanien 1000, 1001, and 1002.

Sturmpanzer

Specifications	
Length	5.80 m (later 5.93 m)
Width	2.86 m
Height	2.45 m (later 2.52)
Weight	24 tons (later 28.2)
Fuel capacity	470 liters
Maximum speed	40 km/hr
Range, on road	200 km
Range, cross country	130 km
Crew	5
Communications	FuG 5 and FuG 2, intercom
Armament	
Weapon, main	15 cm StuH43
Weapon, secondary	7.92 mm MG 34
Ammo stowage, main	32 rounds
Ammo stowage, secondary	600 rounds
Automotive	
Engine make	Maybach
Engine model	HL 120 TRM
Engine configuration	V-12, liquid cooled
Engine displacement	11.9 liters
Engine horsepower	265 @ 2600 rpm

All measurements are given in the metric system.

Above: *A further development of the continued perceived need for a vehicle that could reduce strong points and buildings in urban areas was the Sturmpanzer IV. A unique gun for this vehicle was selected: the 15 cm Sturmhaubitze (StuH) 43 L/12, which had been developed by Skoda. It fired the same shells as the 15 cm sIG 33 heavy infantry gun and was mounted within a large armored superstructure placed on the chassis of the Panzer IV Ausf G. Over three hundred were produced in four distinct types. This early production gun is serving with the Sturmpanzer Abteilung 216 in Italy in 1944.* Patton Museum

Above: *Another gun of the Sturmpanzer Abteilung 216 in Italy. Early production Sturmpanzer IVs can be recognized by the large driver's armored visor located on the left hand side of the hull. This was very similar is appearance and function to that of the Tiger I. Like the Panzer IV that it was based on, the Sturmpanzer IV had 50 mm of armor plated bolted to the lower front hull. The StuH 43 L/12 was unique, in that it was installed in a swiveling ball mount. It fired two-piece ammunition. Initial production of sixty vehicles began in April 1943.* Patton Museum

Above: *Production of the second series Sturmpanzer IV began December 1943. This was again sixty vehicles, built on the Panzer IV Ausf H chassis. Based on combat experience, several improvements were made to the armored construction, the most obvious of which was elimination of the driver's visor. This was replaced with a square armored casemate with a top mounted periscope. A much needed ventilator fan was also fitted to remove combustion gases from the fighting compartment. This is just barely visible at the top left in this vehicle on display at Aberdeen Proving Ground.* Patton Museum

Above: *This Sturmpanzer IV is undergoing evaluation by the British after its capture in Normandy in 1944. Like most German armored vehicles of the time, it is covered in Zimmerit anti-magnetic paste. Although a mount for an MG34, similar to that on the StuG, was intended for the roof it appears to have been rarely, if ever, installed. A circular pistol port is visible here on the upper portion of the armored superstructure. Pushing this armored plug out (it was secured with a small chain) and placing a machine pistol through the opening was the only means of defending the gun against enemy infantry. This hampered the design until its final production.* Patton Museum

Above: *Another improvement in second series production was the introduction of two elaborate mounts on the rear hull for spare roadwheels. They were each formed from a single piece of steel rod, bent into a complex shape. Front wheel failure was another factor that plagued the design of the Sturmpanzer IV, as the armored superstructure and gun placed the majority of the vehicle's weight right over the front two bogie assemblies. The square shapes on the upper rear hull are the covers for the convective ventilators.* Patton Museum

Above: *This largely intact Sturmpanzer IV has ben abandoned by its crew in Italy. This is likely yet another gun of Sturmpanzer Abteilung 216. It featured a full canvas cover for the base of the main gun—an area prone to leak in inclement weather. Moisture in this area could rust and foul the ball mount of the main gun. The right side pistol port has been pushed out, revealing its thickness and its retaining chain. The antenna for the vehicle's radio is visible on the left. It was mounted don the top of the rear right hand ventilator housing.* Patton Museum

ASSAULT GUNS AND THE *STURMGESCHÜTZ*

Sturmmörser

Specifications	
Length	6.28 m
Width	3.57 m
Height	2.85 m
Weight	65 tons
Fuel capacity	540 liters
Maximum speed	37.5 km/hr
Range, on road	120 km
Range, cross country	85 km
Crew	5
Communications	FuG 5, intercom
Armament	
Weapon, main	38 cm StuM
Weapon, secondary	7.92 mm MG 34
	7.93 mm MG 42
Ammo stowage, main	14 rounds
Ammo stowage, secondary	2,550 rounds
Automotive	
Engine make	Maybach
Engine model	HL 230 P45
Engine configuration	V-12, liquid cooled
Engine displacement	23 liters
Engine horsepower	650 @ 2500 rpm

All measurements are given in the metric system

Above: *The final series Sturmpanzer IV addressed most of it shortcomings. The superstructure was redesigned and production began in May 1944 using the chassis of the Panzer IV Ausf J. The roof was now two sections with the forward most one sloped downward. This reduced the size slightly and saved weight. A new gun was also mounted; the StuH 43/1. This was some 800 pounds lighter than its predecessor. Perhaps most importantly, the superstructure was extended at the upper left and an MG34 and ball mount was installed for self-defense. This vehicle was captured by Canadian troops in France in the late summer of 1944. Patton Museum*

Left: *Eventually, the Sturmpanzer IV was considered a failure at its anointed task and a much larger weapon was sought out. The chosen weapon was a complete redesign of a naval mortar known as the 38cm Raketen-Tauchgranatenwerfer L/5,4. For installation in what became known as the 38 cm RW61 auf Sturmmörser Tiger (or simply Sturmtiger), it was designated 38 cm Raketenwerfer 61 and it was mounted on the recycled chassis of a Tiger I. This and the following photos depict a Sturmtiger of the PzStuMrKp 1000 captured and evaluated by the 464th Ordnance Evac. Co. in April of 1945. Patton Museum*

Left: *The 38 cm* Raketenwerfer 61 *at maximum elevation of 85 degrees. The basis for this gun was a 38 cm RTgW L/5,4 rocket propelled depth charge launcher designed by the Kreigsmarine for the defense of naval facilities against submarines. The large, armored mount of the weapon is shown to good advantage here. The lugs seen around the end of the barrel are for the installation of a counterweight. Visible to the lower left is the ball mount for the self-defense MG34. At right, the aperture for the PaK ZF3 sight for the* Raketenwerfer 61 *can be seen with the driver's visor below that. The large hoist for loading the enormous rounds is also visible at the upper left.* Patton Museum

Above: *This and the following photos depict the 464th's prize as the British photographed it during their brief possession of it in the summer of 1945. All* Sturmtigers *constructed had their hulls upgraded to the late Ausf E standard and were updated with newer HL 230 engines and steel rimmed roadwheels. The firm of Alkett in Berlin accomplished all these modifications, including the construction and installation of the larger, armored superstructure. The front of the armored superstructure was 150 mm thick.* Patton Museum

ASSAULT GUNS AND THE *STURMGESCHÜTZ*   123

Above: *Originally, Sturmtigers were to be assigned to special* Panzersturmmörserkompanie *of the Panzer Divisions, each containing fourteen vehicles. This shot provides a good view of the rocket hoist. It could swivel out past the hull and was actuated using a hand crank that was attached to the winch reduction gearbox seen midway up its support shaft. The larger crew entry hatch can just be seen to its left. The cable for the winch and the loop that secured the round are missing here.* Patton Museum

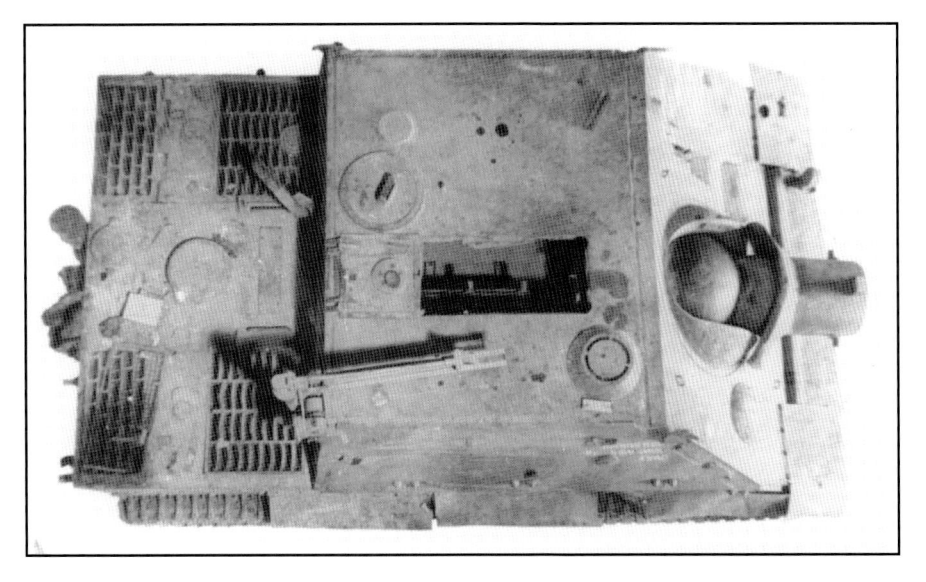

Above: *Full unit strength was never attained due to the extremely low production numbers—only eighteen Sturmtigers were built. Three units were eventually formed, numbered PzStuMrKp 1000, 1001 and 1002, but none of them ever contained more than four vehicles. Later, the responsibility of the units was transferred to the artillery and their designation was changed to Panzersturmmtörserbatterie. This photo provides a view through the loading hatch showing the loading tray and it six rollers. The commander's hatch is to the upper left.* Patton Museum

124 THE COMPLETE GUIDE TO GERMAN ARMORED VEHICLES

Above: *Because the Sturmtiger was based on a refitted vehicle, it often retained the original coating of Zimmerit anti-magnetic paste on the lower hull. Oddly, no coating has been seen on the upper superstructure, in spite of the fact that production of the Sturmtiger began well before the paste was discontinued. The original chassis number of this vehicle has been recorded as 250327, making it a June 1943 model. The cause of the demise of this Sturmtiger was these 76mm hits to the rear plate.* Patton Museum

Above: *The original proposal to use the Tiger I chassis was met with severe resistance in Army circles, due to the extreme need for this vehicle at the front. It was eventually decided that only recycled vehicles would be used as they were returned to Germany for overhaul. The situation remained critical as regard to additional hulls, which was the reason so few Sturmtigers were built. The large and critical housing for the ventilator fan can be seen in the upper center of the photo.* Patton Museum

Above: *The two-piece gun tube of the Raketenwerfer 61 can clearly be seen here. The outer sleeve, containing the vent holes, was connected to the inner, rifled sleeve and allowed the circulation of exhaust gases produced during the launch of the rocket projectiles. The number of holes could differ from vehicle to vehicle, ranging from 20 on the prototype to 30, 31 or even 40.* Patton Museum

Above: *This Sturmtiger was captured in the area of Minden, Germany on April 11, 1945. It was later shipped to Aberdeen Proving Ground in the United States for evaluation and then later placed on outdoor display. The vehicle was then loaned back to the West German government in the 1970s and was then displayed at the WTS Museum in Koblenz. In 1992, it was acquired and partially restored by the Auto+Technik Museum in Sinshiem. Interestingly, the round shaped counterweight appears only on this vehicle.* National Archives and Records Administration

Chapter 3
Jagdpanzers

Germany fielded a number of vehicles intended to combat enemy tanks. While of course there was, at times, tank-on-tank combat, at other times specialized antitank vehicles were used. As seen in previous chapters, while the StuG was specifically originally *not* designed for this use, in time it came to be used almost exclusively for antitank duties. However, Germany fielded two broad types of purpose-built antitank vehicles, the *Panzerjäger* and the *Jagdpanzer*. The former had an open top and rear, while the latter, discussed in this chapter, featured a totally enclosed fighting compartment.

Jagdpanzer 38 "Hetzer"
The Allied bombing of the Alkett plant in November 1943 hampered production of the vehicle that increasingly was the mainstay of Germany's armored force—the StuG. Seeking an alternative, the *Oberkommando des Heeres* (OKH—German Army High Command) considered the Boemisch-Märische Maschinenfabrik (BMM) plant in Prague. While a December 6, 1943, report to Hitler ruled the BMM plant out as a StuG production facility, it presented the possibility of a new light tank killer.

Only eleven days later, design drawings of such a vehicle had been completed. Initially named "*Sturmgeschütz neue Art mit 7.5 cm PaK 39 L/40 auf Fahrgestell* PzKpfw 38(t)," the vehicle was based on proven automotive components. Specifically, the PzKpfw 38(t) *alte Art* and the PzKpfw 38(t) *neue Art*. Armament proposed was the 7.5 cm PaK 39 L/48, the same weapon mounted in the *Jagdpanzer* IV.

A wooden mock-up was built, and it was inspected by the *Heeres Waffenamt* on January 26, 1944. The mock-up was approved, and with only a few changes the vehicle was placed into production. The first three examples were delivered by BMM in March 1944. The next month twenty more were delivered, with production continuing to rise. In order to meet the demand, in July 1944 Skoda began to deliver the vehicles as well.

While even to this day this vehicle is referred to as the "*Hetzer*," in fact this name was never actually assigned to this machine. Rather, that name was intended for the never-produced *Jagdpanzer* E-10 project, but using troops mistakenly applied it to the *Jagdpanzer* 38. Instead, the BMM vehicle was, after November 1944, the "*Jagdpanzer* 38 (SdKfz 138/2)."

Like the StuG it was to fill in for, Allied bombing took a toll on *Jagdpanzer* 38 production, either through strikes on the assembly plants, or those of component suppliers.

Initially, fourteen *Jagdpanzer* 38s were issued to tank-destroyer units within each infantry division. However, shortages caused only ten of the vehicles to be issued to each unit after January 1945. While various minor changes were made during the course of *Jagdpanzer* 38 production, the initial design was sound, and the vehicle did not have nearly as many variations as did most of Germany's armored vehicles.

Above: *Once the 38(t) became obsolete as a battle tank, work began to use its dependable automotive components in a more modern fighting machine. One result was the Jagdpanzer 38(t) Hetzer. This purpose-built chassis mounted the 7.5 cm PaK 39 in a limited traverse mount, surrounded by aggressively sloped armor. The early version seen here can be identified by its relatively small mantlet, 38(t) style drive sprocket and idler wheel, and unadorned paint scheme. Later vehicles had elaborate camouflage applied at the factory.* Hans-Heiri Stapfer

Above: *This mid-production Hetzer now has a larger and wider cast mantlet, as well as a more unique and refined design for its sprocket and idler wheels. Its extremely low silhouette is apparent in this British evaluation photo.* Patton Museum

Above: *This overhead shot of the same vehicle reveals the similarity of the rear lower hull to the older 38(t). The main gun was located well to the right to allow room for the driver and the commander sat to the rear of the gun. The scissor periscope can be seen in place above the hatch. All versions of the* Hetzer *had a remotely operated machine gun mounted in the roof.* Patton Museum

Above: *This late-model* Hetzer *sports an even wider cast mantlet. The manufacturer of the* Hetzer, ČKD, *became well known for its complex factory-applied ambush paint schemes in dark green, red brown and dark yellow. The barrel of the 7.5 cm main gun was threaded for a muzzle brake, but it was rarely seen fitted in the field.* Hans-Heiri Stapfer

Jagdpanzer 38

Specifications	
Length	6.27 m
Width	2.63 m
Height	2.10 m
Weight	16 metrics
Fuel capacity	320 liters
Maximum speed	40 km/hr
Range, on-road	180 km
Range, cross-country	130 km
Crew	4
Communications	Fu Spr Ger f
Armament	
Weapon, main	7.5 cm PaK 39 L/48
Weapon, secondary	7.92 mm MG 34
Ammo stowage, main	41 rounds
Ammo stowage, secondary	600 rounds
Automotive	
Engine make	Praga
Engine model	AC
Engine configuration	6-cylinder, liquid cooled
Engine displacement	7.75 liters
Engine horsepower	150 @ 2600 rpm

Jagdpanzer IV

Specifications	
Length	6.85 m
Width	3.17 m
Height	1.86 m
Weight	24 tons
Fuel capacity	470 liters
Maximum speed	40 km/hr
Range, on-road	210 km
Range, cross-country	130 km
Crew	4
Communications	FuG 5, intercom
Armament	
Weapon, main	7.5 cm PaK 39 L/48
Weapon, secondary	7.92 mm MG 42
Ammo stowage, main	79 rounds
Ammo stowage, secondary	1,200 rounds
Automotive	
Engine make	Maybach
Engine model	HL 120 TRM
Engine configuration	V-12, liquid cooled
Engine displacement	11.9 liters
Engine horsepower	265 @ 2600 rpm

Jagdpanzer IV (SdKfz 162)

Based on the proven *Panzerkampfwagen* IV chassis, the *Jagdpanzer* IV featured a low silhouette much like the *Sturmgeschütz* assault guns. However, the *Sturmgeschütz* was very much a boxy vehicle, while the *Jagdpanzer* IV featured sloping armor for better protection.

Initial work on the *Jagdpanzer* IV began in September 1942. Vomag, the design firm produced a wooden mock-up which was shown to Hitler in May 1943. As designed, the vehicle was to mount a 7.5 cm PaK 39 (L/48) gun. The prototype was delivered in October 1943, while delivery of production examples began in January of the following year, with thirty vehicles. Production of this vehicle, initially dubbed "*Sturmgeschütz neue Art*," ran through November 1944, and totaled 750 units.

During this time several changes were made, including the elimination of the left machine-gun port, and in September, *Flammentoeter* spark-arresting mufflers began to be used, while the application of *Zimmerit* antimagnetic coating was halted. Also in September one return roller was eliminated.

Panzer IV/70 (V) (SdKfz 162/1)

As increased quantities of the PaK 42 L/70 gun became available, these weapons began to be installed in the *Jagdpanzer* IV, increasing firepower over that offered by the standard 7.5 cm PaK 39 L/48. The initial installations of the longer weapon on the assembly line were in August 1944, and by November the PaK 42 L/70 was being installed exclusively.

While the more powerful weapon increased the range of the *Jagdpanzer*, often to the point that it could fire from beyond the range of its opponents, this was partially offset due to reduced mobility. Not only did the added length of

Above: *Perhaps the most unique version of the Hetzer was known as the "Starr." This was a highly simplified version without any recoil mechanism for the main gun. Traverse was also eliminated and all movement of the gun was dependent on the motion of the chassis. The Starr was also uniquely powered by a Tatra eight-cylinder Diesel engine. Only ten were built.* Hans-Heiri Stapfer

Above: *In order to create a specific tank-destroyer version of the venerable Panzer IV, it was decided to mount the deadly 7.5 cm L/48 antitank gun in a fixed superstructure. The result was the Jagdpanzer IV. Although this coincided with the production of the same weapon in the rotating turret of the gun tank, this version was thought to be quicker and less expensive to produce. This photo depicts the mild-steel prototype distinguished by its rounded upper hull and small gun mantlet.* Patton Museum

JAGDPANZERS 131

Above: *This photo of a production vehicle captured by the British in Normandy reveals the sharp, low angles of the upper hull. This made the Jagdpanzer IV an excellent ambush vehicle; however, it was frequently employed as an infantry support tank. This tank is completely covered in Zimmerit antimagnetic paste. Note the threads on the barrel for a muzzle brake.* Patton Museum

Above: *This Jagdpanzer IV was captured by the Americans and later evaluated at Aberdeen Proving Grounds. All versions of the Jagdpanzer IV incorporated suspension components of the Panzer IV H, most notably featuring all steel return rollers.* US Army Ordnance Museum

the gun restrict maneuverability in towns and forests, but the increased length and weight made the vehicle notably nose heavy. Further, the long weapon was affected by vibration during travel, and required greater maintenance to ensure accuracy.

The "V" in the model designation indicated that the vehicle was of the Vomag design. Although Vomag managed to keep the vehicle in production through April 1945, ultimately turning out 970 examples, pressure from Allied bombing steadily reduced the monthly output from its peak of 185 units in January 1945. The *Panzer* IV/70 (V) was used primarily by tank-killer detachments of Panzer divisions, although a few were issued to Independent Panzer Brigades.

Above: *Due to the concurrent production of the L/48 weapon in the turreted version, it was decided to install the 7.5 cm L/70 gun in the Jagdpanzer IV. This weapon had not yet been considered for the Panzer IV. Although more effective, the larger gun overloaded the chassis of the vehicle.* Patton Museum

Above: *This later production Jagdpanzer IV now features only three return rollers. Due to the increased weight of the gun and the strain on the roadwheels, the first set on either side uses steel, rather than rubber, tires. The sloped armor on the transmission was a novel innovation that was not incorporated into regular Panzer IV production.* Patton Museum

Panzer IV/70 (V)

Specifications	
Length	8.50 m
Width	3.20 m
Height	2.00 m
Weight	25.5 tons
Fuel capacity	470 liters
Maximum speed	35 km/hr
Range, on-road	210 km
Range, cross-country	130 km
Crew	4
Communications	FuG 5 and FuG 2, intercom
Armament	
Weapon, main	7.5 cm Pak 42 L/70
Weapon, secondary	7.92 mm MG 42
Ammo stowage, main	60 rounds
Ammo stowage, secondary	1,200 rounds
Automotive	
Engine make	Maybach
Engine model	HL 120 TRM
Engine configuration	V-12, liquid cooled
Engine displacement	11.9 liters
Engine horsepower	265 @ 2600 rpm

Panzer IV/70 (A)

In an effort to supply more of the heavily armed *Jagdpanzers*, the German military turned to Alkett to supplement Vomag's production. Alkett, who had been producing the Panzer IV, set out to mount a *Jagdpanzer* superstructure on an essentially unmodified Panzer IV chassis. However, in order that the breech of the gun clear the Panzer IV fuel tanks, a superstructure taller than that of the Panzer IV/70 (V) had to be devised. In order to do so, essentially an armored box was placed on the chassis, and on top of that, the Vomag superstructure mounted.

The resultant vehicle was thirty-eight centimeters taller than its Vomag counterpart, and because it used the Panzer IV tank chassis, it also lacked the distinctive pointed bow of the Vomag vehicle. Production of the Alkett design began at Nibelungenwerk in Austria in August 1944. When production ceased in March 1945, 278 examples had been completed.

Panzer IV/70 (A)

Specifications	
Length	8.87 m
Width	2.90 m
Height	2.20 m
Weight	27 tons
Fuel capacity	470 liters
Maximum speed	38 km/hr
Range, on-road	200 km
Range, cross-country	130 km
Crew	4
Communications	FuG 5 and FuG 2, intercom
Armament	
Weapon, main	7.5 cm PaK 42 L/70
Weapon, secondary	7.92 mm MG 42
Ammo stowage, main	90 rounds
Ammo stowage, secondary	1,200 rounds
Automotive	
Engine make	Maybach
Engine model	HL 120 TRM
Engine configuration	V-12, liquid cooled
Engine displacement	11.9 liters
Engine horsepower	265 @ 2600 rpm

Jagdpanther

The *Jagdpanther*, or hunting panther, utilized the automotive and chassis components of the Panther medium tank. Typical of *Jagdpanzers*, the vehicle had a fixed superstructure, in which was mounted a powerful 8.8 cm PaK L/71 gun, the same type of weapon used on the Tiger II.

This heavily armed and armored vehicle was conceived not for defense, but rather as an offensive weapon by heavy tank-destroyer battalions. Though heavily armed and armored, like all *Jagdpanzers*, the *Jagdpanther* was vulnerable to infantry attack, and itself had to be protected by infantry and/or tanks.

Krupp displayed a full-sized wooden mock-up of the *Jagdpanther* in November 1942, despite the decision having been made in October to transfer the project to Daimler-Benz.

Above: *Up until July 1944, all Jagdpanzer IV had been produced by Vomag. In order to maximize production of the L/70-armed version of the Jagdpanzer IV, manufacture was opened up to the firm of Alkett. Their design used a simplified superstructure mounted right onto a only slightly modified Panzer IV hull, resulting in a vehicle about forty centimeters higher than its predecessor. Steel-tired roadwheels were used on the first two stations of this version, sometimes known as Jagdpanzer IV (A).* Patton Museum

Above: *These two destroyed Panzer IV/70 (A) produced by Alkett have features common to the last version of the Panzer IV, the Ausf J. Note the stamped idler wheel of the rear tank and the vertical exhaust stacks of the tank in the foreground.* Patton Museum

Specifications

Length	9.88 m
Width	3.45 m
Height	2.72 m
Weight	46 tons
Fuel capacity	700 liters
Maximum speed	46 km/hr
Range, on-road	160 km
Range, cross-country	80 km
Crew	5
Communications	FuG 5 and FuG 2, intercom
Armament	
Weapon, main	8.8 cm PaK 43/3 L/71
Weapon, secondary	7.92 mm MG 42
Ammo stowage, main	60 rounds
Ammo stowage, secondary	1,200 rounds
Automotive	
Engine make	Maybach
Engine model	HL 230 P30
Engine configuration	V-12, liquid cooled
Engine displacement	23.1 liters
Engine horsepower	600 @ 2500 rpm

Mühlenbau und Industrie AG (MIAG) in Braunschweig would take over the project in December 1942. In part because of these repeated transfers, it would be almost a year before MIAG completed two prototype vehicles.

The first group of five production *Jagdpanthers*, amounting to just five vehicles, was completed by MIAG in January 1944. While the company was given a production goal of 150 of the vehicles monthly, the Allies had other plans, with bombers targeting MIAG's Braunschweig plant, causing considerable delays in production.

In an effort to compensate for this, contracts were issued for additional *Jagdpanther* production by Maschinenfabrik Niedersachsen-Hannover (MNH) in Hannover as well as Maschinenbau und Bahnbedarf AG. Nordhausen (MBA) at Potsdam-Drewitz.

The plants of those two firms, as well as that of their suppliers, were also targeted by Allied bombers. As a result, MBA was able to produce only thirty-three *Jagdpanthers*, while MNH completed 112 vehicles; chassis number 303001 through 303112, and MIAG built 268 units, chassis numbers 300001 through 300268.

Ferdinand/*Elefant*

Among the largest of the German tank destroyers was the Ferdinand, which was later modified and renamed *Elefant*.

Left: *The* Jagdpanther *combined the Panther tank chassis, drivetrain, and hull with the powerful 8.8 cm Panzerabwehrkanone PaK 43/3 L/71 gun, mounted in a new, heavily armored superstructure. Initial series production was undertaken by Mühlenbau und Industrie AG (MIAG) of Braunschweig, Germany. After October 1944, the firms MNH and Maschienenbau und Bahnbedarf AG (MBA) also began producing the vehicles. This is one of the earliest MIAG vehicles, as evident from the twin driver's periscopes, a feature that was quickly changed.* Patton Museum

Left: *Only the driver's right periscope is installed in this* Jagdpanther, *however the embrasure for the left periscope remains next to it. Mounted above the armored skirts on the left side of the vehicle is a C-hook, tow cable, and tubular storage container for a bore-cleaning brush.* Patton Museum

These vehicles had their origins in the famed Tiger program, and more specifically, in the creative genius of Ferdinand Porsche, for whom the tank destroyers were initially named.

While Porsche's proposal for the Tiger, the Porsche *Typ* 100, also known as the VK 3001 (P), used a gas-electric drivetrain, the design, which featured two large air-cooled V-10 gasoline engines turning generators, was not selected to be Germany's new heavy tank.

However, vast amounts of raw materials, as well as engineering and labor man-hours, had been devoted to creating one hundred of these so-called Porsche Tigers. Rather than waste these resources, in September 1942 it was decided to convert a significant portion of the Tiger (P) chassis into *Jagdpanzers*, armed with 8.8 cm PaK L/71 cannon.

The superstructure of the new vehicle, dubbed the Ferdinand, was a rear-mounted boxy arrangement, featuring frontal armor an impressive 200 mm thick. Design work for the new vehicle was completed by Alkett in November 1942. The chassis were to be repowered. While a gas-electric drivetrain would be retained, a pair of liquid-cooled Maybach HL120 engines replaced the troublesome Simmering-built Porsche air-cooled engines. Two hulls, which had been completed by Krupp and shipped to Nibelungenwerk, where they had lain dormant following suspension of the Tiger (P) program, were now shipped to Alkett to be made into trial vehicles.

Initially it was planned that once series production began Nibelungenwerk would complete the chassis and Alkett would produce all the superstructures. Those plans changed in February 1943, which it was decided that series production would be undertaken entirely by Nibelungenwerk.

Nibelungenwerk began production of the eighty-nine *Jagdpanzer* Ferdinands in April 1943, and completed the last of the vehicles in May.

With the situation on the Russian Front deteriorating, not surprisingly in June the new vehicles, assigned to *Schwere Panzerjäger-Abteilungen* 654 and 654, were sent to the front, taking part in Operation *Zitadelle*. In December, the forty-eight surviving vehicles were shipped to Nibelungenwerk for rebuilding.

While on the Russian Front, one of the shortcomings revealed in the Ferdinand design was the lack of defense against infantry. Hence, during the post-Kursk rebuild, a ball-mounted machine gun was added at the hull front. This weapon was to be fired by the radio operator.

Also, in order to improve visibility, a cupola was installed replacing the commander's hatch. As a last-ditch defense against infantry with magnetic mines, *Zimmerit* was added to such a height as to protect the vehicle from mines placed by a man afoot.

With the vehicles rebuilt by the end of March 1944, they were issued to *Schwere Panzerjäger-Abteilungen* 653 and dispatched to Italy.

Coincidental with this in February, following Hitler's suggestion, the name of the vehicle was changed from Ferdinand to *Elefant*.

Above: *This* Befehls-Jagdpanther *was captured at Hechtel in September 1944. The* Befehls-Jagdpanther *was a command vehicle with extra radio equipment in the left rear of the superstructure. The vehicle has crosshatched Zimmerit and a single driver's periscope with no rain guard: features consistent with a Jagdpanther produced in July or August 1944. The doors are missing from the commander's and loader's hatches on the superstructure roof. Toward the left front of the superstructure roof is the sliding shield for the gunner's periscope. The right side of the vehicle displays four holes from armored piercing rounds, one toward the rear, and three closely grouped ones below the rear of the superstructure. This* Befehls-Jagdpanther *is now in the collection of the Imperial War Museum.* Patton Museum

Left: *This* Jagdpanther *of schwere Panzerjäger-Abteilung 654, taking part in training at Mailly-le-Camp, France, is missing the front skirt panel on the right side. This vehicle features the sectional, two-piece 8.8 cm gun barrel rather than the earlier single-piece monoblock gun barrel.* Patton Museum

Left: *Two crewmen go about their duties to the front of and on top of a 1944-produced* Jagdpanther. *The typical crosshatched* Zimmerit *pattern is evident on the hull and the superstructure. A* Kugelblende *(ball machine-gun mount) for a 7.92 mm MG 34 was located to the right of the main gun of the* Jagdpanther. National Archives and Records Administration

Above: *The massive tank destroyers, initially known as Ferdinand, were not equipped with close-in defense weaponry as originally produced. This proved a serious weakness when the vehicles were initially deployed on the Russian Front.* Military History Institute

Above: *Somewhere on the Russian Front, a crewman kneels on the roof of the superstructure of Ferdinand number 534. Another man lies on the roof of the massive vehicle. The left engine access cover is open. This vehicle survived the battalion's battles in July and August 1943.* Thomas Anderson

Above: *Ammunition is transferred from a Büssing-NAG 4500 truck to a Ferdinand in Russian Front. The vehicle seems to have just a few splotches of dark paint on the side to interrupt the Dunkelgelb base color.* Thomas Anderson

Above: *Following the loss of almost half of the big tank destroyers on the Eastern Front, the survivors were rebuilt and modified incorporating the lessons learned. Concurrently but coincidentally, the name of the vehicle was changed from Ferdinand to Elefant. During the rebuild, the vehicles were equipped with hull-mounted 7.92 mm MG 34 machine guns.* Ordnance Museum

Above: *The rebuilding program also included the addition of a cupola with vision ports for the commander. The cupola is faintly visible on this captured example, photographed in 1946 at Aberdeen Proving Ground. Also visible is the Zimmerit coating that was applied to the lower portion of the vehicle during the conversion/rebuilding program. Patton Museum*

Specifications	
Length	8.14 m
Width	3.38 m
Height	2.97 m
Weight	65 tons
Fuel capacity	950 liters
Maximum speed	30 km/hr
Range, on-road	150 km
Range, cross-country	90 km
Crew	6
Communications	FuG 5 and FuG 2, intercom

Jagdtiger SdKfz 186

Faced with increasing numbers of increasingly capable Allied vehicles, Germany sought to develop a tank destroyer that was so heavily armed and armored it could absolutely dominate the battlefield.

That armament was 12.8 cm PaK 44 L/55, inspired by the Soviet 122 mm gun. The Germans opted for the slightly larger gun in part to utilize some of the tooling previously created to produce 12.8 cm naval weapons.

While some of these formidable weapons were mounted on towed artillery carriages, two types of mechanized mounts were proposed. One was the German superheavy tank *Maus*. The other was the largest tank destroyer to enter series production, the *Jagdtiger*. It was hoped that not only would this vehicle be effective against enemy tanks, including those beyond the effective range of other guns, but also would be decisive against fortifications.

In order to mechanize the weapon, first a mock-up based on the Panther chassis was created. This style was discarded, and in October 1943 a second mock-up based on the Tiger II chassis, albeit lengthened forty centimeters, was shown to Hitler.

Two trial vehicles were assembled: chassis number 305001 utilized an eight-roadwheel Porsche torsion-bar suspension system, while chassis number 305002 used the Henschel nine overlapping wheel suspension system like that used on the production of Tiger II.

Both were assembled by Nibelungenwerk in February 1944. In total, 150 of the vehicles, dubbed Jagdtigers, were ordered. Ten more of these vehicles were built with the Porsche-designed suspension, while the balance of the seventy to eighty-eight vehicles actually produced featured the Henschel suspension.

Only two units were issued the massive vehicles, the heaviest armored vehicles to see series production during the war, *schwere Panzerjäger-Abteilung* 653 and the *schwere Panzerjäger-Abteilung* 512. Their considerable weight, compounded by the vehicles often being crewed by young, inexperienced men, led to the *Jagdtiger* being of limited usefulness.

Specifications	
Length	10.5 m
Width	3.77 m
Height	2.95 m
Weight	75.2 tons
Fuel capacity	860 liters
Maximum speed	34.6 km/hr
Range, on-road	100 km
Range, cross-country	70 km
Crew	6
Communications	FuG 5 and FuG 2, intercom
Armament	
Weapon, main	12.8 cm PaK 80 L/55
Weapon, secondary	1 x 7.92 mm MG 42 and 1 x 7.92 mm MG 34
Ammo stowage, main	40 rounds
Ammo stowage, secondary	3,300 rounds
Automotive	
Engine make	Maybach
Engine model	HL 230 P30
Engine configuration	V-12, liquid cooled
Engine displacement	23.1 liters
Engine horsepower	600 @ 2500 rpm

Above: *The heaviest armored vehicle fielded by the Germans in World War II was the* Panzerjäger Tiger Ausf B. *This was built on a slightly lengthened Tiger II chassis topped with a fixed casemate and a 12.8 cm PaK 44 L/55 antitank gun. It weighed seventy-nine tons. A few early versions of the* Jagdtiger *had a suspension designed by Porsche, and one such vehicle is seen here. It features staggered 70 cm roadwheels mounted in pairs on the outside of the hull utilizing lateral dampeners, in favor of the torsion-bar suspension of the Tiger II.* Patton Museum

Above: *On April 16, 1945, the remaining* Jagdtigers *of the* schwere Panzerjäger-Abteilung 512 *surrendered to elements of the 7th Armored Division. Much of the large boxy superstructure has been covered in pine boughs for camouflage. The larger roadwheels of the production Tiger II are visible here, as is the huge barrel of the 12.8 cm gun.* National Archives and Records Administration

Chapter 4
Panzerjäger

anzerjäger is the term used for the German army's tank-destroyer service and also the vehicles used by that service. These troops were considered part of the artillery, not Panzer troops, and thus wore the gray army uniform rather than the black Panzer uniform.

The vehicles used by the *Panzerjäger* were often captured enemy tanks that had been rearmed, although in some instances older German tanks were rearmed, and in a few instances, new vehicles built from the ground up.

In each of these cases, unlike the *Jagdpanzer*, the *Panzerjäger* had an open-top fighting compartment—and in some cases only the gun shield provided protection for the crew

Aufklärungspanzerwagen 38 (2 cm) (SdKfz 140/1)

The *Aufklärungspanzerwagen* 38 may seem like an odd choice to open the *Panzerjäger* chapter with, as it is not truly a *Panzerjäger*, but rather a reconnaissance vehicle.

However, by virtue of its being armed with a tank gun, and being open topped, I have chosen to place it in this chapter.

The most commonly used reconnaissance vehicles of the German army—sidecar-equipped motorcycles and four-, six-, and eight-wheeled armored cars—were ill-suited for operations on the Eastern Front, especially in muddy conditions. The *Aufklärungspanzerwagen* 38 was developed to overcome this problem.

The *Aufklärungspanzerwagen* 38 consisted of a turret armed with a 2 cm KwK 38 and a coaxially mounted MG 42, mounted on the proven Czech 38(t) chassis. This is the same turret used on the SdKfz 234/1.

The *Panzerkampfwagen* 38(t) chassis was upgraded by the installation of a more powerful engine, increasing the vehicle's top speed to 45 km/hr. The vehicles, which were built using reconditioned earlier-produced chassis, were equipped with a boxy new upper hull.

The seventy vehicles of the series were contracted to be produced by ČKD (Ceskomoravska Kolben-Danek) in

Aufklärungspanzerwagen 38 (2 cm) (SdKfz 140/1)

Specifications	
Length	4.51 m
Width	2.14 m
Height	2.17 m
Weight	9.75 tons
Maximum speed	45 km/hr
Range, on-road	210 km
Crew	4
Communications	Fu Spr Ger f (9 equipped with FuG 12)
Armament	
Weapon, main	2 cm KwK 38 L/55
Weapon, coaxial	7.92 mm MG 42
Automotive	
Engine make	Praga
Engine model	TNHPS/II
Engine configuration	6-cylinder, liquid cooled
Engine displacement	7754,7
Engine horsepower	180 @ 2800 rpm

Above: *The* Aufklärungspanzerwagen *38 was built to perform high-speed armored reconnaissance. Its basis was the reliable Czech 38(t) chassis. ČKD was the manufacturer of the entire seventy-vehicle series and production of the vehicles occurred during the winter of 1943-1944. The turret of the vehicle was taken from the Sdkfz 234/1 eight-wheeled armored car. The vehicle's primary armament was a 2 cm KwK 38, and a coaxially mounted MG 42 was also provided. Hinged mesh screens were provided to keep objects from entering the vehicle. The vehicles were powered with a 180-horsepower engine, rather than the 150-horsepower engine originally used in the 38(t). Top speed was 45 km/hr.* Patton Museum

Czechoslovakia, which under German occupation was renamed the BMM (Böhmisch-Mährische Maschinenfabrik AG)

Although originally scheduled for production at a rate of five in October 1943, twenty-four in December 1943, and thirty in January 1944, typical of most wartime German armor contracts, there were delays. As a result, the first thirty-seven were accepted by the German army in February 1944, followed by thirty-three in March.

The next month twenty-five of the vehicles were supplied to Panzer-Grenadier-Division "*Grossdeutschland.*" A second group of twenty-five were supplied in September 1944 to the Third Panzer Division, thus the vehicles were used on both the Eastern and Western fronts. Several replacements were also sent to each of these units.

4.7 cm PaK(t) (Sfl) auf PzKpfw I Ausf B

Concerned about encounters with some formidable French tanks, like the *Char B1*, the German army sought to field a self-propelled antitank gun. To create such a vehicle, Panzer I Ausf B were stripped of their turrets, and upon the chassis was mounted the excellent Czech-made Škoda 4.7 cm *kanon* P.U.V vz. 36, known to the Germans as the 4.7 cm PaK 36(t), The resultant vehicles were designated 4.7 cm PaK(t) (Sf) *auf Panzerkampfwagen I ohne turm*, but are more commonly known as the *Panzerjäger I.*

These antitank guns were not war prizes, but rather were new production built for the German military. The weapon lacked the usual wheels, axles, and trails.

Alkett began the series deliveries of the diminutive tank destroyers in March 1940, when thirty were accepted by the army. These were followed by sixty more in April and a further thirty in May. Owing to shortages of the guns, Alkett did not deliver the two final vehicles until September 1940 and July 1941.

Contracts for a second group of these vehicles were issued in September 1940. Only ten of these were to be completed by Alkett; the remaining sixty vehicles on this order were to be assembled by Klockner-Humboldt-Deutz. Ten vehicles were delivered in November 1940, thirty in December and the final thirty the following January. The shape of the gun shield

4.7 cm PaK(t) (Sfl) auf PzKpfw I Ausf B

Specifications	
Length	4.42 m
Width	2.06 m
Height	2.14
Weight	6.4 tons
Fuel capacity	146 liters
Maximum speed	40 km/hr
Range, on-road	170 km
Range, cross-country	115 km
Crew	3
Communications	Fu Spr Ger a
Armament	
Weapon, main	4.7 cm PaK(t)
Ammo stowage, main	74 rounds
Automotive	
Engine make	Maybach
Engine model	NL 38 Tr
Engine configuration	6-cylinder, liquid cooled
Engine displacement	3.8 liters
Engine horsepower	100 @ 3000 rpm

Above: *The role of the* Panzerjäger *was to engage enemy tanks in order to free up other armored vehicles for breakthrough and exploitation. The* Panzerjäger *I was created by marrying the well-regarded Skoda 47 mm kanon P.U.V. vz. 36 gun to the chassis of the Panzer I Ausf B. In German service the gun was known as the 4.7 cm PaK 36(t). Only one variant was produced, with a later model differing slightly in the design of the gun shield. This vehicle was photographed in Belgium in 1940.* Patton Museum

Left: *This shot was taken while the 521 Panzerjäger-Abteilung supported the 71st Infantry Division on the approach to Verdun in early June 1940. In addition to its efficient armor-piercing shell, the 4.7 cm could also fire a 2.3kg high-explosive shell. Infantrymen work closely with the crew to provide accurate firing information. The crew all wears steel helmets, prudent in an open-topped vehicle.* National Archives and Records Administration.

of the second series *Panzerjäger* differed, having seven sides rather than five as found on the first series.

Increasingly capable enemy tanks rendered the *Panzerjäger* I obsolete by late 1943, and it was removed from service.

Panzerjäger Lorraine *Schlepper* 7.5 cm PaK 40/1 (SdKfz 135) "Marder I"

The tank destroyer that came to be known as the *Marder* I has its origins in a field conversion involving mounting an antitank gun on a captured French Lorraine artillery tractor. This conversion was led by Major Alfred Becker, and involved mounting the excellent German PaK 40/1 L/46 7.5 cm antitank gun atop the artillery tractor, which had an open cargo compartment.

Impressed with the efforts of the troops, Hitler ordered that similar conversions be carried out en masse. In order to carry this out, *Baukommando Becker* (Construction Battalion Becker) was formed. The new superstructures were manufactured by Alkett, and shipped to Becker's works in Paris and Krefeld for assembly. During July 1942 104 of the vehicles were assembled, with a final sixty-six being completed in August. These vehicles would be used on both the Eastern and Western fronts for the remainder of the war, gaining fame and known commonly as the *Marder* I.

The relatively thin armor was proof only against small arms and splinters, and was intended to protect the gun crew from infantry, not against tanks. The gun shield of the PaK was placed outside the front of the superstructure. This arrangement permitted the weapon to be traversed 32 degrees either side of center.

Panzerjäger Lorraine *Schlepper* 7.5 cm PaK 40/1 (SdKfz 135)

Specifications	
Length	4.95 m
Width	2.10 m
Height	2.05 m
Weight	8.5 tons
Fuel capacity	110 liters
Maximum speed	35 km/hr
Range, on-road	120 km
Range, cross-country	75 km
Crew	4
Communications	FuG 5
Armament	
Weapon	7.5 cm PaK 40/1 L/46
Ammunition stowage	48 rounds
Armor, gun	shield 10 mm
Armor, hull	8-10 mm
Automotive	
Engine make	DelaHaye
Engine model	135
Engine configuration	6-cylinder
Engine displacement	3.56 l
Engine horsepower	70 @ 2800 rpm

Left: *Several hundred Lorraine artillery tractors had been captured from the French army in 1940. These tractors were designed as supply vehicles for the French army. In order to meet the need for more and more mobile antitank guns, it was decided to mount the 7.5 cm PaK 40 on the chassis with an armored superstructure. Official designation was 7.5 cm PaK 40/1 auf Geschutzenwagen Lorraine Schlepper (f). About 170 conversions were completed at Army workshops in Paris and Krefeld in 1942. They served on both the Eastern and Western fronts and had a crew of four.* National Archives and Records Administration

Panzerselbstfahrlafette 1 für 7.62 cm PaK 36(r) auf Fahrgestell Panzerkampfwagen II Ausf D (SdKfz 132)

Specifications

Length	5.65 m
Width	2.30 m
Height	2.60 m
Weight	11.5 tons
Fuel capacity	200 liters
Maximum speed	55 km/hr
Range, on-road	200 km
Range, cross-country	130 km
Crew	4
Communications	Fu Spr Ger d

Armament

Weapon, main	7.62 cm PaK 36(r) L/51
Weapon, secondary	7.92 mm MG 34
Ammo stowage, main	30 rounds
Ammo stowage, secondary	900 rounds

Automotive

Engine make	Maybach
Engine model	HL 62 TRM
Engine configuration	6-cylinder, liquid cooled
Engine displacement	6.2 liters
Engine horsepower	140 hp

Panzerselbstfahrlafette 1 für 7.62 cm PaK 36(r) auf Fahrgestell Panzerkampfwagen II Ausf D (SdKfz 132)

When MAN's contract to produce 150 examples of Krupp's proposed *Panzerkampfwagen* II, known as the LaS 138, was canceled, all 150 chassis were diverted for production of Panzerjäger by Alkett.

As an indication of the early German successes in the East, the armament for these 150 vehicles was to be captured Russian 7.62 cm antitank guns. In Soviet service these were known as the 76.2 mm F-22 Model 1936 divisional field gun. In German service, the guns were rechambered the weapons to accept 7.5 cm PaK 40 ammunition. The resultant weapon was given the German military designation 7.62 cm PaK 36(r) L/51 antitank gun.

Alkett was scheduled to deliver forty-five vehicles in April 1942, seventy-five in May, and the final thirty in June. Remarkably, and unlike almost any other German armored fighting vehicle of the war, all 150 were completed early, the first sixty in April and the final ninety in May. These vehicles were known as the Marder II.

Contracts were issued to Wegmann in Kassel to produce a further sixty examples, but owing to a shortage of rebuilt Panzer II Ausf D chassis, only fifty-two were completed, all between June 1942 and June 1943.

During the course of the conversion, the superstructure front and sides were raised in order to create a protected fighting compartment for the gun crew. The gun was mounted inside this area on its cut-down field carriage. Stowage was provided for thirty rounds of main gun ammunition, and provision was made to carry a 7.92 mm MG 34 as a close defense weapon. The main gun could be traversed 50 degrees either side of centerline.

Left: *During the initial stages of the German invasion of the Soviet Union, a large number of the highly effective Russian 76 mm antitank guns were captured. In order to quickly put these weapons back into use, the Germans created several novel Panzerjäger designs. What became known as the Panzerjäger II was simply the gun mounted atop the entire chassis of the obsolete Panzer II D. A basic armored superstructure was constructed around it to supplement the gun shield. Also known as the Marder IID, the gun in German service was known as the 7.62 cm PaK 36 r. Patton Museum*

Left: *In order to have the crew platform even with that of the gun, the rear hull was built up with steel plating. Hatches allowed access to ammunition and the engine. The Marder IID had an extremely high silhouette—a serious disadvantage for a tank-hunting vehicle. Only 150 were produced and issued.* Patton Museum

The vehicles began to be used on the Eastern Front in April 1942, primarily by tank-destroyer detachments of Panzer and Panzer-Grenadier divisions, including SS units. By 1944 better tank destroyers had been fielded by the Germany military, and these vehicles were relegated to secondary areas.

7.5 cm PaK 40/2 *auf Fahrgestell Panzerkampfwagen* II (Sf)(SdKfz 131)

By May 1942 the value of the Panzer II as a combat tank had become questionable. At the same time, as noted previously in this volume, the German army badly needed potent self-propelled antitank vehicles.

Thus, with Hitler's authorization, there was a decision to mount the 7.5 cm PaK 40/2 L/46 antitank gun on the Panzer II chassis. Of course, the new gun was far too large to incorporate into the *Panzerkampfwagen*'s turret, so a new, fixed, open-topped fighting compartment was designed to permit the antitank gun's installation. The mounting of the PaK 40 permitted 32 degrees traverse to the left and 25 degrees to the right of the centerline. The standard Ausf F hull and superstructure were utilized in large part, with the driver retaining his former position, and a two-man gun crew riding in the new fighting compartment. This afforded the *Panzerjäger* crew better protection than was afforded for their comrades in *Panzerjäger* I, as there was at least a certain amount of armor along the sides of the fighting compartment, even if it was open at the top and rear. For defense against infantry or aerial attack, the vehicle carried a 7.92 mm MG 34 inside the fighting compartment. A trial vehicle in this configuration was ordered, which was to be completed by June 15, 1942.

7.5 cm PaK 40/2 auf *Fahrgestell* Panzerkampfwagen II (Sf)(SdKfz 131)

Specifications	
Length	6.36 m
Width	2.28 m
Height	2.20 m
Weight	10.8 tons
Fuel capacity	170 liters
Maximum speed	40 km/h
Range, on-road	190 km
Range, cross-country	125 km
Crew	3
Communications	Fu Spr Ger d
Armament	
Weapon, main	7.5 cm PaK 40/2 L/46
Weapon, secondary	7.92 mm MG 34
Ammo stowage, main	37 rounds
Ammo stowage, secondary	600 rounds
Automotive	
Engine make	Maybach
Engine model	HL62TR
Engine configuration	straight 6-cylinder
Engine displacement	6.2 liter
Engine horsepower	140 @ 2600 rpm

Above: *The SdKfz 131 Marder II self-propelled antitank gun comprised the chassis and superstructure of the Panzer II light tank and a semi-enclosed fighting compartment mounting the 75 mm PaK 40/2 L/46 gun, cradle and shield. Officially known as the 7.5 cm PaK 40/2 auf Fahrgestell PzKpfw II (Sf), the sides of the fighting compartment were reinforced with 10 mm armor plate sloped 8 degrees from vertical. Initially, the vehicle was built on a stock Panzer II, but after production of this vehicle ceased, its components were designated specifically for the Marder II and the Wespe 10.5 cm self-propelled howitzer.* Patton Museum

Above: *Like the Panzer II, the Marder II's superstructure is asymmetrically positioned atop the hull. Note the tread pattern on the front mudguards and the wire rope stored on the glacis. Details of the clamp on the gun's travel lock for the gun are visible. This is the later type, without the locking joint. A simple camouflage pattern of green or brown splotches is lightly sprayed over the dark yellow base coat.* National Archives and Records Administration

Production of the new vehicles, based on the Panzer II Ausf F chassis, began the next month by Famo-Ursas. The new vehicle was designated 7.5 cm PaK 40/2 *auf Fahrgestell PzKpfw II (Sf)* (SdKfz 131), but is popularly known as the *Marder* II, making this the second vehicle dubbed *Marder* II. Production of new SdKfz 131 vehicles ended in June 1943. In addition to the 531 new-built vehicles, about 125 more were converted from rebuilt earlier model Panzer IIs. These conversions were done by Skoda, FAMO, and MAN.

The *Marder* IIs was used by *Panzerjäger-Abteilungen* on all fronts from its inception until the end of the war.

Panzerjäger 38 (t) fur 7.62 cm PaK 36(r) (SdKfz 139) "*Marder* III"

Only two days after initiating the project to mount captured Russian 7.62 mm guns on Panzer II chassis, a similar program was begun to mount the same weapon on the chassis of a *Panzerkampfwagen* 38(t).

Much like the Panzer II, the 38(t) was no longer armed or armored to such a level as to be effective on the battlefield, but chassis, running gear, and power plant were proven, reliable, and available.

To create the new gun motor carriage, the design of the chassis of the Panzer 38(t) then in production was modified, omitting provisions for installing a turret as well as the top of the superstructure. At the rear, a flat engine deck was used, rather than the sloping deck found on the tank. A new superstructure was designed, which included a gun mount, upon which was installed the gun and the shield. That shield was proof against only small arms and shell splinters.

Dubbed the *Marder* III, the first production vehicle was delivered by the ČKD plant in April 1942. From April 1942 through July 1942, the gun motor carriage and the 38(t) tank were concurrently produced, in July production of the conventional tank ceased. In total, 344 of the *Panzerjäger* 38 (t) fur 7.62 cm PaK 36(r) (SdKfz 139) vehicles were built in three series from April to November 1942. The final group of 150 vehicles were built with more powerful engines, an attempt to address complaints from the field that the vehicles were underpowered, and thus slowed armored formations.

Panzerjäger 38(t) für 7.5 cm PaK 40/3 Ausf H (SdKfz 138) "*Marder* III"

The next iteration of a *Panzerjäger* built on the 38(t) chassis was also dubbed the *Marder* III. However, it differed from its predecessor in a couple of significant ways.

First of all, the supply of captured Soviet 7.62 cm guns was nearing exhaustion, so the decision was made to arm this vehicle with Germany's own PaK 40/3 antitank gun. Also, the

Panzerjäger 38 (t) fur 7.62 cm PaK 36(r) (SdKfz 139) "*Marder* III"

Specifications	
Length	5.85 m
Width	2.15 m
Height	2.50 m
Weight	10.8 tons
Fuel capacity	218 liters
Maximum speed	42 km/hr
Range, on-road	185 km
Range, cross-country	140 km
Crew	4
Communications	Fu 5 SE 10 U
Armament	
Weapon, main	7.62 cm PaK 36
Weapon, secondary	7.92 mm MG 37(t)
Ammo stowage, main	30 rounds
Ammo stowage, secondary	1,200 rounds
Automotive	
Engine make, early	Praga
Engine model	TNHPS-II
Engine configuration	6-cylinder, liquid cooled
Engine displacement	7.75 liters
Engine horsepower	125 @ 2200 rpm
Engine make, late	Praga
Engine model	AC
Engine configuration	6-cylinder, liquid cooled
Engine displacement	7.75 liters
Engine horsepower	150 @ 2600 rpm

decision was made to retain, with adaptation, the fighting compartment of the 38(t), allowing not only for better protection for the gun crew, but also a notably lower silhouette.

The resultant vehicle, officially classified as *Panzerjäger* 38(t) *für* 7.5 cm PaK 40/3, has become popularly known as a *Marder* III Ausf H—although this was never an official designation.

The chassis used for this vehicle—and thus lending its model designation to the pop-culture name was the

Left: *Another expedient use of the Russian 76 mm antitank gun was its combination with the reliable chassis of the 38(t). Here again, the Germans found a use for a tank that was nearing the end of its combat career. In spite of the shortcomings of the 38(t) as a gun tank, its automotive performance was top notch. The pairing of the two was the start of a large family of vehicles based on the 38(t). The simplicity of the conversion is evident in this profile shot.* Patton Museum

Left: *Officially known as the 7.62 cm PaK 36 r auf GW 38t, it was also known as the Marder III. The expedient nature of the vehicle is apparent in this rear shot. The entire upper hull and engine deck were left intact beneath the riveted superstructure. A large wire basket assembly was placed on the rear to act as a floor for the fighting compartment. Two seats were mounted to the rear for the crew during travel.* National Archives and Records Administration

Panzerkampfwagen 38(t) Ausf H, even though no actual Ausf H tanks were actually built. The PaK 40 was mounted well forward on the chassis, with the driver and radio operator no longer having their own hatches in the hull top. Rather, they entered and exited the vehicle through the fighting compartment.

In addition to submerging the gun crew in the hull, protection was further enhanced by a gun shield, which itself was an improvement over the earlier *Marder* III gun shields.

The sloping shield traversed with the gun, and blended with the sloping side armor of the superstructure. An improved travel lock with remote release supported the gun, which at the same time allowed it to be quickly brought into acton.

Production of this vehicle began with forty-two units delivered in November 1942 and continued through April 1943, with ČKD completing 275 all-new vehicles, plus an additional 175 on rebuilt chassis.

PANZERJÄGER 153

Panzerjäger 38(t) für 7.5 cm PaK 40/3 Ausf H (SdKfz 138) "*Marder* III"

Specifications	
Length	5.77 m
Width	2.10 m
Height	2.50 m
Weight	10.8 tons
Fuel capacity	220 liters
Maximum speed	47 km/hr
Range, on-road	185 km
Range, cross-country	140 km
Crew	4
Communications	FuG 5
Armament	
Weapon, main	7.5 cm PaK 40/3 L/46
Weapon, secondary	7.92 mm MG 37(t)
Ammo stowage, main	38 rounds
Ammo stowage, secondary	600 rounds
Automotive	
Engine make	Praga
Engine model	AC
Engine configuration	6-cylinder, liquid cooled
Engine displacement	7.75 liters
Engine horsepower	150

Panzerjäger 38(t) für 7.5 cm PaK 40/3 Ausf M (SdKfz 138) *Marder* III

Work to develop the final version of the *Marder* began in February 1943. This vehicle, while continuing to utilize a chassis based on the *Panzerkampfwagen* 38(t), was significantly improved. Rather than essentially mounting an antitank gun atop a tank hull, the chassis for these vehicles was heavily customized for the new *Panzerjäger*.

The engine compartment was moved forward to the middle of the vehicle. The weapon was then mounted in the rear. This allowed better weight distribution, reduced the gun overhang (improving maneuverability), and perhaps most importantly, an improved fighting compartment layout. The running gear and suspension were only slightly modified, with the new vehicle having only one return roller on each side, rather than the two previously used.

Among the advantages was a markedly lower crew position, with the gun crew in essence now standing on the floor of the former engine compartment, which both lowered the vehicle silhouette, and in the event of a frontal attack, put the engine between the crew and the enemy. Also, for the first time the *Marder* had armor protection to rear of the crew, albeit only to the mid-torso.

Production of the new model, designated Ausf M (the M designation in this instance indicating *Motor Mitte*, or motor middle), began at the ČKD plant in May 1943.

Compared to earlier models, the fighting ability was improved through a redistribution of the workload among the four crewmen. The driver, of course, drove. The radio operator's station was moved from beside the driver to inside the fighting compartment, allowing the radio operator

Left: *The next stage in the evolution of the* Marder *concept from ČKD was known as the* Marder III Ausf H. *A somewhat more sensible approach to the concept of the original* Marder III, *the Ausf H mounted a 7.5 cm PaK 40 in a larger riveted superstructure. In lieu of the basket-like structure on the rear, a larger stamped tub was installed. The new design lowered the silhouette, and the PaK 40 was a more logistically sound weapon.* US Army Ordnance Museum

Above: *A pair of* Marder *III H in service with the SS Division LAH on the Eastern Front. In spite of all the improvements in the design, the vehicle was still considered to be nose heavy, mostly due to the position of the engine and transmission in relation to the gun. The crew of the nearest vehicle has added an MG 34 to a mount attached to the superstructure. Both vehicles have stanchions for the installation of tarps.* National Archives and Records Administration

to double as the loader. The fourth crewman now served exclusively as the gunner, a duty that in previous *Marder*s fell on the commander.

The driver's station was a compartment that protruded slightly from the superstructure. For most of 1943 this compartment was a combination of cast and bolted construction, but beginning in December 1943 a compartment of welded construction began to be used. At the same time, the hull construction changed to welded as well.

In July 1943, an improved turbocharged engine was installed, raising horsepower to 180, in hopes of improving performance. Unfortunately, the increased intake pressure resulted in frequent head gasket failures. Thus, in November a naturally aspirated 160-horsepower model NS engine began to be used instead.

The early Ausf M also had their exhaust pipes routed internally along the right side of the vehicle, exiting through the vertical tail plate. When the turbocharged engine was introduced, the exhaust system was naturally revised, with the exhaust pipe routed externally, exiting at the rear of the air intake and extending along the side of the hull, then turning to join the rear-mounted muffler.

Some vehicles were produced in *Befelsjäger* 38 Ausf M configurations. Those vehicles were equipped with additional radio equipment, which replaced a 12-round ammunition rack on the right side of the vehicle.

Series production of the *Marder* III Ausf M began at ČKD in May 1943 and continued through May of the following year, during which time 942 of the *Panzerjäger* were completed. *Panzerjäger* detachments on all fronts used these vehicles for the duration of the war.

10.5 cm K. Panzer *Selbstfahrlafette* IVa
Krupp reported in their 1938/39 report that they were engaged in development of a 10.5 cm K. Panzer *Selbstfahrlafette* IVa. This vehicle in time became known colloquially as "Dicker Max," or in English, Fat, or Thick Max. When the project began, the intent was to create a vehicle capable of knocking out the strongest fortifications on the Maginot Line. The development of the vehicle was repeatedly delayed as various suspension systems and engines were considered.

As it was, by the time these matters had been settled, the need to break the Maginot Line had passed, as the German invasion of France bypassed the labyrinth of fortifications.

However, with the invasion of Russia, a new need had arisen—the need for a very heavy tank destroyer. The German military felt that the *Selbstfahrlafette* IVa with

Panzerjäger 38(t) für 7.5 cm PaK 40/3 Ausf M (SdKfz 138) "Marder III"

Specifications	
Length	4.65 m
Width	2.10 m
Height	2.48 m
Weight	11 tons
Fuel capacity	218 liters
Maximum speed	47 km/hr
Range, on-road	240 km
Range, cross-country	140 km
Crew	4
Communications	FuG 5
Armament	
Weapon, main	7.5 cm PaK 40/3
Ammo stowage, main	38 rounds
Automotive	
Engine make, early	Praga
Engine model	AC
Engine configuration	6-cylinder, liquid cooled
Engine displacement	7.75 liters
Engine horsepower	150

its 10.5 K18 L/52 cannon would make an excellent tank destroyer.

The basic chassis was that of the *Panzerkampfwagen* IV Ausf E, however a smaller six-cylinder 180 hp Maybach HL66 Pla engine was used rather than the 265 hp HL 120 V-12 found in the Panzer IV. This engine was coupled to a SSG 46 transmission, which limited the vehicle's speed to 27 km/hr. The 10.5 cm gun used two-part ammunition, and two different types of projectiles were provided, allowing it to be used as either field artillery or an antitank gun.

Krupp completed two trial vehicles in January 1941, several months behind schedule. Had troop trials been successful, production of 100 series vehicles was to have begun in the spring of 1942. In July 1941, the two trial vehicles were assigned to *Panzerjäger-Abteilung* 521 for use on the Russian Front.

The two-part ammunition was blamed for the total destruction of one of the vehicles as they moved into Russia. A fire broke out in one of the vehicles while on a road march. The crew abandoned the *Selbstfahrlafette* prior to the explosion. It is believed that heat from the engine caused the powder to ignite.

The other vehicle fought until late 1941, when it was returned to Krupp for rebuild. It was redeployed to the east after rebuild in mid-1942, where it was lost later that year.

Though the *Selbstfahrlafette*'s gun was lethal, its automotive components were weak and the armor inadequate. Operationally, the necessity of aiming the entire vehicle took

Left: *The final realization of the* Panzerjäger *concept based on the 38(t) was the* Panzerjäger 38(t) für 7.5 cm PaK 40/3 Ausf M, *or as it is more commonly known, the* Marder III M. *It was a completely original design with the fighting compartment moved to the rear and the engine compartment moved to the middle of the tank. This eliminated the long gun overhang evident on previous models and the now coupled the engine directly to the transmission.* Charles Kliment

Left: *A view of the fighting compartment with the rear armor folded down. This aided resupply, as well as gave the crew more room. The gun's rear travel lock, in the engaged position, can be seen as well. As compared to previous* Marder *models, protection for the crew was improved with the* Ausf M, *which had armor surrounding all four sides of the fighting compartment. Main gun ammunition stowage was thirty-eight rounds, reduced to merely twenty-six rounds in command vehicles. It had been forty-eight rounds in the* Marder I *and thirty-seven rounds in the* Marder II. Charles Kliment

Left: *The running gear and suspension were only slightly modified, with the new vehicle having only one return roller on each side, rather than the two previously used. The driver's position was a compartment that protruded slightly from the superstructure. For most of 1943 this compartment was a combination of cast and bolted construction, but beginning in December of that year the vehicles had a more angular welded driver's compartment. This change coincided with the introduction of a welded hull in lieu of the previously used riveted construction.* Bundesarchiv

a heavy toll on the drivetrain and, as with the StuG, limited mobility.

Nashorn

Originally developed as a temporary measure, the *Nashorn* (rhinoceros), originally known as the *Hornisse*, or hornet, ultimately served, with considerable effect, until the end of the war.

When the German army had encountered the British Matilda, French *Char* B1 and then the Russian T-34 and KV-1 tanks, they found that their antitank weapons had little effect. During the 1936–1939 Spanish Civil War it was learned that the high-velocity 8.8 cm FlaK gun made an excellent antitank weapon, and the German army became increasingly reliant on the 88 to counter improving Allied tanks.

Left: *Early Ausf M had their exhaust pipes routed internally along the right side of the vehicle, but beginning in July 1943 the exhaust pipe was routed externally, exiting through the air-intake grille and along the right side of the vehicle. Note the intricate camouflage paint scheme. The radio operator's station in the Marder III was inside the fighting compartment, rather than being adjacent to the driver as in the Panzer 38(t).* Bundesarchiv

Those weapons, however, were towed, and by 1942 there was a high-level demand for a self-propelled version, mounting an improved, more powerful 88.

Developed by Krupp, that weapon, the 8.8 cm PaK 43/1 (the PaK designated anti-tank cannon—*Panzerabwehrkanone*, vs. Flak, or *Flugzeugabwehrkanone*—aircraft-defense cannon) had a 71-caliber (heavy gun calibers are determined by dividing the length of the barrel by the bore) barrel and an 822 mm long cartridge case.

A self-propelled chassis, which had the same hull width as a Panzer III, was created by using the Panzer III final drive, steering unit, sprockets, and transmission, in order to match the desired hull width. Most of the rest of the chassis components were taken from the Panzer IV, including the engine, radiator, track, and suspension. However, the engine was positioned mid-hull, leaving space for a large open fighting compartment at the rear of the vehicle.

A nearly identical chassis was to be used for a 15 cm-armed self-propelled howitzer, and the dual use of the chassis was especially pleasing to Hitler.

Production of the *Hornisse* began in February 1943 and continued until March 1945. This was undertaken by Altmärkische Kettenwerke GmbH (Alkett) in Berlin, who produced 370 of the vehicles, and at the Deutsche-Eisenwerke AG facility in Teplitz-Schönau, who completed 124 of the machines. Alkett stopped building the *Nashorn* in May 1944.

In November 1943, Hitler suggested renaming the *Hornisse* the *Nashorn*, an action which was taken in July of the following year. As mentioned, the *Nashorn* and the *Hummel* share a chassis and superstructure design. However, all *Nashorn* hulls were produced in 1943, thus do

10.5 cm K. Panzer Selbstfahrlafette IVa

Specifications	
Length	7.47 m
Width	2.86 m
Height	2.53 m
Weight	22 tons
Maximum speed	27 km/hr
Range, on-road	170 km
Range, cross-country	120 km
Crew	5
Communications	speaking tubes
Armament	
Weapon, main	10.5 cm Kanone L/52
Ammo stowage, main	26 rounds
Armor	
Front	30–50 mm
Sides	20 mm
Rear	10 mm
Top	10–20 mm
Automotive	
Engine make	Maybach
Engine model	HL 66 Pla
Engine configuration	6-cylinder, liquid cooled
Engine displacement	6.6 liters
Engine horsepower	180 @ 3200 rpm

Above: *The 10.5 cm K Panzer Selbstfahrlafette IVa was the combination of the 10.5 K18 L/52 cannon with the chassis of the Panzer IV. Originally designed in 1938 to tackle fortifications on the Maginot Line, its development continued in order to deal with well-protected Soviet tanks on the Eastern Front. The basic chassis was that of the Panzer IV. However, the smaller six-cylinder 180 hp Maybach HL 66 Pla engine was used rather than the 265 hp HL 120 V-12. The 10.5 cm gun used two-part ammunition, and two different types of projectiles were provided. Krupp completed two trial vehicles in January 1941. In July 1941, the two trial vehicles were assigned to Tank Destroyer Battalion 521 for use on the Russian Front. The troops referred to them as "Dicker Max" (Fat Max).* Patton Museum

Left: *Among the largest* Panzerjägers *produced was the* Nashorn *(rhinoceros). It was the sister vehicle to the Hummel, however rather than the 15 cm howitzer, it was armed with the potent 8.8 cm PaK 43 antitank gun. Like the Hummel, the* Nashorn *was a purpose-built chassis using Panzer III and IV components. The Nashorn was capable of engaging targets at extreme ranges, much to the detriment of its opponents. The combination of the 8.8 cm PaK 43 gun and quality Zeiss Sfl.ZF.la, Rblf36 3 x 8° monocular periscopic sight was a lethal one. Each Nashorn carried forty rounds of ammunition.* National Archives and Records Administration

Nashorn

Specifications	
Length	8.44 m
Width	2.95 m
Height	2.94 m
Weight	24 tons
Fuel capacity	600 liters
Maximum speed	40 km/hr
Range, on-road	260 km
Range, cross-country	130 km
Crew	5
Communications	Fu Spr Ger f
Armament	
Weapon, main	8.8 cm PaK 43/1 L/71
Traverse	manual, +/-15°
Elevation	manual, +20/-5°
Primary gunsight	Sfl. Z. F. 1a (*Selbstfahrlafetten-Zielfernrohr*)
Magnification	5×
Field of view	8°
Indirect fire sight	Aushilfsrichtmittel 38
Magnification	3×
Field of view	10°
Weapon, secondary	MG 34 or MG 42
Ammo stowage, main	40
Ammo stowage, secondary	600 rounds
Armor, Superstructure sides and gun shield	10 mm
Glacis	15 mm
Hull front	30 mm
Hull side	20 mm
Automotive	
Engine make	Maybach
Engine model	HL 120 TRM
Engine configuration	V-12, liquid cooled
Engine displacement	11.9 liters
Engine horsepower	265 @ 2600 rpm

Above: *The later* Nashorn *had spare roadwheel racks located on the rear of the vehicle, and the barrel-style muffler of the early vehicles was eliminated. These entrained vehicles all have their foul weather tarps installed—an essential piece of equipment in an open-topped vehicle. The bands of camouflage on the interior of the rear doors are of interest. The canvas cover provided for the fighting compartment was primarily used in rear areas, or when in transit. It functioned chiefly to protect the weapon and ammunition. The large internal travel lock and its engagement wheel can be seen clearly here.* Patton Museum

not exhibit some of the late production changes seen in the *Hummel*, such as a reduction in the number of return rollers and the enlarged driver's compartment.

With its tall silhouette and relatively thin armor, the *Nashorn* was ill-suited for duels with opposing tanks and armored vehicles. However, its powerful cannon meant that the *Nashorn* was equipped to knock out the enemy vehicles before they closed the range enough for the German vehicle to be taken under fire.

12.8 cm *Selbstfahrlafette* L/61

As previously mentioned, in 1939 the German military was seriously concerned about breaching the French Maginot Line. In addition to the Dicker Max, discussed earlier in this chapter, an alternative vehicular mount for the 12.8 cm K L/61 was developed.

This vehicle, officially known as 12.8 cm *Selbstfahrlafette* L/61 Pz.Sfl.V, but dubbed "*Sturer Emil*" (Stubborn Emil), was based on an extended version of the failed Henschel VK 30.01 tank chassis. The new-built chassis had one additional roadwheel station on each side, and an open-top fighting compartment at the rear of the hull.

By the time the two 35-ton trial vehicles were completed in early 1942, the Maginot Line had been bypassed. However, the German army was encountering formidable Soviet tanks on the Eastern Front. As with the Dicker Max, the decision was made to employ both the 12.8 cm *Selbstfahrlafette* L/61 trial vehicles as tank destroyers.

12.8 cm *Selbstfahrlafette* L/61

Specifications	
Length	9.7 m
Width	3.15 m
Height	2.75 m
Weight	36.5 tons
Fuel capacity	450 liters
Maximum speed	25 km/hr
Range, on-road	170 km
Range, cross-country	80 km
Crew	5
Communications	Fu Spr Ger a
Armament	
Weapon, main	12.8 cm PaK 40 L/61
Ammo stowage, main	15 rounds
Automotive	
Engine make	Maybach
Engine model	HL 116 S
Engine configuration	6-cylinder, liquid cooled
Engine displacement	11.6 liters

4.7 cm PaK(t) (Sfl) auf Panzerkampfwagen 35R 731(f)

Specifications	
Length, without gun	4.20 m
Width	1.85 m
Weight	11 tons
Fuel capacity	168 liters
Maximum speed	20 km/hr
Range, on-road	130 km
Range, cross-country	80 km
Crew	3
Communications	Fu Spr Ger a
Armament	
Weapon, main	4.7 cm PaK(t)
Automotive	
Engine make	Renault
Engine configuration	4-cylinder, liquid cooled
Engine displacement	5.8 liters
Engine horsepower	85 @ 2200 rpm

Above: The 12.8 cm Selbstfahrlafette L/61 "Sturer Emil" was the result of the rush to counter the unexpected threat of the T-34 and KV tanks encountered on the Russian Front. One of the most powerful weapons in the German arsenal at that time was the 12.8 cm FlaK gun. Rheinmetall adapted this into a field weapon, the 12.8 cm K L/61. A suitable chassis was found to mount the massive cannon: the two unused Henschel Tiger I prototype VK30.01 tanks. The hulls were lengthened, and an open-topped fighting compartment mounted on the rear. Both were subsequently deployed to Russia with the Panzerjäger-Abteilung 521 in 1942. The slow speed and lack of turret, as well as their being mechanical orphans, were major hindrances to their utility. However, the long range and high muzzle velocity of their massive cannon offset these disadvantages to a certain extent, with kills at ranges to 4,500 meters. Patton Museum

The slow speed, thin armor, and lack of turret, as well as their being mechanical "orphans" were major hindrances to their utility, as was their low rate of fire due in part to their two-part ammunition. However, the long range and high muzzle velocity of their massive cannon offset these disadvantages to a certain extent, claiming T-34 kills at ranges to 4,500 yards, something no other vehicle could do.

The 12.8 cm K L/61, derived from the 12.8 cm FlaK gun, was one of the most powerful land weapons in the German arsenal. Both vehicles were assigned to the *Panzerjäger-Abteilung* 521 and deployed on the Eastern Front. Both vehicles were lost in the drive to Stalingrad, but not before one of them could claim an impressive thirty-one victories. That vehicle was captured and to this day is on display in Russia.

4.7 cm PaK(t) (Sfl) auf *Panzerkampfwagen* 35R 731(f)

The collapse of France meant that Germany now had possession of hundreds of Renault R 35 tanks. While Germany's tanks were superior, and thus preferred, the *Wehrmacht* hoped to put the R 35 chassis to work as the basis of mobile antitank artillery. The intention was to mechanize additional infantry divisions.

Work on the project was initiated in December 1940, with Alkett completing a mild-steel prototype in February 1941, and demonstrated to Hitler the following month.

Two hundred combat-capable examples were ordered, each of which were created by mounting the Czech 4.7 cm PaK(t) antitank gun on a newly fabricated four-sided superstructure on the R 35 chassis. This design would offer improved protection when compared to the *Panzerjäger* I, which relied solely on the gun shield to protect the crew. Series production of these vehicles was scheduled from August to October 1941.

In July, the new vehicles were dispatched to Russia with *Panzerjäger-Abteilung* 611. There the French-designed chassis quickly failed en masse during the drive east, where the vehicles proved unsuited for long road marches.

This situation was compounded during the severe Russian winter, with units complaining bitterly about the unsuitability of the *Panzerjäger*.

Above: *Captured French R 35 tanks were used to mount the Skoda 47 mm kanon P.U.V vz. 36 gun. The result was the 4.7 cm PaK(t0 (Sfl) auf FgstPzKpw 35 R 731 (f). The German firm of Alkett executed the conversions in 1941. Space was at premium within the vehicle, as the original tank only had a crew of two. The new configuration was intended to have a crew of three, so much of the useable space was obtained in the new superstructure. All ammunition stowage was in the long bustle at the rear. Some two hundred conversions were made, but the vehicle performed poorly due to excess weight and the lackluster nature of the main gun. A command variant armed with a machine gun was also produced. They served on both the Eastern and later, the Western fronts.*

Those vehicles dispatched to the west, in climates that the R35 had been designed for, were substantially more reliable, and were used through at least 1943.

Panzerselbstfahrlafette 1a 5 cm PaK 38 *auf Gepanzerter Munitionsschlepper*

In July 1940 Rheinmetall was charged with the responsibility of designing a light tank destroyer. This vehicle was to be used by airborne troops, as well as dismounted infantry. It was decided that the chassis of the C. F. W. Borgward-built Borgward VK3.02 munitions carrier would serve as the basis for the *Panzerjäger*. Armament was to be in the form of the 5 cm PaK 38 L/60, with the only protection of the gun crew being the thin-armor gun shield, which offered protection only from 7.92 mm armor-piercing ammunition.

While the original plans called for the production of two hundred of these by April 1945, in fact only two trial vehicles were completed. Both were supplied to 19 Panzer Division for troop trials in July 1942. While the details of those trials are unknown, it is known that by that time the 5 cm PaK 38 was no longer a viable antitank gun, and the project was abandoned.

Panzerselbstfahrlafette 1a 5 cm PaK 38 *auf Gepanzerter Munitionsschlepper*

Specifications	
Width	1.83 m
Weight	4.5 tons
Maximum speed	30 km/hr
Crew	3
Armament	
Weapon, main	5 cm PaK 38 L/60
Automotive	
Engine make	Borgward
Engine model	6M RTBV
Engine configuration	6-cylinder
Engine displacement	2.3 liters
Engine horsepower	50 hp @ 3300 rpm

Above: *In July 1940 Rheinmetall was tasked with developing a light tank destroyer suitable for use by airborne troops, as well as dismounted infantry. Using the recently developed Borgward VK3.02 munitions carrier as a basis, a vehicle armed with the 5 cm PaK 38 L/60 was developed. It was known as the Panzerselbstfahrlafette 1a 5 cm PaK 38 auf Gepanzerter Munitionsschlepper. Despite initial plans to produce two hundred by April 1945, only two were completed for evaluation purposes. These were sent forth for troop trials in July 1942. By that time the 5 cm PaK 38 was no longer a viable antitank gun, and the project was abandoned. Patton Museum*

PANZERJÄGER

Above: *In 1941 two pilot light tank destroyers were constructed using Panzer II Ausf G chassis with a 50 mm PaK 38 antitank gun mounted in an open-topped superstructure. The vehicle was designated the* **Panzerselbstfahrlafette** *(armored self-propelled carriage) Ic. It was to have a four-man crew with 30 mm of frontal armor and 20 mm of side armor. Plans for mass production were abandoned and the two pilots were sent to the Eastern Front in 1942.* Patton Museum

Panzerselbstfahrlafette 1c 5 cm PaK 38 *auf Panzerkampfwagen* II *Sonderfahrgestell* 901

In addition to the just-discussed *Panzerselbstfahrlafette* 1a 5 cm PaK 38 *auf Gepanzerter Munitionsschlepper*, July 1940 saw the launch of a second light tank-destroyer program as well. This program, however, was based on the MAN VK9.01 *Panzerkampfwagen* II chassis, and this vehicle too was to be armed with the 5 cm kanone L/60, which was based on the PaK 38.

While the ambitious production plan outlined called for over two thousand of the four-man vehicles to be built and issued, in reality only two trial vehicles were completed. These two vehicles were dispatched to the East for troop trials with the unit ultimately known as the *Panzerjäger-Abteilung* 559.

Despite an impressive 50–60 km/h top speed, the 10.5-ton vehicle was not successful.

Steyr RSO

As Germany's forces pushed east, and were confronted by the Russian snows and mud, they found their wheeled prime movers to be woefully inadequate. Progress was delayed by the ongoing need for tracked and half-tracked vehicles to tow stranded trucks from the mire.

The Russians used STZ-5 crawler tractors, and these became prized war booty for the German forces. In 1942 the *Herres Waffenamt* sought to have a comparable vehicle built with which to equip the German troops.

Steyr RSO/1

Specifications	
Length	4.43 m
Width	1.99 m
Height	2.53 m
Weight	3.5 tons
Fuel capacity	180 liters
Maximum speed	17.2 km/hr
Range, on-road	250 km
Range, cross-country	150 km
Automotive	
Engine make	Steyr
Engine configuration	V-8, air-cooled
Engine displacement	3.5 liters
Engine horsepower	70 hp @ 2500 rpm

Steyr RSO/4

Specifications	
Length	4.71 m
Width	2.13 m
Height	2.10 m
Weight	5.4 tons
Fuel capacity	180 liters
Maximum speed	17.2 km/hr
Armament	
Weapon	7.5 cm PaK 40/1 L/46
Ammunition stowage	42 rounds
Armor, gun shield	2 x 4 mm
Automotive	
Engine make	Steyr
Engine configuration	V-8, air-cooled
Engine displacement	3.5 liters
Engine horsepower	70 @ 2500 rpm

The Austrian firm of Steyr-Daimler-Puch was directed to create such a vehicle, and they did. Utilizing the air-cooled V-8 engine taken from their 4x4 truck line, a new tractor was created. It had, at least initially, an enclosed cab, and open-topped, drop-side bed made of wood, and four roadwheels on each side mounted on quarter-elliptic springs. The vehicle, intended to accompany infantry divisions, was designed with a low top speed.

After successful trials, during which Hitler personally directed that the ground clearance be raised to 600 mm, Steyr began mass production in late 1942. The vehicle was designated *Raupenschlepper Ost*, or tracked tractor for the East.

The demand for these vehicles far outstripped Steyr's ability to produce them, especially since Steyr continued to build 4 x 4 trucks and cars concurrently. Therefore, production contracts were also given to Gräf and Stitt, Wanderer (Auto Union), and Magirus. These later three firms built approximately 4,500, 5,600, and 12,500 RSO each respectively, compared to Steyr's own modest production record of 2,600 pieces. Steyr themselves discontinued RSO production in October 1943, although they continued to be involved in the engineering.

The RSO's contoured pressed-steel cab gave way to a simplified, flat-paneled cab of composite wood and steel construction. This cab was made in both soft-top and closed versions. All Magirus-produced vehicles utilized the soft-top cab. Vehicles with the new cab were designated RSO/2, the original version becoming RSO/1.

The third version of the RSO, the RSO/3 was built in very small numbers by Magirus, and was a considerable improvement over earlier models. Rather than the V-8 gasoline engine of earlier models, it was powered by an air-cooled Diesel. The drivetrain of this vehicle utilized a Cletrac-type final drive, rather than the automotive differential type unit used previously.

One other interesting version of the RSO was produced, and it is this vehicle that resulted in the RSO being included in this chapter. That version was an armored vehicle mounting a 7.5 cm PaK 40/4 antitank gun, not surprisingly designated 7.5 cm PaK 40/4 *auf* RSO. Development of this version began in mid-1943, and trial vehicles were tested that December. Hitler, who had seen preliminary drawings, ordered a limited production run of vehicles even before the test vehicles were completed. In January 1944, the sixty 7.5

Above: *A trio of RSO/1s, artillery in tow, slog through Russian mud. The enclosed cab, air-cooled engine, and fully tracked design were all dictated by the conditions shown here. Though tracked vehicles are not ideally suited for towing semi-type trailers, one of the RSO's biggest drawbacks was its high profile.* National Archives and Records Administration

Above: *The RSO was designed to be used as a prime mover on the Russian Front, hence the name* Raupenschlepper Ost *(tracked tractor for the East). Nonetheless the vehicle served on all fronts, including Normandy, where this vehicle was photographed on June 22, 1944. The RSO/1, shown here, had an enclosed steel cab and a wooden cargo bed with hinged, drop-down sides.* Stefan De Meyer

Above: *This armored RSO with PaK 40 was evaluated at Fort Knox following its capture. Although Hitler was enamored with this variant, the using troops were not favorable in their opinion.* National Archives and Records Administration

PANZERJÄGER

Above: *One of the primary disadvantages is evident here. Even with the sides lowered, there was precious little room for the crew to serve the weapon.* National Archives and Records Administration

Above: *Another problem was access to the ammunition stowage, which was in lockers beneath the deck. To gain access, clearance had to exist between the weapon, and of course the crew couldn't stand on the locker being opened.* National Archives and Records Administration

cm PaK 40/4-armed vehicles that had been produced to that point were issued to Army Group South for troop trials. In March 1944 came a scathing report from the field, which resulted in a June 1944 directive to cease production, declaring that the *Panzerjäger* RSO "has been a complete failure."

Geschützpanzer 39 H(f) 7.5 cm PaK 40(Sf) Hotchkiss
Similar to the 7.5 cm PaK 40/1 auf *Geschützenwagen* Lorraine *Schlepper* (f), the *Geschützpanzer* 39 H(f) 7.5 cm PaK 40(Sf) Hotchkiss were tank destroyers built on captured French chassis. In this instance, the chassis was that of the Hotchkiss H 35 light tank. However, compared to the Lorraine *Schlepper*, the Hotchkiss conversions were much more complicated, resulting in essentially only the floor pans and drivetrains of the French tanks being reused. Armament was the 7.5 cm PaK 40 L/46.

An open-topped fighting compartment housed the weapon and four-man crew. The main weapon had a traverse of 30 degrees left and right, and its gun shield was external to the fighting compartment. As with so many other adapted captured vehicles, the conversion work was done in 1942 at German Army workshops in Paris under the command of Captain Alfred Becker.

Only twenty-four of these vehicles were produced; they were ultimately used in France.

7.62 cm FK36 (r) *Panzerjäger Selbstfahrlafette Zugkraftagen* 5t.
The 7.62 cm FK36 (r) *Panzerjäger Selbstfahrlafette Zugkraftagen* 5t. was the result of an immediate demand from North Africa for a fast, powerful, self-propelled tank destroyer. The then-current and common 5 cm German

Geschützpanzer 39 H(f) 7.5 cm PaK 40(Sf) Hotchkiss

Specifications	
Width	1.85 m
Weight	12.5 tons
Fuel capacity	207 liters
Maximum speed	35 km/hr
Range, on-road	180 km
Range, cross-country	95 km
Crew	4
Communications	Fu Spr Gerd
Armament	
Weapon, main	7.5 cm PaK 40 L/46
Automotive	
Engine make	Hotchkiss
Engine configuration	6-cyliner, liquid cooled
Engine displacement	5.97 liter
Engine horsepower	120 @ 2800 rpm

Above: *Yet another iteration of the self-propelled 7.5 cm PaK 40 was the Geschutzpanzer 39H(f) 7.5 cm PaK 40 (sf). This conversion was based on the captured French Hotchkiss H 39 light tank. The weapon fitted was the somewhat longer 7.5 cm PaK L/46. Production was limited to twenty-four vehicles, all of which were converted in the Paris workshops. All vehicles served on the Western front in the summer of 1944.* Bundesarchiv

Above: *Once of the more interesting German antitank conversions was the 7.62 cm FK36 (r) Panzerjäger Selbstfahrlafette Zugkraftagen 5t. This was a SdKfz 6 5-ton half-track mounting a captured Russian 76 mm gun. The conversion was very basic, with the gun and carriage simply placed on the back of the vehicle. The gun trails were cut to allow more room for the crew to move around and a large armored box was built on the back end as a fighting compartment. Nine of these unique vehicles were produced locally in North Africa for service in the 605th Panzerjäger-Abteilung (motorisiert) in early 1942.* Patton Museum

antitank gun was inadequate against ever-improving Allied armor. However, the German army had captured vast numbers of excellent Soviet 7.62 cm FK36 towed antitank guns, and a limited amount of ammunition on the Eastern Front.

Thus the decision was made to create an expedient Panzerjäger by mounting the complete Russian towed artillery piece, with its wheeled carriage, on the back of a 5-ton SdKfz 6 half-track. It was then wrapped in an open-top box of thin armor. Only nine of these conversions were done, all by Alkett in late 1941.

The resultant vehicles were assigned to *Panzerjäger-Abteilung* 605 in North Africa in March 1942. All of these were lost in action by December of that year.

Had these been more successful, it was planned that these would be followed by serial production of an improved model, code named "Diana," which would again have been armed with the Soviet gun, albeit in this instance rechambered for German ammunition.

As it was, the vehicles, while having a formidable punch, unfortunately stood out readily, themselves becoming prime targets. Further, the armor, which was so tall and thus highly visible, was also far too thin to provide effective protection against even machine-gun fire. Combined with the strain and wear on the overloaded half-track chassis, these flaws meant that no series production of Diana was undertaken.

Ardelt Waffenträger

Faced with increasingly well-armored Allied tanks, Germany began to develop heavier antitank guns, capable of defeating heavy armor at ever increasing ranges. Unfortunately, it seems that the same effort was not put into developing and producing prime movers for these weapons.

Following the loss of seventy PaK 43/41, destroyed on the Eastern Front without having fired a shot, to prevent capture by the Soviets, Hitler demanded that all further heavy antitank guns be self-propelled.

As a result, three different configurations of weapons carriers (*Waffenträger*) were designed and demonstrated, with ultimately an Aderlt-Krupp design selected for limited production at the Ardelt Eberwalde plant. Ten trial vehicles were ordered, with the armament to be 8.8 cm PaK 43. To counter some of the criticism previously leveled at the RSO/4, the gun could traverse through 360 degrees.

The suspension of the vehicle was taken from the Panzer 38(t), while the track was adapted from that of the RSO. Power plant was a Maybach HL 42.

In May 1944, the decision was made to produce eighty-two of the vehicles, with a further eighteen unarmed variants that were to serve as munitions carriers. Ultimately, only seven of the vehicles were completed, and they were immediately used in the defense of Eberwalde in February 1945.

Above: *Among the final Panzerjäger produced during World War II was the Waffenträger. Armed with a 8.8 cm PaK 43, seven of these vehicles were completed by crane manufacturer Ardelt.* Patton Museum

Above: *Krupp, manufacturer of the weapon, made some changes to facilitate mounting the gun on the chassis, including extending the side of the gun shield in order to protect the gunner. While eighty-two vehicles had been ordered, the seven that were actually completed were deployed in defense of the same city that they were built in.* Patton Museum

Chapter 5
Flammpanzers

Man has a primal fear of fire, and it is not surprising that this fear has been exploited by combatants for hundreds of years. In addition to being a terror weapon, flame is also genuinely effective tactically. Unsurprisingly, all the major combatants in World War II utilized flamethrowers, some even going so far as to introduce mechanized flamethrowers.

Germany was no exception to this, and through the duration of the war, the nation fielded numerous variations of mechanized flamethrowers. In this chapter we will cover most of these vehicles, the exception being the SdKfz 251/16 flamethrowing half-track, which is covered in the half-track chapter of this book.

The German military began developing vehicle-mounted flamethrowers in 1939, basing much of their design upon observation of Italy's use of such flamethrowers in 1936. While in 1939 the German military was experimenting at proving grounds with vehicle-mounted flame weapons, in the field, German soldiers were installing man-carried flamethrowers in the turret machine-gun port on Panzer Is and using these weapons in the Spanish Civil War. The effectiveness of these field installations was hampered by the modest range of the flame weapons, which meant that the tank had to close to a vulnerable range before the flamethrower could be fired.

PzKpfw II (*Flamm*) Ausf A and B (SdKfz 122) Flamingo
Development of this flamethrowing tank, based on the *Panzerkampfwagen* II, was begun in early 1939. Prior to this, a few Panzer Is had been retrofitted with flamethrowers by troops in the field. Those field-modified tanks were only marginally successful, as the useable range of the flamethrowers, which were originally man-packs, was too short to use without the tank becoming vulnerable.

The *Panzerflammwagen* (SdKfz 122), later known as the *Panzerkampfwagen* II (*Flamm*) was the first vehicle fielded by the German army as a purpose-built flamethrower, or *Flammpanzer*.

The tank was equipped with two flamethrowers, which were mounted not in the turret, but rather on each front fender. The flame nozzles, known as a *Spritzköpf*, were independently traversable through 180 degrees and were designed to maximize the distance that the flame oil could be sprayed. Each of the nozzles had their own 160-liter supply of flame oil, sufficient for eighty bursts of two to three seconds each.

Compressed nitrogen was used as the propellant to spray the fluid, with an acetylene torch used for ignition. Four gas cylinders inside the tank supplied the nitrogen propellant.

An MG 34 was installed in the turret via a ball mount, providing a modest amount of longer-range firepower.

The initial series of *Panzerkampfwagen* II (*Flamm*) entered production during April 1939.

Series production of the Ausf A began in April 1939. Wegmann built forty-six vehicles on *Panzerkampfwagen* II Ausf D chassis manufactured by MAN by the end of August. Additional flamethrowers were built by Wegmann based on conventional gun tanks' return for conversion. Of these, seventy-three were Ausf D gun tanks, including twenty from the 8th Panzer Division and ten from 7th Panzer Division.

Orders for 150 Ausf B vehicles were placed even before the first series was completed. Production of this series, utilizing newly assembled MAN chassis, began in August 1941, but prior to that date the order had been reduced to ninety vehicles. After that decision was subsequently reversed, new orders came down instructing that the remaining chassis be used to construct tank destroyers. Sixty-two Ausf B flamethrowers had been constructed by that time. These were subsequently converted to tank destroyers, losing their entire flamethrower structure.

PzKpfw II (*Flamm*) SdKfz 122

Specifications	
Length	4.90 m
Width	2.40
Height	1.85
Weight	12.0 tons
Fuel capacity	200 liters
Maximum speed	55 km/hr
Range, on-road	200 km
Crew	3
Communications	FuG 5
Armament	
Weapon, main	2 x *Flammenwerfer*
Weapon, coaxial	7.92 mm MG 34
Flame oil stowage	160 liters
Ammo stowage, secondary	2,250 rounds
Automotive	
Engine make	Maybach
Engine model	HL 62 TR
Engine configuration	straight 6-cylinder
Engine displacement	6.2 liter
Engine horsepower	140 @ 2600 rpm

Above: *Development of the PzKpfw II (Flamm) Ausf A and B (SdKfz 122) "Flamingo" flamethrowing tank, based on the Panzerkampfwagen II, was begun in early 1939. A specially designed flame nozzle, known as a Spritzköpf, was mounted on each front fender. These spray heads were independently traversable 180 degrees. The fluid was propelled by compressed nitrogen that was stored in four cylinders inside the tank. An acetylene-fueled torch provided ignition of the oil. Wegmenn built forty-six vehicles on Panzerkampfwagen II Ausf D chassis manufactured by MAN. Additional flamethrowers were built by Wegmann based on conventional gun tanks returned for conversion. Sixty-two Ausf B flamethrowers had been constructed by that time. Though they saw limited action, these vehicles, like most flame weapons, were very effective.* Thomas Anderson

Above: *The Panzerkampfwagen II (Flamm) was a flamethrower conversion of Panzerkampfwagen II Ausf D chassis. They had a flamethrower in a turret mount on each front fender. The turret was removed from the hull, and a small cupola with a top hatch and a ball-mounted machine gun with an armored visor to each side was installed in its place. This particular tank is an Ausf B, identifiable by its eight-spoked sprocket and lubricated-pin tracks. The Ausf A, on the other hand, had eleven-spoked sprockets and dry-pin tracks.* Thomas Anderson

The Ausf A saw service on the Eastern Front, taking part in Operation Barbarossa.

Panzer B2 (F)

Consistent with the German military practice of reusing or adapting for frontline service those enemy vehicles captured in large numbers, the decision was made to build a flame-projecting tank utilizing the French *Char B* as its basis.

The French hull-mounted 7.5 cm gun was removed, and in its place was installed the same type of *Flammenwerfer-Spritzköpf* that had previously been used on the *Panzerkampfwagen* II (F). Twenty-four tanks were converted in this manner. These in turn were issued to *Panzer-Abteilung* (F) 102, which employed them in Operation Barbarossa.

Development of *Char* B–based flamethrowers continued with a second series. These vehicles differed from the initial production in that a pump was used to induce the flow of the flame oil rather than the compressed nitrogen used previously. The flame oil was stored on the rear of the tank in a fuel compartment made of armor plate. At least sixty of these improved flamethrowers were built beginning in December 1941, and the vehicles served on both fronts for the duration of the war.

Above: *Due to the large number of French vehicles captured in 1940, the decision was made to build a flame-projecting tank utilizing the French Char B heavy tank. Known as the Panzer B2 (F), the hull-mounted 7.5 cm gun was removed and in its place a* Flammenwerfer-Spritzköpf *was installed, similar to the type previously used on the* Panzerkampfwagen II (F). *Wegmann designed the mount for the flamethrower, which replaced the 7.5 cm gun, while Koebe designed the flamethrower itself. Twenty-four tanks were converted.* Bundesarchiv

Panzerkampfwagen B2 (F)

Specifications	
Length	6.86 m
Width	2.52 m
Height	2.88 m
Weight	32 tons
Fuel capacity	400 liters
Maximum speed	28 km/hr
Range, on-road	140 km
Range, cross-country	100 km
Crew	4
Communications	FuG 5
Armament	
Weapon, main	*Flammenwerfer-Spritzköpf*
Weapon, secondary	4.7 cm cannon
Automotive	
Engine make	Renault
Engine model	307
Engine configuration	6-cylinder, liquid cooled
Engine displacement	16.5 liters
Engine horsepower	300 @ 1900 rpm

Above: *A second series was also developed, and these vehicles differed from the initial production in that a pump was used to induce the flow of the flame oil rather than the compressed nitrogen used previously. The flame oil was stored on the rear of the tank in an armored fuel compartment. At least sixty were built beginning in December 1941, and they served on both fronts for the duration of the war. This Panzer B2 (F) was knocked out in Holland in 1944.* Patton Museum

Above: *Shown here is a PzKpfw B2 (Flamm) numbered 125 laying down flame in Ukraine in December 1943. Enough oil was available for two hundred bursts of flame. (BA 708-0293-14). Bundesarchiv*

Above: *One hundred Panzer III Ausf M were converted to Flammpanzers, with a flame projector replacing the main gun. The coaxially mounted machine was retained in the turret, as was a hull-mounted weapon. Many of the Ausf M models were produced with Schürzen side skirts for additional armor protection.* Patton Museum

Panzerkampfwagen III (Fl)

Specifications	
Length	6.41 m
Width	2.97 m
Height	2.50 m
Weight	23.8 tons
Fuel capacity	320 liters
Maximum speed	40 km/hr
Range, on-road	155 km
Range, cross-country	95 km
Crew	5
Communications	FuG 5
Armament	
Weapon, main	14 mm *Flammwerfer*
Weapon, coaxial	7.92 mm MG 34
Weapon, ball-mounted	7.92 mm MG 34
Flame oil stowage	1,020 liters
Ammo stowage, secondary	3,450 rounds
Automotive	
Engine make	Maybach
Engine model	HL 120 TRM
Engine configuration	V-12, liquid cooled
Engine displacement	11.9 liters
Engine horsepower	265 @ 2600 rpm

Panzerkampfwagen III (Fl)

Pleased with the success of the Koebe pump-driven flame system mounted in the second series of *Panzerkampfwagen B2 (F)*, the *Waffenamt* used the same system in the next generation of flame tanks.

These vehicles were based on the proven *Panzerkampfwagen* III. The new tank was essentially a Panzer III Ausf M with the main gun replaced by the 14 mm *Flammwerfer*. A small Auto-Union engine powered the pump, which was fed from two containers holding a combined 1,020 liters of flame oil. Ignition for the flame oil was electrical, as opposed to the acetylene used with the *Panzerkampfwagen* II-based *Flammpanzers*. Through the use of a packing box, the turret and flamethrower could rotate through 360 degrees, just like a normal Panzer III.

The hull-mounted MG 34 was retained, and was supplemented by a second such weapon mounted coaxially with the flame projector.

One hundred of these vehicles, which were designated *Panzerkampfwagen* III (Fl), were completed by Wegmann in Kassel, all on chassis produced by MIAG. These vehicles were used in platoon-sized units in Italy and along the Eastern Front.

Sturmgeschütz-I (Flamm)

In December 1942, Hitler approved the conversion of ten *Sturmgeschütz* into flamethrowers. Initially it was thought new chassis would be used for these vehicles, but in the end it was decided to utilize ten older vehicles that had been

Above: *Flame is an extremely demoralizing weapon and naturally is terribly effective against infantry. However, it has an extremely short range, and the smoke generated makes it fairly easily for opposing artillery to target return fire. On the* Panzerkampfwagen III (F1), *raw oil could be projected fifty meters, while burning oil could reach a little farther, out to sixty meters.* Patton Museum

Sturmgeschütz-I (F1)

Specifications	
Length	5.52 m
Width	2.95 m
Height	2.16 m
Weight	23 tons
Fuel capacity	310 liters
Maximum speed	40 km/hr
Range, on-road	140 km
Range, cross-country	85 km
Crew	4
Communications	FuG 15 or FuG 16, intercom
Armament	
Weapon, main	14 mm *Flammnwerfer*
Weapon, secondary	7.92 mm MG 34
Ammo stowage, secondary	600 rounds
Automotive	
Engine make	Maybach
Engine model	HL 120 TRM
Engine configuration	V-12, liquid cooled
Engine displacement	11.9 liters
Engine horsepower	265 @ 2600 rpm

Above: *At Hitler's request, ten Sturmgeschütz were converted to flamethrowers in 1943. Although issued to an operational unit, no evidence has surfaced indicating that the vehicles saw combat. The superstructure was modified, and an unusual-looking mounting assembly installed rather than the usual gun mount.* Patton Museum

returned for depot overhaul. Nine of these converted vehicles were available in May 1943, with the tenth one being completed the following month.

Very little information about these ten vehicles has surfaced. The vehicles were issued to *Panzertruppenschule* I in June 1943. One was lost due to an accident and had to be rebuilt in July. The rebuilding process took two months.

In January 1944, all ten of the vehicles were returned to an ordnance depot for overhaul and conversion to standard *Sturmgeschütz* configuration with the 7.5 cm StuK 40 L/48. Seven were completed in February, one in March and the final two in April 1944.

Flammpanzer 38

Hitler's special interest in flamethrowers came into play yet again during November 1944. On November 27, he indicated that twenty to thirty *Flammpanzers* would soon be required. The next day, he ordered that an immediate determination be made as to how many could be produced in the next three days.

At that time, he demanded that a large number of flame tanks be made available in a short period of time. The response provided indicated that thirty to thirty-five such vehicles could be produced, some by refurbishing *Panzerkampfwagen* III (Fl), the remainder by fitting flamethrowers to *Jagdpanzer* 38s.

Ordered to proceed, twenty *Jagdpanzer* 38 were drawn from the ČKD factory on December 8, 1944, for conversion to flamethrowers.

The Koebe pump-operated projection system, as used in the *Panzerkampfwagen* III (Fl), was chosen for the *Flammpanzer* 38. Cartridge-type igniters were used with this installation, having been perfected in May 1944. Seven hundred liters of flame oil were carried, which meant that the *Flammpanzer* could fire sixty or so short bursts without refilling. A sleeve was installed around the flame projector tube to camouflage the vehicle as a normal tank destroyer. Unfortunately, this tube was flimsy, and when damaged fouled the flame projector, preventing its operation.

Mechanically, the *Flammpanzer* 38 was identical to the familiar *Jagdpanzer* 38, however the lighter load on the front suspension due to the flame gun improved steering.

The *Flammpanzer* 38 saw their first combat during Operation *Nordwind* during the winter of 1944–1945. The vulnerability of flame tanks to conventional tank and antitank weapons resulted in high losses, but the vehicles continued to be employed well into 1945.

Flammpanzer 38

Specifications	
Length	4.87 m without projector
Width	2.63 m
Height	2.10 m
Weight	16 metrics
Fuel capacity	320 liters
Maximum speed	40 km/hr
Range, on-road	180 km
Range, cross-country	130 km
Crew	4
Communications	Fu Spr Ger f
Armament	
Weapon, main	14 mm *Flammenwerfer* 41
Weapon, secondary	7.92 mm MG 34
Flame oil stowage	700 liters
Ammo stowage, secondary	600 rounds
Automotive	
Engine make	Praga
Engine model	AC
Engine configuration	6-cylinder, liquid cooled
Engine displacement	7.75 liters
Engine horsepower	150 @ 2600 rpm

Above: *On December 8, 1944, twenty Jagdpanzer 38 were drawn from the ČKD factory for conversion to flamethrowers. The Koebe pump operated projection system was chosen for what became known as the Flammpanzer 38. Cartridge-type igniters were used, having been perfected in May of that year. Seven hundred gallons of flame oil were carried, which meant that it could fire sixty or so short bursts without refilling. A sleeve was installed around the flame projector tube to camouflage the vehicle as a normal tank destroyer. This tube was flimsy, and when damaged fouled the flame projector, preventing its operation. The vehicles saw their first combat during Operation* Nordwind *during the winter of 1944–1945 and continued to be employed well into 1945. Patton Museum*

Chapter 6
Flakpanzers—Antiaircraft Tanks

The threat of aerial attack during World War II was constant, but for the Germans, the danger increased steadily during the course of the war as the once-powerful Luftwaffe lost control of the skies. Long-ranging and heavily armed Allied fighters could wreak havoc on German armored formations long before their tank guns were useful, and even the heaviest armor was of little use against 250- and 500-pound bombs.

Not surprisingly, then, the German military sought to equip their units with specialized antiaircraft, or FlaK, vehicles. FlaK is derived from *Flugzeugabwehrkanone*, or aircraft defense cannon.

Initially, these vehicles were based on soft-skinned half-tracks, but in time the increased mobility offered by fully tracked vehicles led to the introduction of the *Flakpanzers*, or antiaircraft tanks, shown in this chapter.

Panzerkampfwagen 38 für 2 cm FlaK 38 (SdKfz 140) Ausf L

The *Panzerkampfwagen* 38 was produced by Českomoravská Kolben Daněk (ČKD), or as it was known under German control, Boemisch-Märische Maschinenfabrik.

This firm, which had recently had begun production of *Geschuetzwagen* 38 *Ausfürung* K "Grille," utilizing the proven Panzer 38(t) components, was tasked with the creation of a *Flakpanzer* based on the same chassis. Armament for the new vehicle was to be the 2 cm FlaK 38 antiaircraft cannon.

Above: *The* Flakpanzer 38(t) auf Selbstfahrlafette 38(t) Ausf L (SdKfz 140), *often abbreviated to Flakpanzer 38(t), was a single 2 cm FlaK 38 L/65 automatic antiaircraft cannon on a Panzerkampfwagen 38(t) chassis. The cannon had 360-degree traverse and elevation of -5 to +90 degrees, and was enclosed in a rigid armored shield with upper panels that folded down when the cannon was in play. The Praga AC six-cylinder gasoline engine was located at the center of the chassis. A total of 140 examples were completed in 1943 and 1944, and the majority of them served with Panzer divisions on the Western Front.* Patton Museum

This weapon was selected because the greatest threat to German armored formations came from low-flying fighter

FLAKPANZERS—ANTIAIRCRAFT TANKS

Above: *The 2 cm gun mount of the* Flakpanzer 38(t) *was equipped with an armored shield that traversed in unison with the gun, and the upper part of that shield is visible above the fixed armored shield mounted above the hull. The left fender of this captured example is badly damaged. Patton Museum*

Above: *On the rear of the captured* Flakpanzer 38(t) *is the insignia of 1st SS Panzer Division "Liebstandarte Adolf Hitler." The exhaust line on the side of the superstructure had become detached from the muffler on the rear of the vehicle. Two leaf hinges were mounted on each folding panel of the armored shield around the cannon. Patton Museum*

Flakpanzerkampfwagen 38 für 2 cm FlaK 38

Specifications	
Length	4.61 m
Width	2.135 m
Height	2.252 m
Weight	9.8 tons
Fuel capacity	218 liters
Maximum speed	42 km/hr
Range, on-road	185 km
Range, cross-country	140 km
Crew	4
Communications	FuG 5
Armament	
Weapon, main	1 x 2.0 cm FlaK 38
Ammo stowage, main	1,040 rounds
Automotive	
Engine make	Praga
Engine model	AC
Engine configuration	6-cylinder, liquid cooled
Engine displacement	7.75 liters
Engine horsepower	150 @ 2600 rpm

bombers, which operated well within range of the rapid-firing (220 rounds per minute) 2 cm Flak.

While this chassis shared many components with the Panzer 38 (t), its engine was mounted midships, like that of the *Geschuetzwagen*.

While resembling the Grille, in fact the superstructure of the FlaK vehicle was different, featuring hinged upper armor sections. When going into action, these sides could be folded down, greatly expanding the cannon's field of fire. With the sides hinged down, the cannon mount could be rotated through 360 degrees, and the barrel depressed enough to engage ground targets. In fact, a third of the vehicle's ammunition load was armor-piercing rounds.

Production of the vehicle, which was designated *Panzerkampwagen* 38 *für* 2 cm FlaK 38 (SdKfz 140) Ausf L, began in November 1943, when fifty vehicles were produced. These were followed by thirty-seven in December, forty-one in January 1944, and a final thirteen in February 1944, making a total production of 141.

The bulk of the new vehicles were assigned in batteries of twelve to FlaK units attached to Panzer units. Forty-eight of the new vehicles were used in Italy, and later a large number were used in Normandy. However, losses were high, and by December 1944 only nine of the vehicles were available on the entire Western Front.

2 cm *Flakvierling auf Fahrgestell Panzerkampfwagen* IV

In May 1943, it was requested that Krupp develop a *Flakpanzer* featuring a quadruple 2 cm antiaircraft gun (*Flakvierling*) mounted on a Panzer IV chassis. This vehicle was to be issued to Panzer units operating the Panzer IV in order to provide organic antiaircraft protection from a vehicle with parts commonality with the units' tanks.

The vehicle's superstructure would consist of an open-top box with hinged double-wall sides of 12 mm armor. The sides were engineered such that crewmen on the inside could lower the sides, allowing the FlaK gun a 360-degree traverse as well as permitting it to engage ground targets.

The pilot vehicle was completed in September 1943, ahead of schedule. The vehicle was driven six and a half hours to Kummersdorf for testing, which was uneventful.

General Guderian was satisfied that the vehicle met the requirements of the Panzer troops, and in October series production was scheduled to begin in April 1944 at a pace of twenty per month.

However, in December 1943, the *Panzerkommission* decided to abandon this vehicle and instead pursue development of a vehicle armed with the 3.7 cm FlaK 43. The planned series production was canceled, and the single trial 2 cm *Flakvierling auf Fahrgestell Panzerkampfwagen* IV was rearmed with a 3.7 cm FlaK 43.

Flakpanzerkampfwagen IV "Möbelwagen"

The decision that was made to abandon the quad 20 mm mount *Flakpanzerkampfwagen* in favor of a single 3.7 cm mount appears to have originated with Hitler himself.

In a January 1944 meeting the decision was announced that per a demand from Hitler, the interim *Flakpanzer* was to be armed not with the 2 cm quad mount, but rather with the 3.7 cm FlaK 43.

In order to expedite development, the 2 cm *Flakvierling auf Fahrgestell Panzerkampfwagen* IV was modified to become the pilot for the new vehicle.

The quad mount was removed, as was its leveling frame, and in its place the 3.7 cm FlaK installed. The mount chosen was the standard 3.7 cm FlaK 43, with a shortened right-side gun shield and other minor modifications. By shortening the right-side gun shield, it became possible for the mount to

FLAKPANZERS—ANTIAIRCRAFT TANKS

Left: In late September 1943, a prototype 2 cm Flakvierling auf Fahrgestell Panzerkampfwagen IV (2 cm Quadruple Antiaircraft Gun on Panzerkampfwagen Chassis) was completed, consisting of a Panzerkampfwagen IV chassis with the turret removed and a quadruple 2 cm automatic-gun mount installed atop the superstructure. Surrounding the gun mount was an armored shield in four panels, which were lowered when the guns were placed in action. *Patton Museum*

Left: The 2 cm Flakvierling is traversed to the rear and elevated, with the sides of the armored shield secured in an extended position outboard, for more working space in the enclosure. Following a successful inspection of the prototype, General Heinz Guderian recommended that serial production of the vehicle begin in the spring of 1944 at a rate of approximately twenty examples per month, but in the end the project was canceled in favor of the 3.7 cm FlaK auf Fahrgestell Panzerkampfwagen IV (sf) (SdKfz 161/3). *Patton Museum*

Above: *The armored shield is lowered on the prototype 2 cm* Flakvierling auf Fahrgestell Panzerkampfwagen *IV, showing the armored shield that was attached to the gun mount. The gunner's seat to the rear of the mount and the right loader's seat are visible.* Patton Museum

Left: *The 3.7 cm FlaK auf Fahrgestell Panzerkampfwagen IV (sf) (SdKfz 161/3), nicknamed* Möbelwagen *("Moving Van") was similar to the 2 cm* Flakvierling auf Fahrgestell Panzerkampfwagen *IV, down to a modified version of the folding armored shield, but was armed with a single 3.7 cm FlaK 43 L/89. A total of 240 examples were completed, with the first ones entering operational service on the Western Front in April 1944.* Patton Museum

FLAKPANZERS—ANTIAIRCRAFT TANKS

Left: *The two hinged panels with the teardrop-shaped slots, located on the front shield, have been swung outward to support the side panels of the armored shield. On the side panel of the shield are two hinged struts, for supporting the side panel when fully lowered, in which state it formed part of a platform around the 3.7 cm gun mount. Patton Museum*

Above: *A 3.7 cm FlaK auf Fahrgestell Panzerkampfwagen IV (sf) is viewed from the right rear with the rear panel of the shield partially lowered and the side panels partially extended. Note the elbow extension attached to the exhaust outlet on top of the muffler. Patton Museum*

Flakpanzerkampfwagen IV Möbelwagen

Specifications	
Length	5.92 m
Width	2.95 m
Height	3.0 m
Weight	25 tons
Fuel capacity	470 liters
Maximum speed	38 km/hr
Range, on-road	200 km
Range, cross-country	130 km
Crew	5
Communications	FuG 5 and FuG 2
Armament	
Weapon, main	3.7 cm FlaK 43/1
Ammo stowage, main	400 rounds
Automotive	
Engine make	Maybach
Engine model	HL 120 TRM
Engine configuration	V-12, liquid cooled
Engine displacement	11.9 liters
Engine horsepower	272 @ 2800 rpm

traverse 360 degrees even without lowering the sides of the vehicle.

The folding sides of the vehicle had been modified when the vehicle was rearmed. Those sides had been shortened by 250 mm.

Per their February contract, Deutsche Eisenwerke AG Werk Stahlindustrie began production of one hundred of the new vehicles on chassis provided by Krupp-Grusonwerk and superstructure from Krupp-Essen, with the initial delivery being in March 1944. Production was to be at the rate of twenty per month.

The first forty-five vehicles had double wall folding platforms, first of 12 mm and later of 10 mm plate. After these were completed, the balance of the 240 Möbelwagens constructed had superstructure sides made of single-thickness 25 mm plates. The 25 mm–thick folding platforms were manufactured by a new contractor, Deutsche Rohrenwerke.

Troops dubbed the new vehicle "Möbelwagen" as its slab sides resembled those of a moving van. The Möbelwagen began to be issued to troops for training in April 1944, and was sent into combat in June.

While the Möbelwagen had from the outset been intended as an interim vehicles, delays in production of the Ostwind meant that additional production contracts for the Möbelwagen were issued. By the time Möbelwagen production ended in April 1945, 243 units had been produced.

Above: *A knocked-out 3.7 cm FlaK auf Fahrgestell Panzerkampfwagen IV (sf) is viewed close-up from the left front. The shield panels except the right one, which is in the lowered position, are missing, as is the left track, except for a remnant wound around the left sprocket.* Patton Museum

Flakpanzerkampfwagen IV Wirbelwind Sd. Kfz 161/4

The 2 cm *Flakvierling auf Fahrgestell Panzerkampfwagen IV* described earlier in this chapter was hardly the final effort at combining the 2 cm quad mount with the Panzer IV chassis.

In mid-1944 the idea was advanced to mount the 2 cm quad mount in an open-top turret, which would then be installed in the Panzer IV standard turret ring.

The design for an open-topped, nine-sided turret to house the *Flakvierling* was completed by June 7, 1944.

Interestingly, to produce the vehicle, the army did not turn to industry, but rather set up their own shop to produce the *Flakpanzers*. Located in Schlesien and known as the *Kommando Ostbau-Sagan*, the facility would produce the vehicles utilizing rebuilt Panzer IV chassis and the new specialized turrets, which were produced by Deutsche-Rohrenwerk.

Flakpanzerkampfwagen IV Wirbelwind

Specifications	
Length	5.92 m
Width	2.90 m
Height	2.76 m
Weight	22 tons
Fuel capacity	470 liters
Maximum speed	38 km/hr
Range, on-road	200 km
Range, cross-country	130 km
Crew	5
Communications	FuG 5 and FuG 2
Armament	
Weapon, main	4 x 2.0 cm FlaK 38
Weapon, ball-mounted	7.92 mm MG 34
Ammo stowage, main	3,200 rounds
Ammo stowage, secondary	1,350 rounds
Automotive	
Engine make	Maybach
Engine model	HL 120 TRM
Engine configuration	V-12, liquid cooled
Engine displacement	11.9 liters
Engine horsepower	272 @ 2800 rpm

Between July 1944 and March 1945, one hundred of the vehicles were produced.

Named the "Wirbelwind," or whirlwind, the new vehicle offered a distinct advantage over the Möbelwagen in that its weapons were immediately employable. The three-man turret crew could immediately bring the guns into play in any direction with the *Wirbelwind*'s turret, whereas in most instances the *Möbelwagen* crew had to lower the sidewalls before their single 3.7 cm gun could be brought into action.

A further advantage offered by the *Wirbelwind* was the protected position of the crew. The *Möbelwagen* crew was totally exposed to ground and strafing fire when in firing order, while the *Wirbelwind*'s crew was protected from small-arms fire as well as shell fragments from all sides except directly above.

Beginning in September 1944, four *Wirbelwind* (as well as four *Möbelwagen*) were issued to *Flakpanzer* platoon.

Flakpanzerkampfwagen IV "Ostwind"

Much like the mounting of the 2 cm FlaK 38-Vierling had transitioned from the initial drop-side Panzer IV chassis to the turret mount of the *Wirbelwind*, in mid-1944 similar

Above: *The Flakpanzerkampfwagen IV (2 cm FlaK 38-Vierling: designated SdKfz 161/4), nicknamed "Wirbelwind" (Whirlwind), consisted of a quadruple 2 cm Flakvierling 38 automatic cannon and mount with an armored, nine-sided, open-topped shield, which traversed in unison with the guns, all mounted on a Panzerkampfwagen IV chassis. The shield armor was 16 mm thick. The hull on this example has been treated with Zimmerit antimagnetic paste. Note the hinged flap on the front of the shield, which was opened to give the gunner a line of sight when the guns were at low elevation.* Thomas Anderson

Above: *The chassis used for the* Wirbelwind *were vehicles that had been returned to the factory from the front lines for major overhauls. In German armored doctrine, the* Wirbelwinds *were intended to work together with the* Möbelwagen: *starting in September 1944, each Panzer antiaircraft platoon was to be equipped with four each of those vehicles.* Thomas Anderson

Above: *The gun crew, a gunner and two loaders, are seated in the 2 cm mount of a* Wirbelwind. *The initial lot of these vehicles consisted of seventeen examples completed in July 1944. By the end of the war, a total of 122 had been completed.* Thomas Anderson

FLAKPANZERS—ANTIAIRCRAFT TANKS

Above: *As seen in an overhead view of a* Wirbelwind, *the rear of the gun shield was narrow, providing just enough room for the seated gunner. Storage racks for 2 cm ammunition magazines are visible on the inner walls of the shield. Ammunition boxes were mounted on both sides of the engine deck.* Thomas Anderson

Above: *The* Flakpanzer IV *(3.7 cm FlaK 3), nicknamed "Ostwind" (East Wind), was a self-propelled 3.7 cm FlaK 43/1 L/60 automatic antiaircraft cannon in a hexagonal, open-topped shield reminiscent of that of the* Wirbelwind, *mounted on a Panzerkampfwagen IV chassis. It was introduced in the summer of 1944 and was intended to be the replacement for the* Wirbelwind. *The Wehrmacht considered the Ostwind preferable to the* Wirbelwind *because of the much greater destructive power and range of the 3.7 cm cannon. An Ostwind is seen here at the left with a Möbelwagen and a* Wirbelwind. Thomas Anderson

Flakpanzerkampfwagen IV Ostwind

Specifications	
Length	5.92 m
Width	2.95 m
Height	2.96 m
Weight	25 tons
Fuel capacity	470 liters
Maximum speed	38 km/hr
Range, on-road	200 km
Range, cross-country	130 km
Crew	5
Communications	FuG 5 and FuG 2
Armament	
Weapon, main	1 x 3.7 cm FlaK 43/1
Weapon, ball-mounted	7.92 mm MG 34
Ammunition, main	400 rounds
Secondary	1,350 rounds
Automotive	
Engine make	Maybach
Engine model	HL 120 TRM
Engine configuration	V-12, liquid cooled
Engine displacement	11.9 liters
Engine horsepower	272 @ 2800 rpm

efforts were made to move the 3.7 cm FlaK 43 found behind the folding sides of the *Möbelwagen* into a turret.

Initially, a prototype with a mild-steel turret somewhat resembling that of the *Wirbelwind*, albeit with only six sides, was produced. Troops at *Kommando Ostbau-Sagan*, where the prototype was fabricated, dubbed the experimental turret *Keksdose*, or pie tin.

Fitted with the cannon from a *Möbelwagen*, the unit was successfully test-fired on July 27, 1944.

With slight changes, the design was approved for production. The vehicle, which would be known as *Ostwind*, or East Wind, would have an open-top, six-sided turret of 25 mm armor.

Orders were placed for one hundred of the vehicles to be produced by Stahlindustrie Duisburg, with Deutsche Roehrenwerke to provide the armor for the turrets. Stahlindustrie was to assemble the vehicles using new chassis supplied by Krupp. Additional turrets were furnished to *Kommando Ostbau-Sagan*, which would assemble *Ostwind* utilizing rebuilt Panzer IV chassis.

Due to various delays and Germany's overall deteriorating war position, despite an ambitious production schedule, by March 1945 Stahlindustrie reported that they had only completed seven *Ostwind*, fifty-three behind schedule.

Kommando Ostbau-Sagan managed to manufacture twenty-two of the vehicles between December 1944 and March 1945.

Left: *The 2.5 cm armored shield came to a point at the front, with a slot for the 3.7 cm cannon incorporated into the front edge. On the right side of the shield, the hinge at the bottom of a flap is visible; the flap was lowered when the gunner was aiming the cannon at low elevation. A conical, perforated flash suppressor is attached to the muzzle of the cannon. Thomas Anderson*

FLAKPANZERS—ANTIAIRCRAFT TANKS

Above: *An Ostwind is viewed from the left side with the 3.7 cm cannon traversed to about the ten o'clock position. The relative thinness of the 2.5 cm-thick armor of the shield is apparent along the edge of the slot for the cannon. Total production for the Ostwind was forty-four: one prototype, thirty-six conversions of remanufactured* Panzerkampfwagen *IV chassis, and seven from new chassis.* Thomas Anderson

Flakpanzer III

By late 1944 the *Sturmartillerie* was growing anxious for their own indigenous antiaircraft protection. It was extremely desirable that this vehicle be based on the *Panzerkampfwagen* III chassis, as this would provide not only parts commonality with their most abundant *Sturmgeschütz*, but similar maneuverability as well.

Toward this end Baurat Alfred Becker was sent to Ostbau Sagan, where Panzer IV–based *Ostwind* and *Wirbelwind* were being assembled in the army's own shops. The management at Sagan, who were convinced that it was impossible to convert a Panzer III to a *Flakpanzer*, were less than helpful.

Becker, who had masterminded much of the Germany army's reutilization of captured French tanks and Russian cannons, felt that the construction of a *Flakpanzer* on the Panzer III chassis was possible.

Becker secured the material to build two trial vehicles at the *Sturmartillerie*'s depot. These vehicles used Panzer III chassis, 3.7 cm FlaK guns, and complete turret bodies as used on the Flakpanzer IV.

Having proven that the *Flakpanzer* III was feasible, authorization was granted to build ninety of the vehicles utilizing the turrets designed for the *Ostwind*. Eighteen of these turrets were diverted from *Ostwind* assembly, while the remaining seventy-two would be placed on order with the turret manufacturer.

Owing to the deteriorating war situation, in mid-March 1945 the Panzer Commission decided to abandon the *Flakpanzer* III project, which had been delayed. The Chief of the *Sturmartillerie* objected, demanding that the eighteen vehicles for which the materials had been set aside be completed.

While no photos of these vehicles have yet surfaced, documentary evidence indicates that the *Sturmartillerie* prevailed, as late March and April 1945 strength reports for various *Sturmgeschütz* units list the *Flakpanzers* as operational.

"Kugelblitz" Leichter Flakpanzer IV mit 3 cm Mk 103 als Zwilling Waffe

By January 1944, the Allies had achieved air superiority, and the need for a *Flakpanzer* capable of delivering a high rate of accurate antiaircraft fire was reaching desperate proportions.

Above: *The only known photograph of a completed* Kugelblitz *is this one, heavily retouched by British Intelligence during the war. Each of the Kugelblitz's 3 cm guns had a rate of fire of 15 rounds per second, and the turret could traverse at a rate of up to 25 degrees per second, and elevate at 20 degrees per second.* Thomas Anderson

As an interim solution, it was proposed to mount the 3 cm FlaK gun with turret, originally developed for use on U-boats, on an unmodified Panzer IV chassis.

Further investigation showed that this was impractical, but, with the concept still appealing, Daimler-Benz was contracted to design a similar new turret as well as the alterations to the Panzer IV chassis necessary to accommodate it.

The new turret, which somewhat resembled an oversized aircraft ball turret, mounted twin 3 cm M103 belt-fed aircraft autocannons.

The new turret required a larger turret ring, and accordingly a Tiger I turret ring was incorporated in the chassis, which required relocating the driver's and radio operator's hatches

In June 1944 three hundred of the vehicles, which were named *Kugelblitz*, were ordered, with Krupp to produce the chassis and Deutsche Roehrenwerke the superstructure. The first five vehicles were scheduled to be assembled by Stahlindustrie in September 1944, with production to ramp up thereafter.

As was the case with many of Germany's armament programs, and in September when the first vehicles were to be rolling off the production line, instead there was a meeting which forecast that the first two vehicles would not be completed until October. Those two would be built by Daimler-Benz, with Stahlindustrie beginning production the next month.

Further delays led to the estimate of initial Stahlindustrie production to be changed again, to February 1945.

As Germany came to its knees, in February 1945 the decision was made to move *Kubelblitz* production to *Kommando Ostbau*. Records indicate that two of the vehicles were actually produced in March.

8.8 cm FlaK *auf Sonderfahrgestell* (PzSfl IVc)

As reported earlier in this book, efforts had been made by Krupp to mount an 8.8 cm FlaK gun on a fully tracked chassis, first intending it to be used as a bunker buster against the Maginot Line, and later as a *Panzerjäger*.

In June 1942, the chassis design was revisited, with modifications, with the intent to create an 8.8 cm-armed *Flakpanzer*. Two trial vehicles were ordered from Krupp which were to be delivered in April and May 1943. Because of earlier experiments, it was decided to use an SSG76 transmission and Krupp-designed steering gear rather than the SSG90 transmission and Henschel L320C steering gear used in the prior efforts. Both the SSG90 and the L320C were found to be not combat serviceable.

In part because of the bombing of the Krupp Essen works, the project fell behind and in October 1943 assembly of the first prototype was transferred to Krupp-Grusenwerk

Left: *Krupp built three examples of the* Versuchsflakwagen *8.8 cm FlaK auf Sonderfahrgestell (Experimental Antiaircraft Vehicle 8.8 cm Antiaircraft on Special Chassis: designated PzSfl IVc) in mid-1943. This constituted an 8.8 cm FlaK 37 or 41 on a mount with a frontal shield, emplaced on a chassis fitted with fold-down side and rear armor shields. The chassis were reworked from an earlier experimental vehicle intended as an assault vehicle. Problems with unsatisfactory drivetrain components and the lack of need for a self-propelled heavy antiaircraft gun ensured the project did not enter serial production.* Patton Museum

8.8 cm FlaK *auf Sonderfahrgestell* (PzSfl IVc)

Specifications	
Length	7.00 m
Width	3.00 m
Height	2.80 m
Weight	26 tons
Fuel capacity	600 liters
Maximum speed	60 km/hr
Range, on-road	300 km
Range, cross-country	200 km
Crew	9
Communications	Fu Spr Ger
Armament	
Weapon, main	8.8 cm FlaK 41
Ammo stowage, main	48
Automotive	
Engine make	Maybach
Engine model	HL 90 P
Engine configuration	V-12, liquid cooled
Engine displacement	9.0 liters
Engine horsepower	360 @ 3600 rpm

in Magdeburg. It was planned that to have the pilot completed the next month. In November, the order for the second prototype was canceled.

The first prototype, armed with an 8.8 cm FlaK 41, began testing and evaluation at Oxbol, Denmark, in early March 1944. Later in the month, it was ordered that the gun be replaced with an 8.8 cm FlaK 37.

The vehicle, designated 8.8 cm FlaK *auf Sonderfahrgestell* (PzSfl IVc) was ill-advised from the outset. The mighty 88 required range-finding gear that would not fit on the vehicle, requiring not only a second vehicle, but also a command-and-control link between the two, which was impractical in the field. Further, the long range of the 88 was of little benefit to Panzer formations, which rarely came under attack from high-flying bombers, but rather were targeted by low-flying fighter-bombers, who operated well within the range of 2 cm and 3.7 cm guns.

However, Germany was a nation increasingly desperate for any type of armament, thus after trials the sole 8.8 cm FlaK *auf Sonderfahrgestell* (PzSfl IVc) was shipped to *Heeres Flakartillerie-Abteilung* (Sf) 304, which was assigned to the 26th Panzer Division in Italy.

Left: *The folding sides and rear of the armored shield of the PzSfl IVc are lowered in this elevated view. The example shown here was armed with the FlaK 41, which is traversed to the right, allowing a view of the left side of the gun, its carriage, and cradle.* Patton Museum

Chapter 7
Self-Propelled Artillery

The German military recognized the value of self-propelled artillery well before they invaded Poland. As far back as 1934 the German war planners had forecast the production of such vehicles, but it would be 1940 before such vehicles were available in quantity. Even then, the first series-produced vehicles were far from ideal.

15 cm sIG auf PzKpfw I Ausf B

The invasion of Poland proved the validity of the *Wehrmacht*'s desire for self-propelled artillery. The fastest way to produce such a vehicle was to roll an unmodified fieldpiece, specifically the 15 cm sIG heavy infantry howitzer, on the chassis of a tank.

Alkett was contracted to produce thirty-eight such vehicles, utilizing the chassis of Panzer IB tanks. Rather than a turret and superstructure, the chassis was topped with two troughs to accommodate the wheels of the howitzer, and the towing eye was secured to a vertical bar at the rear of the vehicle, preventing it from rolling off.

Just ahead of the howitzer, a massive gun shield was installed on the chassis. Although imposingly tall, the soft armor of the shield could protect the crew only from ball ammunition, but was easily penetrated by armor-piercing rifle rounds. The top, rear and much of the sides of the vehicle were open. Four men crewed the vehicle and serviced the piece, a driver, a commander, and two cannoneers.

The vehicle was so crowded only three rounds of ammo could be carried. These were stowed in wicker baskets mounted on the fenders. Additional ammunition was transported by a supporting SdKfz 10 half-track.

15 cm *schwere Infanteriegeschütz* (mot S) PzKpfw I Ausf B

Specifications	
Length	4.42 m
Width	2.17 m
Height	2.70
Weight	7 tons
Fuel capacity	146 liters
Maximum speed	40 km/hr
Range, on-road	170 km
Range, cross-country	115 km
Crew	4
Armament	
Weapon, main	15 cm sIG 33 L/11
Ammo stowage, main	3 rounds
Range	4700 meters
Armor, Chassis	13 mm front 13 mm sides and rear
Armor, Superstructure	4 mm front 4 mm sides
Automotive	
Engine make	Maybach
Engine model	NL 38 Tr
Engine configuration	6-cylinder
Engine displacement	3.8 liters
Engine horsepower	100 @ 3000 rpm

Above: *The 15 cm sIG 33 (schweres Infanteriegeschütz) gun was introduced in 1936 in response to the requirement for a heavy direct-support weapon for infantry units. Normally drawn by the Demag 1-ton prime mover (SdKfz 10), its limited mobility did not meet the needs of the highly mobile Panzer units. Thus a self-propelled solution based on a fully tracked vehicle was required. The first of these early self-propelled guns was based on the Pzkpfw I Ausf B and the combinations were known as 15 cm sIG 33 (Sf) auf Panzerkampfwagen I Ausf B. This gun and its support elements are seen in the town of Montcornet on May 17, 1940. These are guns of the* Infanteriegeschütz Kompanie 706, which was assigned to the 10th Panzer Division. National Archives and Records Administration

Above: *The large boxy armored superstructure of the 15 cm sIG 33 (Sf) auf Panzerkampfwagen I Ausf B encompassed a fully intact 15 cm sIG 33, including its shield, trail, and wheels. Using ramps, the gun could be quickly rolled off the chassis should it become unserviceable. This was a major advantage for a self-propelled weapon. Many viable weapons could be sidelined for otherwise trivial mechanical failures. Six* Infanteriegeschütz Kompanies *were formed, and this gun of the 704 is seen serving in the invasion of Greece in 1941. This unit was subordinate to the 5th Panzer Division, which was assigned to the XIVth Motorized Army Corps.* National Archives and Records Administration

The improvised vehicle had an alarmingly high silhouette, was overloaded, and had a high center of gravity. These factors, combined with its scant ammunition stowage, were severe tactical handicaps. Nevertheless, the vehicles, which were first issued in February 1940, soldiered on until June 1943.

15 cm sIG33 auf Fgst PzKpfw II (Sf)

In October 1940, Alkett successfully produced a trial vehicle which mounted the 15 cm *schwere Infanteriegeschütz* (heavy infantry howitzer) 33 in a Panzer II chassis. However, mounting the large fieldpiece inside the small tank made for a vehicle with a very cramped fighting compartment, making it difficult to service (operate) the fieldpiece.

Alkett was directed to redesign the vehicle, enlarging the chassis in order to make it more practical as a gun carriage.

The redesign included both widening the hull as well as lengthening it enough that an additional roadwheel was required. Additionally, the engine was mounted transversely at the rear, with a transfer case redirecting the power forward along the ride side of the vehicle via a driveshaft that connected to the front-mounted transmission and steering gear. Ultimately, few Panzer II components were actually used beyond track links, drive sprockets, suspension components, and steering gear.

Twelve trial vehicles were produced, seven in December 1941 and five in January 1942. Six were issued to each of two companies of self-propelled heavy howitzers, the 707th and 708th, which were deployed to North Africa. The 708th arrived in Tripoli in February 1942, with the 707th arriving in North Africa in April 1942. In May, the light infantry regiment of the 90th Light Division that they were to support reported that the vehicles were unusable in theater due to being underpowered, and requested assistance with this problem from higher command.

All of the vehicles were lost in North Africa, with the British capturing half of the total production in a local repair shop.

Geschützwagen 38 für sIG 33/1 (Sf) (SdKfz 138/1) "Grille"

Still trying to find a suitable mechanized platform for the 15 cm sIG, the *Waffenamt* next turned to Skoda, but within a year the task was shifted to Rheinmetall-Borsig, the designer of the howitzer, to develop such a vehicle using components of the proven *Panzerkampfwagen* 38(t) chassis.

An all-new mount was designed, although the recoil mechanism and tube of the towed fieldpiece were retained. The new weapon, optimized for mounting in a self-propelled mount, was designated sIG33/1.

15 cm *schwere Infanteriegeschütz* 33B Sfl

Specifications	
Length	5.48 m
Width	2.60 m
Height	1.98
Weight	16 tons
Maximum speed	45 km/hr
Range, on-road	100 km
Crew	4
Communications	Fu Spr Ger a
Armament	
Weapon, main	15 cm sIG 33B
Ammo stowage, main	10 rounds
Range	4,700 meters
Armor, Chassis	30 mm front
	14.5 mm sides and rear
Automotive	
Engine make	Büssing
Engine model	Typ GS
Engine configuration	8-cylinder, liquid cooled
Engine displacement	7.91 liters
Engine horsepower	155 @ 3000 rpm

A trial vehicle was delivered in April 1942, and was well received.

The initial production contract was issued to Českomoravská Kolben Daněk (ČKD), known under German control as Boemisch-Märische Maschinenfabrik (BMM), for two hundred of the vehicles. The vehicles were designated *Geschützwagen* 38 *für* sIG 33/1 (Sf)(SdKfz 138/1), but the vehicle was commonly known as "*Grille*" or cricket.

To create the machine, the Panzer 38(t) chassis was equipped with an all-new superstructure from the fender line up. The new superstructure was made of thin 25 mm armor plate and was open topped. Thus, the crew and on-board ammunition had only basic protection from small arms and splinters. As the vehicle was a howitzer, and thus intended for long-range troop support, this level of protection was deemed adequate.

Right: *Development continued on the self-propelled infantry gun concept using elements of the Panzer II chassis. A new platform was formed that was 24 inches longer and 13 inches wider. A sixth roadwheel was added to better distribute the weight of the gun, crew, and ammunition. Thirty rounds of ammunition were carried. As much of the original gun (minus the wheels) was located within the superstructure, this was still an expedient solution. Officially known as 15 cm sIG 33 auf Fahrgestell Panzerkampfwagen II (Sf), 12 were built by Alkett in 1941. This gun is seen in Marada, Libya, in early 1942.* National Archives and Records Administration

Right: *All twelve guns were shipped to North Africa for use by the* Deutsche Afrika Korps. *They became the newly formed* Infanteriegeschütz Kompanies *707 and 708, which were both part of the 90th* leichte Afrika-Division. *All guns were eventually destroyed or abandoned, like this one, in the general retreat toward Tunisia in 1943. Interestingly,* Infanteriegeschütz Kompanie *708 created at least one replacement gun by using the chassis of a Panzer III.* Patton Museum

SELF-PROPELLED ARTILLERY

Geschützwagen 38 für sIG 33/1 (Sf) (SdKfz 138/1) "Grille"

Specifications	
Length	5.6 m
Width	2.15 m
Height	2.40 m
Weight	11.5 tons
Fuel capacity	218 liters
Maximum speed	42 km/hr
Range, on-road	185 km
Range, cross-country	140 km
Crew	5
Communication	FuG 16
Armament	
Weapon, main	15 cm sIG 33/1
Ammo stowage, main	15 rounds
Range	4,700 meters
Armor, Chassis	50 mm front 15 mm sides and rear
Armor, Superstructure	25 mm front 14.5 mm sides
Automotive	
Engine make	Praga
Engine model	TNHPS/II
Engine configuration	6-cylinder, liquid cooled
Engine displacement	7.75 liters
Engine horsepower	150 @ 2600 rpm

Production of the vehicles began with twenty-five delivered in February 1943, followed by forty in March, fifty-two in April, fifty-two in May, and thirty-one in June. At that time, production of this vehicle, which was based on the Ausf H chassis, was discontinued in favor of a new model, discussed in the next section.

The *Grille* was issued in companies of six vehicles to *Panzer-Grenadier* regiments. The design attained its objective and remained in service for the remainder of the war.

Above: As surplus 38(t) components became available in larger numbers in 1941–1942, work began on mounting the sIG 33 on this more capable platform. The superstructure was partly removed and the sIG 33/1 (the /1 designation denoting that it was modified for use on a self-propelled vehicle) was mounted on a massive trestle in the center. Known as the 15 cm sIG 33/1 Grille Ausf H, it also carried the nickname Grille, German for cricket. This is the first prototype produced by BMM. The vehicle is still finished in plain dark gray. Patton Museum

Above: One of the first production vehicles photographed at the BMM factory. Many of the tools were relocated, with the jack now mounted on the left fender. Loops are spread over the superstructure walls, which were used to secure foliage. A substantial hinged travel lock secured the gun during movement. The vulnerable area underneath the gun was protected during high elevation with a spring-loaded protective plate. The massive superstructure still used riveted construction like the 38(t) parent vehicle. Patton Museum

Geschützwagen 38 M für sIG 33/2 (Sf) (SdKfz 138/1) "Grille"

Specifications	
Length	4.835 m
Width	2.150 m
Height	2.400 m
Weight	11.5 tons
Fuel capacity	218 liters
Maximum speed	42 km/hr
Range, on-road	185 km
Range, cross-country	140 km
Crew	5
Communication	FuG 16
Armament	
Weapon, main	15 cm sIG 33/1
Ammo stowage, main	15 rounds
Range	4,700 meters
Armor, Chassis	20 mm front
	15 mm sides and rear
Armor, Superstructure	10 mm front
	10 mm sides
Armament	
Engine make	Praga
Engine model	AC
Engine configuration	6-cylinder, liquid cooled
Engine displacement	7.75 liters
Engine horsepower	150 @ 2600 rpm

Above: *A good view into the interior of the prototype. The commander's seat is to the left, behind the gun. The loader's sat is to the right. The large central box contained six ready rounds. Compared with the later production vehicle, the location of the Fu 5 radio set is different. Accordingly, the boxes containing the charges were mounted in different places. The perforated plate at lower right was using for packing cartridges and setting fuses. The combustion air inlet was of the standard 38(t) type.* Patton Museum

Geschützwagen 38 M für sIG 33/2 (Sf)(SdKfz 138/1) "Grille"

Without question the *Geschützwagen 38 für sIG 33/1 (Sf) (SdKfz 138/1) "Grille"* was a success, but there was considerable inefficiency in the production of Germany's military vehicles. As can be seen by flipping through this volume, an almost innumerable number of unique chassis were in production.

In an effort to increase production efficiency, the decision was made to mount the 15 cm howitzer in the chassis developed for the *Panzerjäger* 38 Ausf M. As explained in the *Panzerjäger* chapter, the Ausf M was so designated because it featured a mid-engine (*motor-mitte*) layout. The new design further benefited from better weight distribution, and thus suspension loading, more room for the crew, and a smaller silhouette.

Because the sIG was a larger weapon than the antitank gun found in the *Panzerjäger*, the front and sides of the superstructure had to be redesigned.

It was designated the *Geschützwagen 38 Ausf K*, and production was begun by Českomoravská Kolben Daněk (ČKD), or as it was known under German control, Boemisch-Märische Maschinenfabrik, in December 1943. In that month, fourteen of the vehicles were produced. From January through September 1944, a further 148 vehicles

SELF-PROPELLED ARTILLERY 195

Above: *The 15 cm sIG 33/1 Grille Ausf H proved to be successful. It was light and agile with an excellent mobility even in rough terrain. The chassis of the 38(t) had proven to be highly reliable with the tracks and running wheel providing a long service life. To improve and streamline production a new multiuse chassis was created. This was intended to carry either the 7.5 cm PaK 40 (Marder III Ausf M), the 2 cm FlaK 38 (Flakpanzer 38), or the sIG 33. This new design moved the fighting compartment to the rear and the engine compartment was relocated to the middle of the tank. This eliminated the long gun overhang and coupled the engine directly to the transmission. It was designated 15 cm sIG 33/1 Grille Ausf K. Patton Museum*

Above: *A view down into the fighting compartment of the 15 cm sIG 33/1 Grille Ausf K. Many of the same components were used from the Ausf H. The driver now had his own station located in the front right, creating more room for ammunition stowage. The FuG 16 radio set is located to the lower right under a metal rain shield. Cartridge and fuse preparation was now accomplished on the folding rear panel. Stanchions were placed near the four corners for the installation of the tarpaulin. Patton Museum*

Above: *A much simpler travel lock was designed for the 15 cm sIG 33/1 Grille Ausf K. Due to its improved center of gravity, the gun was easier to secure and required a less substantial mechanism to do so. This side view provides a good perspective on the side air intake. This is also where the exhaust pipe exited the engine compartment. Like the Ausf H, the K also had loops around its superstructure for the mounting of foliage as camouflage. Wire can still be seen within the loops in this photo, being essential in keeping the material in place during movement. Patton Museum*

left the assembly line. Production of the *Geschützwagen* 38 Ausf K, which retained the name of its predecessor, "*Grille*," was suspended at that time in order to concentrate on *Panzerjäger* 38 production, which took place in the same facility. Production of the *Grille* resumed in February 1945, when 14 additional units were completed. These were followed by a final three vehicles in March 1945, bringing the total production of the *Geschützwagen* 38 Ausf K to 179 vehicles.

The vehicles were issued on the same basis, and used interchangeably with the earlier *Geschützwagen* 38 *für* sIG 33/1 (Sf)(SdKfz 138/1) "*Grille*," some units operating both types.

15 cm sIG 33/2 (Sf) on *Bergepanzerwagen* 38

Built on a *Bergepanzerwagen* 38 chassis, this vehicle is shrouded in a cloak of mystery. Although since World War II assorted published sources state that up to twenty-four of these vehicles were built, either from rebuilt *Bergepanzerwagen* 38 chassis or new construction, no photos have surfaced but for a handful of photos of the apparent prototype. The images were taken in the fall of 1944 at the Českomoravská Kolben Daněk (ČKD) plant.

Further, no mention is made of production of this vehicle in Českomoravská Kolben Daněk (ČKD) or Skoda records.

The vehicle, whatever its fate, appears to be armed with the 15 cm sIG 33/2 cannon.

LgsFH 13 (Sfl) auf Lorraine-*Schlepper*

When France fell, Germany captured 160 relatively new French Lorraine 37L armored ammunition carriers/prime movers. Seeking to further mechanize their artillery, which at that time still relied heavily on draft animals, the Germans decided to adapt the Lorraines for use as chassis for self-propelled artillery. Sixty were to be armed with 10.5 cm light field howitzers, forty with 15 cm heavy field howitzers, and sixty with 7.5 cm PaK 40 antitank guns.

In June 1942 Hitler demanded that thirty of the vehicles armed with the heavy field howitzers be made immediately available for use by Rommel in North Africa.

Alkett was issued a contract for design and production of these thirty vehicles, which were competed that same month. The vehicles were armed with the 15 cm sFH 13.

These vehicles were immediately shipped to North Africa, although three were sunk in transit in July and four the following month. The remaining twenty-three vehicles performed admirably, but all had been lost in combat by the end of the year. The powerful cannon mounted on the reliable and mobile Lorraine chassis proved an excellent combination.

Meantime, following the Alkett design, a German army depot in Paris converted an additional sixty-four vehicles during July and August 1942. These were issued on the basis of six per battery to *Gepanzerte Artillerie-Regiments* 1 (Sfl) and 2 (Sfl). *Gepanzerte Artillerie-Regiment* 2 (Sfl) was later reorganized as *Artillerie-Regiment* 931 and still later as *Panzer-Artillerie-Regiment* 155 for the 21st Panzer Division. Involved in the fighting at Normandy, by the end of 1944 only one operational LgsFH 13 (Sfl) *auf* Lorraine-*Schlepper* was left.

Above: *Yet another solution for simplified production was this concept based on the* Bergepanzerwagen 38. *Here, the closed superstructure was opened and ringed with armored panels. Mounting of the main weapon was similar to its predecessors, but with much reduced crew space. Some mystery remains as to the production of this vehicle. This photo is believed to be a prototype based on the* Bergepanzer 38(t) *recovery vehicle. Some sources say up to thirty were produced. No photos have yet surfaced of the vehicles in use, nor have records of their assignment to a specific unit.* Hans-Heiri Stapfer

15 cm s Pz H 18/1 auf Fgst Pz III/IV (Sf) (SdKfz 165) "Hummel"

Although the *Heushrecke* (discussed later in this chapter) was under development, German leaders recognized it would be some time before it was ready for series production. Thus, an interim self-propelled mount for the 15 cm field howitzer was needed.

Rheinmetall-Borsig/Alkett were issued a contract to create such a stopgap vehicle. In creating the vehicle, the robust transmission, steering units and final drive from the *Panzerkampfwagen* III were combined with the equally proven engine and suspension of the Panzer IV. The weapon was the 15 cm sFH (heavy field howitzer) 18/1. Only the hull and superstructure were newly designed for the interim vehicle.

The engine was positioned in the center of the vehicle, driving the front-mounted transmission. This arrangement allowed for a spacious rear-mounted fighting compartment. Typical of self-propelled artillery of the era, that fighting compartment was open-topped and only lightly armored, reflecting the intent that the vehicle being used in a support role. The armor was intended to provide protection against shell fragments and infantry rounds up to 7.92 mm.

SELF-PROPELLED ARTILLERY

LgsFH 13 (Sfl) *auf* Lorraine-*Schlepper*

Specifications	
Length	4.40 m
Width	1.85 m
Height	2.20 m
Weight	8.50 tons
Fuel capacity	110 liters
Maximum speed	35 km/hr
Range, on-road	120 km
Range, cross-country	75 km
Crew	4
Communications	Fu Spr Ger a
Armament	
Weapon, main	15 cm sFH13 L/17
Ammo stowage, main	8 rounds
Range	6,200 meters
Armor, Chassis	12 mm front 9 mm sides and rear
Armor, Superstructure	10-14.5 mm front 8 mm sides
Automotive	
Engine make	DelaHaye
Engine model	135
Engine configuration	6-cylinder
Engine displacement	3.56 liter
Engine horsepower	70 @ 2800 rpm

Sometime, apparently in 1944, the hull design was changed slightly, with the number of return rollers being reduced and the driver's compartment being enlarged to span nearly the full width of the vehicle.

Production of the vehicle, designated 15 cm s Pz H 18/1 *auf* Fgst Pz III/IV (Sf) (SdKfz 165), began in February 1943, and continued for the duration of the war.

Ultimately, a total of 884 of the vehicles were reported to have been produced. Given the name "*Hummel*," or bumblebee, the vehicles were deployed in batteries of six, with their first combat on July 5, 1943, while taking part in Operation *Zitadelle*.

Above: *Among the menagerie of converted French vehicles was the 15 cm sFH 13/1 (Sf) auf GW Lorraine Schlepper (f). As the name indicates, this was also based on the robust little French Lorraine tractor. The main weapon was the German World War I 15 cm sFH 13/1 howitzer, many of which still remained in reserve service. Thirty vehicles were built initially and all were intended for the Deutsche Afrika Korps. This is one of seven vehicles captured by the British at El Alamein in December 1942.* Patton Museum

Above: *The right side of the same vehicle shown previously. Alkett was the manufacturer of the first batch of vehicles and they were to be spread among three Panzer Divisions: the 15th, 21st, and 90th leichte Afrika-Division. However, shipping losses accounted for seven of the original thirty. They first went into action in August 1942 and most were reported as lost by early December.* Patton Museum

10.5 cm leFH 16 *Geschützpanzer*

When British troops withdrew from France via Operation Dynamo (at Dunkirk), the German army captured an estimated 40,000 vehicles and weapons. Among these were a number of Light Tanks Mark VI. Six of these were taken over by First Lieutenant Alfred Becker of *Artillerie-Regiment 227*, who had a 10.5 cm light field howitzer mounted on each of

Above: *Ammunition storage was sparse, with only eight shells and eight propellant charges carried. Due to the location of the engine in the Lorraine Schlepper, the gun had to be placed well to the rear. This necessitated the installation of a spade to stabilize the gun during firing. This is one of seven guns captured at El Alamein and sent back to the UK for evaluation. It is believed that all the guns sent to North Africa were painted in overall dark yellow with green bands.* Patton Museum

Above: *This vehicle is part of a group of* Wespe *that are starting to assemble for transport by rail. In this regard, the* Wespe *was quite practical. Weighing only eleven metric tons, it required no special preparation for rail travel. Note the reinforced suspension on the first, second, and fifth roadwheels. There was insufficient room for stowage of personal items and other equipment. To help alleviate this, local workshops often constructed stowage bins, such as those seen here on the front superstructure.* Patton Museum

Above: *The concept of artillery batteries that could keep pace with the advancing Panzer divisions seemed like a natural one for the developers of the blitzkrieg, and it was decided to mount the 10.5 cm gun on a chassis built around the components of the Panzer II tank. The official designation of the weapon was* leichte Feldhaubitze 18/2 (Sf) auf Geschutzwagen II. *It was also known as* Wespe *(wasp), although this was not an official designation. The gun of the* Wespe *was mounted in the rear of the vehicle, and the engine was mounted forward of the fighting compartment and to the right. This created a very stable platform for the gun to both move and fire. Production of the* Wespe *was started in 1942 and continued until January 1945.* Patton Museum

Above: *An overhead view of the fighting compartment of the* Wespe. *Ammunition stowage was to the rear of the gun, and charges could also be stored on the left side of the superstructure. Thirty-two rounds were carried. There was ample room for the crew to service the weapon and keep up a good rate of fire. A travel lock was found underneath the barrel, near the gun shield and another was located at the rear of the gun slide. A radio set was installed at the left rear of the fighting compartment.* Patton Museum

SELF-PROPELLED ARTILLERY

15 cm s Pz H 18/1 *auf* Fgst Pz III/IV (Sf) (SdKfz 165) "*Hummel*"

Specifications	
Length	7.17 m
Width	2.97 m
Height	2.81 m
Weight	23 tons
Fuel capacity	600 liters
Maximum speed	25 km/hr
Range, on-road	215 km
Range, cross-country	135 km
Crew	6
Communications	Fu Spr Ger f
Armament	
Weapon, main	15 cm s.F.H. 18/1
Weapon, secondary	MG 34
Ammo stowage, main	18 rounds
Ammo stowage, secondary	600 rounds
Range	13,250 meters
Armor, Chassis	30 mm front 20 mm sides and rear carbon steel
Armor, Superstructure	10 mm
Automotive	
Engine make	Maybach
Engine model	HL 120 TRM
Engine configuration	V-12, liquid cooled
Engine displacement	11.9 liters
Engine horsepower	265 @ 2600 rpm

Above: *The 15 cm Schwere Panzerhaubitze auf Geschützwagen III/IV (sf) (SdKfz 165) Hummel (Bumblebee) self-propelled armored 15 cm field howitzer was designed to provide the Panzer and Panzergrenadier divisions with artillery support on an armored, fully tracked chassis. The hybrid PzKpfw III/IV chassis was selected for what Army Ordnance meant to be merely an interim solution until a chassis designed specifically as a self-propelled gun platform could be produced. Although components of the PzKpfw III and IV were used, the upper hull and superstructure had to be created. This prototype vehicle featured a muzzle brake that was found to be impractical for production.* Patton Museum

Above: *This Hummel in a training area features spare wheels mounted in brackets on the front hull, as well as wire string along the superstructure for the use of foliage as camouflage. Although built on what was essentially a medium tank chassis, the Hummel, at twenty-four tons, was thinly armored, especially the very high walls around the fighting compartment, necessitated by mounting the sFH 18/1 above the engine.* National Archives and Records Administration

them in an open-topped armored superstructure. Becker's conversions were successful, and in time he was charged with the responsibility of overseeing the conversion and adaptation of scores of vehicles, both captured and of German origin.

The six modified vehicles, designated 10.5 cm leFH 16 Geschützpanzer, entered service in October 1941.

The leFH 16 (light field howitzer of 1916) was itself a proven weapon, with adequate range, firing a round with good bursting qualities. Mounted on the Mark VI chassis, it was found that the vehicle was very stable, and the ground spade only had to be deployed when firing rounds with charge 5.

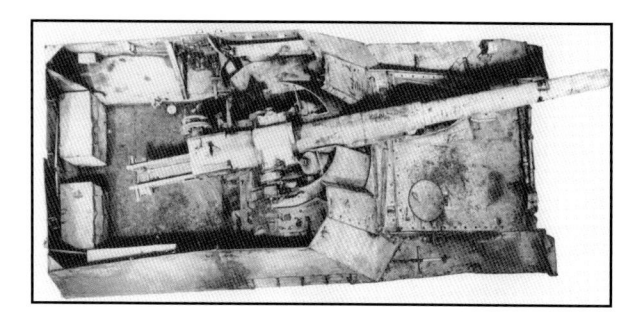

Above: *This overhead view of the fighting compartment of the* Hummel *provides a clear idea of its layout. In many respects, its layout followed that of the* Wespe, *with ammunition stowage at the sides and rear. Eighteen rounds were carried on the vehicle. This is an early production gun. In early 1944, the front crew compartment of the* Hummel *was enlarged to provide additional room. A duplicate vision block and assembly was added to the right side.* Patton Museum

Above: *A* Hummel *of the 9th SS division Hohenstaufen makes its way along a snow track on the Russian Front. The gun has a very neatly applied camouflage scheme of dark gray and dark green. The crew also carries a large section of camouflage netting to conceal its position while firing. A series of wooden poles to support the net are stowed on the travel lock. This vehicle also features an elaborate anti-grenade screen over the crew compartment.* Patton Museum

The vehicles went into combat in October 1941, south of Leningrad. The vehicles won high praise from the troops, not only for the mechanical reliability but also their effectiveness as a weapon.

10.5 cm leFH 16 auf gepSfl FCM

Developed just prior to World War II, the FCM 36 was a design competitive to the R 35. Produced by Forges et Chantiers de la Méditerranée (FCM), this tank featured welded-hull

10.5 cm leFH 16 *Geschützpanzer*

Specifications	
Length	4.00 m
Width	2.20 m
Height	2.00 m
Weight	6.5 tons
Fuel capacity	159 liters
Maximum speed	50 km/hr
Range, on-road	280 km
Range, cross-country	180 km
Crew	4
Communications	Fu Spr Ger d
Armament	
Weapon, main	10.5 cm leFH 16
Range	9,200 meters
Armor, Chassis	11–14 mm front 11–13 mm sides and rear carbon steel
Armor, Superstructure	22 mm front 14 mm side
Automotive	
Engine make	Meadows
Engine configuration	6-cylinder, liquid cooled
Engine displacement	4.43 liter
Engine horsepower	88 @ 3000 rpm

construction and was created to meet the same specifications as its contemporaries, the Hotchkiss H 35 and the Renault R 35. The Diesel-powered FCM 36, although considered to be France's most advanced light tank, was considerably more expensive than the R 35, and only one hundred were procured.

After France capitulated, the German army took possession of several of these vehicles.

During the fall of 1942, eight of them were converted to self-propelled artillery by mounting the proven 10.5 cm leFH 16 field howitzer on the French chassis. In order to do this the turret of the tank was removed and a boxy armored superstructure added to house the fieldpiece.

The eight resultant vehicles were assigned to the 1st and 2nd Batteries of *gepanzerte Artillerie-Abteilung* (Sfl) zBV. By 1944 all eight had been lost.

SELF-PROPELLED ARTILLERY

Above: *The 10.5 cm* leichte Feldhaubitze *16 was the main field howitzer used by Germany in World War I. In early 1941 members of the German 227* Infanterie-Division *converted thirty-four abandoned Vickers Light Tank Mk VIs into self-propelled guns and support vehicles. Among them were six 10.5 cm leFH 16 auf Geschutzwagen auf Fahrgestell Mk VI 736 (e), which utilized the still-reliable weapon. Here is one of those, seen during maneuvers in France.* National Archives and Records Administration

Geschützwagen IVb *für* 10.5 cm leFH 18/1(Sf) (SdKfz 165/1)

In September 1939, WaPrüf 6 received a design proposal from Krupp for a purpose-built self-propelled howitzer. Unlike earlier motorized artillery, this was not an adapted or converted vehicle, but rather expressly designed for this role.

A 10.5 cm leFH 18/1 was mounted in an open-topped turret. The light field howitzer could be rotated in this turret through a 70-degree arc. The sides of the turret were tapered downward toward the rear, allowing excellent side visibility. The new vehicle, initially known as PzSfl IVb, was later designated *Geschützwagen* IVb *für* 10.5 cm leFH 18/1(Sf) (SdKfz 165/1).

Two vehicles were ordered for testing, which were delivered in January 1942. Even before that, during the fall of 1941, a series of ten of the new vehicles were ordered for troop trials. Krupp-Grusonwerk produced these vehicles from August through December 1942. Six of these test vehicles were assigned to *Artillerie-Regiment* 16 of the 16th Panzer Division and deployed to the Russian Front, while the remaining four were issued to a training unit.

Enthusiasm for the new design was such that even before the first vehicle was delivered Krupp was in possession of a contract for two hundred production vehicles. However, none of these were produced because it was found that an adequate carriage could be made from obsolete

10.5 cm leFH 16 *auf* gepSfl FCM

Specifications	
Length	4.60 m
Width	2.14 m
Height	2.15 m
Weight	12.2 tons
Fuel capacity	260 liters
Maximum speed	28 km/hr
Range, on-road	200 km
Crew	4
Communications	Fu Spr Ger d
Armament	
Weapon, main	10.5 cm leFH 16
Range	9,200 meters
Weapon, secondary	7.92 MG
Ammo stowage, main	50 rounds
Ammo stowage, secondary	2,000 rounds
Armor, Chassis	25–40 mm front 20 mm sides and rear carbon steel
Armor, Superstructure	15 mm front 15 mm side
Automotive	
Engine make	Ricardo-Berliet
Engine model	MDP
Engine configuration	4-cylinder, Diesel
Engine displacement	8.49 liters
Engine horsepower	91 @ 1550 rpm

Panzerkampfwagen II chassis, allowing the valuable manufacturing capacity to be put to better use.

10.5 cm leFH 18/3 (Sf) *auf Geschützwagen* B2

The need to create an escort vehicle for the *Flammpanzer* conversions based on the *Char* B was discussed previously in this volume. Such an escort was needed due to the limited range of the flamethrower weapon. Basing the escort vehicle on the same chassis as the *Flammpanzer* would ease the logistical burden by providing a commonality of parts, as

Above: *The Germans captured thirty-seven of the excellent French FCM 36 tanks, known for their innovative sloped armor and reliable Diesel engines. They were initially intended to mount the 7.5 cm PaK 40 antitank gun and those were officially called 7.5 cm PaK 40 (Sf) auf Geschützwagen FCM(f). However, eight of the vehicles were instead converted to mount the 10.5 cm howitzer in a manner and role similar to that of the Wespe. These were known as the 10.5 cm leFH 16 (Sf) auf Geschützwagen FCM (f).v\ Patton Museum*

Above: *The interior of the 10.5 cm leFH 16 (Sf) auf Geschuetzwagen FCM (f) was quite spacious, although much of the room that could have been used for gun laying was devoted to the storage of ammunition. Thirty-seven rounds were carried, along with ammunition for the MG 42 self-defense weapon. The Berliet MDP V-4 Diesel engine generated 91 horsepower and could move the 12.2-ton vehicle along at 15 mph. However, it was a logistical orphan in the predominantly gasoline-driven German war machine.* Patton Museum

Geschützwagen IVb *für* 10.5 cm leFH 18/1(Sf) (SdKfz 165/1)

Specifications	
Length	5.90 m
Width	2.87 m
Height	2.25 m
Weight	18 tons
Fuel capacity	410 liters
Maximum speed	35 km/h
Range, on-road	240 km
Range, cross-country	130 km
Crew	4
Communications	Fu Spr Ger a
Armament	
Weapon, main	10.5 cm leFH 18/1
Ammo stowage, main	60 rounds
Range	10,650 meters
Armor, Chassis	20 mm front 14.5 mm sides and rear carbon steel
Armor, Turret	20 mm front 14.5 mm sides
Automotive	
Engine make	Maybach
Engine model	HL 66
Engine configuration	6-cylinder, liquid cooled
Engine displacement	6.6 liters
Engine horsepower	188 @ 3200 rpm

well as overall familiarity with the vehicle by both crews and support personnel.

The flamethrower-equipped *Char B* tanks were deployed, even before the escort vehicles were completed, to Russia in June 1941. Their use there was not successful, and owing to chassis unreliability, the unit was disbanded.

Nevertheless, production of the howitzer-armed vehicles continued to be scheduled for early 1942.

Five of these vehicles, armed with 10.5 cm leFH 18/3 howitzers in fixed superstructures, were produced in January 1942. Five more were delivered the following month, and the final six in March 1942. The vehicles were designated 10.5 cm leFH 18/3 (Sf) *auf Geschützwagen B2.*

These vehicle were shipped to the 26th Panzer Division, where they were assigned to the *I.Abteilung/Artillerie*

SELF-PROPELLED ARTILLERY

Above: *Early experiments for a self-propelled howitzer led to a new vehicle, initially known as Pz.Sfl. IVb, was later designated Geschützwagen IVb für 10.5 cm leFH 18/1(Sf) (SdKfz 165/1). The SdKfz 165/1 utilized a suspension consisting of six dual roadwheels mounted in tandem pairs on leaf springs. This suspension, with 520 mm diameter wheels, had also originally been proposed for the Panzer IV.* Patton Museum

Above: *The tapered turret sides minimized weight and provided excellent vision for the howitzer's crew of four. The short hull required carefully planned stowage for the myriad of on-vehicle material.* Patton Museum

Regiment 93. As of May 1943, the unit still had fifteen of the 10.5 cm leFH 18/3 (Sf) auf Geschützwagen B2 on strength, fourteen of which were listed as operational. Also on the strength report were twelve replacements for the converted French vehicles, the new *Wespe*. While orders were issued to transfer the 10.5 cm leFH 18/3 (Sf) auf Geschützwagen B2 to the 90th *Panzer Grenadier Regiment*, the final fate of the vehicles is not known.

10.5 cm leFH 18/3 (Sf) *auf Geschützwagen* B2

Specifications	
Length	7.62 m
Width	2.40 m
Height	3 m
Weight	32.5 tons
Fuel capacity	400 liters
Maximum speed	25 km/hr
Range, on-road	140 km
Range, cross-country	100 km
Crew	5
Communications	Fu Spr Ger f
Armament	
Weapon, main	10.5 cm leFH 18/3
Weapon, secondary	7.92 mm MG 34
Automotive	
Engine make	Renault
Engine model	307
Engine configuration	6-cylinder, liquid cooled
Engine displacement	16.5 liters
Engine horsepower	300 @ 1900 rpm

Above: *Sixteen French Char B1 heavy tanks were converted by Rheinmetall-Borsig in 1942 to 10.5 cm leFH 18/3 (Sf) auf Geschützwagen B-2(f). The 75 mm gun in the hull was deleted and the 10.5 cm leFH 18 light howitzer was mounted in an armored superstructure. They took on the same role as the Wespe and other self-propelled variants of the 10.5 cm gun. These vehicles were issued to the I./Artillerie-Regiment 93 of the 26th Panzer-Division and they served on the Eastern Front.* Patton Museum

Geschützwagen Lorraine-Schlepper für leFH 18/4

While, as noted earlier, Hitler had specified that the 160 captured Lorraine 37L carriers be converted into various specifically identified types of self-propelled artillery, on June 4, 1942, this order was amended to allow the specific configuration of the final seventy-eight vehicles to be at the discretion of Field Marshal Keitel.

As a result, twenty-four of these were used to mount the 10.5 cm leFH 18/4. Designated *Geschützwagen* Lorraine-*Schlepper* für leFH 18/4, the vehicle featured an armored superstructure similar to that used with the earlier 15 cm sFH13-armed Lorraine-*Schlepper* conversions. Ammunition stowage was also provided in the open-topped superstructure, as well as seating for four of the crew. The driver, naturally, was in the chassis.

The first twelve of these conversions were completed in September 1942. Six each were supplied to self-propelled artillery regiments 1 and 2 of Battery 6 of the *Gerpanzerte*.

Geschützwagen Lorraine-Schlepper für leFH 18/4

Specifications	
Length	4.40 m
Width	1.85 m
Height	2.20 m
Weight	7.7 tons
Fuel capacity	110 liters
Maximum speed	35 km/hr
Range, on-road	120 km
Range, cross-country	75 km
Crew	5
Communications	Fu Spr Ger f
Armament	
Weapon, main	10.5 cm leFH 18/4
Ammo stowage, main	20 rounds
Range	10,650 meters
Armor, Chassis	12 mm front 9 mm sides and rear carbon steel
Armor, Superstructure	10 mm front 10 mm sides
Automotive	
Engine make	DelaHaye
Engine model	135
Engine configuration	6-cylinder
Engine displacement	3.56 liters
Engine horsepower	70 @ 2800 rpm

Above: *The final variant of the three self-propelled guns based on the French Lorraine tractor was known as the 10.5 cm leFH 18/4 auf Lorraine Schlepper (f). Like the previous conversions, this one was fairly simple. Alkett converted twenty-four examples and they served exclusively in the* Panzer-Artillerie-Regiment *155 of the 21st Panzer Division during the fighting in Normandy in the summer of 1944.* Patton Museum

Above: *The 10.5 cm leFH 18/4 auf Lorraine Schlepper (f) was converted in two batches of twelve vehicles each. The second batch can be identified by the higher and less steeply angled side panel below the midpoint on the superstructure side. These second-batch vehicles are sometimes referred to as the* Baukommando Becker *versions, after the officer who supervised their construction. This is a gun of the 6th Battery, 2nd Platoon,* Panzer-Artillerie-Regiment *155.* Patton Museum

In December 1942, an improved superstructure was designed, and two more vehicles converted with this revision. No further conversions are known to have been made until September–October 1943, when twelve more were produced.

Ultimately, *15 Batterie/Artillerie-Regiment* 227 and *Artillerie-Regiment* 155 of the 21st Panzer Division went into combat in Normandy in June 1944 armed with twenty-four of the *Geschützwagen* Lorraine-*Schlepper für* leFH 18/4.

10.5 cm leFH 18/6 (Sf) *auf Geschützwagen* III/IV "*Heuschrecke* IVB"

The German high command had insisted that a self-propelled howitzer be developed that would permit the weapon to be dismounted and alternately used as towed artillery. Considerable effort over a number of years by a variety of firms went into this objective, but none were considered true successes.

10.5 cm leFH 18/6 (Sf) *auf Geschützwagen* III/IV "*Heuschrecke* IVb"

Specifications	
Length	6.57 m
Width	2.90 m
Height	2.65 m
Weight	24 tons
Fuel capacity	360 liters
Maximum speed	38 km/hr
Range, on-road	225 km
Range, cross-country	120 km
Crew	5
Communications	Fu Spr Ger f
Armament	
Weapon, main	10.5 cm leFH 18/6
Ammo stowage, main	87 rounds
Range	10,650 meters
Armor, Chassis	30 mm front
	20 mm sides and rear carbon steel
Armor, Superstructure	20 mm front
	15 mm sides
Automotive	
Engine make	Maybach
Engine model	HL120TRM
Engine configuration	V-12, liquid cooled
Engine displacement	11.9 liters
Engine horsepower	285 @ 2600 rpm

Above: *One of the odder capabilities put forth in the development of a self-propelled howitzer was that of retaining the ability to dismount the cannon and use it as towed artillery. Krupp's attempt to solve this problem resulted in the 10.5 cm leFH 18/6 (Sf) auf Geschützwagen III/IV Heuschrecke IVB. Basically an extensively modified Hummel chassis mounting a 10.5 cm light field howitzer; a hydraulic system for dismounting the turret was installed as well. Like the SdKfz 165/1, the main gun was similar to that used in the Sturmhaubitze 42.* Patton Museum

Above: *This is what the unusual design was all about. The turret of the Heuschrecke IVb could be dismounted, and either fired from the ground or towed using the carriage stowed on the motor carriage. The wheels for the carriage were stowed on the rear of the final design. The rear of the turret was hinged, providing maximum crew protection while traveling, yet allowing easy ammunition supply and room to man the weapon. A parallelogram-lifting device was used to remove the turret. In this, the final form of the prototype, the dismounting could be accomplished manually.* Patton Museum

Above: *Although the* Heuschrecke *IVb was a purpose-built vehicle, it utilized many components from other designs. Here the parallelogram-lifting device has been collapsed for travel. Elements of the disassembled firing cradle are stowed along the fenders and the wheels are mounted on the rear hull. Note the extended exhaust pipe. This vehicle was sent to the United States after the war and remains in the US Army museum system.* Patton Museum

Geschützpanzer 39H(f) leFH 16 & 18 Hotchkiss

Germany exploited the use of captured equipment to a greater degree than any other country involved in World War II. As seen throughout this volume, captured French vehicles were used en masse to produce a variety of tank destroyers and self-propelled artillery pieces for the *Wehrmacht*.

Above: *Like the 7.5 cm PaK 40 auf Geschützwagen 39H(f), there was also a 10.5 cm armed version of the converted French Hotchkiss light tank: the 10.5 cm leFH 18 (Sf) auf Geschützwagen 39H(f). Interestingly, both the 10.5 cm leFH 18 and the World War I 10.5 cm leFH 16 were used in the conversion, although photos of the latter are rare (only a single recuperator mechanism is present below the barrel of the 10.5 cm leFH 16). Like the FCM 36 conversion, ammunition stowage was copious. A total of thirty-six howitzer rounds were carried.* Patton Museum

Krupp's attempt to solve this problem involved mounting a 10.5 cm light field howitzer on an extensively modified *Hummel* chassis. The engine and cooling system were moved to the rear of the vehicle, in positions much as they were on the *Panzerkampfwagen* III and IV. A new glacis and superstructure was fabricated by Stahlindustrie and installed by Krupp. A hydraulic system for dismounting the turret was installed as well. The cannon itself was based on that used in the ill-fated *Geschützwagen* IVb, modified by the installation of a StuH 43 breech. Ultimately, it was found that the *Geschützwagen* IVb's leFH 18/1 could not be used, and the leFH 18/6 was developed instead.

The mounting and dismounting mechanism for the weapon proved to be a major technological stumbling block.

A trial vehicle was subsequently produced, which began to undergo testing on October 13, 1943. The initial test pointed to several worthwhile modifications, which were made in November. These changes brought about a weight reduction of about 1 ton, as well as facilitating less-costly production. Firing trials were conducted in January 1944. These trials pointed to the need for further modifications being needed, which were subsequently accomplished and further trials began on March 28, 1944. Still further modifications were requested, and the vehicle again was demonstrated on May 31.

At that time, it was determined the turret was unwieldy when removed from the chassis, and the project abandoned.

Above: *Like many of the other French vehicle conversions, the 10.5 cm leFH 18 (Sf) auf Geschützwagen 39H(f) served exclusively with the 21st Panzer Division in Normandy. Although designed to fulfill the traditional role as self-propelled artillery, in the 21st Panzer Division they were assigned to the Sturmgeschütz-Abteilung 200 and served alongside the 7.5 cm PaK 40 (sf) auf GW 39H(f) in both the antitank and infantry support role. A total of forty-eight vehicles were manufactured.* Patton Museum

Geschützpanzer 39H(f) leFH 16 and 18 Hotchkiss

Specifications	
Weight	12.5 tons
Fuel capacity	207 liters
Maximum speed	35 km/hr
Range, on-road	180 km
Range, cross-country	95 km
Crew	4
Communications	Fu Spr Ger d
Armament	
Weapon, main	10.5 cm leFH 16 or 18
Ammo stowage, main	36 rounds
Automotive	
Engine make	Hotchkiss
Engine configuration	6-cyliner, liquid cooled
Engine displacement	5.97 liters
Engine horsepower	120 @ 2800 rpm

The *Geschützpanzer* 39H(f) leFH is one such vehicle. This vehicle was based on the Hotchkiss H 39 medium tank, itself an improved version of the H 35. Hotchkiss referred to the vehicle as the *Char léger Hotchkiss modèle* 38 *série* D, referring to the design year rather than production year.

The German captured over 500 H 35 and H 39 tanks, and in addition to using many of them as tanks, employed them as the basis for artillery conversions.

The vehicle presented here is the result of a September 1943 conversion of a dozen vehicles.

The Germans removed the 37 mm gun-armed turrets from the vehicles, replacing them with an open-top superstructure. Inside of this they installed their own 10.5 cm howitzers, either the leFH 16 or 18. These vehicles, known as *Geschützpanzer* 39H(f), were assigned to *Sturmgeschütz-Abteilung* 200 in September. The following February another dozen similar conversions were also provided to the unit. As with many of the conversions of French vehicles, the *Geschützpanzer* 39H(f) leFH remained in France and were used in the futile attempt to throw back the Allied landings in June 1944. The last of these twenty-four vehicles were lost in the Falaise Pocket in August 1944.

leFH 18/40/2 (Sf) *auf Geschützwagen* III/IV

In addition to the Krupp design discussed previously, Alkett advanced a proposal for a dismountable howitzer using the Hummel chassis. At the rear of the chassis a ramp was installed, making it possible to raise the weapon with the included jib crane, reinstall the trails and wheels (which were stowed on the rear of the vehicle), and roll it down ramps to the ground for conventional use. The howitzer itself was a conventional leFH 18/40/2 installed on a rotating platform recessed in the hull.

Alkett demonstrated their trial vehicle (which survives today and is privately owned) at Hillersleben on March 28,

leFH 18/40/2 (Sf) *auf Geschützwagen* III/IV

Specifications	
Length	7.195 m
Width	3.000 m
Height	2.875 m
Weight	25 tons
Fuel capacity	500 liters
Maximum speed	42 km/hr
Range, on-road	190 km
Range, cross-country	150 km
Crew	5
Communications	Fu Spr Ger f
Armament	
Weapon, main	10.5 cm leFH 18/40/2
Ammo stowage, main	85 rounds
Range	12,300 meters
Armor, Chassis	30 mm front 20 mm sides and rear carbon steel
Armor, Superstructure	10 mm front 10 mm sides
Automotive	
Engine make	Maybach
Engine model	HL 120 TRM
Engine configuration	V-12, liquid cooled
Engine displacement	11.8 liters
Engine horsepower	285 @ 2600 rpm

Left: *Alkett submitted its own design for a dismountable howitzer using the* Hummel *chassis. Known as leFH 18/40/2 (Sf) auf Geschützwagen III/IV, the significant difference of was that it involved the mounting of a conventional leFH 18/40/2 on a rotating platform recessed in the hull. The wheels and trails were carried on the rear of the vehicle. With this arrangement it was possible to raise the weapon, reinstall the trails and wheels, and roll it down ramps to the ground. The empty spindle above the second roadwheel was for the mounting of spare roadwheels, the vehicle's rear deck being kept clear to speed dismounting of the howitzer.* Patton Museum

1944. The heavy weight of the removed components, as well as the confined working area, meant that it took over fifteen minutes to dismount the weapon, a time the military thought was excessive.

Modifications to correct some deficiencies, as well as to allow the weapon to be fired to the rear, were made, and the modified vehicle was demonstrated on May 28.

Despite some lingering problems, the German military made plans to put the vehicle immediately into mass production, albeit utilizing Panzer IV chassis, with initial deliveries scheduled for October 1944. As was the case with many of Germany's AFVs, there were numerous delays in beginning production, and in December 1944 the order was canceled without any production vehicles having been manufactured.

Gerät 040 and *Gerät* 041, "Karl"

Even today, among the largest self-propelled weapons ever built were Germany's superheavy mortars, often referred to as "*Karl.*" Originally conceived in the mid-1930s, by the 1937 Rheinmetall had designed a 60 cm mortar capable of heaving a 2,000 kg shell 4,000 meters. It would be carried on a unique, tracklaying chassis. The vehicle design was such that prior to firing the chassis was lowered to the ground, removing the firing stresses from the suspension components. The breech-loading mortar tube was mounted in a carriage which travelled with recoil, further reducing the abuse transmitted to automotive components. The muzzle faced toward the rear of the vehicle, allowing a quick getaway after firing, although with a top speed of ten or less kilometers per hour, quick was a relative term.

By July 1940 plans for the massive weapon had become a reality, and the first unit was shown to representatives from WaPrüf 4. Enormous consumers of resources, not only in production but in operation and support, only seven of the huge mortars were built, with the last one being completed in 1942. With such a low production number, and being such a huge machine, there was a certain amount of variation between the units.

Gerät 040 and *Gerät* 041, "Karl"

Specifications	
Length	11.15 m
Width	3.16 m
Height	4.78 m
Weight	123 tons (126.4 with 041)
Fuel capacity	1200 liters
Maximum speed	6 km/hr
Range, on-road	42 km gasoline, 60 km Diesel
Crew	21 (18 with 041)
Armament	
Weapon, main	60 cm (54 cm with 041)
Range	4,000 meters with Gerät 040 10,000 meters with Gerät 041
Automotive	
Engine make	Daimler-Benz
Engine model	MB503A (gasoline) MB 507C (Diesel)
Engine configuration	V-12, liquid cooled
Engine displacement	1200 liters
Engine horsepower	580 @ 1850 rpm

SELF-PROPELLED ARTILLERY

Left: *The Karl-Gerät 040 was a heavy siege weapon designed to reduce large fortifications such as the French Maginot Line. The weapon was known as Karl-Gerät 040 after General Karl Becker, head of the evaluation committee. It was also simply known as Gerät 040. It was unique among heavy mortars of its time not only in its size but also in its method of locomotion. The entire mortar was encased in a large steel rectangle that was fully tracked and motorized. This gun is firing on the Brest Citadel on the morning of June 24, 1941. Patton Museum*

Left: *Only seven Gerät 040 were built and only six of those were fielded. Production ran from January through August 1941. The individual guns were known by their production numbers and were expressed in Roman numerals: I–VII. The seventh gun was retained as a test vehicle and was not issued to the troops. This is thought to be that gun: number I, alternatively known by two nicknames, either Adam or Baldur. All Gerät 040 were originally armed with a short 600 mm barrel. Patton Museum*

Originally referred to simply as Project 4, by late 1940 it was known as *Gerät 040*, then *Gerät-Karl* in February 1941. During that month Hitler ordered the range increased by decreasing the bore. Three of the mortars—I, IV and V—were retubed to a 54 cm bore, which also involved some changes to the carriage, although the chassis was unchanged. The smaller-bore version was referred to as *Gerät 041*. In late July 1942 the names were reversed, becoming *Karl-Gerät*, the name they are most widely known by today.

These vehicles were used primarily on the Eastern Front, in the opening stages of Barbarossa, as well as at Sevastopol, Leningrad, and Warsaw. One even fired at the bridge at Remagen in 1945 in an attempt to deny the Allied forces a crossing.

Left: *Other large mortars then in use, such as the Czech 30.5 cm, required transportation in several large loads and many hours of preparation to fire. The Gerät 040 could move into position under its own power at around four miles per hour. Once in position, the entire firing platform was lowered to the ground, also using an onboard engine. The gun was mounted opposite the direction of travel, so the gun could be relocated quickly in the case of counter battery fire. This is gun III, known as Thor, after its conversion to Gerät 041 configuration with the longer 540 mm barrel.* Patton Museum

SELF-PROPELLED ARTILLERY   211

Left: *In order to support 15 cm self-propelled heavy infantry howitzer units, 102 examples of the Munitionspanzer 38(t) were produced using the same type of chassis and hull as the vehicles they supported.* Hans-Heiri Stapfer

Above: *The Geschützwagen III/IV für Munition was mechanically and structurally identical to the Hummel, which allowed the quick conversion of the vehicle into self-propelled artillery if circumstances demanded it. This late-production Munitionsfahrzeug III/IV had the full-width driver's and radio operator's compartment. It is shown following capture by US troops.* Patton Museum

Geschützwagen 38 für Munition (SdKfz 138/1) Ausf K

One of the major shortcomings of the *Grille* was its limited ammunition stowage. In order to support these vehicles in the field, ammunition carriers (munitionspanzers) were built using the same chassis and superstructure.

Českomoravská Kolben Daněk (ČKD), or, as it was known under German control, Boemisch-Märische Maschinenfabrik, produced 102 of these ammunition carriers using *Geschützwagen* 38 Ausf K (*Grille*) chassis and hull. The first five ammunition carriers were delivered in January 1944, followed by ten in February, twenty in March, eighteen in April and the final forty-nine in May.

Inside the superstructure were ammunition racks allowing them to transport forty 15 cm howitzer rounds. The commonality of chassis with the self-propelled howitzer was advantageous for parts supply and driver and support personnel training standpoints. Further, the design of the ammunition carriers was such that the additional ammunition stowage racks could be removed, along with the plating closing the weapon aperture, and a howitzer installed. This allowed the field conversion of the vehicle into an armed *Grille*, providing the units with a ready source of spare chassis for repair.

Geschützwagen 38 für Munition (SdKfz 138/1) Ausf K

Specifications	
Length	4.845 m
Width	2.150 m
Height	2.400 m
Weight	11.5 tons
Fuel capacity	218 liters
Maximum speed	42 km/hr
Range, on-road	185 km
Range, cross-country	140 km
Crew	5
Communication	FuG 5
Armament	
Ammo stowage	40 15-cm rounds
Armor	20 mm hull front
	15 mm hull sides
	10 mm superstructure
Automotive	
Engine make	Praga
Engine model	AC
Engine configuration	6-cylinder, liquid cooled
Engine displacement	7.75 liters
Engine horsepower	150 @ 2600 rpm

Geschützwagen III/IV für Munition (SdKfz 165)

Specifications	
Length	7.17 m
Width	2.97 m
Height	2.81 m
Weight	23 tons
Fuel capacity	600 liters
Maximum speed	42 km/hr
Range, on-road	200 km
Range, cross-country	130 km
Crew	6
Communications	Fu Spr Ger f
Armament	
Ammo stowage	48 15-cm rounds
Armor	30 mm hull front
	20 mm hull sides
	10 mm superstructure
Automotive	
Engine make	Maybach
Engine model	HL 120 TRM
Engine configuration	V-12, liquid cooled
Engine displacement	11.9 liters
Engine horsepower	265 @ 2600 rpm

Geschützwagen III/IV für Munition (SdKfz 165)

The ammunition stowage on board the *Hummel* was extremely limited. The vehicle did not have enough on-board ammunition for a sustained bombardment.

To fill this void, an ammunition carrier was developed that utilized not only the same chassis but also the same superstructure. Such a design ensured that the mobility of these vehicles was similar to that of the *Hummel* (unlike the situation of using half-tracks or trucks for ammunition transport), but operation, repair procedures, and parts were as well.

Frequently called the *Munitionsfahrzeug* III/IV (ammunition carrier), the vehicle was properly designated *Geschützwagen* III/IV *für Munition* (SdKfz 165).

Production of these vehicles began in May 1943, and continued intermittently until November 1944. Production totaled 157 units.

Because these vehicles utilized so much of the standard *Hummel*, this allowed the munitions carriers to be converted to the parent self-propelled howitzer if the situation warranted. This was done by removing the armor plate in the front of the munitions carrier superstructure, which closed the opening through which the gun tube would protrude, removing the ammo racks, and installing the howitzer and mount from a donor *Hummel*.

The munitions carriers were intended two per battery.

Chapter 8
Armored Engineer and Support Vehicles

Although for many, the tanks of an army are the "glamorous" vehicles, the reality is that no army could function without a myriad of support vehicles, both combat engineer vehicles and logistical support vehicles.

These oft-forgotten vehicles are the subject of this chapter. While some are wholly specialized vehicles, built from the ground up for a specific purpose, others are adaptations of combat vehicles, providing a commonality of parts and maintenance requirements.

Abwurfvorrichtungen on Panzerkampfwagen I

For years the *Abwurfvorrichtungen*, translated literally "explosive charge dropper" on *Panzerkampfwagen* I has been misidentified as a *Ladungsleger*, or "explosive charge carrier."

Two arms extending from the rear of the vehicle supported the explosive charge, which could weigh up to 50 kgs. The intent was that the vehicle was to be maneuvered so that it could place (or, more accurately, drop) explosive charges on bunkers and obstacles. The dropping action was controlled from within the armored confines of the tank.

Pursuant to orders issued on December 28, 1939, one hundred *Abwurfvorrichtungen* (the charge dropping device) were to be procured. These devices were to be issued ten per Panzer Division. On March 4, 1940, new orders were

Above: *There were two versions of the explosive-charge-laying PzKpfw I. The idea was to use a buttoned-up tank to deliver an explosive charge against pillboxes and other fortifications. The first was known as* Ladungsleger I auf PzKpfw I Ausf B. *Only two were made. The second, more widely used version was called PzKpfw I (MG) (SdKfz 101) mit Abwurfvorrichtung and it is seen here.* Patton Museum

issued to create a *Panzer-Pionier-Kompanie* (armored engineer company) within each Panzer Division.

Each *Panzer-Pionier-Kompanie* was to have two demolition platoons, each with five Panzer I Ausf B. The *Abwurfvorrichtungen* would be installed on these vehicles.

Above: *The PzKpfw I (MG) (SdKfz 101) mit Abwurfvorrichtung used a cable-operated arm to deploy a charge that weighed up to 50 kg that was detonated by remote control. This vehicle carries a 7th Panzer Division marking on the hull side. Ten of these vehicles were issued to the* Panzer Pionere Kompanie *of the original ten Panzer divisions in two platoons of five vehicles each in 1940.* Patton Museum

B I *Minenräum-Wagen* (SdKfz 300)

This small vehicle was developed by Borgward for use clearing minefields. Capable of being driven either directly or via remote control, the concrete-bodied vehicle was designed to tow a set of mine-clearing rollers, as well as carrying a demolition charge internally. Born of the experiences in Poland, it was intended that this secret vehicle would be used in France.

Development work began in late 1939 and by May 1940 the full order of fifty B I *Minenräum-Wagen* (SdKfz 300) vehicles had been completed. Twenty of these were sent to Kiel for installation of the radio-control equipment, with the remaining thirty sent to Bremen for the same purpose. Once completed, the vehicles were assigned to the *Minen-Räum-Kompanie* of *Panzer-Abteilung* 67 on June 1, 1940. In order to preserve the secrecy of the vehicles, this unit was known as Kompanie Glienicke until ready for service.

Powered by a 1.5 liter Borgward liquid-cooled engine driving through a two-speed transmission, the 1.5-ton vehicle had a top speed of 5 km/hr.

Ultimately, the unit did not see action in France, and the B I *Minenräum-Wagen* saw no service beyond training.

B II *Minenräum-Wagen* (SdKfz 300)

A follow-on vehicle to the B I *Minenräum-Wagen*, the B II was also produced by Borgward. Longer and heavier than the first series, the B II also had armor plate on the front of the concrete hull, protecting the equipment inside from small-arms fire.

While weighing only 2.3 tons, the second-series vehicle could carry a larger charge, up to 300 kg. The concussion of an exploding 300-kilogram charge would detonate mines in a 20-meter radius around the vehicle. A six-cylinder,

Above: *Due to its experiences in Poland, the German Army developed a need to quickly clear minefields. For this task they developed several remote-controlled vehicles. Among the first was the SdKfz 300 Minenräum-Wagen Borgward B I a radio-controlled, 1.5-ton vehicle that towed mine-detonating rollers. Fifty were made and were issued to Minenraum-Abteilung 1 (mine-clearing battalion). This is the prototype.* Patton Museum

Above: *The underside and suspension of the SdKfz 300 Minenräum-Wagen Borgward B I was designed to be proof against the denotation of mines, but this proved to be practical only in the case of small antipersonnel mines. An amphibian version was also conceived, known as the Ente (Duck). These machines were controlled from a Kleiner Panzer Befehlswagen I (SdKfz 265).* Patton Museum

ARMORED ENGINEER AND SUPPORT VEHICLES

49-horsepower engine drove the vehicle through a two-speed gearbox, giving it a top speed of 5 km/hr. Like its predecessor, it could tow mine rollers, or carry a charge that could be detonated by remote control.

The command vehicle, a variation of the Panzer I, could control two *Minenräum-Wagen* simultaneously.

Production of the vehicles began in July 1940, with the first combat use of the vehicle being in the opening stages of Operation Barbarossa in June 1941. Using troops reported the vehicle to be ineffectual, as the chassis was slow, unable to navigate difficult terrain, and their charges were too easily set off.

"Goliath" *leichte Ladungsträger* (SdKfz 302 & 303)

Developed by Borgward, the three versions of this vehicle were among the most interesting German engineered vehicles, at least in the eyes of the average GI or Tommy encountering them.

These tethered remote-controlled demolition vehicles were about five feet long and weighed less than a half ton. Consistent with the tongue-in-cheek naming of certain German vehicles (the 200-ton superheavy tank was named "mouse"), this vehicle's name was Goliath.

Development of the vehicle began in 1940 when Borgward was ordered to create a very small electrically powered vehicle capable of placing a charge of about 50 kgs.

Goliath SdKfz 302

Specifications	
Length	1.50 m
Width	.85 m
Height	.56 m
Weight	370 kg
Fuel capacity	2 batteries
Maximum speed	10 km/hr
Range, on-road	1.5 km
Range, cross-country	.8 km
Armament	
Explosive charge	60 kg
Armor	6 mm front
Automotive	
Power plant	2 x 2.5 kw motor

Goliath SdKfz 303a

Specifications	
Length	1.62 m
Width	.84 m
Height	.60 m
Weight	365 kg
Fuel capacity	6 liter
Maximum speed	11 km/hr
Range, on-road	12 km
Range, cross-country	6-8 km
Armament	
Explosive charge	75 kg
Armor	10 mm front
Automotive	
Engine make	Zundapp
Engine configuration	2-cylinder, 2 stroke
Engine displacement	703 cc
Engine horsepower	12.5 @ 4500 rpm

The design that was approved was powered by two electric motors and carried a 60 kg charge. Control of the vehicle was via a wire which unwound out of the rear compartment of the vehicle as it advanced.

Despite being protected by a 6 mm armor plate at the front, in practice the vehicles were easily defeated either by small-arms fire through the unarmored sides, or by merely severing the control cable.

Production of this vehicle, which was given the *Sonderkraftfahrzeug* (special purpose vehicle—SdKfz) number 302, began in April 1942. The considerable expense of the vehicles, along with the limitations, in particular the vulnerability of the electric drive, led to production being discontinued in January 1944, after 2,635 had been completed.

This was not the end of Goliath, however. In April 1943 a much improved, slightly larger version entered production. Assigned SdKfz number 303, other than a slight increase in size, the most dramatic change was the use of a two-stroke Zundapp gasoline engine to power the diminutive tracklaying vehicle. The frontal armor was upgraded to 10 mm, and strangely the gasoline-powered variant seemed more tolerant of small-arms fire than was the electric model,

Goliath SdKfz 303b

Specifications	
Length	1.69 m
Width	.91 m
Height	.62 m
Weight	430 kg
Fuel capacity	6 liter
Maximum speed	11.5 km/hr
Range, on-road	12 km
Range, cross-country	.6-8 km
Armament	
Explosive charge	100 kg
Armor	10 mm front
Automotive	
Engine make	Zundapp
Engine configuration	2-cylinder, 2 stroke
Engine displacement	703 cc
Engine horsepower	12.5 @ 4500 rpm

Above: The second version of the Goliath was known as the SdKfz 302b (V-Motor). This was powered by a Zündapp SZ7 two-cylinder, two-stroke engine and was larger and could carry more explosives. The manufacturers Zündapp and Zachertz built 325 units by November 1944. Regardless of the type, a control-wire drum was located at the rear of the vehicle that contained a three-strand wire, two strands for driving the vehicle and a third for detonating the charge. For transport the Goliath could be mounted and towed on a two-wheeled trailer. Patton Museum.

Above: Among the most numerous of the German anti-mine vehicles was the Leichte Ladungsträger Goliath SdKfz 302. This was a small wire-guided vehicle designed for minefield clearance, destruction of enemy installations or in extreme cases, as an antitank weapon. The Goliath measured only about 1.5 meters, and the initial version was considered too small and underpowered. This version was known as SdKfz 302a (E-Motor) and was powered by two Bosch MM/RQL 2500/24 RL2 electric motors. Borgward and Zündapp produced 2,650 units of this type from April 1942 to January 1944. Patton Museum

but nevertheless some of the handicaps remained. Among these, the vulnerability of the sides, and the reliance on the rear spooling wire leading to the tethered remote control.

A total of 4,929 gasoline-powered versions of the SdKfz 303 were produced in two models, the SdKfz 303b having a slightly larger payload charge of 100 kgs, compared to 75 kgs for the SdKfz 303a.

The Goliath began to be issued in January 1942, and was first used near Sevastopol in June. Additional units were created and equipped with 162 Goliath each beginning in October 1942. By 1944 the SdKfz 303 was being issued thirty-each to normal Pioneer (Engineer) battalions.

Sprengladungsträger (SdKfz 301) Ausf A and B

While interest in remote-controlled charge layers remained high within the German Army High Command, by October 1941 none of the efforts advanced had produced the desired results. Once again, the *Waffenamt* turned to Borgward, Bremen, as their prime contractor to create a new series of these vehicles.

Unlike the prior efforts, the new design, designated B IV, was not inherently destroyed as a result of its use.

Borgward drew heavily on their VK 302 munitions carrier design. When placing a charge, the premise of the new design was that a driver could advance the vehicle to a point

B IV *Sprengladungsträger* Ausf A

Specifications	
Length	3.650 m
Width	1.800 m
Height	1.185 m
Weight	3.6 tons (4-ton Ausf B)
Fuel capacity	123 liters
Maximum speed	38 km/hr
Range, on-road	200 km
Range, cross-country	125 km
Crew	1
Communications	EP, UKE6 receiver
Armament	
Explosive charge	500 kg
Automotive	
Engine make	Borgward
Engine model	6M 2.3 RTBV
Engine configuration	6-cylinder, liquid cooled
Engine displacement	2.247 liters
Engine horsepower	49 @ 3300 rpm

Above: *The larger Schwere Sprengladungsträger (SdKfz 301) preceded the Goliath by a few years. Designed as a further evolution of the SdKfz 300, it was to be driven to a specific point, where the driver would depart, and then guided to its eventual destination via radio control. A five-hundred-kilogram charge was secured to the front of the vehicle that was to be dropped by the driver and then the vehicle backed away prior to detonation. The Sprengladungsträger could be used multiple times, unlike earlier concepts that were destroyed in use. Patton Museum*

Above: *The SdKfz 301 is occasionally referred to as the Borgward IV, or simply B IV. Two versions of were produced, Ausf A and B. The Ausf A had only a windshield to protect the driver while the Ausf B had side and rear armor in addition to frontal armor. Folding armored flaps were also provided to protect the driver, as well as an escape hatch. The Sprengladungsträger were issued to radio-controlled tank companies. The units were controlled from either Panzer IIIs or Sturmgeschütze. Patton Museum*

near where the charge was to be placed. The driver would then exit the vehicle, and the vehicle continue on its way via radio control. Once in position, the 500-kilogram demolition charge on the front of the vehicle would be released (by radio control), and would slide off the vehicle into position. The now-empty carrier would then be backed out of harm's away prior to detonation of the charge, allowing the carrier to be used again.

Alternatively, the B IV could be driven into a minefield by remote control. Should the B IV hit a mine, the blast pressure would close a belly-mounted pressure switch on the vehicle, setting off the vehicle's own 500-kilogram demolition charge, the concussion from which would then set off any other mines in a 20-meter radius.

Production of a trial series of a dozen B IV a was completed in April 1942. Series production began the next month, and totaled 616 vehicles. This was superseded by the B IV b, which included improvements in the radio system as well as the addition of dry-pin tracks, frontal armor, folding armored flaps to protect the driver, as well as an escape hatch on the right side of the hull. Production of the B IV b reached 260 units before being terminated in December 1943.

Above: *The bin containing the explosives was disengaged by the driver along the sliding front plate of the vehicle. Distance markers were provided to help the operator more precisely gauge the point at which the charge was dropped. The charge was equipped with a delayed-action fuse. Approximately 615 Ausf A, 260 Ausf B and 300 Ausf C were produced. The vehicles were issued and formed into* Panzerabteilungen (Funklenk), *or Tank Battalions (radio controlled).* Patton Museum

Above: *A Schwere Sprengladungsträger (SdKfz 301) Ausf C was introduced in December 1943. It featured increased armored protection and a simplified suspension and was considered cheaper and easier to manufacture. The Ausf C also had a larger 78-horsepower engine compared to the 49-horsepower engine of the Ausf A and B. Immediately apparent here are the thinner and less elaborate roadwheels, as well as the basic-looking dry-pin tracks. The Ausf A and B had more complex lubricated and padded tracks typically associated with German half-tracks.* Patton Museum

The *Sprengladungsträger* were issued to light tank companies, who used *Panzerkampfwagen* III or *Sturmgeschütz* as control vehicles.

Schwere Ladungsträger (SdKfz 301) Ausf C

Reports from the field indicated that there was room for improvement in the B IV, particularly in the areas of protection and maneuverability. Accordingly, the vehicle was redesigned, and the Ausf C introduced. The chassis was lengthened, the driver's compartment was relocated to the left side of the vehicle, and the escape hatch, which had just been introduced with the Ausf B, was eliminated. A more powerful 6-cylinder engine was installed, forcing a redesign of the rear of the vehicle, and armor protection was increased to 20 mm.

Production of this version of the *Ladungsträger* began in December 1943 and continued until a directive from Reich Minister for Weapons, Munitions, and Armaments Albert Speer ordered production halted in October 1944. At that time, just over three hundred of the four hundred vehicles ordered had been completed.

These vehicles were utilized and deployed in the same manner as their predecessors, but Tiger I tanks were frequently used as control vehicles.

B IV c schwere Ladungsträger

Specifications	
Length	4.10 m
Width	1.83 m
Height	1.25 m
Weight	4.8 tons
Fuel capacity	135 liters
Maximum speed	40 km/hr
Range, on-road	250 km
Range, cross-country	125 km
Crew	1
Communications	EP, UKE6
Armament	
Explosive charge	500 kg
Automotive	
Engine make	Borgward
Engine model	6B 3.8 TV
Engine configuration	6-cylinder, liquid cooled
Engine displacement	3,745 liters
Engine horsepower	78 @ 3000 rpm

ARMORED ENGINEER AND SUPPORT VEHICLES

Above: *This rear view reveals details of the box-like hull construction. The side hull was 20 mm thick. The spaced panels over the engine air intakes were 15 mm. Marker lights mounted on stalks helped address the difficulty of seeing the vehicle from a distance in relation to its target. In December 1944, several SdKfz 301 Ausf C were in service with the 301st Schwere Panzerabteilung (Funklenk), where they were controlled by specially outfitted Tiger Is. Very late in the war, improvised tank destroyers were created by mounting rocket launchers in metal frames on the tops of the SdKfz 301 Ausf C. Patton Museum*

Mittlerer Ladungsträger "Springer" (SdKfz 304)

The early discontinuance of the *Schwere Ladungsträger* Ausf C was made possible in part due to the advancing development of this vehicle, the *Mittlerer Ladungsträger*, popularly known as the "Springer." This vehicle marked the abandonment of the concept of the reusable demolition vehicle, and a return to the self-destructive model used early on.

However, for this vehicle the army turned not to Borgward, but rather to the NSU Werke AG at Neckarsulm, Germany, builder of the NSU Kettenkraftrad—the famous German "Half-track motorcycle."

To create the *Mittlerer Ladungsträger*, additional roadwheels and idler were added to the chassis, and the front wheel and steering fork eliminated.

The vehicle, which was powered by an Opel Olympia engine, could transport a 350-kilogram demolition charge, which was carried internally.

Trial vehicles were undergoing troop testing in September 1943, with series production scheduled to begin in May 1945. However, Albert Speer's canceling of manufacturing of the *Schwere Ladungsträger* Ausf C in October 1944 brought with it the beginning of series production of the Springer. The first nine production models were completed in October, followed by sixteen in November, ten in December, and nine in January 1944, with the final six being built in February.

The vehicle was designed to be controlled either by a driver on board or through radio signals. It is not known if the vehicle ever saw combat.

Minenräumgerät mit PzKpfwAntrieb

Little is known about this vehicle, the sole example of which was captured by US forces. Based on the *Panzerkampfwagen* III, the suspension was extended considerably in order to distance the hull from the blast of exploding mines. The design included a forward-projecting boom carrying mine rollers, but this arrangement proved unwieldy and difficult to control.

Schweres Minenraumfahrzeug "Raumer-S"

This odd-looking vehicle was designed by Krupp with the apparent intent of exploding mines with its reinforced wheels. The wheels were heavily constructed to withstand the mine blast, the suspension robust to absorb some of the shock, the wheels large in diameter so as to not be swallowed by a hole in the road, the result of a mine blast, and the crew compartment well elevated above any potential

Springer mittler Ladungsträger

Specifications	
Length	3.15 m
Width	1.43 m
Height	1.45 m
Weight	2.4 tons
Fuel capacity	65 liters
Maximum speed	42 km/hr
Range, on-road	200 km
Range, cross-country	80 km
Crew	1
Communications	KE6, UKE6 reciever
Armament	
Explosive charge	330 kg
Automotive	
Engine make	Opel
Engine model	Olympia
Engine configuration	4-cylinder, liquid cooled
Engine displacement	1.5 liters
Engine horsepower	38

Above: *Further economic measures resulted in the development of the Mittlere Ladungstrager SdKfz 304 Springer. Designed as a replacement for both the Goliath and the Borgward IV, it incorporated many of the components of the Kleines Kettenkraftrad SdKfz 2. As such it was a product of that machine's manufacturer, NSU. Fifty examples were built from October 1944 to February 1945. Like its predecessors, the operator left the vehicle near the target zone and directed it onward using radio control. At 2.4-tons, it weighed less than half as much as the Borgward IV but could carry only 330 kg of explosive.* Patton Museum

Above: *The Kettenkrad lineage is also apparent in this photograph. With the driver's armor collapsed, the vehicle had a very sleek and low profile. The interleaved suspension provided a somewhat more stable operating platform. Although never realized, it had been intended for the Springer to also be used as a basis for a light self-propelled gun, known as a Kleinpanzer Wanze. It would have mounted the 10.5 cm IG recoilless gun.* Patton Museum

Above: *A single prototype of a Minenräumpanzer III was produced, and, as the name implies, it was loosely based on components of the Panzer III. The concept involved raising and reinforcing the hull, allowing mine detonations to dissipate. This side view illustrates how the original torsion bars have been integrated into a new heavy-duty suspension unit. The entire vehicle was meant to anchor a large boom that contained mine-detonation equipment.* Patton Museum

Above: *The prototype Minenräumpanzer III was captured at the end of the war and returned to the United States for evaluation, where these photos were taken. The boom was not part of the recovery, but it is speculated that the vehicle itself was not intended to be the main detonation device; rather that task was designed for the equipment on the boom. The reinforcement of the running gear was only as insurance against those mines missed by the boom. It is interesting to note that the drive sprocket on this vehicle is that of the Panzer III D.* Patton Museum

blast area, and also allowing the concussive force to dissipate out the sides beneath the vehicle.

The articulated machine had an engine and driver's position in each end. Total seating was eight men, with four in each end. In part this was due to the immense size of the 130-ton machine, which meant even with its hydraulic articulation, the turning radius would have been huge. With a driver in each end, the amount of severe turns would be reduced.

Above: *Perhaps the most extreme example of a detonation vehicle is the Schweres Minenräumfahrzeug. Built in 1944 by Krupp, it was loosely based on an earlier three-wheeled concept that used large-track shoes. The Schweres Minenräumfahrzeu weighed in at 130 tons and was composed of two huge wheeled units, each with its own Maybach HL90 engine and attached to one another with an articulated joint. The wheels measured nearly nine feet and each set was spaced to clear a solid path. At the end of the war, US troops captured the single prototype.* Patton Museum

Above: *Due to the number and complexity of the fortifications and water obstacles in Poland and France, the Germans prepared several vehicles to deal with them. Their initial efforts centered on the Panzer I. When this configuration turned out to be insubstantial, the Brückenleger auf Panzerkampfwagen II was created. Chassis of the Panzer II Ausf D and Ausf C were converted by the firm Magirus. It mounted an 11-meter bridge in two sections. The 7th Panzer Division used four while deployed in France in May 1940, where this shot was taken.* Patton Museum

Even though development of this vehicle began in 1942, at the end of the war only a sole example existed, which the US captured at Krupp's Hillersleben works. The vehicle was dismantled to be shipped to 0-644 Ordnance Depot near Paris. US experts opined that there was more planned for the apparatus then they were seeing, as the narrow wheels, even if spaced differently front to rear, could clear only a 1.06 meter lane, far less than one would expect from such a huge machine.

Brückenleger II

Rivers and chasms have delayed advancing armies for time immemorial. It was natural then that Germany developed a means of overcoming these type of obstacles as part of their doctrine of rapidly advancing mechanized warfare. As early as 1939 the *Waffenamt* was developing armored vehicle launched bridges.

For bridges of an 8-ton capacity, the *Panzerkampfwagen* II chassis was selected for the basis. A single trial vehicle was produced and tested, after whch a small production of three vehicles were ordered. MAN completed these three *Brückenleger* on Panzer II chassis in 1939, and additional similar vehicles were created using Panzer II combat tanks. Total production is unknown.

Brückenleger IV

A heavier bridge, with an 18-ton capacity, was designed for installation on Panzer IV chassis. Krupp initially assembled such a vehicle on their proposed BW II chassis, which featured torsion-bar suspension.

In June and July 1939 Krupp completed six *Panzerkampfwagen* IV Ausf C chassis for use as a basis of such vehicles. While Krupp built the pilot and first four production models, they requested that Magirus be tasked with assembling the armored bridgelaying equipment on the remaining sixteen vehicles contracted for at that time.

Ultimately, Krupp would complete ten and Magirus ten of these vehicles, utilizing a mix of Panzer IV Ausf C and Ausf D chassis. All twenty had been completed by the end of April 1940.

These vehicles, except for the mild-steel prototype, were issued in platoons of four to the Engineer Companies of the 1st, 2nd, 3rd, 5th, and 10th Panzer Divisions for use in France and Belgium. Their usage in these areas proved to be less than successful, resulting in the scrapping of plans to produce a further sixty vehicles.

However, an experimental series of four *Brückenleger* IV c was built in January 1941. These were used with some success on the Eastern Front by the 3rd Panzer Division. Of

Left: *Krupp's initial effort to create an 18-ton-capacity armored vehicle–launched bridge was this vehicle, which was based on their BW II chassis.* Patton Museum

Left: *The production 18-ton armored vehicle launched bridge was similar in concept, but utilized the standard Panzer IV Ausf C or Ausf D chassis and was known as the* Brückenleger IV b, *or sometimes as BL IV. The bridge was placed using a pivoting structure activated by cables. The bridging sections could each deploy a stand on the forward end, enabling the creation of a raised platform for surmounting obstacles such as those seen here.* Patton Museum

ARMORED ENGINEER AND SUPPORT VEHICLES 223

Left: *The utility of the forward-mounted stands is clearly demonstrated here, where two bridges are being used to cross a substantial gap. The vehicle here is one of the four experimental Brückenleger IV c built in 1941 and used with some success on the Eastern Front by the 3rd Panzer Division.* Patton Museum

Left: *Only four Panzer IV-based Sturmstegpanzer were produced, all based on the Panzer IV Ausf C chassis and deployed on the Russian Front. Consisting of an aerial firefighting ladder mounted on a tank chassis, the vehicle was intended to provide infantry a rapid means for crossing obstacles.* Patton Museum

note is that in the interest of speed, the bridging equipment of the IV c was transported by truck and transferred to the armored chassis just prior to emplacement.

Brückenleger IV s (Sturmstegpanzer)

Another variation of bridging equipment mounted on the *Panzerkampfwagen* IV chassis was the *Sturmstegpanzer*. These vehicles were created in order to aid infantry in crossing rivers, streams, and ravines. Looking very much like just what they were, aerial firefighting ladders adapted to tank hulls, these ladders could be extended across rivers and gaps. Two vehicles could be parked parallel to each other, the ladders extended, and bridging timbers laid between them to allow even more rapid troop movement. Only four of these vehicles were built in early 1941. The chassis used were those of *Panzerkampfwagen* IV Ausf C. The Third Panzer Division took these vehicles with them to Russia in 1941. There, the vehicles were used on July 16 to cross the Bassin River near Tschauschy. The glowing after-action report stated "the BL IV s *Sturmstegpanzer* has proven to be an excellent bridge for infantry to cross."

Land-Wasser-Schlepper

Work developing these unusual vehicles began in May 1935. It was a result of the combined efforts of Alkett, Huettenwerke, Rheinmetall-Borsig, Sachsenberg, and

Above: *Designed primarily as a towing vehicle for German army engineer units, the* Land-Wasser-Schlepper *was essentially a tracked boat. It was also to be used as a ferry in amphibious operations. The LWS could tow the Kässbohrer amphibious trailer and in that case was capable of transporting up to ten to twenty tons of freight. Weighing seventeen tons, the LWS used the same HL120 engine mounted in the Panzer III and Panzer IV and could carry up to twenty men in addition to its crew of two.* Patton Museum

Above: *Twin rear-mounted tunneled propellers and twin rudders propelled the LWS in the water up to about 7.5 mph. On land, the* Land-Wasser-Schlepper *with its steel-shod tracks and eight bogies could reach a speed of 21 mph. Seven preproduction units has been produced by mid-1940, but its lack of common parts made it a logistical dead end. The LWS saw service on both the Eastern and North African fronts.* Patton Museum

Land-Wasser-Schlepper

Specifications	
Length	9.0 m
Width	3.0 m
Height	3.15 m
Weight	15 tons
Fuel capacity	600 liters
Maximum speed, land	40 km/hr
Maximum speed, water	12.5 km/hr
Crew	3
Automotive	
Engine make	Maybach
Engine model	HL 120 TRM
Engine configuration	V-12, liquid cooled
Engine displacement	11.9 liters
Engine horsepower	265 @ 2600 rpm

Maybach to produce a vehicle to fulfill the army's broad requirement.

The objective was to produce a single vehicle that could be a tractor, tugboat, and a ferry. For such use the vehicle had a boat-shaped hull, beneath which were tracks. During the development period various numbers of roadwheels and return rollers were tried.

As the *Land-Wasser-Schlepper* was intended for use by engineers in a support role, it was neither armed nor armored. Delivery of four trial vehicles began in late 1940 and was complete by the end of December.

These were followed by a small production series, to be delivered at the rate of two per month from March through June 1941. This was to be followed by yet another contract for fourteen further vehicles, to be delivered from July 1942 through September 1943.

With such small production numbers and slow rate of delivery, it is not surprising multiple variations of this vehicle were produced as feedback from the field was incorporated into product improvement.

A Maybach HL120TRM engine drove the vehicle both on the ground and in the water, with water propulsion being through two 800 mm propellers. Its 600-liter fuel tank allowed it to operate for about six hours without refueling.

Little information about the operational use of these vehicles has surfaced, but at least one is known to have been sent to North Africa with *Pionier-Landungs-Kompanie* 778. Four were assigned to Pz Abt 100 to be part of Operation Sea Lion, where in addition to towing assault barges they were also to be used to pull 10-ton and 20-ton capacity amphibious trailers. Others were used in the Ukraine and Estonia.

Panzerfähre

Rather than the Jack-of-all-trades intent of the *Landwasserschlepper*, the *Panzerfähre* was developed especially to transport tanks and other combat vehicles across water while under fire.

The bold concept was that two of these vehicles, with decking between them, would work as a normal ferry, shuttling across rivers and lakes.

Work on these odd armored vehicles began on April 19, 1941, with metalwork starting in July. Magirus did the final assembly, although a host of other firms were also involved in the production of the two experimental vehicles. The vehicles shared a powertrain with the Panzer IV, and had armor protection proof against small-arms fire.

Thirteen months after the project began, two prototypes were delivered. The initial road and water tests indicated

Above: *A more sensible replacement for the LWS was considered, and Marigus was again called upon to produce two prototypes. The* Panzerfähre*, as it became known, was now lightly armored with 14.5 mm of protection. It still weighed in at seventeen tons. The* Panzerfähre *used the drivetrain, motor, and tracks of the Panzer IV Ausf F, making it a more practical vehicle to produce. The driver, co-driver, and radio operator sat in the armored structure just before the air intakes. The first of two prototype vehicles were completed on May 15, 1942.* Patton Museum

Panzerfähre

Specifications	
Length	8.25 m
Width	2.8 m
Height	2.5 m
Weight	17 tons
Automotive	
Engine make	Maybach
Engine model	HL 120 TRM
Engine configuration	V-12, liquid cooled
Engine displacement	11.9 liters
Engine horsepower	265 @ 2600 rpm

that some changes were necessary, but the overall design was sound.

The ferry deck was supported by roller chain, connected to winches on the two *Panzerfähre* supporting the platform. This system, intended to keep the unit stable and level, proved unworkable.

No further *Panzerfähre* were produced.

Chapter 9
Armored Recovery Vehicles

Combat tanks are enormously expensive, and always have been. During World War II on average, less weapons, a Panzer III cost 96,200 *Riechsmarks*, a Panzer IV RM 103,500, and a PzKpfw V Panther RM 117,000. This puts the cost of the Panzer III at roughly $41,000 at the time. As an aside, a US Sherman was priced comparably to the Panzer III and Panzer IV. By comparison, in 1939 a new Cadillac model 61 cost $1,345, an average US house was $4,000, and the average US annual wage was $1,800.

Clearly, all nations had a vested interest in recovering repairable tanks from the battlefield as quickly as possible. In order to do this under difficult conditions, which may include enemy fire, specialized equipment needed to be developed, with emphasis on towing capacity, floatation, and armor protection.

It is not surprising then that many nations, including Germany, adapted tank chassis for use as armored recovery vehicles.

Bergepanzer 38(t)

In order to create a light armored recovery vehicle, Germany utilized the proven Czech 38(t) undercarriage, in the form of the *Jagdpanzer* 38(t) chassis.

Dubbed the *Bergepanzer* 38(t), as initially produced the vehicle was not equipped with a winch or ground spade. Instead, the vehicle was an open-top prime mover outfitted with basic repair and towing equipment. Provisions were made for installing a jib boom on the right side of the vehicle.

Beginning in February, however, the *Bergepanzer* 38(t) became a much more formidable recovery vehicle with the introduction of an internally mounted winch and rear-mounted ground anchor spade. Using both these items in concert allowed the *Bergepanzer* 38(t) to retrieve even vehicles even larger than itself.

Production of the *Bergepanzer* 38(t) (SdKfz 136) was begun in May 1944 by Boehmisch-Mahrische Maschinenfabrik in Prague. The 181 recovery vehicles were produced alongside *Jagdpanzer* 38s through April 1945. Like the *Jagdpanzer* 38(t), a variety of idlers and roadwheels were used throughout production of the *Bergepanzer* 38(t).

One *Bergepanzer* 38(t) was supplied to each Jagdpanzer unit equipped with the *Jagdpanzer* 38(t).

Bergepanzer III SdKfz 144

The original intent of the German military was to use the powerful 18-ton half-track as their recovery vehicle. However, not only could supply not keep up with demand for the big half-tracks, the weight of German tanks continued to climb upward, to the point were it would take several half-tracks to tow a single tank.

Thus the decision was made to begin using tank chassis as recovery vehicles. While initially this was done with the Panther chassis, by March 1944 other tanks began to be adapted to the recovery role as well. To ease maintenance and facilitate parts availability, typically each unit's recovery

Bergepanzer 38(t)

Specifications	
Length	4.87 m without ground anchor
Width	2.63 m
Height	1.97 m
Weight	13 tons
Fuel capacity	320 liters
Maximum speed	40 km/hr
Range, on-road	180 km
Range, cross-country	130 km
Crew	2
Armament	
Weapon, main	7.92 mm MG
Ammo stowage, main	600 rounds
Automotive	
Engine make	Praga
Engine model	AC
Engine configuration	6-cylinder, liquid cooled
Engine displacement	7.75 liters
Engine horsepower	150 hp @ 2600 rpm

Left: *The Bergepanzer 38(t) was an armored recovery vehicle intended to be assigned to Jagdpanzer 38(t) Hetzer units. Essentially, the Bergepanzer 38(t) consisted of a Hetzer chassis and hull with the superstructure lowered to the level of the top of the driver's visor, resulting in an open compartment for equipment and crewmen. A 2-ton jib boom and tow bars were stored on the sides of the superstructure. The first Bergepanzer 38(t) vehicles were available in May 1944; total production was 181, all of which were built by Boehmisch-Mahrische Maschinenfabrik, Prague, Czechoslovakia.* US Army Ordnance Museum

Above: *In an upper-rear view of a Bergepanzer 38(t), the driver's seat and instrument panel are visible in the left front of the open superstructure. Supports for erecting the jib boom were attached to the upper part of the superstructure. One of them is above the driver's compartment, a second one is on the outside of the front right corner of the superstructure, and a third is near the right rear corner of the interior of the superstructure. The tow bars, when in use, were coupled to the beam on the rear of the hull. This example was completed in November 1944.* Patton Museum

ARMORED RECOVERY VEHICLES

Above: Bergepanzer 38(t) chassis number 322678, completed in February 1945, bears a camouflage paint scheme and is equipped with a rear spade and a canvas top. The disassembled jib boom is stored in brackets on the left side of the superstructure. The spade and a winch housed in the right side of the hull were introduced in February 1945. Patton Museum

Above: The spade is raised to its travel position in a right-rear photo of Bergepanzer 38(t) chassis number 322678. Stored in brackets on the right side of the superstructure are the tow bars. A jack is stored on the right rear fender. The winch cable issues out through an opening on the right side of the engine deck; the loop of the cable is jutting to the rear of a cable guide attached to the engine deck. Patton Museum

Bergepanzer III (SdKfz 144)

Specifications	
Length	5.52 m
Width	2.97 m
Height	2.40 m
Weight	20 tons
Fuel capacity	320 liters
Maximum speed	42 km/hr
Range, on-road	155 km
Range, cross-country	95 km
Crew	2
Armament	
Weapon, main	7.92 mm MG 34
Ammo stowage, main	600 rounds
Automotive	
Engine make	Maybach
Engine model	HL 120 TRM
Engine configuration	V-12, liquid cooled
Engine displacement	11.9 liters
Engine horsepower	265 @ 2600 rpm

Right: *In the foreground, an Instandsetzungskraftwagen (maintenance or repair vehicle), a conversion based on a PzKpfw III tank chassis, is parked in front of a PzKpfw III. The Instandsetzungskraftwagen was effected by removing the superstructure, resulting in an open compartment for storing tools, parts, and, according to reports, additional batteries for starting disabled vehicles. A tarpaulin covers the compartment on this example.* Patton Museum

Above: *The* Bergepanzer III (SdKfz 144) *was an armored recovery vehicle based on PzKpfw III chassis. A total of 176 were converted between March and November 1944 and January 1945. The turret of the tank was removed, and a wooden platform was erected atop the superstructure. This platform, which had wooden sides, was used for carrying recovery equipment, including tow bars, a jib boom, and tackle. From the spring of 1944,* Bergepanzer IIIs *serving on the Eastern Front often were furnished with* Ostketten *widened tracks, and these tracks are present on this vehicle. Note the log carried on holders on the left side of the wooden box, and the squared wooden beam on the right side.* Patton Museum

vehicle would share a common chassis with that unit's tanks.

One of these adaptations was the *Bergepanzerwagen* III, which not surprisingly was created using Panzer III chassis. Production of these vehicles, utilizing rebuilt Panzer III chassis as a basis, was begun in March 1944. The construction of these vehicles amounted to installing a heavy wooden box in the area formerly occupied by the tank's turret. This box was used to stow the recovery equipment, which included tow bars and couplings, a jib boom, and a variety of smaller items used in recovery. Because the vehicle was not equipped with a winch, the only recourse that the crew had when winching was an absolute requirement was to break (disconnect links) a track and use the drive sprocket as a windlass.

Production of the *Bergepanzerwagen* III began in March 1944 and continued through November, during which time 167 of the vehicles were assembled. A further nine were produced in the first quarter of 1945. The *Bergepanzerwagen* III were issued to a variety of units which were equipped with either Panzer III or *Sturmgeschütz* vehicles.

Bergepanzer IV SdKfz 164

The Panzer IV–based recovery vehicle, the *Bergepanzer* IV, was, much like the *Bergepanzer* III, a very basic conversion of rebuilt combat tank chassis. A heavy wooden decking was installed over the turret ring, and more heavy planks installed inside the vehicle, the latter to protect the fuel tanks from heavy recovery gear that was stowed internally. Sockets to receive a 2-ton crane were welded to the roof of the vehicle superstructure.

Lacking a recovery winch, the men assigned to the *Bergepanzer* IV had to rely upon using a drive sprocket as a windlass. In order to do this, a track was broken (links separated), and a wire rope was attached to the drive sprocket. The other end of the wire rope was attached to the object to be moved. Placing the *Bergepanzer* in gear caused the sprocket to turn, and the wire rope wound around

Bergepanzer IV (SdKfz 164)

Specifications	
Length	5.92 m
Width	2.88 m
Height	2.10 m
Weight	20 tons
Fuel capacity	470 liters
Maximum speed	42 km/hr
Range, on-road	210 km
Range, cross-country	130 km
Crew	2
Armament	
Weapon, main	7.92 mm MG 34
Ammo stowage, main	600 rounds
Automotive	
Engine make	Maybach
Engine model	HL 120 TRM
Engine configuration	V-12, liquid cooled
Engine displacement	11.9 liters
Engine horsepower	265 @ 2600 rpm

it. Though labor-intensive, this was an effective recovery means.

However, this improvised winching capacity was limited owing to the fact that the *Bergepanzer* IV lacked a ground spade to anchor it, thus requiring the retriever to be anchored to another heavy vehicle or large tree.

Only twenty-one Panzer IV were converted to *Bergepanzer*, all between October 1944 and March 1945.

Bergepanther SdKfz 179

The *Bergepanther* was Germany's first purpose-built armored recovery vehicle, predating all the other vehicles in this chapter.

The earliest, and most basic, type of the *Bergepanthers*—or recovery Panthers—were simply Panther Ausf D chassis without turrets which had a cover fitted over the turret opening. These vehicles were completed by MAN in mid-1943.

These were followed by thirty more elaborate vehicles built by Henschel and based on the Panther Ausf A chassis. These thirty *Bergepanthers* were equipped with a heavy

Bergepanzerwagen Panther

Specifications	
Length	8.86 m with ground anchor
Width	3.42 m
Height	2.70 m
Weight	43 tons
Fuel capacity	1075 liters
Maximum speed	46 km/hr
Range, on-road	320 km
Range, cross-country	160 km
Crew	3
Communications	FuG 5
Armament	
Weapon, main	2 cm KwK 38 (on some models)
Weapon, secondary	7.92 mm MG 34
Ammo stowage, main	600 rounds
Automotive	
Engine make	Maybach
Engine model	HL 230 P30
Engine configuration	V-12, liquid cooled
Engine displacement	23.1 liters
Engine horsepower	600 @ 2500 rpm

towing bracket and provisions for an unditching beam, but little further recovery gear. Forty more units followed that added a superstructure with folding wooden sides to the equipment installed on their predecessors.

In time, the design progressed and the *Bergepanther* began to be fitted with a 40-ton capacity recovery winch fitted in the area normally defined as the fighting compartment. A jib boom for material handling was provided and a hinged ground anchor (spade) was installed on the rear of the vehicle. The latter was to prevent the winch from merely dragging the *Bergepanther* backward during heavy recovery operations.

In October 1944, the *Bergepanther* began to be based on the Panther Ausf G as that model replaced the Ausf A in tank production. Ultimately, MAN built only the twelve original, very basic *Bergepanthers*, Henschel built seventy *Bergepanther* Ausf A, and Daimler-Benz a further

ARMORED RECOVERY VEHICLES 233

Right: *A tank-recovery version of the Panther tank was developed: the Bergepanzerwagen "Panther" (or Bergepanther), SdKfz 179. The conversion to this vehicle involved the removal of the turret and the installation of a jib boom, heavy-duty tow coupling, rear spade, and a 40-ton winch. This rear view of Bergepanzerwagen "Panther" Ausf A chassis number 212161 shows the winch cable and its roller guide, as well as the lowered spade and the erected jib boom.* Thomas Anderson

Left: *Compared to the spade in the preceding photo, the one on this Bergepanther is of a different design, with two extensions on the top to limit the depth the spade could dig into the ground, and with a gap between the extensions to provide clearance for the winch cable and the exhausts. The wooden side on the right side of the superstructure has been removed. To the front of the superstructure is a canvas cover for the driver, shown here folded up. Note the presence of Zimmerit on the lower hull but not on the upper hull. This vehicle, Bergepanther chassis number 175664, was captured by the British and is seen here during testing at the School of Tank Technology.* Patton Museum

Right: *The spade of Bergepanther chassis number 175664 is dug in during evaluations of the vehicle at the School of Tank Technology in England. This vehicle was completed at the Demag factory in September 1944.* Patton Museum

Left: Bergepanther chassis number 175664 is parked in an equipment yard among British tanks after its capture. In addition to the gap between the two extension plates on the top of the spade, there is a V-shaped notch in the top of the spade between those plates, for winch-cable clearance. Patton Museum

Above: *The captured Bergepanther, chassis number 175664, is viewed from the right rear in a shop. Except for the first dozen Bergepanthers, these vehicles were equipped with a 40-ton winch. The jib boom had a lifting capacity of 1.5 tons. Some vehicles had a mount on the front for a 20 mm KwK 38 cannon.* Patton Museum

Above: Bergepanther *chassis number 175664 is seen from the left front in the shop setting after its capture. The jib boom is swung to the left side of the vehicle, and it is equipped with a chain hoist. Note the two grab handles and the "letterbox" bow machine-gun port on the right side of the glacis.* Patton Museum

Above: *This* Bergepanther, *crowded with soldiers, is based on an Ausf G chassis. It has the late-style spade, visible on the front of which are vertical reinforcing ribs.* National Archives and Records Administration

forty. Demag built 123 *Bergepanther* Ausf A as well as 94 *Bergepanther* Ausf G, even though Demag never built any Panther Ausf G combat tanks.

Bergepanzer *Ferdinand*

The massive Ferdinand *Jagdpanzers* which were built on the chassis of the ill-fated Tiger (P) posed a special problem for German armored support personnel. The massive vehicles, weighing sixty-five tons each, well exceeded the towing capacity of the standard German recovery vehicle of the day, the 18-ton half-track. In fact, the vehicles also exceeded the towing capacity of the newly introduced *Bergepanther*.

In order to create a suitable recovery vehicle for the Ferdinand, a further three of the Tiger (P) chassis were converted to recovery vehicles.

The superstructure installed was considerably smaller than that combat vehicles, and the armor was not as thick. The gas-electric power plant, powered by twin Maybach HL 120 engines, as used in the initial design was carried over in the recovery variant. Electric motors drove the rear drive sprockets.

A jib boom was provided, which was stowed on the deck ahead of the superstructure. A 7.92 mm MG 34 for self-defense was fitted in a ball mount on the front of the superstructure. Nibelungenwerk completed the three recovery vehicles in August 1943, and they were supplied to *schwere Heeres Panzer-Jaeger-Abteilung* 653. Ultimately, one was shipped to Italy and the other two to the Russian Front.

At over 60 tons, these were the largest recovery vehicles fielded by the German army during World War II.

Bergepanzer Ferdinand/Elefant

Specifications	
Length	6.97 m
Width	3.38 m
Height	2.97 m
Weight	60 tons
Fuel capacity	950 liters
Maximum speed	30 km/hr
Range, on-road	150 km
Range, cross-country	90 km
Crew	3
Communications	FuG 5
Armament	
Weapon, main	7.92 mm MG 34
Ammo stowage, main	600 rounds
Automotive	
Engine make	2 x Maybach
Engine model	HL 120 TRM
Engine configuration	V-12, liquid cooled
Engine displacement	11.9 liters
Engine horsepower	265 @ 2600 rpm

Above: *Three examples of an armored recovery vehicle based on the Jagdpanzer Ferdinand were produced, with the intention that they would be used for recovering Jagdpanzer Ferdinands when required. These recovery vehicles were referred to by several designations: Bergepanzer Tiger (P), Bergepanzer Ferdinand/Elefant, or Bergepanzer VI. These vehicles featured a shortened superstructure with a roof and round hatch and a detachable jib boom. There was no winch or spade. Patton Museum*

Left: *One of the Bergepanther Tiger (P) recovery vehicles is viewed from the left side. Although not visible here, the jib boom was stored on the deck to the front of the superstructure. Brackets on the upper hull supported the boom when it was erected. An MG 34 machine gun was the only defensive weapon; it was placed in the ball mount on the front of the new superstructure, and that mount is visible here. Patton Museum*

Chapter 10 Armored Semi-Track Vehicles

Leichter Gepanzerter Kraftswagen (SdKfz 250), later designation: le SPW (SdKfz 250)

Although German crews were adequately protected in the Reich's four-, six-, and eight-wheeled armored cars, these vehicles were lacking in the area of cross-country mobility—at least during the early stages of the war. Eight-wheeled armored vehicles, to say nothing of smaller armored cars, struggled just to keep up with heavy tanks in the mud and rough terrain of battlefields, particularly on the Eastern Front.

While Germany's half-tracks were much better suited to operation with Panzer formations, the 1-ton SdKfz 10 and 3-ton SdKfz 11 lacked armor protection—a clear drawback for a reconnaissance vehicle. Accordingly, engineers and builders set out to marry the best of both worlds and provide reconnaissance units with rugged cross-country vehicles that were also armored.

Work on the prototype of the SdKfz 250 was underway in 1939, but the half-tracks only entered production in June 1941. Engineered by Demag, the SdKfz 250 chassis was based on that of the SdKfz 10, albeit with numerous modifications. Büssing-NAG designed the new vehicle's armored body. The SdKfz 250 was intended to carry half of a machine-gun section—i.e., four men. Most of the steering was accomplished using the half-track's front wheels, but during sharp turns, steering brakes on the tracks were automatically engaged, greatly reducing the turning radius.

Chassis for the vehicles were produced by Demag, Adlerwerke, Büssing-NAG, and Mechanische Werke Cottbus. Assembly by Büssing-NAG, Deutsche Werke, Evens and Pistor, Eisenwerk Weserhütte, Wegmann, and Wumag was slow to start but quickly picked up speed. Twelve special-purpose variations of the vehicle were created.

The armored bodies for these vehicles were produced by a variety of firms, some using riveted construction, other firms using welded constructions, as dictated by each firm's capabilities. Further, two styles of Ausf A bodies were used, with about four hundred Ausf A vehicles being completed with an armored superstructure designated *Panzeraufbau* SdKfz 250/Z, the remaining Ausf A vehicles utilizing *Panzeraufbau* SdKfz 250/E superstructures. These are most readily distinguished by the 250/Z body featuring headlights mounted on the sides of the engine compartment instead of on the front of the vehicle as on the 250/E body.

A major watershed development occurred with the introduction of a new, redesigned body, which entered production in mid-1943. The new design cut the number of major armor components from nineteen down to only nine and made for much more efficient output from the manufacturing plants, greatly accelerating production. These vehicles were designated the Ausf B, but are often referred to by enthusiasts as "*neue*" or "new style." The vehicles with the original body were designated Ausf A, but enthusiasts sometimes refer to them as "*alte*" (old) light

SdKfz 250 Ausf A

Specifications	
Length	4.56 m
Width	1.95 m
Height	1.66 m
Weight	5.8 tons
Fuel capacity	140 liters
Maximum speed	65 km/hr
Range, on-road	320 km
Range, cross-country	180 km
Crew	2 to 6, depending on configuration
Communications	Funksprechgerät a (Fu Spr Ger a)
Automotive	
Engine make	Maybach
Engine model	HL42TRKM
Engine configuration	6-cylinder, liquid cooled
Engine displacement	4.198 liters
Engine horsepower	100 @ 2800 rpm

All measurements are in the metric system.

SdKfz 250 Ausf B

Specifications	
Length	4.7 m
Width	1.95 m
Height	1.80 m
Weight	5.38 tons
Fuel capacity	140 liters
Maximum speed	65 km/hr
Range, on-road	320 km
Range, cross-country	180 km
Crew	2 to 6, depending on configuration
Communications	Fu Spr Ger f
Automotive	
Engine make	Maybach
Engine model	HL42TURKM
Engine configuration	6-cylinder, liquid cooled
Engine displacement	4.198 liters
Engine horsepower	100 @ 2800 rpm

All measurements are in the metric system.

Schützenpanzerwagen. Intially, the Ausf B bodies were also produced in both riveted and welded styles, but by mid-1944 the hulls were exclusively of welded construction. In addition, the base SdKfz 250 was also designated SdKfz 250/1.

During June 1942, Büssing-NAG stopped assembling the SdKfz 250. In July 1943 Weserhütte and Wumag converted to SdKfz 251 production, leaving the SdKfz 250 assembly consortium. In February of the next year, Deutsche Werke too converted from SfKfz 250 production to SdKfz 251 production. This left only Evens and Pistor building the light armored half-track. Germany's industrial plans provided for production of the half-track to come to a close sometime before the end of 1945. In the event, obviously, the end of the war in Europe in May 1945 brought all German military production to a halt well before that time.

There were two different loads for both versions of the SdKfz 250. One load provided for the transport of half of a machine-gun section (a "*Halbgruppe*") consisting of four men. Such a vehicle was fitted with two MG 34s and supplied with 2,010 rounds of 7.92 mm ammunition. The other load option provided for the transport of the support "*Halbgruppe*" together with heavy field mountings for the MG 34 machine guns.

During 1943, the German army came to adopt the MG 42 as its standard machine gun, and accordingly, the MG 34 was replaced on all variants of the machine-gun equipped SdKfz 250.

By the end of World War II, 6,628 SdKfz 250 had been built, with slightly more than half of them being the Ausf A configuration. The versatile vehicles saw action on all fronts of the conflict and took on various roles.

All variants were based on either the old- or new-style chassis, so all the vehicles had similar dimensions. Complete tabulated data are given above for the base 250/1 vehicle. Changes unique to individual models are called out in the appropriate text.

Left: *The SdKfz 250 series of half-tracks was designed to meet the need for a compact armored vehicle for use in the recon role. The design requirement was that it be large enough to carry four men in addition to its crew, or a Halbgruppe (half platoon). Over four thousand vehicles were produced in twelve official variants. These variants were designated as SdKfz 250/1, 2, 3 and so on. This SdKfz 250/1 Ausf A was the basic troop carrier version and it is seen here in its intended role in the service of a motorized infantry platoon of the 1st SS Panzer Division in Normandy.* National Archives and Records Administration

Right: *A SdKfz 250/1 Ausf A of the SS-Panzergrenadier Division Leibstandarte advances toward the city of Kharkov in early March 1943. This vehicle was part of SS-PzGrenRgt 1, which attacked the city from the north. This picture was taken in the village of Dergatschi, a sizable obstacle on the road into the city. All SdKfz 250/1 Ausf A carried an MG 34 on a swiveling mount in the center of the superstructure.* Patton Museum

Above: *This SdKfz 250/1 is being used as a training vehicle at the* Fahrschule *(driving school) in 1942. As a fuel-saving measure, most German training vehicles in World War II were equipped with a Holzgas system that converted wood chips and pellets to a combustible gas. As this gas needed to be cleaned and cooled prior to passing into the cylinders of the vehicle, a system of chambers and tubes was necessary. This is an earlier version of the SdKfz 250/1 Ausf A where the headlights are still mounted in front of the fenders.* Patton Museum

SdKfz 250/2 Telephone Vehicle

Combat vehicles may be more glamorous and better known, but in modern, mechanized warfare, in fact many more support vehicles are required than actual fighting vehicles. This was already true during World War II, as exemplified by the SdKfz 250/2 *leichter Fernsprechpanzerwagen*. German reports describe this vehicle as a light telephone section mounted in a light armored personnel carrier. The vehicle housed a telephone and switchboard with ten connections. Also installed in the crew compartment cab was a telephone cable drum. Although 3 percent of all SdKfz 250 production was devoted to this variant from November 1943 through April 1944, by October of that year production had been discontinued.

The 5.44-ton vehicle was manned by a crew of four and came equipped with either an MG 34 or MG 42 for defensive use. SdKfz 250/2 was the base vehicle for Germany's light field cable troops (*leichter Feldkabeltrupp*).

SdKfz 250/3 Light Radio Vehicle

Germany's military strategy—which did its best to make use of the latest technology—accorded radio communications a key role, in an age when for many other countries radio equipment was a rarity, certainly not standard, in military vehicles.

Accordingly, an early development of the SdKfz 250 was the SdKfz 250/3 "*leichter Funkpanzer*" (light radio Panzer). There were four variations of the vehicle, each having a specific type of radio equipment installed, depending on what sort of unit the vehicle was assigned to, and which command center it was expected to be in contact with.

When attached to mechanized forces, the 250/3 was fitted with a FuG 12 radio, Germany's standard radio for land forces. This version of the 250/3 was officially designated the 250/3 I. The radio set was mounted atop the vehicle's fuel tank, which was reshaped to allow for the installation. The FuG 12 medium-wave receiver operated

Above: *The SdKfz 250/2 was known as the* Fernsprechpanzerwagen *and was used by communications troops to lay telephone networks. A large cable reel was mounted on a platform in the right rear of the vehicle, and cable reels were also located on the front fenders. The larger reel has been relocated to the ear of the hull on this vehicle being examined by US troops, and the front reels have been sheared away along with the front fenders.* Charles Kliment

on the 835–3,000 kilocycles-per-second (Kc/s) band, while its 80-watt transmitter functioned on the 1,120–3,000 Kc/s band. Early versions of the vehicle were fitted with a two-meter rod antenna. A star antenna was used on later versions.

Mounted on the right front of the fighting compartment of the vehicle was the antenna for the *Funksprechgerät* f (Fu Spr Ger f), the radio used for inter-vehicular communication. The command antenna was mounted on the left rear. Such radio equipment was installed both in vehicles with the *alte* as well as the *neue* bodies.

Another version of the SdKfz 250/3 came equipped with a specialized FuG 7 VHF receiver/transmitter radio set that comprised an ultra-short-wave receiver and a 20-watt transmitter that operated on the 42,100–47,800 Kc/s band. With a range of 50 kilometers, this radio set was used to contact Luftwaffe support groups and required a two-meter rod aerial. The official designation of this variation was the 250/3 II.

Luftwaffe personnel used a third model of the "*leichter Funkpanzer*" for main divisional command links. This vehicle, designated the model 250/3 III, featured a FuG 4 reciever and a FuG 8 set that comprised a medium-wave receiver/transmitter. The "c" model of the Fu 8 operated on the 835–3,000 Kc/s band, while the earlier "b" model used the 580–3,000 Kc/s band. The early version required a huge frame antenna for the FuG 8, giving the radio a forty-kilometer range. A telescoping eight-meter radio mast with star antenna later replaced the frame antenna and boosted the range to fifty kilometers. License plates of these vehicles typically carried a WL prefix for "*Wehrmacht, Luftwaffe.*"

The fourth SdKfz 250/3 model, the 250/3 IV, was equipped with a FuG 8 medium-wave receiver/transmitter and a FuG 5 high-band HF/low-band VHF transceiver, the standard German tank radio set.

Each of these 5.35-ton radio vehicles was also equipped with a machine gun and carried a crew of four men.

SdKfz 250/4

Originally, the designation SdKfz 250/4 was assigned to a half-track fitted with twin (*Zwillinglafette* 36) 7.92 mm MG 34 machine guns, intended for use as a *Flakwagen*, providing antiaircraft cover. Before the vehicles entered series production, however, plans were changed.

When matters were settled in 1943, the designation SdKfz 250/4 was reassigned to an observation and fire control vehicle to be used by units equipped with self-propelled artillery, such as the *Sturmgeschütz*. FuG 15 and FuG 16 radio sets were installed for communication with such vehicles, and either an MG 34 or

Above: *This is a SdKfz 250/3 Ausf A leichte Funkpanzerwagen. It was a radio liaison vehicle that could be fitted with a variety of radio sets to suit its unit and specific purpose. This particular configuration, with the frame aerial, mounted both the FuG 7 and the FuG 8 radios. The FuG 7 could be used for air-to-ground communication, and the FuG 8 was part of the divisional command net.* Patton Museum

Above: *The armored command section of* Panzergruppe Afrika *had four SdKfz 250/3 Ausf A assigned to it in January 1942. Among them were this vehicle marked with the name* Greif *("griffon"). This vehicle has become closely associated with General Erwin Rommel due to several photos showing him as a passenger, although he did not permanently travel with its crew.* National Archives and Records Administration

Left: *This SdKfz 250/3 Ausf A mounts an antenna on the left rear. The porcelain insulator on the base on the antenna is protected by a small armored enclosure. Because of the sensitive radio equipment located within, the vehicle retains its complete all-weather tarpaulin.* Bundesarchiv

Above: *This SdKfz 250/3 Ausf B is likely a mount of the 9th SS and is seen in its battle against elements of the British 4th Parachute Brigade near Oosterbeek during operation Market Garden in September 1944. The large radio antenna can be seen directly to the rear of the soldier firing the MG 42. Discarded parachutes from supply drops are visible in the background.* Bundesarchiv

ARMORED SEMI-TRACK VEHICLES 245

Above: *Forward recon elements of the 6th Army probe the defenses of Stalingrad in the late summer of 1942. This is SdKfz 250/3 Ausf A (note the dual antenna) and it still retains its all-weather tarp. A name has been stenciled just behind the side-mounted water can.* Patton Museum

Left: *Among the rarer variants of the SdKfz 250 Ausf A was the SdKfz 250/4, leichter Truppenluftschützpanzerwagen, seen here in field trials. Designed as a simple antiaircraft vehicle, the SdKfz 250/4 mounted a twin MG 34 arrangement inside known as a Zwillinglafette 36. The two machine guns were installed on a freely revolving pedestal that provided a stable platform for engaging moving targets. Mechanical sights were installed above the mount. Intended for field artillery units, it is believed that the type was never placed in series production, and thus was never issued to troops in the field.* Bundesarchiv

MG 42 was mounted on the half-track for the four-man crew to use for self-defense.

SdKfz 250/5 Artillery Observation Vehicle
When production of the SdKfz 250 vehicle series got underway in June 1941, the planned range of variants included a *leichter Beobachtungspanzerwagen*, or a light observation vehicle for use by the artillery. A standardized open-topped vehicle, it would serve to augment and replace the closed-topped SdKfz 253, whose production came to an end that same month.

These vehicles underwent the same style changes as the others in the SdKfz 250 series.

When deployed with artillery and armored reconnaissance forces, the 250/5 could be fitted with either of two different radio sets. Vehicles serving with the artillery were fitted with FuG 6 and FuG 2 radio installations, while those assigned to armored reconnaissance troops carried FuG 12 radio sets. Changes in the communication equipment took place as the war progressed. Artillery observation vehicles later were fitted with the FuG 8, FuG 4, and Fu Spr Ger f, while armored reconnaissance 250/5 half-tracks got FuG 12 installations in addition to their Fu Spr Ger f. In 1944, these two sub-variants received the designation SdKfz 250/5 I and SdKfz 250/5 II respectively. As with the previously mentioned versions of the SdKfz 250, the 250/5 vehicles each carried a four-man crew

SdKfz 250/6 Ammunition Supply Vehicle
Introduced in 1941, the SdKfz 250/6 was intended to provide *Sturmgeschütz* units an armored ammunition carrier that was derived from the basic SdKfz 250, rather than the more specialized *leichte gepanzerte Munitionskraftwagen* (armored light ammunition carrier), the SdKfz 252.

In point of fact, no SdKfz 250/6 ever rolled off a factory assembly line. Instead the process of supplying and deploying the vehicles was simplified by building the vehicles as SdKfz 250/1 and then issuing specialized ammunition racks as kits to be supplied by the army rather than in the factory.

Two versions of the kit were produced. The *Ausführung* A (Ausf A) configuration supplied racks for seventy rounds of 7.5 cm *Kanone* ammunition packed in cartridge boxes in pairs. The Ausf B kit included sixty individually packed 7.5 cm *Sturmkanone* (StuK) 40 ammunition.

Above. The SdKfz 250/5 leichter Beobachtungswagen was an artillery observation and communications vehicle that was outfitted with the FuG 8, FuG 4, and Fu Spr f radio sets. These were typically assigned one per battery in self-propelled gun units such as those using the Wespe *and* Hummel. *They were also assigned to certain Tiger units and to the self-propelled Nebelwerfer batteries.* Patton Museum

Above: *A SdKfz 250/5* leichter Beobachtungswagen *Ausf B assigned to a* Werfer-Batterie *during training in France. This SdKfz 250/5 is an Ausf B, sometimes erroneously referred to as Neu. This new hull design was introduced gradually beginning in the second half of 1943 and was considered simpler, cheaper, and easier to produce that the Ausf A version.* Bundesarchiv

Above: *A SdKfz 250/5 Ausf A of the 7th Panzer Division speeds along a road in 1944. This photo may have been taken during the division's deployment to the Baltic States for defensive fighting in Lithuania in the late summer of 1944.* National Archives and Records Administration

Left: *A close-up look at the radio rack installation in a SdKfz 250/5 Ausf B. In German the radio rack was known as a Funkgestell. Radios were securely mounted in the rack and suspended on the side by multiple v-shaped rubber mounts. Just forward of the MG 42 stock is a pivoting bracket for the installation of a scissors periscope. This vehicle is assigned to the Werfer-Abteiling II while serving in Finland.* Patton Museum

Right: *The SdKfz 250/6 Ausf A leichter Munitionspanzerwagen was intended as a replacement for the SdKfz 252 that had been issued to Sturmgeschütz units. It could carry either thirty-five cartridge boxes with two 7.5 cm rounds each or sixty metal tubes carrying a single round each in racks mounted on either side of the interior. Three vehicles were issued to each battery. The SdKfz 250/6 Ausf A also mounted an FuG 16 radio that was specifically designed for communication within Sturmartillerie units.* Patton Museum

SdKfz 250/7 8.0 cm Mortar Carrier

The success of the larger SdKfz 251/2 vehicle with a mounted *schwerer Granatwerfer* 34 8.0 cm mortar led to a decision to mount the same weapon in the smaller SdKfz 250 half-track. Armed with that heavy mortar, the vehicle was designated the SdKfz 250/7. Half-tracks with both the "Ausf A" and the "Ausf B" bodies were constructed in this 250/7 configuration. Three sub-variants of the SdKfz 250/7 were created; the section leader's vehicle, the troop leader's vehicle, and an ammunition vehicle. All carried mortar baseplates and sighting gear. The section leader's vehicle had a crew of five, the troop leader's vehicle a crew of four, and the ammunition vehicle a crew of five.

Mounting the heavy mortar in the half-track required installation of a reinforced baseplate. When so modified, the mortar could be fired from within the vehicle. Also supplied was a conventional baseplate that was stowed on the right rear of the 250/7. The conventional baseplate allowed the mortar to be dismounted and set up as a fire base, in which case the vehicle then served as an ammunition carrier, supplying the mortar crew. In order to give its five-man crew a means of self-defense, the 5.61-ton, 1.8-meter tall 250/7 retained the rear-mounted machine gun of the base-model half-track. The forward machine-gun mount, however, was eliminated so that mortar rounds would have a clear trajectory. The 250/7 was also distinguished by having ammunition stowage bins for sixty-six 8 cm mortar rounds.

Used in pairs, the SdKfz 250/7 crews constitute a mortar squad of an *Aufklärungsschwadron* heavy platoon.

SdKfz 250/8 Self-Propelled 7.5 cm Howitzer

When the *Panzerkampfwagen* IV was being rearmed with long guns, numerous previously used 7.5 cm K 51 L/24 short guns became available. Some of these short guns came to be installed on SdKfz 250 Ausf B half-tracks, a procedure that also involved the installation of a mount earlier developed for the *Sturmgeschütz*. When fitted with these weapons, the half-tracks were designated SdKfz 250/8. Although originally scheduled for production to begin in November 1943, delays meant that the first vehicles, fifty-seven units, were not delivered until December 1943.

Besides the addition of the gun mount, the forward machine-gun mount was deleted and a number of other

Above: *The SdKfz 250/7 Ausf A* leichter Schützenpanzerwagen (sGrW) *was a self-propelled GrW 34 8 cm mortar vehicle. Specifically designed for the fourth platoon of the armored infantry company, the vehicles were deployed in groups of three—only one of which actually carried a mortar. Of the three, one vehicle was intended as an aiming section with a range finder while the other carried sixty rounds of ammunition for the mortar. The combination was known to be quite effective. Both Ausf A and Ausf B versions were produced.* Patton Museum

Left: *The SdKfz 250/7 with the GrW 34 8 cm mortar was commanded by the troop leader, and the weapon was fired from a baseplate mounted permanently within the vehicle. Each of the three sub-variants had this baseplate in order to act as the firing vehicle in an emergency. A separate baseplate was also mounted on the rear hull in order to use the mortar dismounted from the vehicle. It was aimed using a periscopic dual sight, but could also be roughly positioned using the entire vehicle. Later versions had the driver's visor marked to aid in this positioning.* Bundesarchiv

Left: *The SdKfz 250/8 Ausf B leichter Schützenpanzerwagen (7.5 cm) was developed as a heavy support vehicle for reconnaissance units using the same short-barreled 7.5 cm weapon originally mounted in the Sturmgeschütz. Coupled with the lethal MG 42 mounted coaxially, it was a potent offensive weapon. Due to its small size, only twenty rounds were carried for the main gun. Because development began in late 1943, only the Ausf B model was produced.* Patton Museum

Above: *Only very early production vehicles had the coaxial MG 42. This vehicle serving in southern France in the summer of 1944 lacks this mount. The SdKfz 250/8 Ausf B leichter Schützenpanzerwagen (7.5 cm) has a crew of four, although some sources state three. Space was certainly at a premium inside; additional crew members would have been a hindrance to effective gun laying. A similar configuration was to be found in the larger SdKfz 251/9.* Bundesarchiv

radical changes were made to the inside of the 250/8. Several seats were removed and the radio set was relocated so as to accommodate the three-man crew, the infantry support weapon, and stowage for twenty rounds of ammunition. With the cannon installed, the vehicle's weight topped 6.3 tons, and its height rose to 2.07 meters.

The 250/8 half-track was supplied to the Fourth Platoon of light armored reconnaissance companies, which used the vehicle for the duration of the war.

SdKfz 250/9

Authorization was given in March 1942 for the development of an armored reconnaissance vehicle on the chassis of the SdKfz 250. The Gustav Appel company took the pedestal mount with shield that was then being fitted to the SdKfz 222 armored car and adapted it for use on the SdKfz 250 half-track. The SdKfz 222 armament, specifically the 2 cm KwK 38 cannon and coaxial MG 34 machine gun, were retained. The resultant armored reconnaissance vehicle was designated SdKfz 250/9. Intended for the same functions as the four-wheeled SdKfz 222, it was believed that the half-track chassis would give the 250/9 better off-road mobility.

The vehicle's mass production was set to commence in July 1942 at the Evens and Pistor firm and also that of Appel.

In 1943 an extensive redesign of the SdKfz 250 resulted in the introduction of the Ausf B and also involved a redesign of the 250/9. The vehicle received a new turret comprising a six-sided open-top enclosure with the 2 cm cannon mounted on a suspended carriage. A newer MG 42 replaced the coaxial MG 34. The new version of the vehicle, now weighing 6.2 tons, was dubbed the SdKfz 250/9 Ausf B. The 250/9 stayed in production throughout the war and in all, about one thousand of the 250/9 vehicles were produced.

Both the Ausf A and Ausf B carried a three-man crew, a sufficient strength for a vehicle used in reconnaissance units.

Above: *The SdKfz 250/9 Ausf A leichter Schützenpanzerwagen (2 cm) mounted a KwK FlaK 38 2 cm gun in a ten-sided turret with a coaxially mounted MG 34. The open-topped turret was protected by hinged grenade screens and was similar in design to that of the four-wheeled SdKfz 222 armored car. The turret had 8 mm of armor with a shield around the gun of 14.5 mm. The SdKfz 250/9 Ausf A had a crew of three and could carry one hundred rounds for the 2 cm gun.* Patton Museum

Above: *This rear view of the SdKfz 250/9 Ausf A leichter Schützenpanzerwagen (2 cm) reveals details of the back hull stowage, including the low-mounted liquid container and the towrope. The rear hull door is distinctive in this instance due to the presence of a vision port. This picture probably dates from the spring of 1942, so the vehicle remains painted in overall dark gray.* Patton Museum

ARMORED SEMI-TRACK VEHICLES 253

Left: *The SdKfz 250/9 Ausf B leichter Schützenpanzerwagen (2 cm) differed not only in its basic chassis design, but it also featured a new turret. The Ausf B now featured a six-sided turret with sides 9 mm thick and a gun shield of 30 mm. Perhaps the most significant feature was that of the gun mount. Known as a Hängelafette, both the 2 cm and the coaxially mounted MG 42 were suspended from the sides of the turret, rather than on a pedestal mount as on the earlier version.* Patton Museum

Right: *The SdKfz 250/9 represented an effort to field a replacement for the SdKfz 222 light reconnaissance armored car with the same turret but on a more mobile chassis. The open, low-profile turret of the SdKfz 250/9 was armed with the 2 cm KwK 38 automatic cannon and a coaxial MG 34 or MG 42. Production totals were approximately 310 in 1943, 318 in 1944, and 109 in 1945, for a total of 737. Here, troops of the Waffen-SS and Wehrmacht prepare to lay wreaths in front of a church in a village in northern Russia in April 1944; to their front is a Waffen-SS SdKfz 250/9 with 2 cm KwK 38, painted overall in Dunkelgelb.* Bundesarchiv

Above: *The turret of an SdKfz 250/9 is viewed from the front with the guns dismounted but with the anti-grenade shields present atop the turret. The large slot at the center was for the 2 cm KwK 38 automatic cannon; the narrow slot was for the gunner's sight, while the remaining slot was for the 7.92 mm coaxial machine gun.* Patton Museum

Above: *The interior of the turret, including the gun mounts, is visible in a view of the SdKfz 250/9 with the anti-grenade shields open. The plate of armor with the keyhole-shaped opening in it, behind the front center of the turret, was a shield through which the 2 cm cannon barrel was fitted. The shield moved up and down in unison with the elevation and depression of the 2 cm cannon.* Patton Museum

ARMORED SEMI-TRACK VEHICLES

SdKfz 250/10 Self-propelled 3.7 cm antitank gun

When German planners sought to supply platoon leaders with a vehicle that could deliver heavier fire support for the standard 250/1, development led to the introduction of the SdKfz 250/10 *leichter Schützenpanzerwagen* (3.7 cm PaK). These vehicles were built in the both Ausf A and Ausf B configurations. On the 250/10, a 3.7 cm PaK 35/36 was installed in place of the front machine gun. Its mount permitted a thirty-degree left or right traverse. Supplied with the PaK were 216 rounds of ammunition. Meanwhile, the rear 7.92 mm MG 34 was provided 1,100 rounds. The *Zugührerwagen* carried a four-man crew that consisted of the commander, the driver, the loader, and the gunner.

When World War II in Europe was first unfolding, Germany's 3.7 cm weapon was a respectable antitank gun. But after the war with Russia got underway, German forces faced more formidable enemy vehicles. The 3.7 cm gun was no longer effective against new-model Soviet tanks. Though soft targets could still be devastated by a 3.7 cm gun firing high-explosive rounds, its weakness against tanks won it the nickname "door knocker." Accordingly, production of these vehicles came to an end after some 150 units.

SdKfz 250/11

The SdKfz 250/11 *leichter Schützenpanzerwagen* (*schwere Panzerbüchse* 41), *Gerät* 882, represented yet another attempt to come up with an antitank weapon for platoon leaders. Mounted on these vehicles was a 2.8 cm *schwere Panzerbüchse* 41 (sPzB 41 "heavy antitank rifle"), a tapered-bore antitank gun. Tapered-bore weapons embodied the theory that increased back pressure resulted in increased muzzle velocity of the tungsten-based round. Higher velocity meant greater armor penetration. The theory was sound, but tungsten was such a rarity that Germany could not afford to blow up its precious reserves in ammunition. No doubt these were among the factors that led the SdKfz 250/11 to have been discontinued by January 1944. Another factor was the prevalence of scathing reports concerning the ineffectivenesss of the weapon, especially at combat ranges, and the inability of the half-track to withstand the firing stresses.

Above: *The SdKfz 250/10 Ausf A (3.7 cm PaK) Zugfuhrerwagen was issued to each platoon commander of le.SPW platoons to provide heavy fire support. The crew consisted of four: a driver, a gun/vehicle commander, a gunner, and a loader for the 3.7 cm PaK 35/36. The weapon was useful for supporting the normal method of advancing, which was to have two or three groups of vehicles leapfrog through each other's positions, supporting each stage of the move. Carrying 216 rounds of 3.7 cm ammunition on board, space inside for stowage was at a premium and the crew members have stowed much of their gear on the outside of the vehicle.* Patton Museum

Above: *This brand-new SdKfz 250/10 Ausf A (3.7 cm PaK) is being delivered to a Luftwaffe ground unit in Italy in 1943. It is painted in overall dark yellow with a green overspray pattern. The exposed hinges on the engine access doors would be eliminated on later models of the SdKfz 250 Ausf A.* Bundesarchiv

Above: *In order to address the inadequacies of the 3.7 cm PaK gun as an antitank weapon, a new solution was sought to arm the SdKfz 250/10 Zugfuhrerwagen. The answer was found in the schweres Panzerbüchse 41, a remarkable squeeze-bore weapon that had the kill-power of the 5 cm PaK 38, but weighed half as much. Due to its small size, it could be mounted in the same manner as the 3.7 cm weapon. The result was the SdKfz 250/11 Ausf A leichter Schützenpanzerwagen (sPzB 41).* National Archives and Records Administration

Left: *Developed originally as an antitank weapon for paratroopers, the 2.8 cm sPzB 41 was considered portable and a small, wheeled carriage was provided for dismounted use. This was to be stowed on the rear hull of the SdKfz 250/11, along with the trails stowed on the front fenders, but it is not always seen in the field. Twin grips encompassed a trigger on the back end of the weapon, which had a muzzle velocity of 1,400 meters per second. This is a half-track of the Kradschützen battalion of Panzergrenadier Division Grossdeutschland.* Patton Museum

Besides the *Panzerbüchse*, the 250/11 carried either an MG 34 or an MG 42 machine gun for defensive use, mounted on the rear of the vehicle. The main gun was supplied with 168 rounds of ammunition, as well as 1,100 rounds of 7.92 mm machine-gun ammo. The vehicle also carried a field carriage for the *Panzerbüchse*, allowing the antitank weapon to be operated in dismounted mode. Like the 250/10, the SdKfz 250/11 was issued to platoon leaders. The 250/11 had a total weight of 5.53 tons and a height of 2.13 meters.

SdKfz 250/12 Light Armored Survey Section Vehicle
Designed for use by platoon leaders and their assistants in sound-ranging and flash-spotting units, the SdKfz 250/12 is a relatively obscure variant. Moreover, five different sub-variants were planned, with the specific equipment to be fitted varying depending upon their planned use.

The variants were a battery commander's vehicle, an advance warning vehicle, a vehicle for the platoon leader of the sound-ranging section, a vehicle for the flash-ranging section platoon leader, and a flash-ranging vehicle.

Discontinued before January 1944, only fifteen SdKfz 250/12 half-tracks are confirmed to have been built.

SdKfz 251
Based on the SdKfz 11 3-ton half-track chassis, the medium *Schützenpanzerwagen*, or armored personnel carrier, became the backbone of the Reich's armored infantry operations in World War II. Allied intelligence reports from after the war quoted General Heinz Guderian as describing the vehicle as "the greatest saver of blood we possess."

Initially built by Borgward and later by Hanomag, the vehicle's chassis was designated HL.Kl.6p and was based on the SdKfz 11 chassis. The same clutch, four-speed transmission, suspension, and track served both vehicles. Armored and unarmored vehicles were powered by different engines, with the armored vehicles using model HL 42 TUKRM, which included an additional drive for a cooling fan that was separately mounted.

The steering mechanism of the SdKfz 251 differed from that of the SdKfz 11 in having the steering wheel reverse-angled with a slope of forty-five degrees relative to the driver. Unlike the unibody SdKfz 234, the 251 consisted of a chassis upon which a separately manufactured body was mounted—much the way a car body and chassis are brought together.

The body of the SdKfz 251 was initially manufactured by Deutsche Edelstahlwerke of Hannover, and was made in two sections. The forward section ended immediately behind the driver and protected him, the commander, and the vehicle's engine. The body's rear section contained the open-topped area that was originally intended to accommodate ten soldiers. An internal flange allowed the two sections to be bolted together.

Above: *Among the most obscure variants of the line was the SdKfz 250/12 Ausf A leichter Messtruppenwagen. These were to be assigned to special observation units and used to discern the type and range of enemy artillery. Equipped with a variety of optical and sound equipment, the SdKfz 250/12 was further categorized into five sub-variants: a battery commander's vehicle; an advance warning vehicle; a platoon leader vehicle for the sound-ranging section; a platoon leader vehicle for the flash-ranging section; and a flash-ranging vehicle.* Patton Museum

The SdKfz 251 Ausf A, the initial production version of the vehicle, featured two vision slits in the 8 mm armor on each side of the personnel compartment in the vehicle's rear section. These slits were fitted with glass blocks and shielded by an armored flap. This vision slit-feature, absent from successive models of the 251, distinguishes the Ausf A.

The SdKfz 251 entered production in May 1939, and limited numbers of the vehicle served during the German invasion of Poland that September. After about 232 of the Ausf A vehicles had been produced, production shifted to the SdKfz 251 Ausf B. The Ausf B differed from its predecessor only in details, such as the elimination of the vision slits in the rear of the body. A lack of supply of these vision slits was cited as the reason that SdKfz 251 output failed to meet requirements for the month of September 1939.

Other material shortages also affected SdKfz 251 output in 1939. Armor plate used to construct the vehicle's body was also in short supply. This difficulty led to the production of the *mittlerer ungepanzerter Mannschaftstransportkraftwagen* [Mannsch Trsp Kw] (SdKfz 251)—that is, the "SdKfz 251 troop transport vehicle with mild steel body." A total of 305 of these mild-steel vehicles were turned out between June and December 1939. More production was under consideration, indeed orders were placed for the vehicles, but in December 1939 it was decided that the SdKfz 11 would be built instead, using the chassis that had been intended for the additional unarmored SdKfz 251 half-tracks.

Internal stowage aboard the 251 Ausf B was slightly rearranged, most significantly, the radio was moved from behind the co-driver to in front of his position. In addition, the front machine-gun mount was transformed into a simple pivot type, and the guns were provided with gun shields. The radio antenna moved from the right front fender to a location nearer to the radio set itself. It appears that in all, about 350 Ausf B half-tracks were produced.

The SdKfz 251 Ausf C entered production in January 1940 and more producers now joined the list of manufacturers. The F. Schichau-Werke in Elbing, East Prussia, began to undertake final assembly, making use of the chassis manufactured by Hanomag. These chassis were additional to the ones on which Hanomag was doing in-house mounting of armored bodies.

Maschinenfabrik Niedersachsen Hannover (MNH) was also contracted to turn out the SdKfz 251 chassis; indeed MNH replaced Borgward (Hansa-Lloyd und Goliath) in this role of 251 chassis producer. Borgward-built chassis instead were employed in the production of the SdKfz 11.

With demand for the half-track fairly high, welded armored bodies were also ordered from Schoeller-Bleckmann Stahlwerke in Ternitz, Lower Austria, which began delivering its products in March 1940. Even this addition to the output of Deutsche Edelstahlwerke was insufficient to meet demand, so yet more bodies were ordered from Bohemia's Böhmisch-Leipa in the Sudetenland. Since that company was not able to weld armor plate, the Bohemian-based firm used riveted construction in producing SdKfz 251 Ausf C bodies.

Nomenclature for the half-track was meanwhile also evolving. By November 16, 1940, the previous name for the vehicle—"*mittlerer gepanzerter Mannschaftskraftwagen*"—had been replaced by "*mittlerer Schützenpanzerwagen.*"

In addition to Hanomag and MNH, which did some of their own final assembly, and the previously mentioned F. Schichau AG, the companies Gollnow und Sohn, Eisenwerk Weserhütte, and Wumag all mounted armored SdKfz 251 bodies on chassis turned out by Hanomag or MNH.

Apart from the fact that some of the half-tracks had riveted rather than welded bodies, the change in producers was not apparent. The SdKfz 251 Ausf C is easily distinguished from other models, however. The front plate of the engine compartment on the Ausf C was constructed of a single, flat armor plate, presented the most obvious change from the earlier versions, in which front of the engine compartment had been formed from two intersecting pieces of armor. In addition, the front bumper present on the Ausf A and B was eliminated from the Ausf C, which had no bumper.

Another difference was the fact that the Ausf A and B had pulled engine-cooling air down through a grille on the top front of their armored engine hoods, but the Ausf C drew engine-cooling air up behind the armor plate. To protect the cooling air exhausts, the Ausf C was fitted with armored covers: large box-shaped structures on both sides of the engine compartment. The fenders over the Ausf C tracks were redesigned with a slight upsweep near the front.

Internal changes introduced on the Ausf C included the addition of lockers for stowage in back of the troop seats. The vehicle's front seats were reconfigured to fold down, and they could also easily be removed for maintenance.

Design work for the SdKfz 251 Ausf D was completed by Büssing-NAG before December 1, 1942. Deutsche Edelstahlwerke, in Krefeld, the Prussian Rhineland, launched production of the Ausf D on May 18, 1943, and new bodies began to arrive from Deutsche Edelstahlwerke, Steinmüller in June. Bohemian Böhm-Leipa; Schoeller-Bleckmann/Ternitz; Ferrum Kattowitz's Laurahütte plant near Auschwitz, Poland; and Poldi-Hütte in Kladen, Central Bohemia, all joined in manufacturing Ausf D bodies.

To ensure that output levels would be maintained while allowing Hanomag to discontinue its final assembly operation (though it would still produce chassis), F. Schichau GmbH, Maschinen und Lokomotivwerk, Elbing, signed a contract to do assembly. Schichau made its first delivery in November 1943. Schichau's sprawling complex in Elbing, East Prussia, included a shipyard with 18,000 workers in 1944, reportedly including 2,000 drawn from the Stutthof concentration camp. Elbing fell to the Soviets by February 1945, and it was planned that production would be transferred to Weserhütte und Wumag Waggonfabrik, Görlitz, Lower Silesia.

Production of the chassis had to be adjusted as well. MNH turned away from manufacturing the SdKfz 251 in March 1943 to focus on turning out the Panther tank instead. Adlerwerke stepped in to make up the loss, beginning delivery in that same month of March. Auto Union, where the first SdKfz 251 deliveries started in May and Skoda, which started output in July 1943, also joined the team of SdKfz 251 producers.

The Ausf D body was easier, cheaper, and presumably quicker to manufacture than the earlier 251 versions had been. The half-track's rear was totally redesigned. A simple flat plate, set at an angle and with hinged doors, replaced the complicated clamshell doors that featured on previous versions.

Integral stowage bins along the sides of the vehicle replaced the storage boxes that previously had been mounted atop the fenders. The bins embraced the whole space between the top of the track guards and the armored body. The Ausf C half-track had had large air ducts on both sides of the engine compartment, but the Ausf D eliminated those ducts.

Meanwhile armament was also evolving. In line with a directive dated January 27, 1944, the 7.92 mm MG 34s were replaced with 7.92 mm MG 42 machine guns.

Internally, the layout of the vehicle's equipment was little changed from earlier SdKfz 251 versions, but with the Ausf D, wood was used where metal or leather had earlier been employed.

The importance of the SdKfz 251 may be judged by the fact that the half-track was included on the emergency production program for armored vehicles, announced on February 28, 1945. Under this program, production of this vehicle was to continue until April 1945.

Many SdKfz 251 variations (*Ausführungen*) were produced, but not all models came out in every (Ausf A, B, C, and D) body style. The designation for the basic vehicle or armored personnel carrier was SdKfz 251/1. After the end of World War II, Czechoslovakia slightly modified the design of the vehicle to produce a Diesel-powered, fully enclosed, armored half-track transporter known as the *Obměný transportér* 810 (OT-810), 1,500 of which were turned out between 1958 and 1962. The last OT-810 vehicles were removed from the Czech army's warehouses as recently as 1995.

Rocket Launchers

A common modification made to the SdKfz 251, beginning in 1941, was the installation of rocket launchers. Called a *schwere Wurfgerät* or "heavy launch system," the device could fire off 28 cm or 32 cm rockets using the *Wurfrahmen* 40 or "launch frame [19]40." The launch frame consisted of three adjustable baseplates that were fitted along both sides of the body of the half-track. Traverse of the rockets was controlled by the positioning of the vehicle, and aim was facilitated by aiming rods attached to the half-track's front.

SdKfz 251/1 Ausf D

Specifications	
Length	5.80 m
Width	2.1 m
Height	2.1 m
Weight	8.5 tons
Fuel capacity	160 liters
Maximum speed	53 km/hr
Range, on-road	300 km
Range, cross-country	150 km
Crew	2
Communications	FuG Spr Ger f
Automotive	
Engine make	Maybach
Engine model	HL42 TUKRRM
Engine configuration	6-cylinder, liquid cooled
Engine displacement	4.170 liters
Engine horsepower	100 @ 2800 rpm

Above: *This is the first model of the SdKfz 251, the Ausf A. Its characteristics included a tubular front bumper, two-piece frontal plates on the body, a ventilation grille on the top of the front of the body, pioneer-tool stowage on the sides of the body toward the rear, and two fixed vision ports on the side of the body in addition to the driver's and assistant driver's hinged side visors. Both armored bodies and unarmored bodies were built, and this example has the armored body.* Patton Museum

Above: *A total of 305 SdKfz 251s were built with unarmored bodies in 1939, due to a shortage of armor plate. Once such vehicle, designated* ungepanzerte *(unarmored), is seen here during urban maneuvers. Distinguishing features of this model are the two vision slits on small, flat panels to the rear of the driver's-side visor. These panels were nearly flush with the body.* Bundesarchiv

ARMORED SEMI-TRACK VEHICLES 261

Above: *An SdKfz 251 Ausf A crests an embankment during the invasion of Greece in 1941. The recommended tire pressure is marked on the edge of the fender: 2.75 atü. This is a measure of air pressure used by the Germans where 1 atü is equal to 1 technical atmosphere, or 14.695 psi. On very early models of the SdKfz 251 the radio antenna was mounted on the dip in the right fender. Later the antenna was moved to a mount midway on the top of the body.* Patton Museum

Above: *An SdKfz 251 Ausf C operates with a SdKfz 250/3* leichte Funkpanzerwagen *during the campaign in the Soviet Union in 1942. On the side of the SdKfz 251, a faded white* Balkenkreuz *is visible just to the rear of the vehicle number 136. Also visible on the left side is the collapsed Lafette tripod mount for the MG 34, important when committing motorized troops to a sustained assault on a fixed position.* Bundesarchiv

Above: *The final model of the SdKfz 251 was the Ausf D, and it entered operational service in 1943. The Ausf D had a faired structure from the fender up to the bottom of the upper side plates of the body, with three bottom-hinged access doors. The Ausf C had three box-type stowage compartments on each fender. The vehicle depicted here is a SdKfz 251/1 and was the basic type configured as a Panzergrenadier armored personnel carrier.* Patton Museum

Above: *Beginning in 1941, the SdKfz 251 was used as a platform for the* schwere Wurfgerät 40. *Six of the launcher racks and rockets were mounted on a heavy launching frame known as the* schwere Wurfrahmen 40. *There were three units per side. Either a 28 cm high-explosive rocket or a 32 cm rocket with a napalm-like mix of oil and high explosive could be used. The ignition system for the rockets was electrical. The elevation of the launchers was adjustable, but to adjust the azimuth, the entire vehicle was aimed at the target.* Patton Museum

The rockets' elevation had to be adjusted on each launcher. The rockets came in three calibers: 280 mm and 300 mm high-explosive rockets, or 320 mm incendiary rockets. The rockets were shipped in crates that also served as the launch housing. These were hung on the baseplates fitted alongside the half-track. The range of these rockets varied from 975 to 4,550 meters.

Because of the rocket exhaust, crewmen were required to leave the vehicle prior to launch. These rocket launchers were mounted on infantry carriers as well as engineering half-tracks. The crew of such rocket-launching vehicles consisted of a driver, two gunners, and a vehicle commander.

SdKfz 251/2 Mortar Carrier
In September 1940, a mortar carrier based on the SdKfz 251 entered development. In the spring of 1941, a vehicle equipped with a *schwerer Granatwerfer* 34 8.0 cm mortar was successfully tested. Configured so that the mortar could fire from inside the half-track when stationary, the vehicle was designated the SdKfz 251/2. The trajectory of the mortar shell made it necessary to delete the forward machine gun. The mortar could also be dismounted and fired, thanks to a conventional mortar baseplate that the half-track carried externally.

Most of the mortar carriers used earlier bodies, but some mortar carriers were constructed using the Ausf D body. The 8.64-ton half-track when equipped as a mortar carrier was fitted out with stowage for sixty-six rounds of mortar ammunition, and also had room to transport its eight-man crew.

SdKfz 251/3 *Funkpanzerwagen*
In the D-660/7 loading manual issued on August 13, 1942, the SdKfz 251/3 was described as an artillery-towing vehicle. Reality intervened, however, and by February 10, 1943, the 251/3 was being classified as a *Funkpanzerwagen* or communications vehicle. Most SdKfz 251/3 half-tracks were based on the Ausf D body, though the Ausf C body was the basis for a certain number of the 251/3.

As of August 8, 1944, the following were the seven sub-variants of the SdKfz 251/3:

- SdKfz 251/3 I equipped with FuG 8, FuG 4 and Fu Spr Ger f
- SdKfz 251/3 IIa equipped with FuG 8, FuG 5, FuG 4 and Fu Spr Ger f
- SdKfz 251/3 IIb equipped with FuG 12, FuG 5, FuG 4 and Fu Spr Ger f
- SdKfz 251/3 III equipped with FuG 7, FuG 1 and Fu Spr Ger f
- SdKfz 251/3 IIIa equipped with FuG 12, FuG 1 and Fu Spr Ger f
- SdKfz 251/3 IV equipped with FuG 11 and FuG 12
- SdKfz 251/3 V equipped with FuG 11

The SdKfz 251/3 IV took the place of the SdKfz 251/6 and received the designation mFunkPzWg (KdoWg), or medium radio command vehicle.

Each of the versions of the vehicle carried a seven-man crew. The half-tracks initially were fitted with two 7.92 mm MG 34 machine guns, which by January 27, 1944, had been replaced by two 7.92 mm MG 42 machine guns (depending on year) with 2,010 ammunition rounds.

SdKfz 251/6 *mittlerer KommandoPanzerwagen*
Though often confused with the SdKfz 251/3, the eight-man, 8.5-ton SdKfz 251/6 was fitted with both an eighty-watt FuG 12 and a fifteen-watt FuG 19 radio set. Some of these vehicles also carried the well-known Enigma cryptographic machine.

Luftwaffe units received the SdKfz 251/6 half-tracks for use by "flivos" (*Fliegerverbindungsoffiziere*) or Air Force Liaison Officers—basically, forward air controllers. These 251/6 vehicles were sometimes equipped with ten-meter pole anntennas. A map table was field installed in the driver's compartment of some of the half-tracks with Ausf A and Ausf B bodies.

SdKfz 251/7 *mittlerer PionierePanzerwagen*
The SdKfz 251/7, produced from vehicles with hulls from Ausf C and Ausf D vehicles, was an improvement on the earlier SdKfz 251/5. It carried extensive stowage for engineer equipment in special internal compartments—as had the 251/5. The 251/7, however, carried two portable bridge sections of 8-ton capacity on racks, one on each side of its body.

Weserhütte produced the *mittlerer Pionierepanzerwagen* from its introduction in late 1940 through March 1945, almost the end of the war. The first of the vehicles were armed with the MG 34, but the eight crewmen of later models defended themselves with two MG 42 machine guns. Every second vehicle in a given platoon—numbers 2, 4, and 6—also packed a PzB 39 antitank rifle. Later, an MP 40 machine pistol replaced one of the MG 42 machine guns on the vehicles in November 1944. While some early vehicles lacked a radio, starting in 1942 engineer half-tracks carried the Fu Spr Ger f radio set, which was fitted in front of the co-driver. As of 1943, some of the 251/7 vehicles

Above: *The first numbered variant of the SdKfz 251 was the SdKfz 251/2, an armored carrier for the 8 cm GrW 34 mortar. The interior of an SdKfz 251/2 is viewed from the right side. The mortar base rests in a socket on the floor between the crew seats, and the upper part of the mortar tube is supported by a bipod. To the right is the cab, and to the left are the rear doors. The weapon could be fired from within the vehicle, or it could be set up on a baseplate outside, and it had a maximum range of 2,624 yards.* Patton Museum

Above: *During an inspection of the 12th SS Panzer Division Hitlerjugend, Field Marshal Gerd von Rundstedt and his staff walk past a pair of SdKfz 251/2 mortar carriers and a SdKfz 251/9 Ausf D Stummel. This photo was taken at the Beverloo training camp in Belgium in early 1944. These vehicles lacked front machine-gun mounts, which would have impeded the forward fire of the mortars. The nearest two vehicles are radio-equipped.* Bundesarchiv

ARMORED SEMI-TRACK VEHICLES   265

Left: *The first iteration of the SdKfz 251/3 was an artillery prime mover, but by early February 1943 that designation had been bestowed on a new sub-model, the* mittlerer Funkpanzerwagen *(medium radio carrier). Several different types of antennae were in use on SdKfz 251/3s, depending on the radio sets carried. Two are visible on this vehicle: a 2-meter star antenna on the left rear of the body, and a 9-meter winch mast, a telescoping-mast design shown in the lowered position.* National Archives and Records Administration

Above: *The SdKfz 251/6* mittlerer Kommandopanzerwagen *was a medium armored command half-track. Assigned to upper-echelon commanders, they were equipped with FuG 12 and FuG 19 radio sets, decoding and encoding equipment, and, from 1942 on, a Funksprechtgerät radio. The SdKfz 251/6 featured a prominent frame antenna above the vehicle, as seen on this Ausf A example.* National Archives and Records Administration

Above: At a site near Bir es Sfiri, Libya, in May 1942, a SdKfz 251/6 Ausf B is set up for the use of a Fliegerverbindungsoffizier, or aircraft liaison officer. These officers were forward air controllers, who called in air strikes on enemy positions on the ground. They were nicknamed "flivos." In addition to the frame antenna, a large telescoping winch mast is fitted to the right rear of the vehicle. National Archives and Records Administration

Above: Two SdKfz 251/6 command vehicles configured for flivo operations are operating in mountainous terrain. Both vehicles are equipped with the large telescoping winch masts. Note the star antenna on the farther vehicle and the wire lead on the closest vehicle. The closer vehicle is an Ausf B. Equipment. A vehicle such as this led to successful intraservice cooperation and was essential to the early successes of the Wehrmacht. Patton Museum

Above: *The SdKfz 251/7 was designed for use by the armored engineer companies, known as Panzer-Pionier-Kompanie. The SdKfz 251/7 was outfitted with four brackets, two on each side, for transporting two bridge sections with a capacity of 8.8 tons. These bridges were sufficient for spanning trenches and small streams. This vehicle, an Ausf C, has* Elch/2 (Moose 2) *painted on the ventilator cowl and is towing a 2.8 cm* schwere Panzerbüchse 41 *antitank weapon.* Patton Museum

were equipped with the Fu. 5 radio. Such half-tracks were classified as SdKfz 251/7 II.

SdKfz 251/8 *mittlerer Krankenpanzerwagen*

Specially fitted out as a battlefield ambulance, the SdKfz 251/8 mounted no weapons. It featured a large water container mounted on the floor above the transmission, and in the place of normal seating and equipment storage facilities, it was fitted out with special seats and litter racks. On some occasions, conventional SdKfz 251 half-tracks were converted to ambulance service, but such vehicles retained weapons mounts (though not the weapons themselves). The 7.47-ton field ambulances were served by a two-man crew.

SdKfz 251/9 *mittlerer Schütz Pz Wg (7.5 cm K) Kanonenwagen "Stummel"*

As the German army increasingly felt the need for a fire support vehicle that was based on the medium half-track, developers rearmed the *Sturmgeschütz* with long guns. Commissioned from Büssing-NAG in March 1942, the design for the SdKfz 251/9 provided for installing 7.5 cm K51 L/24 short guns as they were removed from the assault guns that were being rearmed. The mounting developed for the *Sturmgeschütz* was the basis for the mount used on the SdKfz 251/9. The resultant SdKfz 251/9 with its short barrel earned the vehicle its nickname "*Stummel*," meaning "stump."

The installation of the guns necessitated some other significant modifications to the half-track. The forward machine-gun mount was eliminated. Much of the frontal armor was removed in the area usually used by the co-driver. This change was designed to minimize the height of the vehicle by partially insetting the new gun into the half-track's profile. To create space for stowage for thirty-two rounds of main-gun ammunition, the left rear seat was taken out. To accommodate the cannon and mount, the vehicle's radio set was moved to the left side wall.

With the *Kampfwagenkanone* (KwK) mounted, the weight of the half-track rose to 8.53 tons, and its height increased to 2.07 meters.

After successful testing of two trial vehicles on the Eastern Front, production of the 251/9 got underway in June 1942. By the time the design was changed in December

Above: *The German armed forces developed an armored ambulance designated the SdKfz 251/8* mittlere Krankenpanzerwagen. *The vehicle could transport three stretcher patients or up to eight ambulatory patients. All four* ausfuhrung *of the SdKfz 251, from Ausf A to Ausf D, were used, such as this Ausf D vehicle assigned to Panzer-Division Hermann Göring in Italy in 1944. A Red Cross banner is on a rigid frame at the front of the personnel compartment, and a soldier is holding a Red Cross flag.* Bundesarchiv

Above: *The SdKfz 251/9, also designated* mittlerer Schützenpanzerwagen (7.5 cm Kanone), *was developed in early 1942. It mounted the 7.5 cm Kanone 37 L/24, a weapon previously used on the Sturmgeschütz. Initially, the gun protruded through a cutout in the right side of the frontal plate of the cab. The vehicle had a carrying capacity of thirty-two rounds of 7.5 cm ammunition, consisting of a mix of high-explosive and shaped-charge rounds.*

1943, a total of 630 SdKfz 251/9 vehicles with the 7.5 cm K 51 L/24 had been manufactured.

In December 1943, the SdKfz 251/9 began to be made using the 7.5 cm K51 (sf) with a simplified mounting that no longer required cutting away part of the vehicle's frontal armor. Now the weapon would be fitted atop the superstructure above the driver and co-driver. A new armored shield would protect the crew in this otherwise more exposed position. The new mounting not only expedited production, it also raised the side-to-side traverse to 20 degrees left or right, instead more limited traverse of the 7.5 cm *Kanone* L/24, which was 12 degrees right and 10 degrees left. On the right side of the gun shield was mounted a flexible MG 42 machine gun. In all, 1,090 examples of the new half-track model with the 7.5 cm K51 (sf) cannon were produced between January and November 1944.

The SdKfz 251/22 superseded production of the SdKfz 251/9 by order of Adolf Hitler and Wumag rolled out the last two *Stummel* vehicles in December 1944.

SdKfz 251/10 mittlerer Schützenpanzerwagen (3.7 cm PaK)

Armed with a 3.7 cm antitank gun, the SdKfz 251/10 was intended for use by platoon leaders, with the hope that it would give each platoon a heavier impact and provide an integral defense against tanks and other hard targets. In May 1941, Rheinmetall delivered a trial vehicle and regular output began soon thereafter. In July and August 1941, eighty units of the 251/10 were delivered, in what was the first installment of output that continued until at least October 1943. By January 1944, however, a decision had been made to discontinue production of the /10, replacing it organizationally with the SdKfz 251/17.

The SdKfz 251/10 featured a 3.7 cm PaK 36 fitted above the driver and co-driver, occupying the position normally reserved for a machine gun. A variety of gun shields were employed, ranging from the standard shield for the PaK 36, to various low-profile shields, to a shield positioned on only one side. In some cases, the weapon had no shield at all.

With a crew of five or six men, the 251/10 weighed 8.01 tons and carried 168 rounds of ammunition. On the rear of the vehicle was mounted either an MG 34 or an MG 42. The machine gun was supplied with 1,100 rounds of ammunition.

SdKfz 251/11 mittlerer Fernsprechpanzerwagen

Initially manufactured in the Ausf C body, the SdKfz 251/11 was intended for the task of laying telephone cable and housing telephone exchange equipment. These specialized half-tracks began to be delivered in August 1942, with production expected to continue until February 1945.

Above: *The SdKfz 251/10, or mittlerer Schützenpanzerwagen (3.7 cm PaK 36), entered production in mid-1941 and saw use in the infantry-support role to engage infantry concentrations, soft-skin vehicles, and lightly armored vehicles. The example shown here was based on an Ausf C vehicle. A similar role was played by the smaller SdKfz 250/10 half-track.* Patton Museum

Above: *A British soldier is at the controls of the 3.7 cm PaK 36 on this SdKfz 251 Ausf B captured in North Africa. Field modifications were permitted and, in fact, encouraged. As a result, the designs of the mounts varied from unit to unit. This gun is mounted on a box-shaped base on the cab roof, giving the gun a higher position than a factory-installed mount.* Patton Museum

Above: *The SdKfz 251/11 mittlerer Fernsprechpanzerwagen was a field-telephone vehicle, equipped with a telephone switchboard and equipment for laying telephone lines. Equipment included a cable reel and holder on the right fender and a reel holder in the rear of the personnel compartment. The officer in the rear of the Ausf C example is holding a wire pike, a lineman tool consisting of a wooden pole with a hook and roller on the end, for laying or recovering paid-out telephone lines.* Patton Museum

There were two versions of this telephone cable laying vehicle. One version was fitted with the *leichter Feldkabelträger* 6 (light field cable carrier). The other version was equipped with the *mittlerer Feldkabelträger* 10. In both versions the two right-side bench seats were replaced by a cabinet with cable reels and telephone equipment. On the vehicle's left fender was mounted a third cable reel. The five-man crew used long staffs to suspend cable in trees and bushes.

The SdKfz 251/11 weighed 8.5 tons and retained the standard two-machine-gun armament typical of most SdKfz 251 half-tracks.

SdKfz 251/12 mittlerer Meßtrupp und Gerätpanzerwagen,

SdKfz 251/13 mittlerer Schallaufnahmepanzerwagen,

SdKfz 251/14 mittlerer Schallauswertepanzerwagen,

SdKfz 251/15 mittlerer Lichtauswertepanzerwagen

These half-tracks, which were to be fitted out with equipment for *Messtruppen* (sound and flash ranging teams) for Panzer divisions, appear in the operators' manual issued in July 1943. No record, document, or photograph, however, has yet emerged to prove that any of these vehicles were ever actually manufactured.

SdKfz 251/16 *mittlerer Flammpanzerwagen*

In January 1943, the SdKfz 251 Ausf C was first used to mount flamethrowers. When the Ausf C body was superseded by the Ausf D, production of the flamethrower version based on the Ausf C chassis nevertheless continued and ultimately more than 350 were manufactured.

Initially configured with two mounted 14 mm flame projectors and one portable but tethered 7 mm projector, the flamethrowing half-track was classified as the SdKfz 251/16.

ARMORED SEMI-TRACK VEHICLES

Above: *To give its troops a mobile, armored flamethrower capability, the* Wehrmacht *ordered the development of the SdKfz 251/16* mittlerer Flammpanzerwagen. *It was armed with two 1.4 cm projector tubes on pivoting mounts, known as* Strahlrohren. *These had armored shields converted from machine-gun shields. One mount was on the upper part of the body on each side of the personnel compartment. A handheld 7 m flamethrower with extension hoses was available for use off from the vehicle. This equipment is stored on the rear of this Ausf C vehicle.* Patton Museum

The 14 mm projectors were fitted, in a staggered arrangement, on either side of the hull with mountings that allowed a traverse of 160 degrees. Two containers for flame oil, one located inside each rear sidewall, had a combined capacity of seven hundred liters. This capacity permitted the operator to fire about eighty one-second bursts. Powered by a separate Auto Union 28-horsepower engine, a Koebe pumping system pushed fuel to the flamethrower projectors, whose range was fifty to sixty meters. The 14 mm flame projectors had an electric ignition system, while the portable projector used a cartridge ignition.

Changes were made to the flamethrower system on the SdKfz 251/16 in May 1944. The electric ignition used by the fixed side-mounted flamethrowers was replaced with a cartridge ignition. Meanwhile, the little-used handheld flamethrower was eliminated altogether, as it was seen to be impractical and cumbersome.

Besides their flame projectors, the four crewmen of the *mittlerer Flammenpanzerwagen* also had the forward MG 34 for the defense of themselves and their 8.62-ton vehicle. The commander of the vehicle also served as radio operator, the two mounted projectors each had a crewman to operate it, and the remaining crewman was, of course, the vehicle's driver.

SdKfz 251/17 *mittlerer SchützenPanzerwagen* (2 cm)

Throughout the war, some medium half-tracks were modified to serve as antiaircraft vehicles, but until the SdKfz 251/17 no official antiaircraft half-track had been produced. The plan was for production of the 251/17 variant to begin in November 1944 and 390 examples were to be completed by Schichau and 822 by Weserhütte by the end of December 1945. But an inventory list produced by the *Panzerkraftwagen und Zugkraftwagenabteilung Amtsgruppe für Industrielle Rüstung—Waffen und Gerät* (Tanks and Tractors Branch, Group for Weapons and

Above: *The two 1.4 cm flamethrowers were staggered, with the one on the right side more forward. Flexible hoses conducted flame oil from two tanks in the rear of the compartment to the flamethrowers. Each flamethrower had a lever for aiming the weapon, with a trigger lever below the handle. To the front is an MG 34 and armored shield—a highly potent and lethal combination. In addition to the two flame-oil tanks, there was a motor for driving a Koebe flamethrower pump.* Patton Museum

Above: *In 1943 a new, armed variant of the* mittlerer Schützenpanzerwagen *was developed. It was designated the SdKfz 251/17, and it featured a 2 cm KwK38 automatic cannon on a pedestal mount, with an armored shield. The gunner, seated behind the gun, used his weight and movements to aim the weapon. A loader was seated to the front of the pedestal. This knocked-out SdKfz 251/17 Ausf D is being examined by US troops.* NARA

Equipment Manufacture) dated September 1, 1944, already showed fifty-four Sd.Kfy. 251/17 vehicles available.

Pedestal mounted at the rear of the half-track was a 2 cm KwK 38, with the gunner's seat attached to the mount. The seat moved together with the gun as it was traversed and elevated using handwheels. Twenty-round magazines fed ammunition to the weapon. To enable the four-man crew to defend themselves and their vehicle, the rear MG 42 was retained. The SdKfz 251/17 proved less than totally successful, in part due to the cramped quarters within the vehicle's hull.

SdKfz 251/20 mittlerer Schützenpanzerwagen (Uhu)

Already in the late 1930s efforts were underway to develop the German army's night-fighting capabilities. A night-fighting system for the Panther tank was developed by 1944, but one of its shortcomings was its limited visibility range. Mounted on the Panther was a 20 cm infrared (IR) searchlight whose range of vision was only 100–200 meters.

Above: *The 2 cm KwK 38 automatic cannon mount on the same knocked-out SdKfz 251/17 Ausf D is depicted here. The shield, which was 1 cm thick, is severely damaged and the body plate to the rear of the driver's side vision slit (lower left) has been blown off. Below the gun breech is the upper part of the pedestal mount. NARA*

A larger, more powerful infrared searchlight was the obvious next step, but space on the tank was limited. It was decided, therefore, to mount a larger searchlight on the SdKfz 251 Ausf D half-track.

Designated the SdKfz 251/20, one of these 9.3-ton infrared half-tracks was to be attached to each six infrared-equipped Panther tanks. The SdKfz 251/20 featured a 60 cm IR searchlight in the rear, set up on a mount that rotated and pivoted. In addition, just in front of the windshield, the cowl was fitted with a smaller, 20 cm IR searchlight. The half-track also carried the BG 1251 and FG 1252 infrared scopes, an MG 42 machine gun, and radio equipment. The combination of the IR searchlight and scope received the code name "*Uhu*," "great horned owl." The Wumag firm was tasked with assembling the infrared half-tracks, an operation that got underway in January 1945.

Only one use of this equipment has been documented: an action on March 26, 1945, in which 1.*Kompanie/Panzer-Abteilung* 101 of the Führer-Grenadier Division had three SdKfz 251/20 *Uhus*, served with 10 Panther tanks that had FG 1250 infrared sights on them.

It has been reported that generators and large searchlights were removed from some of the *Uhu*-equipped 251 half-tracks, allowing the partial IR-equipped vehicles to serve as armored personnel carriers for infantry support. *Falke* ("Falcon") was the name given to this vehicle. The *Falke* retained the smaller searchlight, walkways, and other features of the 251/20 and the stencil "SdKfz 251/20" continued to appear on their shipping data.

SdKfz 251/21 *mittlerer Schützenpanzerwagen* (MG 151S)

As the war continued, the Allies acquired and intensified their air superiority, compelling the Germans to develop mobile antiaircraft defenses for their infantry and armor.

The SdKfz 251/21 was one such vehicle intended to play this role. Mounted on the rear of this medium half-track—drawn up in July 1944—was a triple 1.5 cm machine-gun mount called the *Drilling* ("Triplets").

274 THE COMPLETE GUIDE TO GERMAN ARMORED VEHICLES

Above: *Late in World War II, the Germans undertook a limited effort to mount infrared lighting and sighting devices on armored vehicles. One such vehicle was the SdKfz 251/20, also referred to as mittlerer Schützenpanzerwagen (Uhu). Uhu is German for "great horned owl." The vehicles were intended to be part of a system to illuminate the battlefield, working in conjunction with infrared-equipped Panther tanks. Key features of the SdKfz 251/20 were a 60 cm infrared searchlight on a pedestal mount above the personnel compartment, a 20 cm infrared searchlight at the center of the frontal plate of the cab, and an FG 1252 infrared sight on the front.* Patton Museum

Left: *The powerful 60 cm infrared searchlight of the SdKfz 251/20 provided broad IR illumination of a battlefield. Below the searchlight is the infrared sight associated with the searchlight. A protective cover is fitted over the front of the sight. Special platforms were set up at the top of each side of the body of this test vehicle.* Patton Museum

ARMORED SEMI-TRACK VEHICLES 275

Left: *Some examples of the* mittlerer Schützenpanzerwagen (Uhu) *lacked the 60 cm infrared searchlight mount but were equipped with the driver's BG 1251 infrared searchlight and FG 1252 sight as well as an MG 42 with an FG 1250 infrared scope, as seen on this example photographed at the special training center for Panzer troops at Fallingbostel, Germany, in March 1945.* NARA

Above: *The same* mittlerer Schützenpanzerwagen (Uhu) *shown in the preceding photo is viewed from a different angle, showing the infrared searchlight on the upper right of the MG 42 and the FG 1250 infrared scope on the upper left of the machine gun. On the side of the driver's compartment is a shipping label that includes the nomenclature of the vehicle, SdKfz 251/20.* Tank Museum

Above: *Introduced in 1944, the SdKfz 251/21 featured a pedestal-mounted triple antiaircraft gun mount with an armored shield originally developed for the Kriegsmarine. The weapons were MG 151 1.5 cm automatic cannons mounted side by side. They were fed ammunition by belts from three magazines, with 250 rounds for the outboard cannons and 500 for the center one. The first 85 SdKfz 251/21s carried 3,000 rounds of 1.5 cm ammunition. Additional ammunition was stowed in bins inside the vehicle.* Patton Museum

Originally developed as aircraft weapons, the Mauser MG 151 had since been superseded on aircraft. Mounted on half-tracks, they were aimed manually, using first optical, and later ring-and-bead sights. A single-person seat on the right rear of the 251/21 and two single-man seats on the left rear replaced the standard rear bench seat. Also inside the vehicle's rear were three ammunition bins, one large and two small ones. The outer guns were fed ammunition from chests that each contained 250 rounds. A center chest with four hundred rounds fed the center gun. Fired shell casings accumulated in the pedestal. Remaining on the rear of the half-track was the MG 42 machine gun used by the crew for self-defense.

The SdKfz 251/21 was produced from August 1944 into December 1944, at which time more powerful 2 cm MG 151 heavy machine guns began to replace the 1.5 cm weapons. Although it is known that the 251/21 remained in production into February 1945, records for the later period have disappeared.

Above: *The Drilling mount of the SdKfz 251/21 had an armor shield that protected the front and the sides. In addition, a four-sided armor shield was added to the top of the vehicle for added protection. The gunner traversed and elevated the guns by body motion. His seat was designed so that his body weight counterbalanced the front-heavy cannons. To the front of the gunner's face is the gunsight with padded eyepiece.* Patton Museum

ARMORED SEMI-TRACK VEHICLES

SdKfz 251/22 mittlerer Schützenpanzerwagen (7.5 PaK)

Late in 1944, Adolf Hitler ordered that all suitable motor vehicle chassis be adapted to serve as *Panzerjäger*. With a mounting similar to the one on the SdKfz 234/4 armored car, the 7.5 cm PaK 40 was fitted into a medium half-track.

The foundation for the gun mount consisted of two heavy steel beams installed in the rear hull, sloping down toward the rear. The mount itself was similar to that used by the PaK 40 towed weapon, except that it had no carriage. The gun shield was also modified, part of the lower corners being cut back to permit traverse. In addition, part of the roof over the driver's compartment was removed so that the gun's recoil cylinder would have clearance. Interior stowage was also heavily modified. The commander's seat, forward rear seats, and rifle racks were deleted. Outside the vehicle a travel lock was added and inside ammunition lockers were installed. The vehicle's four-man crew had an MG 42 machine gun for self-defense.

Production of the SdKfz 251/22—which was concentrated at Wumag—began in December 1944. After Wumag fell to the Soviets in February 1945, there were efforts to field modify half-tracks—mostly SdKfz 251/9 vehicles—into 251/22 configuration.

2 cm FlaK 38 *auf Schützenpanzerwagen* SdKfz 251

About a dozen SdKfz 251 Ausf C half-tracks were modified to act as antiaircraft vehicles for the *Luftwaffe*, ten of them being gun vehicles, two being command vehicles. A complete 2 cm FlaK 38 mount was fitted into the vehicle's rear. Side plates of the hull were extended to allow clearance for the mount. The resultant vehicle bore a certain resemblance to the SdKfz 250 *alte* version. At the same time, though, much of the hull sides were hinged, as was the extension so that they could be folded down. The gun thus acquired a traverse of 360 degrees, but it could also be depressed sufficiently to engage ground targets. The redesign also ensured the crew sufficient room to service the weapon.

Although these half-tracks took part in field trials, they were too complex and their conversion too expensive for them to be adopted as standard vehicles. Not to be confused with the 2 cm FlaK 38 *auf Schützenpanzerwagen* SdKfz 251, the later SdKfz 251/17 lacked folding side armor.

Le gep Munitionskraftwagen (SdKfz 252)

The small SdKfz 252 was designed and built as a frontline armored ammunition resupply vehicle for *Sturmgeschütz* units. Conceived as early as 1936, manufacture of the 252 only began in mid-1940.

The 1-ton half-track chassis served as the basis for the 252, albeit shortened slightly, and the number of roadwheel

Left: *A mobile antitank gun was developed in late 1944, known as the SdKfz 251/22, or mittlerer Schützenpanzerwagen (7.5 cm PaK). It featured a 7.5 cm PaK 40 L/46 on a limited-traverse mount. A special platform was constructed at the front end of the personnel compartment of the vehicle for the gun, upper carriage, traversing table, and shield—all taken from a towed 7.5 cm PaK 40.* Patton Museum

Left: *An armored, mobile antiaircraft vehicle was developed for the Luftwaffe known as the 2 cm FlaK 38 auf Schützenpanzerwagen. Armed with the 2 cm FlaK 38 automatic cannon, a radical modification was made to the body of the vehicle to provide clearance for the gun mount. This comprised a bulged panel, hinged at the bottom on each side.* Patton Museum

Above: *When the 2 cm FlaK 38 was placed in action, the hinged body sections would be lowered to allow more room for the gun and the crew to maneuver. Hinged arms at the front and the rear of the side panel acted to hold it in the lowered position.* Patton Museum

ARMORED SEMI-TRACK VEHICLES

Le gep *Munitionskraftwagen* (SdKfz 252)

Specifications	
Length	4.70 m
Width	1.95 m
Height	1.80
Weight	4.73 tons
Fuel capacity	140 liters
Maximum speed	65 km/hr
Range, on-road	320 km
Range, cross-country	180 km
Crew	2
Communications	FuG 15
Automotive	
Engine make	Maybach
Engine model	HL 42 TRKM
Engine configuration	6-cylinder, liquid cooled
Engine displacement	4.17 liters
Engine horsepower	100 @ 2800 rpm

All measurements are in the metric system.

stations was cut by one to compensate for the greater weight of the armored body. The rear was designed with a steep slope, to reduce the amount of armor—and hence weight—of the half-track.

Demag and Büssing-NAG produced the redesigned chassis, which was designated D7p. The armored body of the 252 was put together by Boehler, but it was the Wegmann and Kiel companies that actually installed the bodies on the chassis. Manufacture evidently was completed in the latter part of 1941, and in all just fewer than four hundred of the small half-tracks were produced. The SdKfz 252 vehicle was designed for use as a shuttle between ammunition trucks and *Sturmgeschütz* armored, tracked assault guns. It is considered unlikely that any 252 half-tracks were still extant after early 1944.

Le gep *Beobachtungskraftwagen* (SdKfz 253)

The need for armored ammunition resupply vehicles for *Sturmgeschütz* batteries became apparent even in 1937. As the supply vehicle needed to combine both relatively high road speed with mobility comparable to that of the StuG, it is not surprising that a half-track was developed to fill this requirement. Starting with the SdKfz 10 Type D7 1-ton half-track, a new vehicle was developed, featuring one less roadwheel and a correspondingly shorter chassis. Upon this was mounted an armored body with sloping armor and

Right: *The SdKfz 252 leichte Gepanzerte Muntionskraftwagen is not considered a true member of the 250 family, as it was built well ahead of its brethren. Designed specifically for use in Sturmgeschütz units, it featured a fully enclosed armored superstructure and a long sloping back hull. Within this long hull plate were two large doors that when opened revealed a large interior stowage bay for ammunition. This is a vehicle of the StuG Abt. 210 immobilized near Demidov—a town on the Kasplya River near Smolensk Oblast, Russia.* Bundesarchiv

Left: *Here an SdKfz 252 of the StuG Abt. 249 bombs up a StuG in the town of Kolonha in Crimea. The utility of the large rear doors is apparent here. It is thought that the SdKfz 252* leichte Gepanzerte Munitionskraftwagen *could carry up to two hundred rounds of 7.5 cm ammunition. An additional thirty-six rounds could be carried in a specially designed trailer known as the Sonder-Anhänger (Sd Ah) für Munition (7.5 cm) (Sd Ah 32/1). The SdKfz 252 was eventually replaced by the SdKfz 250/6.* National Archives and Records Administration

Above: *This is a SdKfz 252 of the StuG Abt. 210 immobilized near Demidov—a town on the Kasplya River near Smolensk Oblast, Russia. From this angle, the rooftop enclosure is clearly visible.* National Archives and Records Administration

Le gep *Beobachtungskraftwagen* (SdKfz 253)

Specifications	
Length	4.70 m
Width	1.95 m
Height	1.80 m
Weight	5.7 tons
Fuel capacity	140 liters
Maximum speed	65 km/hr
Range, on-road	320 km
Range, cross-country	210 km
Crew	4
Communications	FuG 6, FuG 2
Automotive	
Engine make	Maybach
Engine model	HL42 TRKM
Engine configuration	6-cylinder, liquid cooled
Engine displacement	4.198 liters
Engine horsepower	100 @ 2800 rpm

M *gepanzerter Beobachtungskraftwagen* (SdKfz 254)

Specifications	
Length	4.50 m
Width	2.47 m
Height	2.33 m
Weight	6.4 tons
Fuel capacity	72 liters
Maximum speed	75 km/hr
Range, on-road	500 km
Range, cross-country	100 km
Crew	4
Communications	FuG 6, FuG 2, Tornister Funkgerät
Automotive	
Engine make	Saurer
Engine model	CRDv Diesel
Engine configuration	4-cylinder, liquid cooled
Engine displacement	5.3 liters
Engine horsepower	70 @ 2000 rpm

featuring an amored roof enclosure. The pilot models were available for testing in the fall of 1937.

Designated the *leichter Gepanzerter Beobachtungskraftwagen* (SdKfz 253), or light armored observation vehicle, the first twenty-five vehicles were built in March through June 1940. These vehicles were issued in groups of five to *Sturmgeschütz* batteries.

Following the successful employment of these vehicles, 260 more SdKfz 253 were assembled by June of the following year.

M *gepanzerter Beobachtungskraftwagen* (SdKfz 254)

This unusual vehicle equipped with both wheels and tracks was developed in 1936 by Saurer-Werke for the Austrian army. Classified as the *Raeder-Raupenfahrzeug 7*, 160 of the vehicles were ordered. By the time Germany annexed Austria in March 1938, the vehicle had been renamed the M36 gg 2/2 t ZgWg.

Although undecided what role it would play in their plans, the German military was nonetheless interested in the vehicle. Three chassis were complete and shipped to Daimler-Benz where superstructures were installed, then the vehicles were forwarded to the Kummersdorf proving ground for testing.

Delivery of production vehicles began in June 1940 and continued sporadically through March 1941 until ultimately 128 were built. In March 1940, the German army redesignated the vehicle as *gepanzerter Artillerie-Beobachtungskraftwagen* auf RK7 (SdKfz 254).

The vehicles served on the African and Russian Fronts with the artillery regiments of various Panzer divisions. The operator's manual refers to the vehicle as *mittlerer gepanzerter Beobachtungskraftwagen* (SdKfz 254) *auf Raeder-Kettenfahrgetell* RK7.

Mun Kw fur Nebelwerfer (SdKfz 4) and 15 cm Panzerwerfer 42 auf Sf (SdKfz 4/1)

The half-track known as the *Maultier* came about by converting cargo trucks to half-tracks to meet pressing mobility requirements on the Russian Front. In 1943, Opel was asked to create a version of the *Maultier* with an armored body equipped for the mounting of the 15 cm *Nebelwerfer*. This would both increase the mobility of the Nebelwerfer battery and increase protection for the crews. This increase in

Above: *The SdKfz 254 was a unique variation on the half-track concept in that the vehicle could be operated in either the fully tracked or fully wheeled configurations. This was accomplished by having retractible wheels mounted on what in essence was a fully tracked vehicle.* National Archives

Above: *A disabled SdKfz 254 is inspected in the desert.* National Archives

protection was twofold. Not only were they protected from enemy small-arms fire, they were also protected from the launching blast, negating the time-consuming need to dig the protective trenches used by conventional *Nebelwerfer* batteries.

Mun Kw *fur* Nebelwerfer (SdKfz 4) and 15 cm *Panzerwerfer 42 auf Sf* (SdKfz 4/1)

7.5 cm *Selbstfahrlafette* L/40.8 *Modell* 1

This specialized half-track tank destroyer was designed by Büssing-NAG in the mid-1930s. Two different trial vehicles were built, on two different chassis, both designated 7.5 cm *Selbstfahrlafette* L/40.8 *Modell* 1. The first *Selbstfahrlafette*, or self-propelled carriage, were on the rear-engined BNL6(H) chassis. This chassis had five roadwheels. An alternate prototype was also constructed utilizing the BN10(H) chassis, this can be distinguished by its six roadwheels.

Both vehicles had armored bodies and mounted a Rheinmetall-Borsig 7.5 cm L/40.8 cannon in a turret designed by the gun's maker. It is believed that three trial vehicles were produced.

3.7 cm *Selbstfahrlafette* L/70

This experimental half-track was built between 1935 and 1936 by Hansa-Loyd for use as a *Panzerjäger*. The HL kl 3 (H) chassis was a rear-engine design with tracks extending three-quarters of the way forward. It was armed with a 3.7 cm PaK L/70 mounted in a turret, both the gun and turret being designed by Rheinmetall-Borsig. An unknown number of vehicles were built, none of which it is believed were used in combat.

Schwerer Wehrmachtschlepper (gep Ausf)

The sWS was envisioned to be the German Army's standard heavy towing tractor, a status that it never attained. However, its increased load-carrying capacity and mobility compared to the Maultier meant that it was natural that the army would want to use the sWS as the basis for their *Nebelwerfer*-armed half-tracks, and in mid-1944 they did just that.

An armored body, similar to the one developed for the rocket-armed *Maultier*, was installed along with the ten-tube launcher. The sWS-based vehicle had the added advantage of increased ammunition stowage capacity over the *Maultier* vehicle.

Another armored cab was also developed along with a body with fold-down sides in order to allow the effective mounting of the 3.7 cm FlaK 43 L/89.

Both these variants saw service from mid-1944 through the end of the war.

Above: *The basic vehicle shown here is an Opel 3-ton* Maultier, *based in turn on the Blitz truck. In 1943, an armored version of the* Maultier *was introduced.* Walter J. Spielberger

Left: *Six hundred of the armored* Maultier *were produced from April 1943 through March 1944. One half of these were equipped with a ten-tube 15 cm Nebelwerfer launcher.* Patton Museum

Left: *The* Nebelwerfer *was not a terribly accurate weapon, lending itself rather to area use, such as bombardment prior to an assault. Their use, however, was quite demoralizing to opposing troops.* National Archives

Left: *This Rheinmetall-built rear-engined half-track mounting a 7.5 cm antitank gun was photographed January 27, 1940. Despite its powerful gun, it was not considered a success.* Patton Museum

ARMORED SEMI-TRACK VEHICLES   285

Left: *The 3.7 cm Selbstfahrlafette L/70 was an experimental rear-engined half-track developed in the mid-1930s. It was intended as a nimble, lightly armored, tank destroyer.* Patton Museum

Above: *A few of the sWS, or heavy army towing tractor, half-tracks were built with armored bodies. It was intended to use these as platforms for the mounting of 3.7 cm FlaK guns and Nebelwerfer rocket launchers.* National Archives

Chapter 11
Armored Cars

Maschinengewehrkraftwagen (Kfz 13)/ Funkkraftwagen (Kfz 14)

Two of the earliest armored cars that Germany built as part of its rearmament immediately prior to World War II were the *Maschinengewehrkraftwagen* (Kfz 13) and the *Funkkraftwagen* (Kfz 14). They were based on reinforced Daimler-Benz and Adler chassis for automobiles and proved far from ideal as armored vehicles.

Regardless of which chassis was employed, the two vehicles resembled each other. Daimler-Benz converted its own chassis as well as those from Adler and fitted the armored bodies onto the vehicles. The most that the thin armor could resist was 7.92 mm fire. Even then, only the front of the vehicle was protected against armor-piercing shells.

The *Maschinengewehrkraftwagen* Kfz 13, as implied by its designation, was armed with a 7.92 mm MG 13 machine gun. Pedestal mounted, the gun could rotate a full 360 degrees. The Kfz 13 was equipped to carry one thousand rounds of ammunition for the machine gun.

The radio-equipped *Funkkraftwagen* Kfz 14 carried no machine gun; its interior space was occupied by a 5-watt transmitter and receiver that could handle both voice communications and key operation.

Between 1933 and 1935, thirty radio vehicles and 116 machine-gun carriers were built. It is considered unlikely that any of those machine-gun or radio vehicles ever saw service on the front lines of World War II.

Kfz 13 and Kfz 14-Daimler-Benz Construction

Specifications	
Length	4.20 m
Width	1.70 m
Height	1.46 m
Weight	2.1 tons
Fuel capacity	45 liters
Maximum speed	70 km/hr
Range, on-road	250 km
Range, cross-country	150 km
Crew	2
Communications	Fu9 SE 5 in Kfz 14 only
Tire size	6.00-20
Armament	
Weapon, main	7.92 mm MG13 in Kfz 13 only
Ammo stowage, main	1,000 rounds
Automotive	
Engine make	Daimler-Benz
Engine configuration	6-cylinder, liquid cooled
Engine displacement	2.6 liters
Engine horsepower	50

ARMORED CARS

Above: *The* Maschinengewehrkraftwagen *(Kfz 13) was a simple armored car built on a commercial car chassis and equipped with 8 mm steel plate. Designed for the interwar Reichswehr, they were intended to provide basic training to motorized troops. Armament was the MG13 7.92 mm machine gun mounted on a pedestal and protected by an armored shield also of 8 mm thickness. There was a radio-equipped version known as the* Funkkraftwagen *(Kfz 14).* National Archives and Records Administration

SdKfz 221

Specifications	
Length	4.56 m
Width	1.95 m
Height	1.70 m
Weight	3,85 tons
Fuel capacity	110 liters
Maximum speed	80 km/hr
Range, on-road	350 km
Range, cross-country	200 km
Fording depth	60 cm
Crew	2
Communications	none from factory
Tires	210-18
Armor	5.5 mm to 8 mm thick, sloped
Armament	
Weapon, main	7.92 mm MG 34
Ammo stowage, main	1,050 rounds
Automotive	
Engine make	Horch
Engine model	801
Engine configuration	V-8, liquid cooled
Engine displacement	3.5 liters
Engine horsepower	75 @ 3600 rpm

SdKfz 221

The *Sonderkraftfahrzeug* SdKfz 221 was, unlike its predecessor, built on a chassis specially designed by Auto-Union's Horch works for armored cars. This difference was the basis for the different designation of *Sonderkraftfahrzeug*—a specialized vehicle rather than a simple *Kraftfahrzeug* vehicle. The first trial chassis was completed in July 1934. Upon acceptance, the same facility began series production of the chassis, which was designated *Typ* 801. Armored bodies for the SdKfz 221 were built by Deutsche Edelstahlwerke in Hannover, Boehler Werk Kapfenberg, and Schoeller Bleckmann, Muerzzuschlag.

With its four-wheel drive and four-wheel steering, coupled with a fairly powerful engine for its era, the SdKfz 221 had adequate off-road as well as on-road capability.

Atop the roof of the SdKfz 221 was a manually rotated open-topped gun shield that at first glance gave the appearance of a turret. Folding screens afforded additional protection against grenades being hurled into the enclosure behind the gun shield.

Initial production of the SdKfz 221 was divided among four production lots, corresponding to various contracts. The chassis (*Fahrgestell*) numbers of these groups were 810001–810359, 810360–810485, 810486–810817, and 810818–810414. It is important to note that these are *chassis* numbers, and some chassis within each of those ranges were used for armored cars other than the SdKfz 221.

The military soon decided that a more powerful engine and more robust chassis were needed for the armored cars (even the operator's manual warned that the vehicle,

Above: *The* leichte Panzerspähwagen *SdKfz 221 was the first of many four-wheeled armored cars fielded by the Germans in World War II. It was based on the Horsch 801 heavy car chassis and featured a rear-mounted engine, four-wheel drive, and front-wheel steering. Armor protection was 8 mm, and it was armed with an MG 34 in an eight-sided turret. Two series were produced, and this is an earlier Series 1 vehicle. Patton Museum*

SdKfz 223 Ausf A

Specifications	
Length	4.56 m
Width	1.95 m
Height	1.75 m
Weight	4.2 tons
Fuel capacity	100 liters
Maximum speed	85 km/hr
Range, on-road	300 km
Range, cross-country	200 km
Crew	3
Communications	FuG 10 SE 30
Tires	210-18
Armament	
Weapon, main	7.92 mm MG 13 or 34
Ammo stowage, main	1,000 rounds
Automotive	
Engine make	Horch
Engine configuration	V-8, liquid cooled
Engine displacement	3.5 liters
Engine horsepower	75 @ 3600 rpm

with its allotted equipment, was loaded to the maximum). Accordingly, in 1939 efforts were made to upgrade the chassis, resulting in the *Typ* 801v chassis. These chassis included a 90-horsepower version of the Horch engine, new transmission, shock absorbers, and power brakes.

Originally, the improved chassis was to be used on the SdKfz 221 as well as other variants (SdKfz 222, SdKfz 223, SdKfz 260, SdKfz 261), but the lackluster performance of the type on the Eastern Front led to the cancellation of orders for several chassis, with the result that the improved chassis, while used on some of the variants listed above, was not used in SdKfz 221 production.

Early SdKfz 221 vehicles were fitted with an MG 13, but later MG 34 machine guns were retrofitted. In the end, some of the SdKfz 221 vehicles were fitted with the 2.8 cm *schwere Panzerbüchse* 41 (sPzB 41).

By the time production ceased in August 1940, a total of 339 SdKfz 221 had been produced.

SdKfz 223

Also built on the Horch 801 and 801v chassis specially engineered for armored cars, the SdKfz 223, like the SdKfz 221 and 222, all which featured four-wheel drive and four-wheel steering. Slightly heavier than the SdKfz 221, the 223 used the same Horch 801 V-8 power plant and therefore its performance was somewhat inferior. The additional weight was the result of radio equipment and radio operator, features that distinguished this vehicle from the SdKfz 221.

Three men—a driver, radio operator, and commander/gunner—made up the crew of the SdKfz 223.

Production of the 535 vehicles built was divided into four groups. Horch 801 chassis serial numbers 810001–810359 included 117 SdKfz 223, with twelve assembled by Daimler-Benz, sixty-four SdKfz 223 assembled by Deutsche-Werke and forty-one SdKfz 223 assembled by Schichau. Serial numbers 810700 through 810817 included 118 SdKfz 223, all of which were assembled by MNH, Hannover between June 1939 and September 1940. The same facility produced a further 112 between September 1940 and December 1941, those using chassis in serial number range 810818 to 810414. The final group of 208 SdKfz 223 used chassis in the serial number range of 8110004 to 8110994, with seventy-two being assembled by Wegmann between July 1942 and February 1944, and 136 by Weserhuette, from April 1943 to February 1944. These 208 vehicles were the Ausf B variant, while the prior groups were all Ausf A vehicles.

SdKfz 223 Ausf B

Specifications	
Length	4.80 m
Width	1.95 m
Height	1.75 m
Weight	4.48 tons
Fuel capacity	100 liters
Maximum speed	85 km/hr
Range, on-road	300 km
Range, cross-country	200 km
Crew	3
Communications	FuG 12 SE 80
Tires	210-18
Armament	
Weapon, main	7.92 mm MG 34
Ammo stowage, main	1,100 rounds
Automotive	
Engine make	Horch
Engine configuration	V-8, liquid cooled
Engine displacement	3.8 liters
Engine horsepower	90 @ 3600 rpm

Above: *A modification to the original SdKfz 221 concept was the leichte Panzerspähwagen (Fu) SdKfz 223. This differed from the 221 by featuring a radio system. Six series of the SdKfz 223 were produced, with each subsequent offering incremental improvement in automotive performance and construction method. The hull of the SdKfz 223 was somewhat wider, and the turret was mounted further back than on the earlier vehicle. It also featured a larger engine and four-wheel steering.* National Archives and Records Administration

Above: *The SdKfz 223 initally carried the FuG 10 radio set, which was a medium wave transceiver (with both a receiver and transmitter) that was used in command tanks. It had a transmit power of 30 watts and was used with a frame antenna. Later series of the SdKfz 223, such as this one undergoing evaluation at the US Army's Aberdeen Proving Ground, featured cast vision visors and an armored cover over the radiator grills.* Patton Museum

Above: *This rear view clearly shows the armored cover of the later Series SdKfz 223. These vehicles were assigned to reconnaissance units that ranged far ahead of armored formations. With their speed and radios they were able to act as the long-range eyes of the armored commanders in order to exploit any weakness in the enemy's strength.* Patton Museum

Atop the roof of the SdKfz 223 was a manually rotated open-topped gun shield that at first glance gave the appearance of a turret. Folding screens afforded additional protection against grenades being hurled into the enclosure behind the gun shield. Early SdKfz 223 vehicles were fitted with an MG 13, but from March 10, 1938, the vehicles were armed with MG 34 machine guns instead.

Radios were a feature of all the 1935 through February 1944 production-run SdKfz 223 vehicles. 30-Watt FuG 10 SE 30 radios were fitted to the SdKfz 223 Ausf A vehicles, but the Ausf B vehicles had factory-installed 80-Watt FuG 12 sets instead. These more powerful radios were also retro-fitted to the older SdKfz 223 vehicles.

Kleiner Panzerfunkwagen (SdKfz 260 and 261)

The SdKfz 260 and 261 were *kleiner Panzerfunkwagen*, or small radio cars, built on the *Typ* 801 and 801v chassis. The radio cars featured the four-wheel drive and four-wheel

SdKfz 260 and SdKfz 261 Ausf A

Specifications	
Length	4.83 m
Width	1.99 m
Height	1.78 m
Weight	4.3 tons
Fuel capacity	110 liters
Maximum speed	75 km/hr
Range, on-road	320 km
Range, cross-country	200 km
Crew	4
Communications, SdKfz 260	kl.Pz.Fu.Tr.c, FuG 7 SE 20, Fu Spr Ger a
Communications, SdKfz 261	kl.Pz.Fu.Tr.d, FuG 10 SE 30, Fu Spr Ger a
Tires	210-18
Armament	
Weapon	none
Automotive	
Engine make	Horch
Engine configuration	V-8, liquid cooled
Engine displacement	3.5 liters
Engine horsepower	75 @ 3600 rpm

SdKfz 260 and SdKfz 261 Ausf B

Specifications	
Length	4.80 m
Width	1.95 m
Height	1.75 m
Weight	4.36 tons
Fuel capacity	100 liters
Maximum speed	85 km/hr
Range, on-road	320 km
Range, cross-country	200 km
Crew	4
Communications, SdKfz 260	kl.Pz.Fu.Tr.c, FuG 7 SE 20, Fu Spr Ger a
Communications, SdKfz 261	kl.Pz.Fu.Tr.d, FuG 12 SE 80, Fu Spr Ger a
Tires	210-18
Armament	
Weapon	none
Automotive	
Engine make	Horch
Engine configuration	V-8, liquid cooled
Engine displacement	3.5 liters
Engine horsepower	90 @ 3600 rpm

steering of the other vehicles in the series, but unlike them, the radio cars lacked armament.

Strictly intended for communications, the SdKfz 260 was set up for ground-to-air communications, while the SdKfz 261 boasted a large frame antenna that facilitated long-range ground communications.

Both the *Typ* 801 and *Typ* 801v chassis were employed in the manufacture of these communication vehicles. The Ausf A vehicles utilized the *Typ* 801 chassis, while the Ausf B used the typ 801v chassis, which featured a ninety-horsepower engine, rather than the seventy-five-horsepower engine of the *Typ* 801. Although delays caused both the trial vehicles and the production vehicles to miss their scheduled completion dates, in the end, 132 SdKfz 260 were built between April 1941 and April 1943. Thirty-six of these were Ausf A vehicles assembled by Weserhuette between April

Above: *Utilizing the same armor and automotive improvements seen on the SdKfz 223, the kleine Panzerfunkwagen SdKfz 260/261 was conceived to provide communication for the signal units of swiftly moving Panzer groups. The two vehicles can be distinguished by the presence of the large frame antenna, which is indicative of the SdKfz 261. Neither vehicle carried a weapon, so the forward hull was clear for stowage as on this Afrika Korps example. Four Series were produced.* Patton Museum

Above: *This SdKfz 261 is being prepared for rail movement. The screen arrangement that protected the radio compartment is raised here and can be seen to good advantage. A small generator is installed in the stowage box on the left-hand side. This was used to test the radios when the engine was shut down. The fuel hose can be seen dangling from the corner of the box. This vehicle bears the markings of a signals unit of the 5th Panzer Division. The dark areas around the insignia appear to indicate this vehicle has been repainted overall dark yellow.* National Archives and Records Administration

Above: *The SdKfz 261 carried a FuG 12 radio set, which was also a medium wave transceiver (receiver/transmitter) used for tank command networks. It differed from the FuG 10 in that it was more powerful with a transmit power of 80 watts. The SdKfz 260 carried a FuG 7, which was a VHF transceiver. It was usually used with the 1.4-meter antenna, so this vehicle would have differed only in the appearance of the frame antenna. Interestingly, this radio was matched with the Luftwaffe transceiver FuG 17 for ground support operations. This vehicle is part of a substantial reconnaissance patrol and has its frame antenna in the collapsed position.* Patton Museum

1941 and July 1941, and 96 were Ausf B vehicles assembled by the same firm from April 1942 until April 1943.

Concurrently, 352 of the SdKfz 261s were produced, with 215 of them being Ausf A built from April 1941 through March 1942, followed by 137 Ausf B produced from April 1942 through April 1943. Weserhuette assembled all of these at Bad Oeynhausen.

SdKfz 222

The SdKfz 222 shared the Horch *Typ* 801 (and later, *Typ* 801v) with the SdKfz 221, but rather than being armed with a machine gun, the turret of the SdKfz 222 carried a heavier armament, specifically the 2 cm KwK 38 cannon and coaxial MG 34 machine gun.

Like the SdKfz 221 and 223, the SdKfz 222 was initially built on the Horch *Typ* 801 chassis, which featured four-wheel drive and four-wheel steering. While the chassis gave the vehicles acceptable off-road operation, drivers were instructed that the vehicles were to be opeated on-road whenever practical, and that four-wheel steer was to be used only when operating off-road, or at slow speed in close quarters. Use of four-wheel steer at highway speeds was forbidden, due to safety concerns.

SdKfz 222 Ausf A

Specifications	
Length	4.80 m
Width	1.95 m
Height	2.00 m
Weight	4.8 tons
Fuel capacity	110 liters
Maximum speed	70 km/hr
Range, on-road	300 km
Range, cross-country	180 km
Crew	3
Communications	none from factory
Tires	210-18
Armament	
Weapon, main	2 cm KwK30 up to September 1940, 2 cm KwK 38 thereafter
Weapon, secondary	7.92 mm MG 13 up to March 1938, MG 34 thereafter
Ammo stowage, main	180 rounds
Ammo stowage, secondary	1,050 rounds
Automotive	
Engine make	Horch
Engine configuration	V-8, liquid cooled
Engine displacement	3.5 liters
Engine horsepower	75 @ 3600 rpm

SdKfz 222 Ausf B

Specifications	
Length	4.80 m
Width	1.95 m
Height	2.00 m
Weight	4.8 tons
Fuel capacity	100 liters
Maximum speed	85 km/hr
Range, on-road	300 km
Range, cross-country	180 km
Crew	3
Communications	Fu Spr Ger a or f
Tires	210-18
Armament	
Weapon, main	2 cm KwK38
Weapon, secondary	7.92 mm MG 34
Ammo stowage, main	180 rounds
Ammo stowage, secondary	1,100 rounds
Automotive	
Engine make	Horch
Engine configuration	V-8, liquid cooled
Engine displacement	3.8 liters
Engine horsepower	90 @ 3600 rpm

Three men—a driver, loader, and commander/gunner—made up the crew of the SdKfz 222.

A total of 990 SdKfz 222 were built in five groups, four groups of which were the Ausf A, while the final group were the Ausf B. The first group of seventy-two vehicles were built from 1935 through 1937, with Daimler-Benz assembling ten examples, thirty-six by Schichau, and twenty-six by Deutsche-Werke. Production of the seventy-two vehicles in the second series began in April 1938 and continued through November of the same year. The third group, consisting of only sixty-four vehicles, was assembled by Schichau from June 1939 through January 1940. The fourth and final group of Ausf A vehicles were built at the same plant from September 1940 through December 1941, and was the largest yet, including 232 vehicles. The main armament was changed at that time, with the KwK38 being installed, and elevation increased five degrees, to eighty-five degrees. The final group of SdKfz 222 were the 550 Ausf B vehicles, which were built from May 1942 through June 1943, with 350 flowing from the Büssing-NAG assembly line, and two hundred from the Schichau facilty.

As with other members of the light armored car family, on March 10, 1938, it was ordered that the MG 34 machine gun be installed rather than the previously used MG 13.

Beginning in 1941 and continuing until the end of production, radios were installed in the SdKfz 222 vehicles. Similar equipment was to be retrofitted to earlier production vehicles.

ARMORED CARS 293

Left: *The* leichte Panzerspähwagen *SdKfz 222 (2 cm) was designed to provide the armed might behind the reconnaissance arm. Outfitted with the reliable 2 cm KwK 30 or KwK 38 cannon, it also carried an MG 34 in a coaxial mount—all ensconced in an eight-sided rotating turret with 8 mm of armor. Using the same improved armored body and chassis as the SdKfz 221 and 223, the SdKfz 222 also had increased armored protection on the front of 30 mm. Five different series were produced.* National Archives and Records Administration

Left: *The SdKfz 222 continued to serve on all fronts until the end of the war. This vehicle is seen here while engaged on the Normandy front in the summer of 1944. This later series vehicle mounts the distinctive and elaborate formed wire guards over the turn signals (upper middle hull) and the Notek light (front left fender). The triangular armored guards for the wheel hubs were abandoned after the third Series. The SdKfz 222 carried only the FuG Spr Ger radio for short-range communication.* National Archives and Records Administration

Above: *This late Series SdKfz 222 is undergoing evaluation by the British. It is missing most of its external sheet metal stowage boxes. Although the main gun is missing here, the mount has been elevated to nearly a vertical position—useful to engage aerial targets. Both weapons were mounted on a sophisticated pedestal system known as Sockellafette. Attached to a large frame that was integrated into the floor of the vehicle, it featured seats, as well as elevation and traversing handwheels. Patton Museum*

Above: *In Germany during the early 1930s, the Army Weapons Office Test Unit 6 (WaPrw 6) experimented with several different prototype armored cars based on a 6-Rad (six-wheel) truck chassis. The several prototypes included this one with a hexagonal turret, drum-shaped cupolas for the front and rear drivers, and no frontal plate with visor for the driver. Patton Museum*

SdKfz 231

Germany's first successful heavy armored car was the *Kraftfahrzeug* (Kfz) 67, which was later designated the *sonder Kraftfahrzeug* (SdKfz) 231 (6-Rad). The SdKfz 231 (6-Rad) and its radio-equipped counterpart the SdKfz 232 (6-Rad) were both based on modified contemporary German 6 x 4 truck chassis. One of the modifications was the fact that the chassis was lengthened so as to allow for a second, rear-facing driver's position. The Daimler-Benz G3A chassis was used for most SdKfz 231 vehicles. Vehicle bodies were produced by armor manufacturers. Aside from the Daimler-Benz chassis, other notable chassis were produced by Büssing-NAG, which provided the G31P, and Magirus, which furnished the M206A. The armor applied to the vehicle was intended to protect the occupants of the vehicle from 7.92 mm armor-piercing rounds fired from at least thirty meters away.

The SdKfz 231 design retained the conventional truck chassis layout with the engine in front, but the inclusion of an additional driver's position at the rear of the car allowed the vehicle to reverse directions even when there was insufficient space for a 180-degree turn. Atop the vehicle was a

SdKfz 231 (6-Rad)

Specifications	
Length	5.57 m
Width	1.82 m
Height	2.25 m
Weight	5.7 tons
Fuel capacity	105 liters
Maximum speed	70 km/hr
Range, on-road	250 km
Tire size	6.00-20
Crew	4
Armament	
Weapon, main	2 cm KwK30
Weapon, coaxial	7.92 MG 13
Ammo stowage, main	200 rounds
Ammo stowage, secondary	1,500 rounds
Automotive	
Engine make	Daimler-Benz
Engine model	M09
Engine configuration	6-cylinder, liquid cooled
Engine displacement	3.7 liters
Engine horsepower	65

ARMORED CARS 295

Left: *Developed during the 1930s, the SdKfz 231 (6-Rad) was the first German heavy armored car to enter production. It saw considerable combat in the early stage of World War II. The SdKfz 231 (6-Rad) was characterized by a single front axle, two rear axles, a long front end, and a revolving turret housing a 2 cm KwK 30 cannon and a 7.92 mm MG 13.* Bundesarchiv

Left: *The rear of the turret of the SdKfz 231 (6-Rad) was curved, with a two-panel door with a rain gutter over it. A dome-shaped hatch and a hinged visor were provided for both the front driver and, as seen here, the rear driver. A two-panel door on the rear of the hull provided access for the rear driver.* Bundesarchiv

Left: *On the left side of the front of the turret of the SdKfz 231 (6-Rad) was a visor with two hinges on top, above which was a curved rain gutter. The front driver had visors to the front and to the left side.* Bundesarchiv

Left: *A disarmed SdKfz 231 (6-Rad) manufactured by Magirus, center, is part of a display of military equipment, next to a radio-equipped SdKfz 232 (6-Rad) parked to the right. The registration plate is the Reichswehr type, in use until September 1935. Behind that plate is the muffler.* Thomas Anderson

manually traversed gun turret fitted with a 2 cm cannon and coaxial MG 13 machine gun.

The six-wheeled SdKfz 231 was in production from 1932 through 1937, when it was superseded by eight-wheeled armored cars that boasted improved off-road mobility.

During the course of production in 1935, manufacturers began installing an antiaircraft machine gun outside the vehicle's turret. A spare tire was also added. Although this pioneer German heavy armored vehicle suffered from limitations, it did see limited service in Austria, Poland, and France.

SdKfz 232 (6-Rad)

Initially designated the *gepanzerten Kraftwagen* (Fu) (Kfz 67a), the radio-equipped version of the SdKfz 231 heavy reconnaissance car was later, in April 1936, reclassified to the designation that is now more familiar: *schwerer Panzerspähwagen* (Fu) SdKfz 232 (6-Rad). Most of the vehicles were constructed on the Magirus chassis, which was introduced in the middle of the 1930s. A few of the radio-equipped vehicles were also manufactured using Daimler-Benz and Büssing-NAG chassis. All the chassis used in making the SdKfz 232 boasted electrical generators that were larger than those used on the SdKfz 231 chassis. Additional output was necessary to run the Fu Ger 11 SE 100 medium-range radio and the Fu Spr Ger "a" short-range radio set featured in the vehicle.

Although it expedited production, the use of commercial 6 x 4 commercial truck chassis as the basis for their design meant that both the SdKfz 231 and the SdKfz 232 6-*Rad* were somewhat hampered as combat vehicles. The truck chassis was known as a reliable automotive powertrain, but was never intended for off-road use. Off-road use was, however, inevitably a necessity in a combat vehicle—even if it was a reconnaissance vehicle.

The use of the truck chassis left the SdKfz 231 and SdKfz 232 with low ground clearance and relatively limited suspension articulation, and as a result, the vehicles tended to become high-centered in rough terrain. Lacking all-wheel drive, the addition of even relatively light armor resulted in these vehicles getting easily mired. Because of these shortcomings, the 231 and 232 were withdrawn from the front lines after the invasion of France.

The shortcomings of the SdKfz 231 and 232 were instructive, however, and the next vehicle series retained the same SdKfz numbers but otherwise reflected a totally new design.

SdKfz 263 (6-Rad)

In the middle of the 1930s, a decision was made to convert a dozen of the newer Kfz 67a (SdKfz 231 6-*Rad*) vehicles into radio cars that would serve with the signal battalions of a number of Panzer divisions. The vehicles' turret was fixed, with a flat plate forming its face. An MG 13 machine gun in a ball mount was fitted in the vehicle as its one weapon.

Within the vehicle, a hundred-watt radio set was attached to an exterior frame antenna. A telescoping aerial was also fitted. Built on chassis from Magirus, the new vehicles were dubbed the Kfz 67b—a classification replaced in 1937, when the vehicles were barely a year old, by the designation SdKfz 263 (6-*Rad*).

SdKfz 231 (8-Rad)

In a bid to tackle the problem of off-road mobility of the six-wheeled armored cars, the *Waffenamt*'s WaPruf 6 automotive design office made a request to Büssing-NAG to come up with a design for an all-new vehicle.

The WaPruf 6 request resulted in the SdKfz 231 (8-*Rad*), an eight-wheeled armored car that entered production late in

SdKfz 232 (6-Rad)

Specifications	
Length	5.57 m
Width	1.82 m
Height	2.87 over antenna
Weight	6 tons
Fuel capacity	110 liters
Maximum speed	62 km/hr
Range, on-road	250 km
Tire size	6.00-20
Crew	4
Armament	
Weapon, main	2 cm KwK30
Weapon, coaxial	7.92 MG 13
Ammo stowage, main	200 rounds
Ammo stowage, secondary	1,500 rounds
Automotive	
Engine make	Magirus
Engine model	s88
Engine configuration	6-cylinder, liquid cooled
Engine displacement	4.6 liters
Engine horsepower	70

Left: *Originally designated the (FU) Kfz 67A until April 1936, the subsequently renamed SdKfz 232 (6-Rad) was the radio version of the SdKfz 231 (6-Rad). It was fitted with a large frame antenna, supported by two struts on the rear of the body and a bracket on the turret with a pivoting support, allowing the turret to enjoy full traverse. The vehicle shown here was made by Büssing-NAG.* Patton Museum

Left: *Two SdKfz 232 (6-Rad) heavy armored cars are running in opposite directions in dusty conditions. The turret of the closer car, traversed to the rear, displays the early design of mantlet; to the side of the mantlet, the gunner's visor is open.* Patton Museum

Left: *One of the fifty-four SdKfz 232 (6-Rad) heavy armored cars built by Büssing-NAG from 1933 to 1937, this vehicle exhibits the armored shields that frequently were bolted to the wheels, to provide protection to the bearings. The shields for the front wheels were round, while those for the rear wheels were triangular with rounded corners. The designs of the supports for the frame antenna are also apparent. Thomas Anderson*

1936. Purpose built, the vehicle had independent suspension and eight tires with self-sealing innertubes. All eight wheels had power and could be steered. Powering the new armored car was Büssing's eight-cylinder L8V/G.S.36 engine.

As had been the case with its predecessor, the SdKfz 231 had a driver's position at both ends of the vehicle, which could cruise at 85 km/hr in either direction. A four-man crew of driver, co-driver, commander, and gunner served on the vehicle, whose armament and armor were comparable to those of the six-wheeled armored cars. The SdKfz 231, however, boasted a turret of a different configuration.

A 2 cm automatic cannon plus a coaxial 7.92 mm MG 13 machine gun were fitted in the vehicles, which had stowage of 1,125 rounds of 7.92 ammunition and 180 rounds of 2 cm shells—enough when the cannon was operated as a single-shot weapon. Producers began to install a belt-fed MG 34 with flexible mount in May 1939, in lieu of the previously installed MG 13. Initially the KwK 30 was the 2 cm cannon used in the SdKfz 231, but in 1942 that weapon was replaced by the KwK 38 that lacked the KwK30's tapered configuration.

Despite having a drivetrain that was overburdened and armor that could be penetrated by anything equal to or greater than a US M2 HB .50 caliber machine-gun round, the eight-wheeled SdKfz 231 continued to be produced into 1943, and remained in frontline use until the German surrender in May 1945.

SdKfz 232 8-*Rad*

Sharing almost every component part with the SdKfz 231 8-*Rad* was the SdKfz 232 8-*Rad*, which went through development alongside it. Like the six-wheeled SdKfz 232, the SdKfz 232 (8-*Rad*) was designed to facilitate long-distance radio communication for the heavy platoon of the armored reconnaissance company of each reconnaissance battalion. To fulfill this role, three SdKfz 232 vehicles served with every heavy platoon, being fed information via Morse code from a light platoon of SdKfz 223 four-wheeled armored cars.

In the beginning, the 232 was distinguished from the 231 by the massive frame aerial that loomed atop the 232. The antenna served together with the powerful hundred-watt FuG 11 SE 100 radio. When the vehicle was halted, the radio with its big antenna boasted a voice range of 70 km. To augment this equipment, a turret-mounted *Funksprechgerät* a was added in 1941. The SdKfz 231 also began to incorporate the *Funksprechgerät* a at the same time. These 24.11 to 25.01 megahertz (MHz) radios only had a range of one kilometer when the vehicle was moving. Early in 1943, the 19.9 to 21.4 MHz *Funksprechgerät* f replaced the *Funksprechgerät* a, and increased the radio range to three kilometers when the vehicle was in motion.

The FuG 11 radios began to be replaced on SdKfz 232 vehicles by 80-Watt FuG 12 SE 80 radio sets with their distinctive, but considerably smaller "star" aerials in July

Left: *Wehrmacht troops assess the damages in the aftermath of an accident in which an SdKfz 232 (6-Rad) burst through an iron fence along an elevated roadway, crashing the front end on pavement below. The guns have been retrieved from the turret.* Thomas Anderson

ARMORED CARS

Above: *Another type of radio-equipped heavy armored car was the SdKfz 263 (6-Rad), which was distinguished from the SdKfz 232 (6-Rad) by having two support struts for the frame antenna located to the immediate front of a fixed, not-traversing turret. The rear antenna supports were similar to those on the SdKfz 232 (6-Rad). Fewer than thirty SdKfz 263 (6-Rad) heavy armored cars were built, including the one shown here crossing a pontoon bridge.* National Archives and Records Administration

1942. The voice range of the Fu 12 SE 80 was 60 km when the vehicle was standing still, and 25 km when the vehicle was moving. The new antenna made it more difficult to distinguish the SdKfz 232 from the SdKfz 231—in itself a substantial tactical advantage. Between 1936 and 1943, 610 SdKfz 231 and 232 (8-*Rad*) armored cars were manufactured.

SdKfz 233

Armored reconnaissance units acquired a more formidable weapon than they had previously had when they began to acquire the heavily armored scout vehicle armed with 7.5 cm cannon—the *schwerer Panzerspähwagen* (7.5 cm), designated the SdKfz 233. The 2 cm automatic cannon of the SdKfz 231 and 232 eight-wheeled vehicles had been effective against lightly armored adversaries, but the 7.5 cm StuK on the SdKfz 233 was much more effective against fortifications, and was even somewhat effective against medium tanks. The lightly armored chassis of the SdKfz 233 was, however, far less than what armored combat vehicles were built around.

The 7.5 cm StuK guns became available when it was decided to rearm the *Sturmgeschütz* assault guns with weapons of higher velocity. Schichau built 135 SdKfz 233 armored vehicles. Most were purpose built from the ground up, but a few were made by cutting down superstructures of rebuilt SdKfz 263 vehicles. That modification was fairly easy to effect, given that the SdKfz 233 body was based on the 263 design. The SdKfz 233's mounting allowed a twelve-degree right traverse and nine-degree left traverse, with an elevation from -4 to +20 degrees. The vehicles had four-man crews, three of whose members—the commander, loader, and gunner—occupied the open-topped fighting

SdKfz 263 (6-Rad)

Specifications	
Length	5.57 m
Width	1.82 m
Height	2.25
Weight	5.7 tons
Fuel capacity	105 liters
Maximum speed	70 km/hr
Range, on-road	250 km
Tire size	6.00-20
Crew	4
Communications	FuG Spr Ger 'a'
Armament	
Weapon, main	7.92 MG 13
Ammo stowage, main	1,500 rounds
Automotive	
Engine make	Magirus
Engine model	s88
Engine configuration	6-cylinder, liquid cooled
Engine displacement	3.7 liters
Engine horsepower	65

SdKfz 231 (8-Rad)

Specifications	
Length	5.85 m
Width	2.20 m
Height	2.35 m
Weight	8.50 tons
Fuel capacity	180 liters
Maximum speed	85 km/hr
Range, on-road	300 km
Range, cross-country	170 km
Crew	4
Communications	none
Tire size	210-18
Armament	
Weapon, main	2 cm KwK30 to July 1942, 2 cm KwK 38 thereafter
Weapon, coaxial	7.92 mm MG 13 or 34
Ammo stowage, main	180 rounds
Ammo stowage, secondary	2,100 rounds
Automotive	
Engine make	Büssing-NAG
Engine model	L8V/GS
Engine configuration	V-8, liquid cooled
Engine displacement	7.91 liters
Engine horsepower	155 @ 3000 rpm

compartment. The gunner aimed the weapon, using a Sfl.Z.F.1 periscopic sight with 5X magnification.

Having originated as an armored car, the SdKfz 233 had one serious drawback—its chassis. Intended for use in light and mobile reconnaissance cars, the chassis was overburdened by the StuK 40 gun. In addition, the fighting compartment on the SdKfz 233 was so overcrowded that ammunition stowage was limited to only thirty-two rounds.

First used in Tunisia in November 1942, the SdKfz 233 vehicle for the most part saw action on the Eastern Front. The vehicle remained on the front lines until the end of World War II.

SdKfz 263 8-Rad

Intended as a mobile base station for Panzer unit communications, the SdKfz 263 was expected to operate in rear areas. Accordingly, their only armament was a 7.92 mm MG 34 machine gun in a ball mount for use in close-in defense.

As was the case with other vehicles in the family, the 263's armor was thin—providing protection only against 7.92 mm armor-piercing rounds or less.

In place of a turret, fixed stationary on top of the vehicle was a hexagonal truncated pyramid. This structure housed the crew as well as a powerful m.Pz.Fu.Tr.b with FuG 11 SE 100 radio set. Besides the frame antenna that had become standard German communications equipment, the *Panzerfunkwagen* also boasted a nine-meter telescoping antenna that was fitted behind the hexagonal superstructure. The vehicle's crew consisted of five men—a commander, two drivers, and two radio operators.

From the automotive point of view, the SdKfz 263 was the same as the SdKfz 231 and 232 8-*Rad* vehicles.

Left: *The* schwerer Panzerspähwagen 231 (8-Rad), *also referred to as the SdKfz 231 (8-Rad), was a heavy armored car designed by Büssing NAG. It went into production in 1936. In many ways it was similar in basic lines to the SdKfz 231 (6-Rad) except with the body turned end-for-end, and with eight wheels instead of six, and the addition of a redesigned turret. Separate, boxy fenders were supplied for the two front wheels and the two rear wheels on each side. Armament was one 2 cm KwK 30 or 38 cannon and one 7.92 mm MG 34.* Thomas Anderson

Left: *Attached to the front of this SdKfz 231 (8-Rad) is a Zusatzfrontplatte, a supplementary armor fixture introduced in 1940, featuring 10 mm plate mounted on a substantial frame. A jerrican liquid container is stored on the side of that frame. Powering the vehicle was a Büssing-NAG L8V/G.S.36 V-8 motor, located in the rear of the armored car.* Bundesarchiv

Left: A SdKfz 231 (8-Rad) fresh out of the factory in 1937 is seen from the front with the weapons yet to be installed in the turret. Note the visors on the front and sides of the driver's compartment, and the double-panel entry door for the driver on the front of the body. Patton Museum

Left: A rear view of the SdKfz 231 (8-Rad) shows, top to bottom, the doors on the rear of the turret; the rear driver's visors, the engine deck, ventilating louvers on the rear of the body, the two registration plate holders, rear service headlights for use during nighttime driving in reverse, and, on the fenders, the mufflers. Patton Museum

Above: *An elevated photo of a captured SdKfz 231 (8-Rad) includes a view of the turret roof with its single hatch, the driver's open doors, the visors and vision slits on the body and the turret. A smoke discharger on the side of the turret displays the layout of the hatches on top and at the rear of the turret, as well as a closer view of the smoke discharger on the side of the turret. On the engine deck are the air intake and a two-panel access door. Patton Museum*

Left: *The angular body of the SdKfz 231 (8-Rad) was designed to increase the effective thickness, and thus, stopping power of the armor. The armor ranged in thickess from 5 mm to 15 mm in thickness. This vehicle seems to be the same one shown in the preceding photo, with the turret turned slightly to the right and with a British-style smoke-grenade projector on each side of the turret. Patton Museum*

SdKfz 232 (8-Rad)

Specifications	
Length	5.85 m
Width	2.20 m
Height	2.90 m
Weight	8.50 tons
Fuel capacity	180 liters
Maximum speed	85 km/hr
Range, on-road	300 km
Range, cross-country	170 km
Crew	4
Communications	FuG 11 SE 100
Tire size	210-18
Armament	
Weapon, main	2 cm KwK30 to July 1942, 2 cm KwK 38 thereafter
Weapon, coaxial	7.92 mm MG 13 or 34
Ammo stowage, main	180 rounds
Ammo stowage, secondary	2,100 rounds
Automotive	
Engine make	Büssing-NAG
Engine model	L8V/GS
Engine configuration	V-8, liquid cooled
Engine displacement	7.91 liters
Engine horsepower	155 @ 3000 rpm

Above: *The SdKfz 232 (8-Rad) was the command and communications version of the SdKfz 231 (8-Rad), with a frame antenna mounted above the vehicle and a FuG 11 SE 100 radio set inside the vehicle. A Notek blackout headlight is mounted above the Zusatzfrontplatte on an SdKfz 232 (8-Rad) named after Friedrich Wilhelm von Seydlitz, a Prussian cavalry general of the eighteenth century. This vehicle served with the 2nd Company, 8th Armored Reconnaissance Battalion, 5th Panzer Division, in the Balkans in 1941.* National Archives and Records Administration

Above: *Two fixed support struts on the rear of the body supported the rear part of the frame antenna. Aside from the antenna and its supports, the SdKfz 232 (8-Rad) appeared virtually identical to the SdKfz 231 (8-Rad) from the rear.* Patton Museum

Above: *An SdKfz 232 (8-Rad) is seen from the front with the armaments not installed in the turret. A bracket on the turret supporting the forward part of the frame antenna was equipped with a pivot connection to the antenna, allowing the turret to freely traverse.* Patton Museum

Left: *The SdKfz 232 (8-Rad) nicknamed "Seydlitz" is making its way through a town in Greece on April 23, 1941. The wedge-shaped object strapped to the right fender is a fifteen-liter container for Kraftstoff Explosionssicher (explosion-proof fuel). Next to the turret on the body is a turn-signal device with its guard.* National Archives and Records Administration

Left: *Starting in July 1942, the* Sternantenne *(star antenna) replaced the frame antenna on the SdKfz 232 (8-Rad) command and communications vehicles. The* Sternantenne *consisted of a mast on a special base, with radiating rods at the top of the mast that had somewhat the appearance of the rays of a star. The* Sternantenne *on this vehicle is mounted on a box-shaped structure on the right side of the body.* Thomas Anderson

Above: *The* schwere Panzerspähwagen *(7.5 cm), also designated the SdKfz 233, was a fire-support heavy armored car, consisting of a 7.5 cm StuK 37 L/24 mounted on a modified SdKfz 231 (8-Rad) chassis. The gun was located on the right side of the driver, with the barrel and cradle protruding through a new armored shield at the front of the fighting compartment. A column of SdKfz 233s is seen here filing through a harbor area. Three smoke dischargers are on the fenders of each vehicle.* Patton Museum

Above: *A British or Commonwealth soldier stands next to a captured SdKfz 233, apparently in good condition. Visible above the fighting compartment to the rear of the 7.5 cm gun is its periscopic sight. Crew doors on the lower part of the body between the front and rear wheels remained a constant throughout heavy armored car production. Note the open door for the storage compartment in the rear fender.* Patton Museum

SdKfz 233

Specifications	
Length	5.85 m
Width	2.20 m
Height	2.25 m
Weight	8.70 tons
Fuel capacity	150 liters
Maximum speed	85 km/hr
Range, on-road	300 km
Range, cross-country	170 km
Crew	3
Communications	Fu.Ger. a or f
Tire size	210-18
Armament	
Weapon, main	7.5 cm Kanone 37
Weapon, secondary	7.92 mm MG 42
Ammo stowage, main	32 rounds
Ammo stowage, secondary	1,500 rounds
Automotive	
Engine make	Büssing-NAG
Engine model	L8V/GS
Engine configuration	V-8, liquid cooled
Engine displacement	7.91 liters
Engine horsepower	155 @ 3000 rpm

Orders for the *Panzerfunkwagen* were placed in 1937 and the vehicles remained on assembly lines until January 1943, when the orders for those vehicles that still remained were changed to the 7.5 cm-armed SdKfz 233. Schichau built all 297 of the SdKfz 263 vehicles, just as it constructed all the other vehicles in the series.

PanzerMesskraftwagen mit Aggregat

Perhaps the most unique member of the SdKfz 231 vehicle family was the *Ballistik-Messfahrzeug auf schwere Panzerspähwagen* (8-Rad). Although it is frequently stated that the one SdKfz 231 captured by US forces at the Hillersleben Proving Ground in Germany in 1945 was the only vehicle of its kind, there is photographic evidence suggesting that there were at least two 234s manufactured.

The voluminous body of the SdKfz 231 accommodated a range of equipment for ballistic data recording. In contrast to the normal arrangement on 231-series vehicles, on the *Panzermesskraftwagen mit Aggregat* the engine and radiator were positioned in the front of the vehicle, whereas in other SdKfz 231 vehicles, these were located in the vehicle's rear.

It is also noteworthy that one of these vehicles had dual rear wheels on both of the trailing axles. Given the tight clearances and fundamental difficulty of steering dual wheels, this configuration raises questions about just how many of the axles on this particular version of the 231 had actual steering capability.

Located at the far back end of the vehicle was a box containing reels of cable for connecting monitoring instruments. Besides serving conventional artillery, the *Panzermesskraftwagen mit Aggregat* was reportedly employed in conjunction with the testing of the German *Vergeltungswaffe*-2 (V-2) rockets.

Schwerer Panzerspähwagen (2 cm) (SdKfz 234/1)

Work commenced in August 1940 on a new generation of heavy armored cars. The eight-wheeled 8-*Rad* vehicles had indeed boasted significantly improved mobility as compared with the earlier 6-*Rad* vehicles, but there was still room for improvement. As the war progressed, the Germans encountered ever more formidable weaponry and, accordingly, there was constant pressure to increase armor protection. The new design—designated SdKfz 234 *schwerer Panzerspähwagen*—responded to both these concerns, in addition to improving engine cooling, and the first production vehicle of the type rolled off the assembly line in June 1944.

In contrast to the earlier six- and eight-wheeled series vehicles, the *schwärer Panzerspähwagen* had an armored hull to which, much as on a tank, other components were mounted. Earlier armored cars consisted of an armored body attached to a truck-style chassis, as was the case with the earlier 8-*Rad* vehicles.

Büssing-NAG was the main contractor for the series. A twelve-cylinder Tatra air-cooled Diesel engine powered the vehicle.

The open-topped turret of the 234/1 was armed with a 2 cm KwK38 together with a coaxial MG 42 machine gun. The hand-traversed turret sat a crew of two—the commander to the left and the gunner to his right. The vehicle carried 250 rounds of 2 cm shells and 2,400 machine-gun rounds. Radios were fitted in only a few of the approximately two hundred vehicles built.

Left: *A German column halted in a town in Yugoslavia in the last half of 1943 includes an SdKfz 233 in the foreground. A Notek blackout headlight is on the left fender, on the inboard side of which is the horn.* Bundesarchiv

Schwerer Panzerspähwagen (5 cm) (SdKfz 234/2) Puma

Like the other SdKfz 234 vehicles, the SdKfz 234/2 relied on a Tatra twelve-cylinder air-cooled Diesel engine that drove all eight wheels by means of a six-speed transmission. An air-cooled engine was introduced in part because the eight-wheeled vehicles had suffered from overheating when operating in North Africa. The 234/2 had an on-road range of 1,000 kilometers and 600 kilometers cross country, thanks to 360-liter fuel tanks. The vehicle's drivetrain was designed to facilitate driving equally effectively and quickly in either direction, running at nearly 50 miles per hour.

As compared with the earlier 8-*Rad* vehicles, the 234/2 had slightly thicker frontal armor of 30 mm, but side armor was relatively thin—plate of 8 mm thickness. The vehicle's top speed was raised to 80 km/hr with the phenomenal range of 1,000 kilometers.

The SdKfz 234/2 was originally to be armed with a 2 cm KwK 38, but instead a 5 cm KwK 39/1 replaced it even before the first vehicle rolled off the assembly lines.

Despite the improvements in armor and armament, these heavy armored cars were still inferior to Allied tanks.

The 5 cm KwK39/1 mounted in the turret had 360-degree rotation and elevation of -10° to +20°. Coxial with the cannon was a 7.92 mm MG 42 machine gun. The vehicle carried fifty-five shells for the main gun.

First designated the SdKfz 234 but later relabeled as the SdKfz 234/2, the vehicle was in production from December 1943 through March 1945, and in all 101 vehicles were produced.

Schwerer Panzerspähwagen (7.5 cm) (Sd. Kfz/ 234/3)

Basically a modernized version of the SdKfz 233 8-*Rad* vehicle, the SdKfz 234/3 incorporated the larger and more powerful Diesel-powered chassis of the *schwerer Panzerspähwagen* (heavy armored car). It had the same armament as its predecessor—the 7.5 cm StuK 51 L/24, together with an MG 42 machine gun for antiaircraft and antipersonnel use. This MG 42 was particularly useful, since the SdKfz 234/3, like the SdKfz 233, had an open-topped fighting compartment. Weapons and three of the four crewmen were housed in the vehicle's interior, as were 50 main gun rounds and 1,950 rounds for the machine gun. Also contained inside the vehicle was a 19.9 to 21.4 MHz *Funksprechgerät* f radio system. Located in the center of the fighting compartment of the SdKfz 234/3 was the 7.5 cm gun. This configuration differed from that on the SdKfz 233 in which the 7.5 cm gun was located to the right side. Fitted to the right of the main gun was an MG 42 machine gun. Only eighty-eight examples of the SdKfz 234/3 were produced.

Schwerer Panzerspähwagen (7.5 cm PaK 40)(SdKfz 234/4)

The most heavily armed vehicle in the *schwerer Panzerspähwagen* family was the SdKfz 234/4—a favorite of the German *Führer*, who personally expedited the vehicle's development. Despite Hitler's interest, only eighty-nine were produced between the onset of production in December 1944, and March 1945, when production ceased.

Confronting a relentless tide of Allied armor, the Germans, now on the defensive, badly needed a powerful, mobile antitank weapon. Marrying the proven reliable chassis of the SdKfz 234 with the 7.5 cm PaK 40, one of World War II's finest antitank weapons, appeared to be a very good option.

Work began on the project in October 1944. In November that year, the project was a topic when Hitler met with the Armaments and Munitions Minister, Albert Speer. The vehicle entered production in December, speeded along by the use of chassis that had previously been earmarked for use in the SdKfz 234/3.

The base of the standard PaK 40 was adjusted and mounted on a formation of steel girders inside the vehicle's fighting compartment. The standard PaK 40 gun-shield was kept but modified by cutting out its lower edges to permit a traverse of about twenty degrees in either direction. The gun was laid using the normal optics associated with a PaK 40—a 3X magnification PaK-*Zielfernrohr* with an eight-degree field of view. The installation of the weapon allowed an elevation range of -5 to +22 degrees. Weight and space limitations, however, then allowed stowage of only thirty-six rounds for the cannon.

S gl gep Personenkraftwagen (SdKfz 247)

The intended use of the *schwerer geländegängiger gepanzerter Personenkraftwagen* or "heavy cross-country armored staff car," was as a command vehicle for armored reconnaissance staff.

The six-wheeled earliest version used the Krupp limber—the Krupp L2H143 chassis, which had been developed especially for the military. Powered by Krupp's horizontally opposed engine, ten of these vehicles were manufactured between 1937 and January 1938.

The open-topped vehicle's armor could protect the driver and five passengers from 7.92 mm armor-piercing rounds—provided that they were fired from at least thirty yards distant.

In 1938 another fifty-eight of the cars were ordered, but these would be substantially different vehicles. The German

SdKfz 263 (8-Rad)

Specifications	
Length	5.85 m
Width	2.20 m
Height	2.90 m
Weight	8.10 tons
Fuel capacity	150 liters
Maximum speed	85 km/hr
Range, on-road	300 km
Range, cross-country	170 km
Crew	5
Communications	FuG 11 SE 100
Tire size	210-18
Armament	
Weapon, main	7.92 mm MG 34
Ammo stowage, main	1,050 rounds
Automotive	
Engine make	Büssing-NAG
Engine model	L8V/GS
Engine configuration	V-8, liquid cooled
Engine displacement	7.91 liters
Engine horsepower	155 @ 3000 rpm

army's SdKfz numbers were assigned based on the use of a vehicle, not on its design. This practice was in contrast to the approach followed by the US Army in its Standard Nomenclature List, or the SNL G-numbers. Accordingly, even though the vehicles that were produced later had only four wheels and were constructed on the basis of the *Horch Einheitsfahrgestell* II ("uniform chassis II"), they retained the SdKfz 247 designation.

A four-wheel-drive vehicle, the SdKfz 247 had only two-wheel steering—in contrast to Germany's other contemporary four-wheel armored vehicles.

The launch of production hit several snags and only finally began in July 1941. Daimler-Benz finished its contracted fifty-eight vehicles in January 1942. The four-wheeled SdKfz 247 could carry a driver and five passengers, as could the six-wheeled versions. No provision was made for mounted armament, however, or for communications equipment. In both the four-wheeled and six-wheeled

Left: *The* Panzerfunkwagen, *designated SdKfz 263 (8-Rad) and also referred to as Gerät 95, was developed at the same time as the SdKfz 231 (8-Rad) and shared the same chassis. Intended as a mobile, armored, radio base station for Panzer units, it had a sizeable superstructure above the body to accommodate sophisticated m.Pz.Fu.Tr.B and FuG 11 SE 100 radio equipment and crew. A frame antenna and a nine-meter telescopic antenna were mounted on the vehicle.* Patton Museum

Above: *The same* Panzerfunkwagen *is viewed from the rear. The nine-meter telescopic antenna, which was detachable and was mounted to the rear of the superstructure, is not installed here. A two-panel door is on the rear of the superstructure above the rear driver's visors.* Patton Museum

Above: *The nine-meter telescopic antenna is installed on the rear deck of this* Panzerfunkwagen. *On the side of the body to the front of the left rear support strut for the frame antenna is a* Schwenkarm für Flugzielbeschuss: *a pivoting mount for an antiaircraft machine gun. This device was discontinued in 1939.* Thomas Anderson

versions, the engine was positioned in the front of the vehicle.

Production delays meant that by the time the vehicles had been actually manufactured, they were no longer needed for their original purpose. Instead, the SdKfz 247 vehicles were assigned for headquarters use in motorcycle units.

Above: *A real rarity, the Ballistik-Messfahrzeug auf schwere Panzerspähwagen (8-Rad) (Ballistic Measuring Vehicle on Heavy Armored Scout Car) was based on the SdKfz 231 chassis. Photographic evidence indicates that two such vehicles were completed, one of which US troops captured at Hillersleben Proving Ground, Germany, in 1945. The oversized body contained equipment for recording ballistic data during the testing of artillery. The engine was in the forward part of the body.* Patton Museum

Above: *The windows of the Ballistik-Messfahrzeug auf schwere Panzerspähwagen (8-Rad) were equipped with hinged, armored flaps, which were swung down while the crew of the vehicle was observing and recording data of artillery tests. There were also flaps, shown raised here, to protect the wheels during firing. Note the two steps cut into the body between the first and second wheels.* The Tank Museum

Polizei-Panzerkampfwagen ADGZ

Originally made from 1935-1937 for the Austrian army, twenty-seven vehicles constructed by Austro-Daimler-Puch

SdKfz 234/1

Specifications	
Length	5.86 m
Width	2.33 m
Height	2.10 m
Weight	11.5 tons
Fuel capacity	360 liters
Maximum speed	80 km/hr
Range, on-road	1,000 km
Range, cross-country	600 km
Crew	4
Communications	FuG 12 SE 80 and Fu Spr Ger f
Tire size	270-20
Armament	
Weapon, main	2 cm KwK38
Weapon, secondary	7.92 mm MG 42
Ammo stowage, main	250 rounds
Ammo stowage, secondary	2,400 rounds
Automotive	
Engine make	Tatra
Engine model	103
Engine configuration	V-12, air-cooled Diesel
Engine displacement	14.825 liters
Engine horsepower	220 @ 2250 rpm

were of no interest to the *Wehrmacht* after the *Anschluss*, and were, accordingly assigned to the Reich's state police.

In 1942, however, an additional twenty-five of the vehicles were produced, some of which were employed by the German army and SS, although only briefly.

Unusual in appearance, the vehicles featured dual wheels on their central axles and single wheels on the forward and trailing axles. Mounted in the vehicle's rotating turret was a 2 cm KwK 35 (L/45) cannon. Manned by a crew of six, the vehicle had armor that was 11 mm thick.

A vehicle of somewhat marginal use at the best of times, by late 1944 they were employed solely for training purposes.

S gl LKW 4.5t für FlaK (Sf)

By the middle of the war, the Allies were asserting superiority in the skies over the battlefield. Strategic bombing of Axis

Above: *The schwere Panzerspähweagen (2 cm), or SdKfz 234/1, was the first of four versions of heavy armored car based on a new and improved chassis to replace the aging SdKfz 231 (8-Rad) and SdKfz 233 (8-Rad). The basic vehicle included new wheels, single fender units with storage compartments, redesigned body, and other improvements. Power was provided by the Tatra 103 engine through a gearbox with six forward and six reverse gears. The first model of the vehicle, the SdKfz 234/1, featured a low, open-topped turret, traversed to the rear in this photo. The turret was armed with a 2 cm KwK 38 L/55 automatic cannon and a 7.92 mm MG 42.* Patton Museum

Above: *The same SdKfz 234/1 shown in the preceding photo is observed from above, showing the layout of the front of the hull with a hatch on the right side, the turret, and the engine deck. A folding anti-grenade screen was mounted on each side of the open turret; the right screen is in the lowered position, and the left screen is missing, as is the MG 42.* Patton Museum

Left: *As illustrated in this view of an SdKfz 234/1 with a tarpaulin over its turret, in autumn 1944 simplified fenders were introduced, with the two center storage bins on the side omitted, and the remaining doors being equipped with leaf hinges on the tops, instead of the former piano hinges on the bottom. Four jerricans are strapped to the fender. Stefan de Meyer*

SdKfz 234/2

Specifications	
Length	6.80 m
Width	2.33 m
Height	2.38 m
Weight	11.7 tons
Fuel capacity	360 liters
Maximum speed	80 km/hr
Range, on-road	100 km
Range, cross-country	600 km
Crew	4
Communications	Fu Spr Ger f
Tire size	270-20
Armament	
Weapon, main	5 cm KwK39/1 (L/60)
Weapon, coaxial	7.92 mm MG 42
Ammo stowage, main	55 rounds
Ammo stowage, secondary	2,850 rounds
Automotive	
Engine make	Tatra
Engine model	103
Engine configuration	V-12, air-cooled Diesel
Engine displacement	14,825 liters
Engine horsepower	220 @ 2250 rpm

transport and industry and tactical bombing of men and materiel took an increasingly heavy toll.

The German answer was to increase development of antiaircraft weaponry. One new addition in this field was the 5 cm FlaK 41. Though fewer than 100 of the FlaK 41 were manufactured, some of them were mounted on the seasoned Mercedes-Benz L 4500 A 4.5-ton truck to produce a mobile antiaircraft weapon.

The cabs of these trucks were fitted out with armor plating and an armored splinter shield was added in front of the radiator. To allow the bed to become a working platform for an antiaircraft gun crew, the sides of the bed were hinged so that they could fold down to serve as a work space and to allow 360-degree rotation of the weapon mount. The trucks were equipped with outriggers for stability when the gun was in use.

Given the paucity of the FlaK 41, these antiaircraft trucks were rare vehicles.

Above: The SdKfz 234/2, also called by its nickname, the Puma, shared the same chassis as the SdKfz 234/2 but had an armored, fully enclosed turret armed with a 50 mm KwK 39/1 for use against light armor and a coaxial 7.92 mm MG 42. The gunner sat to the left of the 50 mm gun, while the commander/loader sat to the right of it. A total of 101 of these vehicles were produced. The disabled SdKfz 234/1 shown here, registration number WH-1542744, was photographed in France in the summer of 1944. National Archives and Records Administration

Above: This SdKfz 234/2, registration number WH-1542940, from Panzer Aufklarungs Abteilung 2 was captured by the British, who applied stenciled shipping labels to the vehicle. On top of the turret, an antenna mount and covers for the periscopes on the commander's (right) and gunner's (left) hatches are visible. Smoke dischargers are on the side of the turret. A battered muffler is present on the right rear fender, but the left muffler is missing. The Tank Museum

SdKfz 234/3

Specifications	
Length	5.86 m
Width	2.33 m
Height	2.22 m
Weight	11.5 tons
Fuel capacity	360 liters
Maximum speed	80 km/hr
Range, on-road	1,000 km
Range, cross-country	600 km
Crew	4
Communications	Fu Spr Ger f
Tire size	270-20
Armament	
Weapon, main	7.5 cm K 51 (L/24)
Weapon, secondary	7.92 mm MG 42
Ammo stowage, main	50 rounds
Ammo stowage, secondary	1,950 rounds
Automotive	
Engine make	Tatra
Engine model	103
Engine configuration	V-12, air-cooled Diesel
Engine displacement	14.825 liters
Engine horsepower	220 @ 2250 rpm

Left: *The SdKfz 234/3 was the fire-support version of the SdKfz 234 family: in effect, an improved version of the SdKfz 233 (8-Rad). The SdKfz 234/3 was armed with the 7.5 cm KwK 51 L/24 gun. A low shield of 14.5 mm armor atop the car's body gave the gun crew some protection, but not from artillery airbursts and overhead fire. Approximately ninety examples were completed by the end of production in December 1944.* Patton Museum

ARMORED CARS 319

Above: *The British captured this still operable SdKfz 234/3, registration number WH-1751008; it is preserved at the Tank Museum at Bovington. The 7.5 cm gun had a limited amount of play: twelve degrees to either side of the center, and an elevation range from -10 degrees to +12 degrees.* The Tank Museum

Above: *The same captured SdKfz 234/3, registration number WH-1751008, is observed from the left side, showing the design of the side of the armored shield above the body, which tapered down in height from the front to the rear.* The Tank Museum

SdKfz 234/4

Specifications	
Length	5.86 m less gun
Width	2.33 m
Height	2.38 m
Weight	11.5 tons
Fuel capacity	360 liters
Maximum speed	80 km/hr
Range, on-road	1,000 km
Range, cross-country	600 km
Crew	4
Communications	Fu Spr Ger f
Tire size	270-20
Armament	
Weapon, main	7.5 cm PaK 40
Ammo stowage, main	36 rounds
Automotive	
Engine make	Tatra
Engine model	103
Engine configuration	V-12, air-cooled Diesel
Engine displacement	14.825 liters
Engine horsepower	220 @ 2250 rpm

Left: *Of all of the vehicles of Germany's heavy armored scout cars in World War II, the one that packed the greatest firepower was the SdKfz 234/4. It mounted a 7.5 cm PaK 40 L/46 in an open-topped fighting compartment with just a low shield on the body of the car and the stock two-ply armor shield that came with the towed version of the gun. This example was photographed in Prague, Czechoslovakia, and had a three-color camouflage scheme.* Thomas Anderson

Left: *Eight soldiers, enough to crew two of these vehicles, pose for their photograph with an SdKfz 234/4 near the end of World War II. Approximately ninety of these armored cars were completed in a short span of time late in the war, from December 1944 to March 1945. The 7.5 cm PaK 40 L/46 gave armored car scout units firepower capable of defeating many but not all Allied armored vehicles, but the SdKfz 234/4 entered service too late to make much of a mark. Stefan de Meyer*

schwerer gelandegängiger gepanzerter Personenkraftwagen SdKfz 247 (6-Rad)

Specifications	
Length	5.20 m
Width	1.96 m
Height	1.70 m
Weight	5.2 tons
Fuel capacity	110 liters
Maximum speed	70 km/hr
Range, on-road	350 km
Range, cross-country	220 km
Crew	1 + 5 passengers
Communications	none
Armament	
Weapon, main	none
Automotive	
Engine make	Krupp
Engine model	M305
Engine configuration	4-cylinder, opposed
Engine displacement	3.5 liter
Engine horsepower	65 @ 2500 rpm

Polizei-Panzerkampfwagen ADGZ

Specifications	
Length	6.26 m
Width	2.16 m
Height	2.56 m
Weight	12 tons
Maximum speed	70 km/hr
Range, on-road	450 km
Crew	6
Armament	
Weapon, main	2 cm KwK35 L/45
Weapons, secondary	3 x 7.92 mm MG 34
Ammo stowage, main	100 rounds
Ammo stowage, secondary	2,500 rounds
Automotive	
Engine make	Austro-Daimler
Engine model	M612
Engine configuration	6-cylinder, liquid cooled
Engine displacement	12 liters
Engine horsepower	150 @ 1800 rpm

Above: *The SdKfz 247 armored car was initially built by Daimler-Benz as a six-wheeled vehicle (6-Rad) for use by staff officers. The second, more numerous production batch utilized a four-wheel (4-Rad) configuration and two-wheeled steering. Neither was equipped with a weapon, or oddly for a command vehicle, a radio set. Both were lightly armored with 8 mm plate. This SdKfz 247 has been outfitted with two additional sirens on the left front fender, the better to announce the arrival of its important occupants. Fifty-eight of the 4-rad version were produced.* Patton Museum

Above: *The ADGZ was a massive twelve-wheeled armored car designed in 1934 for the Austrian Army. It had 6 mm of armor plate and was armed with a 2 cm KwK 35 L/45 auto cannon. Twenty-seven ADGZs were delivered, but after annexation in 1938, the Germans used them to equip SS and military police units. Their official designation was M35 mittlere Panzerwagen. Twenty-five additional vehicles were ordered in 1941 by the SS and used in the Balkans with several notably going to the Prinz Eugen division for anti-partisan duties. This is thought to be one of those later vehicles.* Patton Museum

Above: *The Mercedes Benz L 4500 A truck was large and robust all-wheel drive 4.5-ton Diesel truck that had been heavily used by the German army as a cargo vehicle. As the truck was being phased out of production in 1944, it started to be utilized as a mount for various FlaK weapons. In many instances, the truck cabs and radiators were lightly armored as on this example. The typically mounted weapon was the 3.7 cm FlaK with an armored shield, but this version mounts the somewhat rare 5 cm FlaK 41. The outriggers would have provided much-needed stability for the larger weapon.* Patton Museum